THE CARE OF THE SELF
AND THE CARE OF THE OTHER

The Care of the Self and the Care of the Other

FROM SPIRITUAL EXERCISES TO
POLITICAL TRANSFORMATION

Daniel Louis Wyche

Columbia University Press
New York

Columbia University Press
Publishers Since 1893
New York   Chichester, West Sussex

Copyright © 2025 Columbia University Press
All rights reserved

Library of Congress Cataloging-in-Publication Data
Names: Wyche, Daniel Louis, author.
Title: The care of the self and the care of the other : from spiritual exercises to political transformation / Daniel Louis Wyche.
Description: New York : Columbia University Press, [2025] | Includes bibliographical references and index.
Identifiers: LCCN 2024044824 | ISBN 9780231207805 (hardback) | ISBN 9780231207812 (trade paperback) | ISBN 9780231557122 (ebook)
Subjects: LCSH: Self (Philosophy) | Other (Philosophy) | Spiritual exercises. | Hadot, Pierre. | Friedmann, Georges, 1902–1977. | Foucault, Michel, 1926–1984. | King, Martin Luther, Jr., 1929–1968. | Lorde, Audre.
Classification: LCC BD438.5 .W93 2025 | DDC 126—dc23/eng/20241204

Cover design: Milenda Nan Ok Lee
Cover art: Erik Ruin, *Wanderers (Trees)*, 2014

GPSR Authorized Representative: Easy Access System Europe,
Mustamäe tee 50, 10621 Tallinn, Estonia, gpsr.requests@easproject.com

For my grandparents

CONTENTS

ACKNOWLEDGMENTS IX

Introduction 1

Chapter One
Pierre Hadot: Ancient Spiritual Exercises and
Contemporary Spiritual Demands 46

Chapter Two
Georges Friedmann: From the Great Disequilibrium
to the Interior Effort 90

Chapter Three
Michel Foucault: From the Analytics of Power
to the Care of the Self 141

Chapter Four
The Practice of Dignity: Martin Luther King Jr., Self-Purification,
and the Montgomery Bus Boycott 182

Conclusion
Audre Lorde: Survival, Immediacy, and Poetry as a Way of Life 235

NOTES 257
BIBLIOGRAPHY 309
INDEX 319

ACKNOWLEDGMENTS

In many ways, this project began while I was an undergraduate at Rutgers University, in Professor John McClure's seminar on Religion and Contemporary Literature, many years ago now. And for that, I must first thank John, whose mentorship and insights have stayed with me.

I would also like to thank three of the most generous people I have ever met: Arnold I. Davidson, Bernard E. Harcourt, and Curtis J. Evans, who each in their own ways contributed to the cultivation of the concepts and methods that make up this book. I am grateful to Arnold for many years of both close reading and close listening, and for understanding the role that music, and above all improvisation, have played in the elaboration of these and other ideas. I am grateful to Bernard for always being available whenever I have needed his help and for facilitating so many of the richest conversations I have been lucky to take part in. I am especially grateful to Curtis for such unwavering support across the development of this project, which has been invaluable with regarding to my ability to read King, Thurman, and other figures in the American context. My engagement with those sources would have been impossible without his help and guidance.

Profound appreciation is also due to the friends who have been my closest interlocutors: Davey Tomlinson, Sean Hannan, Dalmar Hussein, Greg Chatterley, Maureen Kelley, Marie Satya McDonough, Tuomo Tiisala, Ted Gordon, Adam Stern, and Sunny Yudkoff. I owe you all a debt of gratitude that I look forward to reciprocating for a long time. Special thanks are also due to my dear friend and collaborator Niki Kasumi Clements, whose support and insight have been indispensable across the process of researching, writing, and editing this book. I would also like to thank Tom Durkin for his generosity and support over many years. Further thanks are due Wendy Lochner at Columbia University Press, for her patience and guidance in this process.

Finally, I thank my family, and above all, I thank Claudia and Gracie.

THE CARE OF THE SELF
AND THE CARE OF THE OTHER

INTRODUCTION

> The school of a philosopher is a surgery. You are not to go out of it with pleasure, but with pain; for you do not come there in health; but one of you has a dislocated shoulder; another, an abscess; a third, a fistula; a fourth, the headache. And am I, then, to sit uttering pretty, trifling thoughts and little exclamations, that, when you have praised me, you may each of you go away with the same dislocated shoulder, the same aching head, the same fistula, and the same abscess that you brought? And is it for this that young men are to travel? And do they leave their parents, their friends, their relations, and their estates, that they may praise you while you are uttering little exclamations? Was this the practice of Socrates? Of Zeno? Of Cleanthes?
>
> —EPICTETUS, *DISCOURSE* 3.23.31-32

> Did we have a leader? Our leaders is just we ourselves.
>
> —CLAUDETTE COLVIN, SUPREME COURT TESTIMONY, *BROWDER V. GAYLE*, MAY 11, 1956

I. OVERVIEW

The goal of this book is to describe and develop a class of concepts and practices that I will very generally refer to as practices of ethical self-change, even as a particular term is much less important than what it denotes. For this reason, I will sometimes use the general language of self-transformation, self-overcoming, or "practices of the self." Alternately, I will often simply default to the language of "spiritual exercises." I approach this task through the introduction, elaboration, and critique of five distinct but overlapping concepts, as they are articulated by five twentieth-century thinkers, which comprise but by no means exhaust this general category. Each of the following chapters takes up one of these figures and their attending articulations.

First, the concept of "spiritual exercises," as described and elaborated by the French classicist and philosopher Pierre Hadot (1922–2010). This concept is at the heart of Hadot's philosophical and philological lifework, especially his rereading and understanding of ancient Greco-Roman philosophy, and thus philosophy in general. It is worth noting that Hadot also sometimes invokes the language of "the care of the self" among other terms, although "spiritual exercises" remains both his core concept and primary usage. If for no other reason than his influence on Michel Foucault, Hadot's work has been decisive in introducing and reintroducing this set of concepts and concerns to contemporary audiences over the past several decades, or at least in setting the terms of those conversations. For these and many other reasons, I will often default to Hadot's language and conceptual resources.

Second, there is what Georges Friedmann (1902–1977), the father of French sociology of labor and a philosopher in his own way, referred to as both the "interior effort" and "spiritual exercises." Friedmann is somewhat unknown to Anglophone audiences, although his role in France in the introduction of Marx to major intellectual circles, his status as a kind of "intellectual ferryman" to the USSR in the 1930s,[1] as well as the development of the sociology of labor and technology following the war, are all formative. As I elaborate later, this language of the "interior effort" and "spiritual exercises" does not explicitly appear in his major sociological landmarks or his first-person and ethnographic accounts of "machine culture," even as it informs that work at its foundations. Nor are these terms really articulated in his handful of more traditional philosophical works. Rather, these themes are primarily found in a sprawling and complex philosophical "quasi-memoire," *La puissance et la sagesse* (Wisdom and Power), published in 1970, several years before his death in 1977. They also appear, although often implicitly, in another case of "writing the self," his posthumously published *Journal de guerre, 1939–1940* (War journal).[2] As we will see, the nature and form of these sources is significant. From the vantage of these more challenging texts, it becomes possible to see the role of these concepts, or perhaps the more fundamental concerns that generate them, in his firsthand sociological studies of the human wages of labor and automation in the mid-twentieth century.

Third, we have a range of concepts invoked and articulated by Michel Foucault (1926–1984), primarily over the course of the last decade of his life and career. This is often referred to as Foucault's "ethical" period, reflecting a guiding concern with something he calls "the ethics of the care of the self" or simply "the care of the self." In later lectures and interviews, Foucault also speaks of "technologies of the self," the "concern for the self,"

INTRODUCTION

and invokes Hadot's language of "spiritual exercises," among several other terms. Although there is some ambiguity across Foucault's publications, lectures, and various interviews in this period, it is possible to read all of these concepts and practices as fitting within the more fundamental idea of "the relationship of the self to itself."[3] As I have already intimated, Foucault often uses the term "ethics" somewhat interchangeably with concepts like "the care of the self" and above all "the relationship of the self to itself." In this usage, it generally denotes concepts like "ethical self-fashioning," "self-transformation," and the like. What many refer to as Foucault's "ethical period" is thus concerned with ethics in this sense, not in the more familiar sense of determining and acting upon morally correct views or behaviors. It is not about parsing out what is right or wrong and why. At the same time, his use verges on things like virtue ethics and moral perfectionism, although such comparisons are for another time. What matters here is that Foucault's "ethics" is related to but distinguished from "morals" or "morality," even as there is overlap across terms. I generally follow Foucault's distinction and use the term "ethics" in his sense across this book.

Fourth, there is the concept and practice of political "self-purification" invoked by the American philosopher, theologian, political theorist, organizer, orator, and so much else, Martin Luther King Jr. (1929–1968), in his 1963 "Letter from Birmingham Jail." As the third of King's "four basic steps" in a nonviolent campaign, this self-purification is identified as a necessary precondition for direct action, even as the term is underspecified in the "Letter." However, by 1963, this concept already had a long theoretical and practical history within the Gandhian nonviolent tradition, a tradition with which King was intimately familiar. It appears in other forms in the writings of figures like Bayard Rustin (1912–1987), one of King's primary advisors and mentors.[4] King's overall view and usage is also influenced by perhaps his greatest mentor, the polymath Howard Thurman (1899–1981). I argue that Thurman, a kind of patron intellectual of the long Civil Rights era, is also among the most sophisticated and decisive twentieth-century theorists of the subject and power. In all of these cases, the idea of political self-purification is always reinterpreted and reshaped to meet the spiritual and political needs of a given moment and campaign.

Finally, I conclude this work by turning to a series of themes untreated in the primary arc of the main text, some of which are invoked in this introduction. I do so through a brief but directed close reading of the poet, theorist, and activist Audre Lorde's (1934–1992) often-invoked statement that "caring for myself is not self-indulgence, it is self-preservation, and that is an act of political warfare."[5] What she means here is tied to both her personal circumstances in writing these lines—dealing with cancer and finding treatment—and the larger intersectional shifts in activism and political work in the post–Civil Rights period in the United States that figures like Lorde helped to define. As I say in the conclusion, I do not end with Lorde as an afterthought. Rather, I end with Lorde because in many ways I would like to begin with someone like Lorde. That is, her work raises a set of questions for the conclusions that I draw across this book as a whole that I can only pose once the former are established, and which for that reason constitute the beginning of new and important lines of investigation. Indeed, many of the aspects of Lorde's work that I find most relevant to this study are more adjacent to or branching from the main throughlines that I pursue here and the conclusions that I arrive at in chapter 4. They are, however, all the more valuable and illuminating for that adjacency, especially in the ways that this oblique orientation raises and re-raises new questions and challenges to the claims developed in the preceding chapters. Lorde thus allows this conversation to set the stage for new questions and new approaches to those I establish here. Finally, Lorde allows us to begin to address a set of questions that arise within the preliminary stage-setting of this introduction, questions I think can only be addressed on the other side of the main throughlines of this investigation.

With reference to Lorde, and regarding the taxonomy of terms that I have begun to class here, it is worth noting that at the time of this writing, the concept and practice of something called "self-care" is popular if not ubiquitous. Within that constellation, many practitioners and writers invoke Lorde and her statement in *A Burst of Light*. However, Lorde does not use the nominalization "self-care," and her claim, taken in context, is concerned with something rather different from many—though not all—of the varied of forms of self-care that appear in popular discourse today. Now, to be as clear as possible, my goal is not to disparage or dismiss the contemporary concept and practice of self-care, but rather to place it outside this study, with some qualifications. This is because on my view self-care is not a general term or name for the overall class of concepts and practices that concern me here, and it is not a synonym for spiritual exercises or even "the care of the self." Instead, I understand it to be it a historically,

INTRODUCTION

practically, and conceptually specific concept, with particular features, limits, and defining characteristics. If anything, it is one historical iteration that may fall within this larger frame, although a complex and ambiguous one that requires far more specification than I can provide here. It is only on the other side of analyses like these that I believe I may have anything at all to say about it and spiritual movements, discourses, and practices like it.

It is also worth repeating that I do not take these figures and their attending conceptions to either exhaust the category of practices of the self or the questions that emerge from it. There are a number of other authors and themes that could have been explored in a book like this, at least in a world without page and word limits. For readers familiar with this literature, the fact that the Czech phenomenologist, student of Husserl, and Charta 77 signatory Jan Patočka's idea of the "care of the soul" does not appear may be notable.[6] Similarly, anyone familiar with both this literature and the secondary literature around it, including many of my own primary interlocutors and mentors, will note that the voice of Stanley Cavell, the notion of Emersonian perfectionism, and the "unattained but attainable self," are a kind of absent presence here.[7] To be clear, Cavell is very much in the background across this book, especially in cases where some form of perfectionism is invoked or stands as an informative contrast. Finally, and speaking of specters, chapter 2 and my discussion of Friedmann make clear that Marx, too, is, as always, in the background of my thinking across the many sources and contexts that I attempt to traverse here. At some point, it could be fascinating to think through the implications of all that emerges within this book in light of the third thesis on Feuerbach and the notion of "self-change" or *Selbstveränderung* invoked there.[8] Such a study would, of course, need to establish whether or not there are in fact any implications to speak of, beyond a set of passing resonances.

These are just a few of the more immediate fellow conceptual travelers that intuitively emerged for me in researching this project. Others will just as intuitively present themselves to other readers and other perspectives. All of these possibilities represent major themes and resources that deserve the kind of dedicated treatment that I hope can build on any foundations established here. However, an already crowded bibliography and a status adjacent to my central goals meant bracketing these rich and important contributions, relying instead on far briefer invocations that appear only as needed. This latter point is important: despite the richness of the resources that I have chosen to bracket, I have done so above all because they are not strictly necessary for the story I wish to tell.

Returning then to the specific sources and the class of practices that concern me, and borrowing some language from Pierre Hadot as I often will, it should already be clear that there is both unity and great diversity among the members of this broader conceptual family.[9] Borrowing further from Hadot, I collectively define this class of formulations according to his specific understanding of spiritual exercises as "an effort to modify and transform the self,"[10] or more precisely, as "voluntary, personal practices intended to bring about a transformation of the individual, a transformation of the self."[11] Each of these initial criteria require further specification and will be subject to a great deal of elaboration over the course of this project. At the same time, this foundational definition serves well enough for all of the thinkers that I engage and thus as a starting point for the general category under which I have gathered them.

For Hadot, spiritual exercises can refer to an entire range of practices, and like his definition, his examples are representative:

> By this term, I mean practices which could be physical, as in dietary regimes, or discursive, as in dialogue and meditation, or intuitive, as in contemplation, but which were all intended to effect a modification and a transformation in the subject who practiced them. The philosophy teacher's discourse could also assume the form of a spiritual exercise, if the discourse were presented in such a way that the disciple, as auditor, reader, or interlocutor, could make spiritual progress and transform himself within.[12]

To this list, we may add any number of exercises, some more clearly philosophical, others recognizably on the order of religious practice: forms of prayer; chanting, singing, the creation of devotional objects, and other kinds of artistic activity; pilgrimage and other practices of travel and physical hardship; and so on. Whatever the exercise or regimen, however, spiritual exercises are taken up in order to bring about some kind of change within the practicing subject. This last part, the goals or aims of given exercises, constitute what Foucault calls the *telos* of practices of the self, another term that I borrow across this project.[13]

It is also worth being clear at the outset, as it may or may not be apparent from Hadot's strict definition, that this general idea of spiritual exercises, practices of self-change, or whatever we may call them should hold no specific normative weight. In other words, these terms are meant to represent a general description of a form of activity. As I reemphasize in chapter 3, a practice is not "good" (or "bad" for that matter) insofar as it is a spiritual exercise. Moreover, spiritual exercises in general do not produce the criteria of their own judgment, except in those cases where recognizably discursive philosophical and theoretical practices devoted to that particular task also constitute forms of spiritual exercise. This also means that the role of the more familiar, discursive forms of philosophical and theoretical work remains fundamental even to "philosophy as a way of life"—and even to Hadot, as noted in the passage cited earlier, and as I discuss in chapter 1. Although all of the examples that I engage here seek what most would agree are desirable outcomes in forms of moral or political growth that at least claim goals related to human flourishing, that does not mean that such practices will naturally produce positive or desirable forms of life.

One may, and many have, engage in practices of self-transformation to prepare oneself to commit acts of moral or political violence, forms of terrorism, and the like. Acts of religious violence often present some of the clearest examples of such cases, but this phenomenon is by no means unique to that domain. Closer to the ground, practices of immoral or normatively undesirable self-transformation can occur anywhere, at any time, and can be taken up by anyone, even in the most mundane and unspectacular ways. After all, and as I repeat later, we spend a great deal of time and effort transforming ourselves into monsters, whether we know it, intend it, or not. To be clear however, this book does not explore the problem of immoral or politically undesirable forms of self-transformation; that remains yet another project for yet another time. I only raise this point to clarify the general neutrality of the primary class of concepts, even as I focus on what I take to be exercises that entail some kind of liberatory potential, or at least aspiration.

As I have already begun to suggest, neither Hadot's foundational definition nor this preliminary list of examples can exhaust the kinds of exercises that motivate the group of thinkers in question here or the category of practices of self-overcoming on the whole. Indeed, I use terms like "class," "family," and "category" rather than referring to a singular "concept," because while it is clear that this group of notions can be taken as a kind of conceptual cluster, it is equally clear that the development of each is marked by precise forms of specification and are tied to an entire range of motivations, attending philosophical questions, historical concerns, and material conditions. Further, one of my primary goals is to challenge, elaborate, and develop this general category and thus the concepts and definitions that constitute it. For this reason, Hadot's specification and his brief list of representative examples will serve a benchmark or touchstone, a kind of preliminary working definition. It sets a foundation for the critical work that emerges from the category and from those definitions themselves. In other words, and to paraphrase Hadot, the general unity allows us to explore the diversity and to understand what each articulation has to offer to the others, to the conceptual family as a whole, and to us.

It is from this shared if still ambiguous point of departure that I elaborate and develop the differing ways that the figures and concepts noted here understand, theorize, critique, and deploy practices, of whatever kind, taken up in order to bring about some change in the practicing subject, however that subject itself is understood, for whatever reasons, and to whatever ends. As noted already, each of the following chapters takes up a given figure, generally introduces their respective conception of practices of the self, explores and illuminates the conceptual resources they provide, marks out lacunae in their articulations, specifies the important questions that emerge from these treatments, and so on. Often, a given figure raises core questions that can only be addressed through resources cultivated within a different perspective or body of work. Indeed, on the scale of the book as a whole, this is essentially the relationship of King to the French theorists that precede him. He and the concepts and practices around him provide an entire range of possibilities to the questions that the former writers help develop and specify but do not, and perhaps cannot, answer themselves. In other cases, given lines of investigation or conceptual resources only emerge through the broader collective dialogue. In this way, each chapter at once presents a singular focus and builds upon preceding discussions, although in a way that is at times nonlinear, as necessitated by the material in question.

While I address a range of concerns over the course of this project, and while it is in some sense meant to provide a general introduction to this material, the overall study is fundamentally motivated by at least three positive questions. Each of these themes consistently appears in and around this literature. The first two are important but in some sense "minor" questions, as those discussions give way to the third, major question. First, there is the question of practicing, articulating, and recognizing spiritual exercises in the present, or what I sometimes call "properly contemporary" spiritual exercises. Second, we have the long-standing problem of religious and philosophical specialists who primarily populate and author the major texts and sources and, conversely, the formulation of "everyday" practices developed, adapted, and taken up by "average" people, non-elites, and non-specialists. Third and finally, there is the major question of the political content and consequences of practices of self-change. To some extent, the relationship between the minor and major questions guides and determines the overall compositional structure of this book. It unfolds as it does according to the ways that pursuing the first two questions produces certain conceptual resources for addressing the major political question.

First, we have the question of taking up ancient or past spiritual exercises in the present and the attending challenges of articulating, practicing, and refining "properly contemporary" practices of the self. Although each does so in their own way, all of the figures that I engage in this book are concerned with the possibility of how to effectively—with this term itself under a great deal of scrutiny—take up practices of the self under contemporary historical, political, material, religious, and other conditions. The answer to this question may seem obvious: clearly people practice spiritual exercises, the care of the self, religious practices, and forms of self-care all the time. However, as Hadot helps demonstrate, much more fundamental and much more interesting questions emerge from this otherwise uncontroversial fact. Those themes come into sharp relief when refracted through specific historical, moral, and political concerns and when we think more clearly about the relationship of given practice to given telos.

Each chapter engages the often differing ways that this question arises within the work of the figure and frame in question. However, for compositional and conceptual reasons, it receives the most directed attention in chapter 1, with my discussion of Hadot. If, as Hadot argues, the practice of spiritual exercises is an ancient one, and if the contexts and commitments of those who developed such traditions matter for the substance and nature of those exercises themselves, it is not as simple as merely "importing" a practice and all of the conceptual scaffolding that co-constitutes it into another time, place, and set of problems without a substantive work of translation. Hadot most adamantly insists on this challenge, although

Foucault too recognizes it. As he says, "You can't find the solution of a problem in the solution of another problem raised at another moment by other people."[14] In many ways, this tension also sits at the heart of Friedmann's entire project. Similar, if at times greater, challenges emerge when attempting to understand or specify wholly new forms of spiritual exercise, which may emerge in response to wholly contemporary "spiritual demands," formulated in and though wholly contemporary conceptual and practical resources.

Chapter 1 further demonstrates that the question of contemporary practices of the self also goes beyond the various concerns that initially motivate a given thinker's interest in this category. Through a tension within the overlap between what I refer to as Hadot's prescriptive and descriptive projects, I argue that the question of contemporary spiritual exercises reduces to the problem of understanding the emergence (whether whole cloth or in translation) of new forms of practice in general, in any time and place, and under any given set of conditions. For a given regimen of spiritual exercises, it is always an issue of the relationships between the varying practical and theoretical aspects that constitute them and the overall relationship of what Foucault calls a given "morality" to "the reality in which it is situated."[15] That, in turn, with Hadot's help, leads to the specification of a set, however incomplete, of formal criteria necessary for any attempt to translate or adapt ancient spiritual exercises into a contemporary context, to specify and deploy new forms of practice, or finally and perhaps most intriguingly, to recognize given practices as genuine forms of spiritual exercise, where any number of factors would typically preclude or obscure such recognition. As is so often the case here, Hadot shows us why such a translation process is so important, and even models many of the necessary criteria for any such project, but does not take up the task himself. These criteria are also indispensable for addressing the second and third guiding questions of this study.

Second, there is the problem of specialists, tied in many ways to the problem of translation. The majority of ancient and often modern primary sources in this literature are the result of elite authorship of some kind, especially those that Hadot and Foucault primarily draw from. This may mean economic and political elites, religious and philosophical specialists, and often both. As invoked in chapter 1, in his influential landmark *The Varieties of Religious Experience*, William James identifies his goal of looking to such specialists, what he called religious "geniuses" and "pattern-setters" as the primary objects of his massive study. Here, the average believer, practitioner, or subject of religious experience is described as an "imitator" whose experience exists as a "dull habit," and so on.[16] To be sure, few scholars subscribe to this kind of top-down view now, and this is reflected in the majority of social scientific work and work in religious studies on religious belief and practice. Nonetheless, it persists implicitly and helps illuminate a problem integral to many of the historical sources that many rely upon. (This is conversely a tension that Friedmann, King, and Lorde are quite sensitive to.) Because the documents that outline the practice of spiritual exercises come from either economic and political elites or from specialists leading lives devoted to such practice, it is often unclear how they were or are taken up in daily life. Beyond simply "following instructions," we must ask how such sources are translated and adapted by average people in everyday practice, for reasons, to ends, and in ways that are by definition fundamentally different from those of given elite articulators.

Furthermore, even removing the gap between specialist and everyday wisdom, it is simply the case that spiritual exercises are always subject to translation, and that can be in any direction. Such adaptation is not simply from elite to everyday, but laterally across differing communities, and from the ground up as it were. Someone who buys a popular spiritual guide or self-help book today will likely adapt it in some way to their own needs and goals. It is also very often the case that refined articulations are a systemization, if not appropriation, of popular beliefs and practices. In all cases, I argue that the unique perspectives, experiences, and practices of non-elite, nonspecialists are important in their own right, and cannot be subsumed by or assimilated to whatever textual articulation we—or even they—may happen to be drawing from. Chapter 1 develops this line of thinking with regard to one of Hadot's favorite examples, "the view from above." I ultimately argue that for this concept to have any ongoing purchase, let alone any political significance, *the view from above must be a view from below*.[17] This position emerges from my first question, is shaped in discussion of the second, and directly informs my articulation of the third, the primary concern of this book as a whole: what I call the politics of self-overcoming.

Finally, there is the major question, which I pose, revise, and rephrase in several forms over the course of this book. What are the political content, consequences, and general status of ethical practices of self-change?

Without reducing the collective, systemic, and material nature of the political to the mere aggregation of the ethical self-constitution and moral lives of individuals, and without conversely reducing ethical life to a kind of by-product of given political and material conditions, how and under what conditions can we understand spiritual exercises in terms of political practice? What is the relationship of the ethical transformation of the self to the political transformation of the world, and vice versa? In what ways do these domains intersect with, determine, or co-constitute one another? How can we understand, articulate, and recognize practices of ethical self-formation that cultivate and sustain, rather than preclude, just ethical and political relations with others?

The particular question of how we might understand the politics of spiritual exercises can be understood as a concretization of what is arguably the most fundamental question motivating this project, which, although for the most part implicit, provides its overarching structure and goals at the greatest level of abstraction: what is the relationship—or rather, what are some of the possible relationships—between ethics and politics? At its most foundational level, this work is concerned with the imbrication of ethical and political life, or rather with the specification of one possible form that this relationship may take. Although this general, foundational concern remains in the background, it appears explicitly at regular points in the following discussions, and it is thus worth being clear about it from the outset. I argue that understanding the political relationship of the kinds of ethical practices that concern me here means that we can reframe the practical and conceptual relationships between individual moral action, ethical self-formation, and collective and systemic political life, in at least one set of cases.

However, beyond these general articulations, I more often and more precisely pose the guiding questions of this book through the specific concerns and particular language of the authors and texts that constitute its substance. In the clearest and most basic terms, and in language that we find in both Hadot and Foucault, the central goal of this book is to ask how, in what form, and under what conditions, we may identify or articulate a form of the care of the self that is at once identical to or coterminous with the care of the other?[18] Phrased in this way, this is primarily a moral and ethical question, but may also take on a political form: what forms of the care of the self are at once "indissolubly" care of plural *others*, of the community, or of the city? How, paraphrasing Friedmann's self-critical articulation at the outset of his *La puissance et la sagesse*, might we place what he calls moral and even "spiritual" concerns neither in front of nor behind, but rather alongside economic and social conditions?[19] What forms must "caring for oneself" take, especially in relation to others, such that it does not amount to "self-indulgence" and can even claim, as Lorde does, the status of "political warfare?" How is "self-purification" a properly political exercise, rather than, say, something that is at best adjacent to and at worst a distraction from the critical work of direct action? How can an intervention on the level of what Foucault calls "the relationship of the self to itself" also amount to an intervention into the systemic, institutional, and material political conditions that on some level and to whatever degree, necessarily co-determine that relationship, and vice versa? Indeed, what does Foucault mean, or could he mean, when he so concisely and yet so enigmatically states that "there is no first or final point of resistance to political power other than in the relationship one has to oneself"?[20] In some sense, it would only be a slight exaggeration to say that this project as a whole can be read as a kind of extended meditation on this statement.

The political question in turn raises the primary negative criteria, the challenge and charge that face any attempt to understand the politics of spiritual exercises, which I have already invoked in discussing the problem of reductionism. What again is the relationship of the collective, systemic, and material nature of political life to the ethical self-constitution and moral lives of individuals, with the former necessarily understood as something wholly other than the mere aggregation of the latter? This latter premise, that the political does not amount to the ethical "scaled up," that its systemic and material nature has a life of its own outside and beyond the moral behavior and ethical self-formation of individuals taken in sum, serves as one of the major guiding threads of this work. It also produces the two primary negative criteria against which all of my readings and arguments here are measured, structured, and determined. These are what I refer to, following Friedmann, as the problem of ethical "spiritualism" and its attending counterpart in political "moralism." I elaborate these concepts in detail later.

These concepts and constraints emerge from the concerns and articulations of the figures and sources that constitute the substance of this overall investigation. However, at the outset of any such analysis, they can be obscured by a range of other, surface concerns that may appear more immediate. Before moving on, it is important to address these initial problems of obscurity and misdirection, what I paraphrase Foucault in calling the problem of "connotations and overtones." It is no coincidence that in this literature the language of the "spiritual" is consistently shadowed by an attending vocabulary, centered around a series of important distinctions and disclaimers. These specifications reflect a fundamental, persistent, and indeed intelligible anxiety on the part of these writers and many readers about the language of "spirituality," "spiritual exercises," the "care of the self," an "interior effort," and the idea of "self-purification." An entire range of negative associations accrues to such terms, and there is a looming and consistent threat of misunderstanding that emerges from them. Some of these are superficial, others constitute real challenges, and some are superficial on their own while lending clarity to our more substantive questions in context.

II. WHAT IS THE "SPIRITUAL"?

In the representative article "Spiritual Exercises," Pierre Hadot begins to articulate that foundational concept by almost immediately laying out the trouble that tends to follow the idea of "spirituality." Hadot's description proceeds from an opening invocation of a favorite passage from Georges Friedmann's *La puissance et la sagesse*, and I will return to both that passage and Hadot's fascination with it often. Building on Friedmann's own use of the term "spiritual exercises," Hadot begins to muse on the reasons they both insist on using the admittedly uncomfortable language of the "spiritual," maintaining that in the end no other term will really do for the conceptual and practical phenomena at the heart of their shared concern.

As Hadot says, in direct response to Friedmann, "'Spiritual exercises.' The expression is a bit disconcerting for the contemporary reader. In the first place, it is no longer quite fashionable these days to use the term 'spiritual.'"[21] As he suggests, the language of "spirituality" does not seem to generally inspire much philosophical confidence, among numerous other reliably negative associations that attach to the term. An awareness of this disconcertion, indeed the disconcertion itself, is paralleled in Friedmann's work, where he characterizes what he calls the "spiritual dimension" that he seeks to resituate alongside the economic and political as something "so despised today."[22]

INTRODUCTION

These diagnoses of "the spiritual" as something either disconcerting, despised, or both, no doubt remain as accurate today as they were for Hadot and Friedmann in the 1970s, at least for a certain shared audience. And as evinced by these disclaimers, they are both aware of the possibility that either misreading or outright dismissal could follow from the use of the language of the spiritual. Here they are joined by Foucault and Lorde, as all are well aware that a certain early ambiguity, if left unchecked, can develop into an antipathy that would leave their own projects vulnerable to misreading on multiple levels. In deploying the vocabulary of "spirituality" and "the spiritual," they all do so in a way that evinces a consistent concern that their work and their claims not be taken for something beyond the strict definitions and examples that they invoke.

Friedmann is representative here. In a way that reflects Hadot's early disclaimers, he opens *La puissance et la sagesse* by immediately specifying what the language of the "spiritual" does not mean for him. In an endnote to an early and important passage,[23] he distances his own work from what he calls *spiritualism*: "This term, 'spiritual,' will surprise, and perhaps even shock, certain readers. I was myself somewhat disturbed by its resonances, its association with 'spiritualist' doctrines or dogmas, which are so foreign to me."[24] In other words, Friedman recognizes that it is not without some good reason that the "spiritual dimension" has come to be "so despised," as concepts and practices that he does find genuinely contemptible have attached to the term. These latter fall under the category of what he refers to here as spiritualism, which I adopt from that text, and elaborate further over the course of this book as one of two primary negative criteria against which my arguments will be measured.

The shared forms of contempt and disconcertion in question for Hadot and Friedmann stem in no small part from the strong association of both the term "spiritual" and the notion of "spirituality" with seemingly unsophisticated and capricious forms of "vulgar religiosity" or "pop spirituality," ranging from late nineteenth- and early twentieth-century forms of spiritualism proper and Theosophy, to New Age practices, drugstore self-help literature, and so much else besides. As the American sociologist of religion Robert Wuthnow describes it, such forms of religious life and their attending discourses are often associated with claims of the sort that one is "into yoga and very spiritual," or somehow "spiritual but not religious," and are taken to be aesthetically and affectively uncomfortable or doctrinally without substance. As Wuthnow puts it, "Some observers . . . wonder whether 'spiritual' has become synonymous with 'flaky.'"[25]

Now, my goal here is not a critique or defense of those maligned forms of popular religious life, to whatever extent either is called for. Rather and again, I want to begin by simply noting that Friedmann and others are very much aware of the kinds of associations the concepts in question carry with them—and indeed share a certain antipathy toward them—and yet insist on retaining a qualified and more precisely rendered technical vision of terms like "spiritual," "spirituality," and "self-purification," among many others. If we are to understand what Hadot and Friedmann mean when they use the language of the spiritual, it is worth beginning with the simple observation that they explicitly do in spite of both the negative connotations it tends to carry with it, and the ambiguity that surround it.

The task is to specify that antipathy, which on my reading in no way amounts to superficial forms of either aesthetic discomfort or metaphysical disagreement. It is instead the result of what I take to be the most substantive challenge to any of these formulations, which is already evinced in the language that all of these thinkers marshal in their respective disclaimers. If Foucault is at pains to distance his "ethical" work from the "Californian cult of the self"[26] and what both he and Hadot call a kind of "moral dandyism,"[27] then what must they mean when they invoke this kind of language? The problem is in fact already evinced by the way that I have phrased the question, as we must avoid confusing the specific philosophical, ethical, and political questions that Friedmann, Foucault, Hadot, Lorde, and King are trying to raise on the one hand, with the kinds of popular concerns and associations that attach so immediately to a term like "spirituality" on the other. We need to be just as clear and precise about what these thinkers are rejecting and why as we are about what it is that they are endorsing.

At the same time, it should be equally clear that it is not simply a matter of clarifying what Hadot and Friedmann *do* mean by distinguishing it from what they do *not* mean, and then dispensing with the latter. Rather, here the problem of spiritualism is directly related to the relevant understanding of spirituality, for at least two reasons. First, because it is not always clear what does or does not fall under the category of spiritualism. To understand the beliefs, practices, and general forms that the writers in question want to include also allows us to see why some doctrines or practices that may appear "spiritualist" on the surface may not be, and thus cannot simply be dismissed or declared irrelevant. Second, what seem like simple disclaimers on the part of these authors in fact begin to reveal why and how what we are calling spiritualism does indeed present real problems and genuine challenges to what it is that much of the present work concerns itself to articulate.

In order to gain that purchase, however, we need untangle a knot in several stages. The consistent first hurdle is the conflation of the spiritual in general with what are taken to be the more undesirable trappings of spiritualism, which so often redirect the kinds of questions that I want to raise and thus prevent any such conversation from so much as getting off the ground. In chapter 3 and elsewhere, I refer to this as the problem of aesthetic misdirection. To reject or pass up an analysis of given beliefs and practices for immediate aesthetic or affective reasons—that is, because they "seem flaky"—is completely superficial. But even recognizing this fact raises a second and more important problem: the conflation of a rejection of those trappings with a series of much more fundamental theoretical and ethical concerns.

If we think that Friedmann dismisses spiritualism for superficial reasons, that then obscures our ability to see the substantive issues that motivate him without even knowing that we have done so. We need to be as clear as possible about what is important to identify and reject, and what is ultimately a distraction. To assume that any strong response to what we are calling spiritual practices is merely superficial, and thus unfair, is to already begin to miss the more fundamental critique and therefore the line of thinking that leads to the positive specification of the criteria of spirituality.

"Connotations and Overtones"

Regarding the first hurdle, the problem of misdirection, two general points lend some clarity. First, the term "spiritual" may suggest a category marked by certain metaphysical concerns—in the popular sense of that term—including, perhaps above all, belief in varying forms of interaction with objects taken to exist beyond nature, in either a more traditional religious sense or in the terms used by the subjects of Wuthnow's study, for example. However, it is clear from the texts in question that when Friedmann, Hadot, or Foucault use the term "spiritual," they do not mean it in the sense of either "having to do with spirits" or the divine in general.

The problem is still more complex, however: Friedmann does not distinguish spirituality and spiritualism in order to exclude given forms of practice based on metaphysical commitments. The issue is not that these criteria exclude a given example from the domain of spirituality, but rather that they are irrelevant to the definition of that category. The adjudication of the truth content of metaphysical statements about the existence of objects or beings beyond nature, as we would find in some traditional philosophy of religion, is irrelevant to both this project and the thinkers it engages, even those with clear religious commitments.

That Wuthnow's subjects believe in ghosts, angels, and the like, and that this may indeed be a source of discomfort for someone like Friedmann, cannot be denied. But if the "spiritual" here does not necessarily imply a concern with objects beyond nature, it does not necessarily exclude them either. If "metaphysical content" is not a definitional criterion of what we mean when we use the technical term "spiritual," it is an equally irrelevant criterion of dismissal from that category. For that reason, if the spiritual is not synonymous with such beliefs, there is indeed still room for certain forms of the latter within the former as it is reconstructed here. Thus, in a way that will perhaps appear puzzling (to some readers at least), the metaphysical content of a given view is irrelevant to the notion of the spiritual as I use it. This also means that neither spirituality nor spiritualism are synonymous with "religion."

Second, alongside any metaphysical confusion, there is the possibility that given beliefs and practices may seem doctrinally incoherent. This is one possible reading, or even definition, of what Wuthnow means when he rehearses the concern that certain beliefs and practices seem "flaky." Certainly, New Age thought, yoga studio philosophy, or contemporary invocations of self-care can appear this way: rather than a cohesive set of beliefs and practices, we may observe something akin to the metaphor of the shopping cart full of spiritual odds and ends, chosen and brought together haphazardly for their affective purchase rather than any more robust criteria, pragmatic or otherwise.

Among the many problems with this view is that it lacks its own criteria for the assessment not simply of the coherence of such practices, but of a notion of coherence itself appropriate to the task, let alone an argument that "coherence" matters much at all. There may be forms of seemingly incoherent constellations of doctrines and practices that do fit the criteria of spirituality, but we do not yet have those criteria, and thus cannot yet judge. Thus, any rigorous reapproach to such material—on my part, at least—can only occur on the other side of the present work. There may well be a place for certain forms, or even simply aspects, of what seems like spiritualism within what these thinkers call spirituality, but the proper standards by which such a judgment can be made are not obvious at this juncture, at least not to me. And although this problem falls outside the bounds of this project, the production and specification of the resources we would need to appraise such traditions and practices are also productive for my guiding concerns here.

All of this is to say that there are far more pressing matters than "spirits" and "flakiness" at issue. The disclaimers of Hadot and Friedmann should not serve to dismiss such trappings outright, but to draw our attention to the fact that whereas they seem quite important in popular discourses around spirituality, they are irrelevant here.

Egoism and Withdrawal

"Spiritualism" has come to already serve as a kind of foil, although it should be clear that the term does not necessarily apply to the forms of popular religious life referenced earlier. Neither metaphysics nor aesthetics nor affect is a constitutive criterion of either the spiritual or spiritualism on this model, and is, on its own, grounds for neither endorsement nor dismissal. In other words, there is nothing about the work of any of the figures that I engage here that would discount an analysis of, for example, contemporary New Age practices or self-care through the framework of the ethics—or politics—of practices of self-overcoming.

What then is "spiritualism"? What is the substantive concern behind the disclaimers that I have rehearsed, and why must all of these thinkers take it seriously as a genuine challenge to their respective analyses of the category of practices of self-overcoming? This is the second hurdle I mentioned, the next part of the knot to untie, and the most important one. Foucault is especially clear on this point, identifying what I take to be the fundamental criterion for a working distinction between the spiritual and the spiritualist. The real danger, the genuine challenge to any invocation of the spiritual, and therefore the central criterion of spiritualism, is egoism.

With words of caution redolent of Hadot's and Friedmann's own disclaimers, Foucault begins to describe this challenge in the opening passages of *The Hermeneutics of the Subject*, in his elaboration of the idea of the care of the self:

> I think we can say that there is something a bit disturbing for us in this principle of the care of the self. Indeed, going through the texts, the different forms of philosophy and the different forms of exercises and philosophical or spiritual practices, we see the principle of care of the self expressed in a variety of phrases like: "caring for oneself," "taking care of oneself," "withdrawing into oneself," "retiring into the self," "finding one's pleasure in oneself," "seeking no other delight but in the self," "remaining in the company of oneself," "being the friend of oneself," "being in oneself as in a fortress," "looking after" or "devoting oneself to oneself," "respecting oneself," etc. Now you are all well aware that there is a certain tradition (or rather several traditions) that dissuades us (us, now, today) from giving any positive value to all of these expressions, precepts and rules, and above all from making them the basis of a morality. All these injunctions to exalt oneself, to devote oneself to oneself, to turn in on oneself, to offer service to oneself, sound to our ears like . . . a sort of challenge and defiance, a desire for radical ethical change, a sort of moral dandyism, the assertion-challenge of a fixed esthetic and individual stage. Or else they sound to us like a somewhat melancholy and sad expression of the withdrawal of the individual who is unable to hold onto and keep firmly before his eyes, in his grasp and for himself, a collective morality (that of the city-state, for example), and who, faced with the disintegration of this collective morality, has naught else to do but attend to himself. So, the immediate, initial connotations and overtones of all of these expressions direct us away from thinking about these precepts in positive terms.[28]

As Foucault concludes, "We have the paradox of a precept of care of the self which signifies for us either egoism or withdrawal."[29]

I return to this passage in chapter 3. For now, it suffices to note that Foucault's conclusion is resonant with Hadot's rejection of any conception of a "care of the self" that seems "focused far too much on the 'self.'"[30] Friedmann is perhaps closer, when he argues that "the first condition is, on the level of the individual, that we do not accept the withdrawal into the self."[31] What Friedmann thus calls the "escape into *spiritualism* or mystical

INTRODUCTION

comforts," then, is characterized by and reflective of "a negative and desperate attitude . . . and religious or secular forms of retreat from the world."[32] Such a "retreat" into oneself is a form of self-absorption, a way of "looking inward" that does not result in productive relations outward. It does not cultivate, but rather precludes robust ethical relations with the other and positive political relations with and within larger human communities, including and especially relations of solidarity.

Spiritualism, then, is characterized by *an egoistic relationship to oneself that precludes robust ethical relations with the other and liberatory political relations with others*. All of these terms are subject to a great deal of further specification, and I further distinguish the ethical and political variations of this problem later. For now, if Wuthnow's "flakiness" means anything substantive, it is this egoism—accompanied of course by all of the uncomfortable affective sheen that, for whatever reason, so often attaches itself to a relation to oneself marked by the abnegation of concern for others. In Foucault's terms, it is the form of life of the moral dandy, the one committed to the "Californian cult of the self" with "naught else to do but attend to himself." As I have intimated, there are also political consequences here. On my reading, we find such challenges at the heart of Lorde's concern when she not only rejects any charge of self-indulgence, but directly opposes it to political practice. For King, his work can only operate—that is, take concrete form in mass direct action—from a perspective and within a practice that already excludes the forms of egoism in question, even as it remains a constant danger. Furthermore, such forms of *spiritualist*—rather than *spiritual*—exercise also very predictably result in harm to oneself. Indeed, as King so often emphasizes, the mistreatment of others is coterminous with one's own dehumanization and moral disfiguration.

In all cases, it is clear that spiritualism presents both an ethical challenge and entails an attending set of political consequences. This problem of retreat and withdrawal is the first and most immediate, although by no means the only or even primary challenge (I will return to the second and more pressing problem later). Friedmann is again particularly clear here, emphasizing that a withdrawal into the self is not only subject to ethical criticism, but may also constitute a retreat from everyday life and an abnegation of larger social and political responsibilities. As he says of the "wisdom" (the *sagesse*) invoked in the title of *La puissance et la sagesse*, "Its title [*Wisdom and Power*] is likely to bring about a misunderstanding, but one which should dissipate with this preface. The wisdom which is so necessary today is not a form of contemplation, [it is not] a retreat from the unrest and abominations of the century. . . . It is an unquiet wisdom, one that is active and audacious, and which, in the eyes of some, appears more or less ridiculous, but so be it."[33] For Friedmann, the spiritualism he rejects and the "spiritual dimension" he seeks to explicate are already political categories, just as they are already ethical categories. And the "unquiet wisdom" he pursues must not be mistaken for quietism, a contemplative "retreat" from the political domain. For someone like Friedmann, as we will see in chapter 2, the catastrophes that marked the midnight of the twentieth century lend the greatest urgency to his insistence. The same is very clear for King and Lorde, and indeed for anyone, at any time, living through the political nightmares and systemic injustices so familiar to so many.

At the same time, and as I have insisted, it is not always clear on the surface just what constitutes egoism, retreat, or withdrawal. For example, there are kinds of "retreat" that take the form of monasticism or hermeticism, a withdrawal from the world to engage in some regimen of spiritual exercise. Such "monastic forms" may take on any political or ethical valence depending on any number of contextual factors. Moreover, "monasticism" here need not refer to actual monastic institutions in their familiar religious iterations, but can rather denote any institutional withdrawal from daily work and life, whether for a lifetime or a weekend, alone or in the company of others, to take up some regimen of self-change. And for that reason in turn, alongside their familiar religious counterparts, monastic forms may be political, artistic, educational, and so much else.

It is significant that none of the figures that I engage here outright dismiss this category of what I have begun calling "monasticism" in a technical sense. In fact, as Friedmann himself puts it, "asceticism as means of spiritual progress" does not necessarily amount to the forms of retreat that concern us.[34] Some monastic forms may well constitute either a direct cultivation of positive relations with others or serve as preparatory practice for the care of others. Rosa Parks's visit to the Highlander Folk School in the summer of 1955, four months before her famous refusal to give up her seat on a Montgomery city bus, is an ideal example here, and one that I invoke in chapter 4. Conversely, as King and others warn, one may cultivate cancerous egoism even in the midst of an otherwise flourishing political community (as every organizer knows so well), just as one may well engage in "retreat" or withdrawal in the very midst of everyday life, among the masses of other people.

All this is to say that "retreat" and "withdrawal," as I will follow Foucault and Friedmann in using these terms, understood as an egoistic dereliction of one's moral or political obligations, do not necessarily correspond to any particular form of practice, or even to physical or social isolation. They are not synonymous with monasticism or asceticism per se. This is why spiritualism must be a criterion in itself, and not a proxy for given aesthetic trappings, metaphysical commitments, or even institutional forms. It is spiritualism that allows us to understand those latter phenomena in the terms that I am articulating, rather than the other way around. Here, further, we can see just how this idea of spiritualism, generally understood in terms of the ethical problem of egoism, can produce a first or preliminary political consequence in the self-regarding abnegation of duties to plural others, systemic injustices, and so on. It also helps us see, just a little more clearly, when and how removing oneself, alone or in the company of others, may sometimes be the very condition of robust moral relationships and just political action.

Productive monasticism aside then, and as I have indicated, this problem of abnegation in no way exhausts the political challenges to the accounts I explore and the class of concepts and practices that concern me. Nor is it even remotely the primary danger. The real problem, on Friedmann's account, and in a way that is at least entailed by the work of someone like Foucault, is what the former calls political *moralism*, understood as a kind political counterpart to ethical spiritualism. And it is this moralism that presents the primary challenge to which all of the conceptions discussed in this book and any synthetic positive account on my part must respond.

The Problem of Moralism

At least at its most mild, this kind of spiritualist abnegation, the retreat and withdrawal described earlier, represents a kind of negative conception, a quietism that claims or assumes a perhaps impossible "apolitical" status. This "hands-off" perspective is grounded in the idea that one may simply "attend to oneself" in forms of life devoted to practices of self-change that somehow do not intersect or impact the political and material conditions that shape human life. Whether, how, under what circumstances, and in which cases genuine neutrality is so much as possible is another question. Actual monasteries, after all, have always been political institutions. The point is that as I am using these terms, they represent a conception that does not really claim a politics, even as they entail one. This is what I mean when I say that such quietism is by definition a negative view. It either does not have a politics as it claims, or shades into and pragmatically amounts to a form of the major political challenge to these authors and conceptions: what I again follow Friedmann in calling political moralism.

The real problem, as Friedmann argues, is far more pressing, because it represents a positive and indeed prescriptive conception of the relationship of ethics to politics, even if it is at times deployed only implicitly. As we will see in chapter 2, within his ongoing reflections on the lessons of the USSR and Western criticisms of the Soviet project, Friedmann is concerned by any reduction of economic and material concerns to the aggregated behaviors of individuals. It is this impulse that Friedmann calls moralism:

> I have indicated several of these grand problems which today call for a combat to designate goals and give rise to values. There are certainly many others which are essential in the countries and on the continents which I have not yet visited. But, wherever they implant themselves on the planet, these efforts are present and tied to one another. They all demand *coordinated action* because it is their spirit and their flesh, collective struggles in order to ameliorate institutions and organize societies. . . . It is moral (and we must qualify that), but is in no way a "moralism"—the more or less conscious illusion, the pride and hypocrisy of those who pretend to bring a "morality" to human beings, without addressing or attending to the material conditions necessary for a truly human life: the elements fundamentally required for our well-being, without which there is no question, for the immense majority of human beings—setting aside for the moment the case of asceticism as means of spiritual progress, whether explicitly religious or not—of "morality," or happiness. I recall here, deliberately, the notion of happiness that certain critics of "consumer society" include in their confused condemnations.

Friedmann goes on to reemphasize his foundational commitment to the importance of material and economic conditions understood as something other than and beyond the ethical: "Habitat, food, housing, adaptation to one's work, reduction of fatigue, breaks and relaxation: needs that have long been at the center of my studies. They have lost nothing of their importance in my eyes. Their satisfaction is the prerequisite to any humanization that amounts to more than words."[35]

Whereas "moralism" typically refers to the habit of "moralizing," of casting judgment on the ethical behaviors or principles of others, Friedmann uses the term in a different sense. Moralism, for him, amounts to a primary emphasis on ethics and behavior that is not founded in a concern for material and economic well-being or any robust understanding of the many and complex ways that the latter may shape and determine the former. Moralism sees the material and economic as the mere consequence of the ethical. In my use, and following Friedmann, moralism will thus refer to the *reduction the systemic, material nature of the political to the mere aggregation of the ethical self-formation and moral lives of individuals*. Such a view may be explicitly and aspirationally posited in theoretical articulations or just implicitly assumed, but as Friedmann emphasizes, it has also been pragmatically enacted in various forms of political life.

Such a moralism is, for example, evinced by the facile critiques of consumerism that Friedmann invokes above: the idea that shifts in consumption habits, or ambiguous claims about the effects of certain forms of consumption on "character," can somehow, someday, scale up to material justice. In our own context, such claims often appear in the form of virulent critiques of the personal behaviors of the poor and working classes or arguments around so-called cultures of poverty, as if these have any substantive bearing on systemic economic and material conditions, their operations, or their effects on individuals. (It is, incidentally, in these cases that the two meanings of "moralism" most overlap.)

More broadly, such a view is either implicitly or explicitly evinced in neoliberal discourse and policy, the particular forms of twentieth- and twenty-first-century American conservatism, and countless other historical iterations. For example, Chief Justice John G. Roberts's famously dismissive statement regarding systemic racism in the United States: "The way to stop discrimination on the basis of race is to stop discriminating on the basis of race," in the U.S. Supreme Court's 2007 *Parents Involved* decision, is an archetypical claim of moralist politics.[36] In such cases, whether "conservative," classical liberal, neoliberal, or otherwise, politics in this case is simply ethics writ large; the systemic and material political whole is nothing beyond the mere sum of its ethical parts.

Moralism, in this sense, is thus the political consequence or incarnation of ethical spiritualism. It can be distinguished from quietism, even as this third term is ultimately not a primary concern for me in this book. Indeed, I take it that many claims to political quietism pragmatically shade into moralism—or even liberatory political relations—under scrutiny. In either case, a study of political quietism on the terms I develop here would be worthwhile on its own, although it would certainly amount to its own project.[37] Once again then, moralism is a positive view that implicitly or explicitly holds that the aggregation of moral transformation brought about the practice of spiritual exercises on a mass scale by discrete individuals would on its own result in desirable political change, including material and economic justice, however construed. For the remainder of this book, then, I will use "ethical spiritualism" or simply "spiritualism" to refer to the ethical domain, and "moralism" to refer to the political. As should be clear, the relationship between the two is complex.

The Other Reductionism

As we will see in chapter 2, Friedmann does very briefly contrast this moralism with what he takes to be its quasi-antithesis, which he describes as the *marxisme naïf* of his own youth,[38] defined by a "mechanistic interpretation of Marxism," which I'll more simply refer to as "naïve materialism." Now, it is worth being clear at the outset that this is not a major concept for either Friedmann or myself. It does not carry the same weight and receives little further attention in this book, where moralism is the central challenge. Insofar as it is not, on my reading, a major threat or challenge either to my case or those of the figures I take up here, it receives much more limited, though precise, attention. This is in part because it in no way amounts to either a rejection of materialism itself or the construction of what Foucault would call "counterarguments that are symmetrical and contrary," a perfect inversion of moralism or some kind of both-sides parallelism.[39] This concept does, however, help illuminate something important about the kinds of critiques that can be, and often are, leveled at the literature and figures I engage—challenges to which they are indeed vulnerable, as is my own project. For that reason, it is worth dwelling on a moment.

INTRODUCTION

As Friedmann describes it:

> The element that most effectively explains the penetration of this amoral "realism" among certain Western intellectuals (of whom so many are, in fact, honest people) and among the people is the following: in the mechanistic interpretation of Marxism, we rely exclusively on the importance of economic and social transformation, which would allow for the creation of a new society, and "new human beings." Suppress capitalism and the private ownership of the means of production, and the individual, as a materially liberated being, will also be morally liberated. Automation. Transform the *setting* (I employ this term as an image) of human life, and it will find itself upended.[40]

The view critically articulated here does not simply prioritize the economic, material, and large-scale systemic conditions of human flourishing, but rather takes the ethical life of the individual to be either reducible to or a mere by-product of those conditions. "Transform the setting" and the rest will take care of itself; wind up the right political mechanism, let it go, and ethical life will fall into place on its own.

At best and at least, such a view would hold that the ethics of the self constitutes a separate domain that is either unrelated or a kind of overlay to political transformation, something to take care of once other political problems are solved. In strategic and tactical terms, I am more sympathetic to the latter position, even as I hold that such a distinction is both practically and theoretically impossible—and likely amounts to another causal view in the end anyway. That too is a conversation for another time. The important thing is that this naïve materialism is again defined by another merely causal relationship between the ethical and the political. Its disagreement with moralism is simply in the direction of effect. It remains within the same framework and terms as political moralism and does not reconceive—perhaps does not think to reconceive—those foundational concepts and relationships.

Now again, and as detailed in chapter 2, it is important to understand that Friedmann does not reject materialism. He is as clear as possible that holding to a robust materialism is important for his project and for my own—indeed, this is perhaps his greatest contribution here—whereas moralism misconstrues actual and possible ways of understanding and enacting the relationship of the ethical to the political. Rather, he rejects this mechanistic or "naïve" form, against which he seeks to offer an internal corrective. In other words, naïve materialism, insofar as it is a materialism, does get something right about the ways that material and economic conditions shape and condition the ethical self-formation and moral lives of individuals. This is why the qualifier "naïve" is so important here, and it is that naïveté alone that must be exorcised.

This concept is relevant, because even as a nonparallel counter-discourse or reverse-discourse to moralism, it operates according to a very similar form of reasoning, though with an inverted set of values and conclusions. That is, rather than an ethical reductionism, it represents an economic, material, and political reductionism that seemed significant enough for Friedmann to note in the limited ways that he does in *La puissance et la sagesse*. It matters for my purposes, because it is the view, or perhaps more accurately the impulse or intuition, from which the standard criticisms of the idea of a politics of self-overcoming are likely to emerge. In other words, it is from the perspective of naïve materialism that the very charges of ethical spiritualism and political moralism may be leveled at the class of practices in question here.

It is the naïve materialist position that is most likely to either dismiss the category of practices that concern me for superficial reasons on the one hand, or for a misconstrual of the deeper political and theoretical questions at issue on the other. This is because, as we will see in chapter 3, I argue that Foucault's conception of the care of the self entails a reformulation of the relationship of ethics to politics in which neither is taken to be prior to the other, and thus abandons the terms by which spiritualism, moralism, and Friedmann's naïve materialism all operate. Friedmann, too, is clear at the very outset of *La puissance et la sagesse* that such a fundamental revaluation is among his goals.[41] For my part, such a reformulation is, as I have noted, at the heart of this project. But a care of the self that is coterminous with the care of others will look like a reduction of politics to ethics if it is viewed from a perspective whose fundamental terms and form are themselves reductionist. Within such a framework, any reformulation is likely to come across as a mere inversion, because it cannot see options outside those terms.

If the charges of spiritualism or moralism most likely to be leveled at the figures I engage emerge from what amounts to a form of naïve materialism, it is because such a perspective can overlook the ways that a robust politics of self-overcoming entails—or *can* entail—a reformulation of the relationship of ethical self-formation to political life and transformation. A care of the self that is genuinely coterminous with the care of others entails a nonreductive governmentality, one that does not operate according to the basic terms of the critique. The irony is that the very framework of the critical position causes it to overlook the fact that thinkers like Friedmann and Foucault are also concerned about spiritualism and moralism for the same reasons: they do not want to fall into a mere ethical reductionism. The naïve view is thus unaware that in order to do so, Foucault, for example, can and must reenvision the forms of reasoning by which the former operates and from which that very charge is leveled. Without an explicit understanding of that reformulation, the care of the self and the interior effort reliably end up looking like spiritualism. This is what I mean when I say that such a critique does get something right: the dangers it illuminates are real. Indeed, they constitute one of the most important challenges to the framework I wish to articulate here. At the same time, it misrecognizes the ways the thinkers in question at the very least evince an awareness of those challenges and at best attempt to avoid them. This because that critical perspective can easily find itself locked in a conceptual frame that only allows for an either/or choice of reductive possibilities.

Now, to be clear, it is entirely possible to read such a perspective into the late Foucault, for example. On that reading, the political consequence of his "turn" to ethics is at best an abandonment of political concerns and at worst a facile commitment to a reductive "politics of the self." However, as I argue in chapter 3, such a view results from a misunderstanding of the very notion of the care of the self that Foucault is either implicitly after in his later work or is at least a consequence of that work. Such a reading also fails to see that Foucault himself criticizes any vision that entails ethical egoism and political withdrawal. In fact, this is the major problem with the "California cult of the self," *not* that it takes up an aesthetically unpleasant or affectively suspicious way of life. Moralism is also the likely critique of any politically minded reading of Hadot, just as it looms large in the background of all of Friedmann's engagements. In the case of Friedmann, the problem is that his criticism of any quasi-exclusive emphasis on the material can be misread as a wholesale abandonment of Marx or the socialist vision. The fact that such a reading is so much as possible, let alone so easy to make, is itself evidence of the problem at hand, and of the real threat of spiritualism and moralism.

On my reading, Friedmann and Foucault would have to agree that we cannot simply recycle or handshake our way to human liberation, even as these kinds of charges way well be leveled against them upon the invocation of the idea of the "spiritual." Nor does King's nonviolent political strategy amount to an attempt to bring about large-scale political change through somehow appealing to the "hearts" of the oppressor, one at a time. Such a view misconstrues the ways in which nonviolent tactics work to provoke political crisis, because those tactics and their critics operate according to different forms of reasoning. If naïve materialism assumes that the practitioner and theorist of exercises of self-change is working from a partial, incorrect, or inverted view of its own perspective, it is little wonder that such practices can be uncritically reduced to a form of spiritualism.

What I ultimately hope to articulate here is an approach and perspective that exits this overall frame: a care of the self that is coterminous with the care of the other and of others, a vision of the relationship of the self to itself whose circuit passes through liberatory political transformation, and vice versa. There are of course exegetical issues here. With regard to the sources that I have gathered in attempting to both frame that challenge and articulate an answer, there is some admitted ambiguity that is worth noting at the outset. It is clear on my reading that Friedmann, Foucault, and even Hadot are aware of and concerned with the dangers and challenges I have articulated. The textual evidence given earlier is explored further in the following chapters. It is also clear that Friedmann, at very least, and Foucault, on my reading, both picture a different, nonreductive relationship between the ethical and the political. It is less clear whether anyone other than Friedmann is carrying that kind of analysis much further.

Several things are clear though. On my reading, all of the resources that I gather are aware on some level of the dangers and challenges in question, and legitimately so. In all cases, the problems of ethical spiritualism or political moralism are real challenges to these accounts and to my own. However, they all show or help in some way to show why the kind of reformulation that interests me is so important. In some cases, even if they do not say this themselves, it is clear that such a reformulation is also a consequence of their other arguments. At the same time, and to be clear, none of the texts that I engage have to explicitly or intentionally address the issues I raise in order to help articulate core questions and provide crucial resources for addressing them. It is ultimately irrelevant to my goals whether or not my questions are their questions. Indeed, aware or not, it is not clear that any of these texts and figures are able to provide that reformulation on their own. Taken together however, I argue that they collectively provide historical and theoretical resources for articulating both the terms of those challenges and an understanding in which distinctions between the care of the self, the other, and the community are ultimately effaced. All of this comes together in chapter 4, with King and the Montgomery boycott. The latter, I argue, provides a representative space in which caring for oneself and caring for others are coterminous, where changing selves are inextricably bound up with changing material conditions.

Implications and Guiding Threads

I have felt it necessary to begin with this set of perhaps overly detailed disclaimers, as it is inevitable that certain questions and concerns arise immediately at the invocation of any discussion of this kind. It is easy for a discussion of the spiritual to be confused with an endorsement of a spiritualism, and not just because the terms are similar. Rather, without a great deal of care and specification, given spiritual exercises can very well appear as *spiritualist* exercises, and vice versa. Further still, it is possible that the same formal practice could very well amount to either under differing circumstances, and the distinction may only be apparent with scrutiny: the practitioners that someone like Wuthnow describes cannot be judged based on surface-level readings of whatever it is they happen to be doing, whether that means attending yoga classes in an office complex or a prayer or meditation retreat in a traditional religious setting. Many bristle at terms like "spiritual," and without addressing those superficial forms of discomfort, whatever their origins, a project of this kind will never even get off the ground. It has been my hope to dispense with these kinds of ultimately irrelevant aesthetic or affective hesitations in order to take up the more difficult, genuine challenges that these themes and this body of work present.

  Others are subject to a more sophisticated form of discomfort, in that they understand that ethical egoism and its counterpart in political moralism are the central problems that these themes face. But they then presume that these flaws simply and uncritically accrue to the work and thinkers in question here. And in some very real sense, this critical view is correct: spiritualism and moralism constitute the substantive challenge to any conception of exercises of self-change in general, and any attempt to understand and articulate the political content and consequences of such practices in particular. What that view misses, however, is that this is a problem that all of these thinkers take seriously on some level and a charge from which they all seek to distance themselves. This perspective assumes that thinkers like Friedmann or Foucault are either unaware of these dangers, despite all of the disclaimers they provide, or are conceptually fated to them. That in turn increases the likelihood that one will overlook the possibility that some aspect of their work can either be read as a response to it, or at least that their work can provide crucial resources for such a response. Such a perspective is also likely to produce charges of a "spiritualization" of politics, which amounts to the spiritualism—that is, the moralism—I have already begun to describe. All told, that general impulse is likely to preclude a study of this kind at all.

The irony is that such readings do recognize a real problem, but assume on the one hand that there are no solutions, and on the other that thinkers who write about practices of the self are blind to it. They also, therefore, tend not to recognize that there are solutions to this tension. Here it bears reemphasizing that even if it is exegetically true that any or all of the figures I engage in this book do not explicitly escape the challenges in question on their own, I argue that, with their help, we still can. On the account that I present, the way out entails articulating a particular conception of the relationship of the ethical to the political, which means recognizing and critiquing the causal and reductionist terms through which we recognized the problem in the first place.

I argue that Foucault, Friedmann, Hadot, and Lorde are all aware, to varying degrees, of the spiritualist challenge, as evinced by the many early disclaimers that we have begun to rehearse here. I argue further there is rather robust textual evidence that spiritualist egoism is in some form or another an ever-present concern within all of this literature. I argue, finally, that while this problem also presents a challenge to someone like King, we require a detailed analysis of the other thinkers represented here to understand how it may intersect with his work and thought, in at least two major ways. First, we must understand how and why spiritualism and moralism may also be potential problems for him. Second, doing so against the backdrop of all that comes before allows us to recognize how and why his philosophical, theological, and political work on the whole presents thorough, unique, and exciting counter-challenges to those problems.

This project as a whole can thus be understood as a rebuttal to the idea that any research in this direction is fated to egoism, and thus to moralism. At the same time, it must also be made clear that I seek to develop a formal, philosophical–theoretical category, with the help of some historical investigation. Here, historical resources, and the work on King, the Montgomery bus boycott, and the history of nonviolent organizing in the twentieth century in general that constitute chapter 4, serve a positive theoretical role in challenging and developing the conceptual apparatus that precedes them.

To the extent that this is a theoretically and methodologically synthetic and constructive project on my part, it is also because these analyses together open up new possibilities for the theorization of the role of ethical and religious practice more generally, and within the field of religious studies in particular. Among the other implicit goals here is to lay the theoretical groundwork for using these varying conceptions, together or individually, to analyze religious practice and other exercises of self-change. I am especially interested in those places where such ethical pursuits intersect with structural and political questions and more general questions of the relationships of individual practitioners to the communities they inhabit. The constructive, synthetic thread within my work emerges in part because none of the conceptions I explore provide the full range of tools required to diagnose and address the political question on their own or to provide the new theoretical lens I hope to deploy elsewhere in the future.

With all of these qualifications in place, the book proceeds as follows.

CHAPTER SUMMARIES

Chapter 1. Pierre Hadot: Ancient Spiritual Exercises and Contemporary Spiritual Demands

Pierre Hadot sets the conceptual and historical stage of this project, by introducing ancient spiritual exercises in all of their historical specificity, and as a model for any formulation of practices of this kind. In this way, Hadot's work provides the basic vocabulary and methodological tools for the project as a whole. I briefly rehearse some of Hadot's privileged examples from the ancient sources, especially those like the Stoics and Epicureans, with whom he seems to find the greatest personal affinity. I describe important examples such as exercises of the "premeditation of evils" and the "view from above," which reappear as themes and threads over the course of this book.

I highlight the distinction between Hadot's "prescriptive" and "descriptive" projects in order to draw attention to the ambiguous but productive tension between them within Hadot's research. The "descriptive project" constitutes the great bulk of Hadot's oeuvre, and consists in his rich, textual-critical contributions to understanding ancient philosophical life. The "prescriptive project" seeks to "offer contemporary mankind a way of life" in some way grounded in ancient spiritual exercises. It is from the prescriptive project that the three motivating problems of this book emerge, and it is from the productive tension between them that some of the major methodological principles of this book are established.

First, Hadot raises the question of how to practice spiritual exercises in the present, whether by taking up ancient spiritual exercises, generating what I call "properly contemporary" spiritual exercises, or adopting some complex combination of translation and creation.

Second, an ambiguous but productive tension exists between the prescriptive goal Hadot articulates and the sources he engages. That tension helps illuminate what I call the problem of specialists. In other words, it is clear that the historical articulations of both spiritual exercises and philosophical diagnosis typically come from either social, political, and economic elites, *or* religious, philosophical, and spiritual specialists whose lives and general focus are devoted to philosophy, religion, or asceticism as a dedicated way of life. While many of their conclusions are certainly universalizable, I argue that this is often only true in very general terms. The specificity of the lives, experiences, and goals of the working class, the disinherited, and even the average person going about daily life, work, and worry, demand that any efficacious, let alone morally or politically liberatory, engagement with practices of the self or philosophy as a way of life must address the fine-grained detail of those lives and forms of experience. Hadot himself wrestles with this tension, as I note in chapter 1. It is from this perspective that I argue that *the view from above must be a view from below*.

Third, although Hadot does not really address the political content and consequences of spiritual exercises in the kind of detail that I would find satisfying, he does raise this question in a preliminary way. With the first two questions again in productive contrast with the latter as a general impulse or suggestion, we have enough to begin to articulate (again still in an ambiguous way at this stage) the question of a genuine politics of spiritual exercise. We can ask how, under what conditions, and in what forms we may engage in genuinely collective practices of the self, *and* how such exercises can, if ever, constitute an intervention on the level of the systemic, material nature of political institutions, economic relations, and so on.

Finally, there is a productive tension between Hadot's scholarly work and this prescriptive impulse that is present throughout his interventions, and one that feeds back into the three preceding questions. This tension further allows me to draw some general conclusions that I then apply in my readings of Friedmann in chapter 2 and King in chapter 4, while setting up my reading of Foucault in chapter 3. I highlight the ways that Hadot's analyses of ancient spiritual exercises are guided by the injunction that they must always be situated in their own cultural, historical, and literary conditions of emergence. I further highlight the ways that Hadot's methodology demonstrates a rich connection between the forms that given practices take, the philosophical diagnosis of human suffering that motivates one to both articulate and take up such practices up, and the goals or ideals toward which one aims in such exercises. However, his articulation of that goal is often very general, pointing to what he takes the ancient Greco-Roman traditions to have to offer us, or in some cases, what they have already offered us.

The principles that guide his descriptive work demonstrate that there is no question of simply taking up given ancient practices, even those that would seem appropriate on the surface. Rather, by his own arguments, the forms that any properly contemporary practice would take would need to be tailored to the specificity of the historical conditions—political, economic, religious, technological, and so on—that give rise to the motivation to take up such practices or to the "spiritual demands" that they are meant to address. I argue that his historical researches also provide the kind of model required to so much as begin to translate ancient spiritual exercises into any differing historical contexts and to constitute and recognize new forms of practice appropriate to new and different spiritual demands. It is not, however, simply that his method provides a kind of model. Rather, I argue that Hadot's work demonstrates that the form such contemporary analyses must take are a direct consequence of his very conception of spiritual exercises.

However, Hadot's project stops here, and he does not deploy the same kind of historical analysis to present conditions as to the ancient, even as he shows us quite clearly what such an analysis would need to look like. As I insist over the course of this book, to note the limitations and boundaries of a project is not to level a criticism at that project. Hadot does not take up a comparable analysis of the contemporary world he seeks to aid in anything like the detail that he engages the ancient context that he wants to bring to us. That is fine however, as he does give a sense of what such attention would need to look like, and why it is so vital. Hadot provides the clearest and most foundational sense of what it is we are talking about when we talk about spiritual exercises or practices of the self, details critical resources for identifying the objects of this study, aids in identifying and articulating the questions that I pursue and why they are so important, further clarifies the formal criteria that any study of this kind must adhere to, and so much else. From the borders of his work, I turn to Georges Friedmann, who Hadot so often invokes (and, frankly, because Hadot so frequently invokes him), who in many ways picks up where Hadot leaves off.

Chapter 2. Georges Friedmann: From the Great Disequilibrium to the Interior Effort

Chapter two engages Georges Friedmann, who is generally credited with founding the sociology of labor in France following the war, even as his work is less well known in the English-speaking world.[42] An early French Marxist and fluent Russian speaker, Friedmann visited the USSR on multiple occasions in the 1930s and facilitated communication between French and Soviet intellectuals, while studying developments in labor and technology in the Soviet world. Despite these connections, or rather because of them, Friedmann broke with the party in the late 1930s. Nonetheless, the influence of Marx, commitment to Marxism, and a lifelong concern for the Soviet project remain a foundational influence across his work. Although nascent in this period, it is only after the war that Friedmann's major sociological landmarks and his studies of what he calls *machinisme* appear, which among much else reflect the human wages of rapid technological change and its attending economic and social transformations.

Alongside his sociological output and some early writing on philosophical themes, Friedmann write at least two philosophical journals. His

Journal de guerre, 1939–1940 recounts his time in a mobile hospital unit on the French front, but was only published posthumously. Nearer the end of his life, Friedmann published *La puissance et la sagesse* (Wisdom and Power), a kind of philosophical memoir, in 1970. As already noted, Hadot makes consistent, if partial, reference to Friedmann's *La puissance et la sagesse* due to the latter's invocation of the notion of "spiritual exercises," even as that invocation takes on a different valence when read against Friedmann's political commitments and sociological output. Among the most consistent throughlines of *La puissance et la sagesse* is his critical reading of distinctions between "interior" (ethical/spiritual) and "exterior" (political/systemic) efforts to promote human flourishing. It is in this context Friedmann models a version of the core question of this book: how to understand the relationship of what he calls the "interior" to the "exterior" effort, such that neither is considered prior to the other.

Although Hadot does not explore this dynamic in general, it is this tension and concern within texts like *La puissance et la sagesse* that constitute Friedmann's primary contribution to my own concerns. I argue that Friedmann's sociological studies of labor conditions and technological change over the course of the twentieth century, when put into context with his political–philosophical reflections, reflect just the form of analysis called for by the confluence of Hadot's own methods and goals. It is in this way that, on my reading, Friedmann picks up where Hadot leaves off. I engage Friedmann's work through the lens of his relationship to Marxism, direct sociological methodologies, and specific philosophical commitments to draw out several other consequences that are at best implicit in Hadot.

First, and as we have already seen in this introduction, Friedmann helps identify and clarify the two major negative concepts that I engage: what I call ethical "spiritualism" and political "moralism." Indeed, I borrow this language from Friedmann, even as I clarify it beyond his initial usage. Although these terms have already been introduced, they are further elaborated over the course of this book.

Second, by reading his sociological studies of factory work and machine culture like *Industrial Society: The Emergence of the Human Problems of Automation* alongside philosophical memoirs like the *Journal de guerre* and *La puissance et la sagesse*, I argue that Friedmann provides one rich model of what any investigation of properly contemporary "spiritual demands" would need to look like. It also demonstrates, as I begin to emphasize in chapter 1, how and why technological and economic transformation matter in any conversation of this kind. I argue that it is in this way that his philosophical and sociological work together provide the kind of thorough preparatory analysis that Hadot's oeuvre necessitates but does not take up.

Third, these same analyses describe the mutually determining relationship of human subjects to the built environment. This perspective allows us to begin to understand just how what Friedmann and Hadot call "spiritual demands" are also, necessarily, material and political demands. Through the example of rapid technological transformation, what Friedmann calls "the technological adventure of human beings in the twentieth century," which produces what he further calls "the great disequilibrium," Friedmann provides an initial model for understanding how the systemic mutually informs the "spiritual."[43] In this way, Friedmann allows us to see that, as a consequence of Hadot's own project, any attempt to articulate or analyze properly contemporary forms of spiritual exercise is itself a necessarily political project. In turn, Friedmann helps illuminate just how what might initially seem to be merely "ethical," "spiritual," or "individual" attempts to address those demands may themselves constitute forms of political work. These general insights lay the groundwork for several claims that I elaborate in chapter 3 with Michel Foucault, regarding the ways that given material or institutional conditions shape us in "who we are" and the political and ethical consequences for transformative action within this general framework.

However, while Friedmann does provide the kind of analysis called for by Hadot, his project also seems to stop short at the articulation of its own consequences. He does not fully explore the mutually constitutive relationship of laboring subject to the environment. Nor does he provide the kind of positive analysis of the kinds of spiritual exercises that would enable those same subjects to intervene in the "Great Disequilibrium" he argues has emerged within that relationship due to the radical pace and form of contemporary technological change. In other words, while he identifies certain spiritual demands, effectively models the kind of analysis required to understand such demands, and calls for the integration of an "interior" effort to external struggles, his work does not then model the kinds of political–spiritual exercises that should follow from those analyses.

INTRODUCTION

Chapter 3. Michel Foucault: From the Analytics of Power to the Care of the Self

Chapter 3 takes up Michel Foucault's late "ethical" work (roughly the late 1970s to his death in 1984) within the context of the more explicitly "political" period of analysis that is said to precede it in the early to mid-1970s. Using the theoretical resources garnered thus far, I argue that Foucault's late "ethics" is neither a "turn" from his political work nor a form of moralism. It is instead a coherent extension of his analytics of power with potentially misunderstood political consequences. I argue that Foucault's "ethical" material, including the notion of the care of the self, proceeds from the "analytics of power" found in texts like the first volume of the *History of Sexuality* or even *Discipline and Punish*. I describe the ways that the concept of "resistance" in Foucault, as underspecified and underdeveloped as it is, emerges from his analyses of relations of power and in turn lends directly to the formulation of what we call his ethics. There is, in other words, a politics to his ethics, at least potentially. But by this I do not mean that this ethics entails any particular political outlook or program on a normative level. Rather, his ethical work entails a range of theoretically fruitful consequences for the analysis of relations of power in political terms, and vice versa. However, these political consequences must again be extracted from the texts and clarified, as Foucault generally does not do so himself.

Although interesting in their own right, I take up these Foucauldian exegetical issues in the service of further elaborating my own concerns here. I argue that Foucault's ethical writing entails (but may also in fact rest upon) an underspecified but crucial reformulation of the relationship between ethics and politics. On my reading, that reformulation reflects Friedmann's concern, elaborated in chapter 2, to resituate the ethical and political such that neither is necessarily prior to the other, or are at least more intimately linked in a way that does not amount to mere moralism. To be clear however, without understanding just how ethics proceeds from the analytics of power, or how these dynamics entail a nonreductive and mutually co-constituting relationship between the "ethics of the care of the self" and the politics of institutions and relations of power, it is very much possible to read Foucault's ethics as a form of reductive moralism. However, this challenge itself is in fact highly productive, drawing attention to aspects of Foucault's arguments and demanding fine-grained close readings that illuminate a great deal about the late ethical period, among much else. I argue that the premises of any such reading are neither supported by the texts themselves nor by the relationship between these texts, and that Foucault is implicitly or explicitly concerned with what I call moralism. Furthermore, when understood properly, the relationship between the ethical and the political that I argue is at least entailed and at most endorsed in these later texts constitutes an important step in the elaboration of a nonreductive theorization of the relationship between ethical and political life.

Specifically, if relations of power, as he argues in the 1970s, are productive and creative, and what they create is subjects, people, or "who and what we are," then the subject itself can be a site of political contestation. However, it is possible to assume that this entails a contentless "politics of the self," which leads to forms of self-formation that are political in name only and do not amount to any robust or effective intervention into the systemic, institutional, or material conditions that constitute the relations of power in question. Often enough, such forms of life ultimately amount to ethical spiritualism and political moralism. However, it would be a misreading to take such examples as the only or necessary consequences of Foucault's claim. Rather, any such struggle can take on a number of forms and locate itself in multiple points of intervention.

On this basis, I argue that the relationship of the self to itself is a circuit that passes through any number of social relations, forms of experience, institutional realities, and material conditions. In some cases, a direct intervention on the level of "who one is" may constitute a significant enough strategic shift in given relations of power to allow for further transformation. I raise a series of preliminary questions around the challenges of this kind of intervention in the conclusion and my brief remarks on Audre Lorde, without by any means reducing Lorde's life and work to only this kind of intervention—even as I do read her as one of the more exciting and efficacious models of this kind of political work. Alongside this more "immediate" form, I argue that as a consequence of Foucault's analytics of power, more familiar forms of political work, insofar as they target institutions and conditions that shape us as subjects, also by consequence amount to forms of spiritual exercise. It is here, however, that Foucault's project also meets its own horizons.

Like Hadot, Foucault lacks a historical articulation of representative practices that fit either his own criteria or those drawn out in preceding chapters. Specifically, and perhaps surprisingly, this late work lacks any thoroughgoing analysis of mass movements or of "collective" practices of the self in general. Even as Foucault invokes the idea of a genealogy of "revolutionary subjectivity" in texts like the *Hermeneutics of the Subject* and *Speaking the Truth About Oneself*, this promising concept is abandoned alongside so many others. Foucault does not provide the kind of analysis required to articulate the kind of model that I argue his own work entails and that the project I develop here requires. For this reason, I argue that Hadot is indeed correct, at least in one sense, in his critique of the notion of the "care of the self" as something that "is focused far too much on the self." Chapter 4 and the conclusion work to provide these missing analyses.

Chapter 4. The Practice of Dignity: Martin Luther King Jr., Self-Purification, and the Montgomery Bus Boycott

Against all of the theoretical resources articulated and new questions raised in the preceding chapters, chapter 4 consists in a kind of elaborated historical–theoretical analysis of the idea of "self-purification" identified by Martin Luther King Jr. as a necessary component of direct action. It is through this concept and this analysis that this chapter reapproaches the core question of this book: How and under what conditions can the care of the self be understood as coterminous with the care of the other, others, the city, and vice versa? How, and under what conditions, does the transformation of the self amount to the transformation of the world, and vice versa? Finally, how, and under what conditions, can we understand spiritual exercises as a form of genuine political practice, and vice versa?

I take up these questions through a historical–philosophical close reading of the events of the 1956–1957 Montgomery bus boycott, one of the watersheds of the Civil Rights era in the United States through the lens of King's notion of political "self-purification." I do so for several reasons. First, because on my reading, the events in question demonstrate a concrete elaboration of what King means by a form of political self-purification that is a condition, and indeed a form, of direct action. Second, because within the strict limits of its immediate goals, the boycott was a success. It sought to desegregate the bus system in one city, and to provide a model for similar movements at the same time. Whatever one might think of nonviolent principle and strategy, we can understand this campaign to be successful on its own terms. Lastly, and as I note elsewhere, I do not take up this reading as a kind of final "example" that is meant to illuminate the conclusions of the preceding theoretical chapters. Rather, I do not take those chapters to reach any substantive conclusions regarding the major questions I am asking. Instead, they are meant to help frame those questions and develop some of the resources for answering them. It is this last analysis that is instead meant to complete many of the lacunae left in previous chapters and to provide clear answers to many of these core questions. In other words, I end with King and Montgomery because they provide historical and theoretical insights that the previous authors set up but do not themselves finalize.

I begin with an analysis of the system of legal segregation and an argument that any reading that approaches it in purely juridical terms is insufficient to account for the way it seemed to operate logistically on a day-to-day basis, at least on King's account. Using King's personal reflections from a number of sources, as well as other major figures in the nonviolent tradition, especially Howard Thurman, I argue that practices of dehumanization, humiliation, and so on—whether ultimately "successful" or not—are integral rather than tangential to the functioning, in this case, of legal segregation. The chapter thus begins by centering an analysis of various reports and discussions of the psychological, physical, and spiritual effects of the system of legal segregation, leading into an argument of the role of these effects in the apparatus of the system itself.

From here, I continue the analysis of the boycott movement itself, specifically the political role of certain directed and organized practices of self-overcoming, and the ways that those practices mediate the relationship of the individual to the group. This larger argument occurs through the integrated analyses of several of the constituent events of the boycott: the practice of walking to work, the organization of large groups of people, training to manage fear and engage in direct action, and so on. Here, I rely on a number of historical and first-person accounts that are, as mentioned earlier, approached through a close reading of Bayard Rustin's "Lesson Plan on Nonviolent Action," an unpublished archival document held at the Swarthmore Peace Collection. That reading is in turn further specified against Glenn Smiley's description of the nonviolent workshops at Montgomery in his brief pamphlet *Nonviolence: the Gentle Persuader*. The practices described in these and other texts are self-identified forms of self-transformation, crafted and deployed along lines familiar from Hadot and Foucault, and thus constituting spiritual exercises in their own right.

I read these latter practices as tactical interventions into both the former conditions and the infamous repressive countertactics deployed by the police, the city of Montgomery, and the white political structure in general. It is from these analyses that I conclude both this chapter and the arc of this book as a whole. I demonstrate just how practices like walking to work or certain forms of training to face violent police repression constitute both a direct intervention into the relationship of the self to itself *and* a systemic intervention into the relations of political power that constitute, in this case, the work of legal segregation. This analysis brings several of the horizons left in the preceding chapters into sharp relief, including the claims made in chapter 3 regarding some of the consequences of reading Foucault's ethics and politics together, which the latter never concretely illustrates. In the cases I end with, we see how the kind of political organizing taken up in places like Montgomery is at once a direct transformation of oneself, a direct intervention into existing systemic political conditions, and, perhaps above all, a case in which direct political action facilitates and co-constitutes a transformation of the self.

It is on this basis that I conclude that organizing, the mass movement, is the paradigmatic case of political–spiritual exercise. It constitutes at least one vision of the ways in which the care of the self, the care of the other, the care of ourselves, and the care of the community may exist in an irreducible reciprocity. It is for this reason, further, that such a conception will be resistant or immune to charges of spiritualism and moralism, and thus provides a standard for adjudicating the political consequences not simply of the kinds of practices of ethical self-overcoming that concern me here, but the larger category, including religious practices, as a whole. That model in turn serves to clarify the ways that certain practices that would not be intuitively placed under the rubric of the care of the self may indeed be analyzed as such. Finally, it allows us to see just what genuinely collective spiritual exercises look like, a vision that never really crosses the horizons of Hadot, Foucault, or even Friedmann.

Conclusion. Audre Lorde: Survival, Immediacy, and Poetry as a Way of Life

The conclusion takes the famous claim of Audre Lorde that caring for herself constitutes a form of "political warfare" as the basis for raising, though by no means answering, a series of new questions for understanding the political content and consequences of ideas of "spiritual exercises," "the care of the self," and so on. Lorde's life, poetry, and prose all raise profoundly challenging questions for both this category of practice as a whole and for all that I claim in this book. At the same time, her work constitutes something of a branching trajectory, moving in new and different directions from the main body of my arguments here. For that reason alone, I cannot provide the kind of thorough analysis of Lorde that I would prefer, and it remains far more productive to begin to specify those questions for the sake of future investigations. The goal, in other words, would be to both read Lorde against all that I have claimed so far, and then reread those analyses, the very questions asked, and the methods of answering them back against much of what Lorde provides. I raise roughly three themes in conclusion.

First, Lorde's attention to, indeed embodiment of, intersectionality raises resonances with the importance of the particular demands and conditions that any practice of the self must undertake. This point is important when attempting to understand what she means when she says that "caring for herself" is a form of "political warfare." This claim is not an injunction to, say, "treat oneself." It rather reflects a crucial conception of "survival," which she contrasts with the illusion of mere "safety," and serves as a guiding thread across her work. When understanding the politics of "caring for oneself," it is vital to see what that means for someone who was "never meant to survive," whose life itself is a site of political contestation. This reemphasis on the hyperparticular raises existing questions in new ways and leads them in new directions, while raising further challenges for our understanding of the universality of the concepts explored here.

Second, and following this initial point, the work of figures like Lorde, and Thurman and King before her, is shot through with a necessary urgency and immediacy, for vital and familiar reasons. And yet, ancient philosophical texts are often read to emphasize the contemplative life of philosophical reflection as characterizing "the good life." But for those who Thurman calls the "disinherited," those who live "with their backs against the wall," contemplation is tied to action, especially political action. Much more importantly, such figures often directly contest the idea that "leisurely" contemplation holds some inherent value or actually constitutes an ideal. Rather, the greatest freedom and the greatest flourishing emerge in the practice of becoming free and of cultivating liberation in others. How, then, does this entire form of life, which is more than a view or perspective, challenge existing conceptions of "philosophy as a way of life," and to what extent does it constitute a rich resource for understanding the politics of "caring for oneself?"

Finally, I note that in contrast to the more explicitly organizing-based forms of political–spiritual practice discussed in chapter 4, Lorde's life and outlook again evince a kind of immediacy, though in this case in a different form. In the case of Lorde, the politics of the self can be said to pass more directly through the self and then outward toward given conditions. While in many ways much more intuitive, I argue that this way of understanding the political transformation of the self as a kind of systemic intervention is much more challenging to understand, especially as it can be confused for forms of spiritualism or moralism. I suggest that we may read Lorde's understanding of poetry as something that is not a luxury, as she so famously puts it, as something that is also, for that very reason, a way of life. I suggest further that we may understand this form of life in terms of the *parrhesia* that so interests Foucault, as briefly noted in chapter 3. We may then read poetry as a parrhesiastic form of life in at least three ways: in poetic practice itself; in Lorde's powerful public excoriations of any number of racist, sexist, and homophobic institutions; and in her life itself, the way she chose to live it, and perhaps especially in her relationship to her cancer diagnosis.

Lorde, perhaps more than any of the other figures I engage here, raises a question that constitutes one of the primary, if often tacit, throughlines of this work as a whole, and one that it is worth reading the rest of this book against: If, for someone like Hadot, the practice of spiritual exercises is one of liberation, how much more so are those practices of the self that at the same time work to liberate others?

Chapter One

PIERRE HADOT

Ancient Spiritual Exercises and Contemporary Spiritual Demands

I. CONSUMED BY WORRIES, TORN BY PASSIONS

In both the final remarks of "Forms of Life and Forms of Discourse," his inaugural address as chair of the History of Hellenistic and Roman Thought at the *Collège de France* on February 18, 1983, and the opening of the representative essay "Spiritual Exercises," Pierre Hadot cites a passage that appears toward the end of Georges Friedmann's *La puissance et la sagesse*, dated August 3, 1942:

> To take flight each day! At least for a moment, however brief, as long as it is intense. Each day a "spiritual exercise,"—either alone or in the company of another who also wishes to become better.
>
> Spiritual exercises. Step out of duration. *Struggle* to rid yourself of your passions and vanities, the hunger for talk about your name (which, from time to time, can burn like a chronic illness). Avoid gossip, and abandon pity and hatred. Love all free human beings. Become eternal by transcending yourself.
>
> This interior effort is necessary; this ambition is just. Many are those who are entirely absorbed in militant politics, in preparation for social Revolution. Rare, very rare, are those who, in order to prepare for the revolution, wish to become worthy of it.[1]

In "Spiritual Exercises," following this citation, Hadot remarks that, "with the exception of the last few lines," this passage could well be "a pastiche of Marcus Aurelius," and speculates that Friedmann had not been "aware of the resemblance." Hadot further wonders aloud why Friedmann did not "ask himself about value of the philosophical tradition of Greco-Roman antiquity" in his attempt to "re-source himself," after coming to the conclusion "that there is no tradition—be it Jewish, Christian, or Oriental—compatible with contemporary spiritual demands."[2]

Hadot poses this question of Friedmann due to a philosophical affinity that begins with the invocation of the idea of spiritual exercises. By this concept Hadot again means practices "aimed at a modification, an improvement and a transformation of the self," which can include forms of "meditation, dialogue with oneself, examination of conscience, or exercises of imagination such as the view from above of the cosmos or the earth," among a range of other examples.[3] But where Friedmann's concerns sit squarely in the present, Hadot emphasizes that the idea of spiritual exercise is rooted in those forms of life particular to the philosophical schools of antiquity. So despite this shared philosophical affinity, and indeed a shared concern with addressing what Hadot calls contemporary "spiritual demands," it is for Hadot, by definition, to the ancient world that we must first turn.

In "Spiritual Exercises," following his invocation of Friedmann, Hadot charts the notion of *Exercitia spiritualia* back through Ignatius of Loyola to the early Latin Christian tradition, the corresponding Greek Christian concept of *askesis*, and finally to the philosophical world of classical antiquity, where he argues askesis "must be understood not as asceticism, but as the practice of spiritual exercises."[4] And despite an extensive religious education,[5] it is not to Loyola or even to the Christian tradition that Hadot looks to understand the class of practices called spiritual exercises.[6] Instead, Hadot is adamant that "in the final analysis, it is to antiquity that we must return in order to explain the origin and significance of this idea of spiritual exercises, which, as Friedmann shows, is still alive in contemporary consciousness."[7]

Building upon his invocation of Friedmann, Hadot's stated goals in "Spiritual Exercises" (and indeed throughout his career) are "to delimit the scope and importance of the phenomenon [of spiritual exercises in Greco-Roman antiquity], and to show the consequences which it entails for the understanding not only of ancient thought, but of philosophy itself,"[8] including contemporary philosophy and contemporary life. On Hadot's account, to understand ancient philosophy without a notion of spiritual exercises is to not understand ancient philosophy at all, or perhaps philosophy in general.

Hadot's reading, his argument across his large and varied oeuvre, that ancient philosophy must be understood in some fundamental relation to a conception of spiritual exercises may or may not surprise or challenge contemporary readers.[9] But if, as he often insists, a core aspect of his conception of ancient philosophy is foreign to at least certain dominant threads within professional academic practice,[10] the origins of his insight are still rooted in a meticulous attention to his sources: "It was my interpretive work on the philosophical texts of antiquity that led me to an awareness of the importance of what we could call 'spiritual exercises.'"[11] In fact, Hadot was led to his conception of ancient philosophy by way of a standing exegetical and philological puzzle. "If I came to conceive of this notion of spiritual exercises," he tells us, "it was because, like many of my predecessors and contemporaries, I was struck by a well-known phenomenon: that of the inconsistencies, even the contradictions, that one encounters in the works of the philosophical authors of antiquity."[12] Of this problem, Hadot gives numerous examples: "Whether it is a matter of Augustine, Plotinus, Aristotle, or Plato, modern historians never cease to deplore the blunders in philosophical exposition, and the compositional defects which are found in their works."[13] Among the most privileged, a text to which he continually returns as both an instance of misreading and a rich source of rereading, are the Stoic writings of Marcus Aurelius, especially the *Meditations*—a book whose title Hadot notes is better translated from the Greek as *Exhortations to Himself*.[14]

In a number of articles and books, Hadot surveys the many interpretations of the *Meditations* that attempt to make sense of its seemingly scattered and repetitive structure, alongside those commentators who "please themselves in denouncing the pessimism, resignation, and even sadness of the philosopher-emperor."[15] Regarding the issue of composition, it was once argued that "the apparently disjointed character of Marcus Aurelius' *Meditations* came from the fact that he had written a systematic treatise that had been destroyed and that someone had tried to put back into order,"[16] or that it was simply a collection of notes or extracts for a lost or never-completed treatise.[17] Others attempt to explain the "shocking images and brutal descriptions of naked reality [which] abound in the *Meditations*" by pathologizing the text and its author.[18] Thus, famous passages, such as those that refer to the imperial purple as merely "sheep's wool dipped in the blood of a shellfish" and sex as "the friction of a piece of gut and, followed by a sort of convulsion, the expulsion of some mucus,"[19] or the practice of envisioning the courts of great emperors or entire generations "engulfed by time,"[20] are accounted for in any number of extratextual ways. Hadot catalogs an entire range of retroactive physical and psychological diagnoses that claim that the emperor suffered from everything from an identity crisis to gastric ulcers, opium addiction, or a general "disgust for life." While some of the stranger accounts may be dismissed, even sympathetic modern readers may still find something off and unfamiliar in the content and organization of a text like the *Meditations*. Thus, even in milder cases, Hadot argues that much of the reception history of the text has anachronistically "projected the literary prejudices of [its] own epoch back onto the *Meditations*" and other ancient sources.[21]

His own approach is inspired in no small part by the work of his wife, Ilsetraut Hadot (b. 1928), among a handful of other scholars of classical antiquity, the early church, and philosophy.[22] But Hadot's methods and insight are also motivated by a historically early encounter with Ludwig Wittgenstein (1889–1951), who Hadot helped introduce to French readers.[23] Following Wittgenstein, Hadot took up the idea that "the philosopher is always situated within a language game: that is to say, situated in a form of life or a certain attitude," and it is therefore "impossible to understand the sense of philosophers' theses without situating them within their language game."[24] It thus becomes clearer and clearer to Hadot that "the works of antiquity are produced under entirely different conditions than those of their modern counterparts," and on his reading that difference is decisive.[25]

From this perspective it is almost never a question of how disorganized or unsystematic a text is, but rather one of understanding the particular principles of systematicity and the organizational forms native to the ancient texts, genres, and "ways of life" that frame their sense and intelligibility.[26] In other words, Hadot begins "with the very simple principle that a text should be interpreted in light of the literary genre to which it belongs."[27] This methodological point is "the origin of the notion of the spiritual exercise as an effort to modify and transform the self," as the core interpretive principle for Hadot's reading of ancient philosophical practice and for him the decisive feature of ancient philosophy in general.[28]

While Hadot's insight is simple in principle, its methodological consequences are complex and demanding. He demonstrates that in order to understand these authors, "we must take account of all of the concrete conditions in which they wrote, all the constraints that weighed upon them: the framework of the school, the very nature of philosophia, literary genres, rhetorical rules, dogmatic imperatives, and traditional modes of reasoning."[29] It is not, moreover, only a question of excavating and detailing the forms of life internal to the ancient schools and their doctrines, but of understanding the range of larger political, economic, linguistic, religious, and other circumstances that condition everything from the emergence of the schools to the questions that they ask.

On this reading, a text like the *Meditations* and the figure of Marcus Aurelius are placed within the history and context of the Stoic school. Hadot then analyzes the text through the framework of well-attested Stoic spiritual exercises, refracted through the particular circumstances of the Roman context, the emperor's position, power, and so on. Hadot thus argues that these *Exhortations* may be recognized as a form of a collection of *hypomnemata* (*commentaria* in Latin)—that is, notes, exhortations, or "communings" with himself "written on a daily basis for the author's personal use."[30] The larger text in turn contains a number of other spiritual exercises and formal features that emerge from its practical–philosophical status. The statements evincing the author's famous "pessimism" are rather examples of recognizable Stoic practices such as the so-called premeditation of evils or practices of "objective representation" and "definition," among many others.[31] The text is repetitive because the exercises which constitute it are just that: practices that refine the subject through repetition, as in the cultivation of any skill. Other textual features, including certain structural elements and doctrinal themes, are the result of the influence of figures like Epictetus.[32] From this perspective, the *Meditations* are not the disjecta of a lost treatise or the fragmented visions of an ulcer sufferer, but rather the body of a "dialogue with oneself," left by someone "training to be a human being."[33]

This idea of "becoming human" or our "humanization" is a recurring one, and can be read as one of the defining features of spiritual exercises as they are understood across Hadot's work, that of a fundamental transformation of the practitioner.[34] Indeed, for Hadot, the change that one undergoes is not merely a modification of one's beliefs or the comprehension of some idea, however complex or challenging: "we are not dealing with mere knowledge, but with the transformation of our personality."[35] In fact, if the modifier "spiritual" denotes anything distinctive, it is this capacity for and depth of transformation:

> As we can glimpse through Friedmann's text, these exercises in fact correspond to a transformation of our vision of the world, and to a metamorphosis of our personality. The word "spiritual" is quite apt to make us understand that these exercises are the result, not merely of thought, but of the individual's entire psychism. Above all, the word "spiritual" reveals the true dimensions of these exercises. By means of them, the individual raises himself up to the life of the objective Spirit; that is to say, he re-places himself within the perspective of the Whole ("Become eternal by transcending yourself").[36]

The changes in question are so fundamental that Hadot describes them in the language of conversion: "The philosophical act is not situated merely on the cognitive level, but on that of the self and being. It is a progress which causes us to *be* more fully, and makes us better. It is a conversion which turns our entire life upside down, changing the life of the person who goes through it." Or, as he says later, "the same thing happens in every spiritual exercise: we must *let* ourselves be changed."[37]

Hadot insists that among the ancients, all philosophical practice is marked in some way by spiritual exercises. Although "each school has its ... method," and despite the "richness and variety of the practice of spiritual exercises in antiquity," on a level more basic than "this apparent diversity ... there is a profound unity, both in the means employed and in the ends pursued," as well as in the motivations for which one would take up such practices.[38] On his reading, "All schools also agree that man, before his philosophical conversion, is in a state of unhappy disquiet. Consumed by worries, torn by passions, he does not live a genuine life, nor is he truly himself." But, he continues, "All schools also agree that man can be delivered from this state. He can accede to genuine life, improve himself, transform himself, and attain a state of perfection."[39] The goal of all spiritual exercise, and of the philosophical way of life, is thus "precisely to bring about this transformation."[40]

Of course, "such a transformation of vision is not easy, and it is here that spiritual exercises come in. Little by little, they make possible the indispensable metamorphosis of our inner self." Thus ancient philosophy "did not consist in teaching an abstract theory—much less in the exegesis of texts—but rather the art of living. It is a concrete attitude and determinate lifestyle, which engages the whole of existence" meant to mitigate our unhappy disquiet.[41] The ancient schools thus provided more than a conceptual framework or system of understanding, but instead an entire "way of life" comprising spiritual exercises meant to transform practicing subjects. Thus, as Hadot argues, if contemporary philosophy has been defined by the discursive and the conceptual, for the ancients, "the parts of philosophy were not only theoretical discourses, but exercise themes, which had to be practiced concretely if one wanted to live as a philosopher."[42]

The state of perfection, the "genuine life" in which one is "truly oneself"—whatever the concepts of "truth," "one," or "self" might mean—was often personified in an ideal exemplar, the figure of the sage. Generally, the sage was both modeled on the ideal principles of a school and embodied those principles. Thus, each school "will elaborate its rational depiction of this state of perfection in the person of the sage, and each will make an effort to portray him."[43] The sage personifies the ideal state in which suffering no longer holds sway, even as the understanding of what it means for the causes of our suffering to "hold sway" differed from school to school. The same is true for the ways in which those causes were understood to mark the daily lives of normal people *and* the life of the sage. In some views, given foundational troubles are still present within the perfected state, and the sage has simply learned to live with them. In other cases, such problems may no longer "exist" because they are the products of our ignorance, which the sage has vanquished.

However, because the ideal of the sage "represented absolute perfection, which admits of no degrees," it was often understood to be just that, an ideal.[44] Although coterminous with the philosophical ideals of a school or tradition, the model that one aspired to emulate, the sage could be taken as neither a living (or even deceased) exemplar nor even an attainable state:

> It is true that this transcendental ideal will be deemed almost inaccessible; according to some schools there never was a wise man, while others say that perhaps there were one or two of them, such as Epicurus, this god among

men, and still others maintain that man can only attain this state during rare, fleeting moments. In this transcendent norm established by reason, each school will express its own vision of the world, its own style of life, and its idea of the perfect man.[45]

Thus, although the practitioner devotes a lifetime to its pursuit, "the philosopher also knows that this wisdom is an ideal state, almost inaccessible." In this way, "the philosophical life will be an effort to live and think according to the norm of wisdom, it will be a movement, a progression, though a never-ending one, toward this transcendent state."[46] For many of the cases Hadot surveys, the issue then is not the attainability of this ideal, but rather its approachability, the ability to walk toward it, even if one may never arrive. As he says, "Self-transformation is never definitive, but demands perpetual reconquest."[47]

There were, it seems, no illusions that the value of the model of the sage lay in its attainability, but rather in its ability to crystallize the teachings of the school in an ideal model. The sage served as an embodiment of what Foucault calls the telos, toward which the one would strive and against which progress could be measured.[48] Conversely, there were also no illusions regarding the concrete reality of the spiritual demands that differing ideal states of sagacity and wisdom were meant to redress. Thus, despite the many differences among the schools in their descriptions of either of these poles, "each school, then, represents a form of life defined by an ideal of wisdom," personified in the sage and formulated in response to a diagnosis of the causes of our unhappy state.[49]

Understood in this way, the ancient schools did not simply recognize human suffering as a philosophical problem, but rather acknowledged it as *the* philosophical problem. But they also offered a solution, in the form of a conception of philosophy that is, Hadot says, "a spiritual exercise because it is a mode of life, a form of life, and a choice of life."[50] Whether attainable in this life or not, one approaches the ideal state of resolution through "exercises designed to ensure spiritual progress toward the ideal state of wisdom, exercises of reason that will be, for the soul, analogous to the athlete's training or to the application of a medical cure."[51] Thus, for Hadot, philosophy is ultimately "a therapeutics" in which "we must concern ourselves with the healing of our own lives" through the practice of spiritual exercises that are unequivocally "required for the healing of the soul."[52]

Like Friedmann, Hadot does not simply feel an intellectual affinity for a vision of philosophy conceived in this way. Something, after all, is indeed always wrong, and he argues that it is possible that ancient philosophical exercises may still have something to offer us in understanding, mitigating, and healing the particular troubles that mark contemporary life. The question is, of course, for the ancients as for us, just what it means to "heal our own lives."

Contemporary Spiritual Demands

Hadot's life's work, devoted to the explication and elaboration of ancient spiritual exercises, is expansive in its historical breadth and its reassessment of philosophy both ancient and modern. And for all that, Hadot is clear that his is not a just historical project, a way of setting the historical record straight regarding the nature of philosophy in the ancient world, nor is it simply an intervention internal to the contemporary academy. Rather, it is also marked and motivated by the explicitly prescriptive project of providing answers to "those who, like Friedmann, ask themselves the question: how is it possible to practice spiritual exercises in the twentieth century?"[53] It is a prescriptive concern that he also recognizes in the late work of Michel Foucault, whose "description of the practices of the self—like, moreover, my description of spiritual exercises—is not merely an historical study, but rather a tacit attempt to offer contemporary mankind a model of life."[54]

This prescriptive project is tied to the "descriptive" historical work that constitutes the bulk of Hadot's output. However, in her introductory remarks to *The Present Alone Is Our Happiness*, Jeannie Carlier describes the two threads within Hadot's work in terms of a "discrepancy between the two projects." "On the one hand," she says, "to inform the reader of a set of facts that show . . . that for the Greeks philosophy was not the construction of a system, but a choice of life; and, on the other, to discreetly 'turn' this reader toward philosophy understood in this sense."[55] Borrowing a phrase from Victor Goldschmidt that Hadot himself so often invokes, Carlier describes Hadot as someone who seeks to "form as he informs."[56] His work proceeds in the hope that through his historical-philosophical readings of ancient texts, his readers will "hear a call" that will somehow draw them toward the practice of spiritual exercises.[57] And yet, this description of a "discrepancy" between "two projects" is misleading. Far from a "discrepancy," the complex juncture of Hadot's descriptive and prescriptive projects is rather a site of productive tension, and for that reason I take it as my point of departure here.

But perhaps there is a "discrepancy" after all: not within Hadot's project itself, but in the ways in which it is possible for that work to be received. It is certainly possible for secondary discussions of Hadot to focus on the descriptive project, even despite themselves. On the one hand, any reading of Hadot invariably takes place within the contemporary academic setting that he argues has held little place for philosophy as "a way of life." On the other hand, despite Hadot's departure from some of the standard frameworks of contemporary philosophy, his work still remains within the domain of recognizably philosophical and philological pursuits. After all, Hadot's interest in spiritual exercises as a concept emerges from familiar problems of textual exegesis and philosophical interpretation, and he engages the metaphysical, ethical, and logical commitments of ancient thinkers. His writing consists of claims and arguments about the nature, context, content, and role of philosophy in antiquity, which can be assessed using the familiar armature of contemporary academic research. In other words, insofar as Hadot's work and the responses to it are ultimately comprised of the interpretation of texts and the critical analysis of concepts and claims, regardless of the content of those claims, this work largely remains within the clear bounds of contemporary scholarly practice.

This point is simple enough, though it can be obscured, and for good reason. Hadot's project situates familiar philosophical pursuits (reading, writing, dialogue, physical and metaphysical speculation, etc.) within the larger category of practices he calls spiritual exercises. He further argues that those familiar philosophical activities were taken up within certain historical contexts to ends either unrecognizable or potentially uncomfortable to contemporary readings. It is for this reason that this descriptive project remains embedded within those forms of contemporary academic practice that he argues have wandered from their ancient forebears. And it is for these same reasons that this descriptive project may remain the center of academic attention to his work. We can ask, after all, using *our* methods, whether Hadot is "right" about the ancient world, or whether his claims about the composition of the *Meditations* of Marcus Aurelius hold up to historical and philosophical scrutiny, or whether certain practices constitutive of various Christian traditions really do have their origins in ancient forms of philosophical life, among many other examples.

Conversely, the prescriptive aspect of his work may appear anywhere on an interpretive spectrum of absurd and anachronistic to obvious and thus lacking any real need for detailed attention. In the case of the former, it is not difficult to imagine charges of spiritualism or careless wishful thinking leveled at Hadot. In the case of the latter, it seems easy enough to understand what Hadot means by spiritual exercises, and even easier to go about practicing them. If, after all, the *Meditations* are just a kind of journal, what could be more familiar and easier to adopt into our own daily lives, even at a distance of centuries?[58] Doesn't Hadot himself suggest as much in his question to Friedmann? If death, for example, is among *the* universal human experiences, can we not learn something about how to face it, in ways that are applicable to our own lives, from the ancient thinkers in question? Aren't spiritual exercises in one form or another ubiquitous in contemporary cultures? And if so, is it not simply a question of integrating those that Hadot has reintroduced into one's "repertoire," as it were?

Both of these sets of assumptions are at once misguided and productive for the project at hand, though my work here does not take the form of a direct response to either. I do not argue for the coherence or inaccuracy of Hadot's readings of the ancient texts. Indeed, I am neither qualified nor interested in doing so. Nor does this chapter make any claims assessing the value of Hadot's thoughts on practicing spiritual exercises in the present, and instead takes that aspect of his work as just that, a core feature that must be situated within his larger overall project. My goal here is neither to make Hadot's case regarding the nature of philosophy for him nor to endorse the view of ancient philosophical practice that he puts forward. Rather it is to understand Hadot himself as a thinker, to elaborate his own philosophical commitments as they are woven through his treatment of ancient spiritual-philosophical life.

In other words, this chapter aims to say very little about antiquity, only a little about the present, and instead a great deal about Hadot in order to specify the details, limits, and consequences of his conception of spiritual exercises. I do not approach this goal by solely engaging Hadot's descriptive project and setting the prescriptive impulse to one side. Instead, I take the latter feature of Hadot's work seriously, placing it at the center of my reading. As undeveloped as they in fact are in his own texts, I argue that Hadot's prescriptive claims have yet-unspecified consequences for his understanding of the ancients, his more general philosophical commitments, and thus the idea of "spiritual exercises" in and beyond his own work.

If Hadot can ask why Friedmann does not look to the ancients, we may just as easily ask why he believes that he can and that we should. On the one hand, there may be something fundamental in Friedmann's work in *La puissance et la sagesse* that Hadot has either missed, or at least underappreciated, regarding the specificity and import of the term "contemporary" as it is used there, as a modifier of both "spiritual exercises" and "spiritual demands." On the other hand, I argue that it is also a necessary concern for Hadot, as a consequence of an implicit thread within his descriptive work regarding the relationship between spiritual exercises and the spiritual demands that they are meant to address. For this reason, I lean heavily on this question of what the term "contemporary" could mean here, in order to motivate the lines of questioning I want to explore both in this chapter and throughout this book.

To be clear, I am not so much concerned with identifying forms of contemporary spiritual exercise as I am with understanding the practical and theoretical methods and resources by which such forms would need to be understood, identified, and determined. If my first goal in this chapter is to introduce Hadot, I do so in the service of the second: to bring to light certain productive tensions that arise between what I am calling his prescriptive project and the general formal features of spiritual exercises throughout his oeuvre. This will in turn help identify the limits of Hadot's larger project, the place in which his own work seems to end, just as it poses a series of questions, the answers to which Hadot himself only gestures toward.

Although Hadot is motivated by an interest in offering forms of ancient spiritual exercise to contemporary spiritual demands, he only partially explains what that would look like in a handful of instances. However, I argue that Hadot's analyses of ancient spiritual exercises provide the kind of formal model required to develop methods capable of either translating ancient spiritual exercises into a historical present, or to develop and recognize properly contemporary forms of spiritual exercise, even as Hadot does not take up this work himself. These latter questions can be understood to reduce to the more general problem of the emergence of new forms of spiritual exercise in any context. For that reason, I first address the general question of how to specify the criteria that would allow us to determine the appropriateness and potential efficacy of spiritual exercises in any time and place, and thus under the conditions of any "spiritual demand." Indeed, the general framework, or at least the beginnings of one, required to understand the applicability of a given practice or regimen to a given context is implicit within Hadot's approach to the ancient texts. I argue that the foundations of that method are to be found within the analysis of the practical-philosophical coherence and integrity of the three poles of the philosophical diagnosis of given "spiritual demands"; spiritual exercises themselves; and the telos, or ideal principles, within the ancient schools.

However and again, although Hadot acknowledges the impossibility of simply introducing practices and concepts from one historical context to another without some reliable method of doing so, he stops short of articulating any such method. He simply does not take the next step of showing us just what the preliminary analysis and concrete specification of the forms that any properly contemporary regimen of spiritual exercises would have to look like. Moreover, the few examples that Hadot provides of spiritual exercises in the present do not ultimately meet the criteria that I reconstruct from his work, and thus fail to meet his own implicit standards. In other words, it is quite possible that Hadot cannot fully answer his own question to Friedmann, at least not without the kind of exhaustive analysis of contemporary conditions entailed and modeled by his own work on the ancients. And so, while the question of contemporary spiritual exercises is much more central to Hadot's project than it may seem, he ultimately leaves the task of answering it to others, and we come up against the limits of his project. I do not take this to be a flaw on Hadot's part: his oeuvre is capacious and methodical. Indeed, I do not take the fact of boundaries and limitations, or our ability to locate them, to be a flaw in any project. Quite the opposite, it is a testament to any work that it raises new questions beyond its own borders, a principle that stands for all of the authors I engage in this book. We can ask, however, what the consequences of Hadot's descriptive work are for his own prescriptive goals, and vice versa. In other words, how can or should his historical understanding of spiritual exercises inform the possible contours of practices taken up in times and places different from those of their origin, or new forms of practice cultivated to meet unique historical demands?

These questions serve as both motivation and guiding thread in my discussion of Hadot. And they have great implications for the larger questions already outlined in the introduction: first, that of the theorization of the emergence of new practices, which I only begin to treat here; second, that of the possibility of a proper politics of self-overcoming, to which later chapters will be more generally devoted, even as it also begins to take shape here. The former questions, those I ask directly of Hadot, will allow us to more fully understand the broader category of practices of the self by identifying fundamental problems that the later questions, those that guide this book as a whole, must answer. Indeed, it is in no small part because this productive tension within Hadot's work has such wide-ranging consequences that I have chosen to begin this project with him. In order to properly motivate either of these lines of investigation, and to contextualize them appropriately, we must begin with a more general sense of what we mean when we talk about spiritual exercises in the first place. And if the broader issues I want to pursue here emerge from a reading of Hadot, then it is with his rich investigations of ancient spiritual exercises that we must begin.

II. "NOT WITHIN THINGS": HADOT ON ANCIENT PHILOSOPHICAL LIFE

Despite the difficulties inherent in the textual record, Hadot elaborates the spiritual exercises and forms of life taken up among the range of ancient philosophical practitioners across the Greek and Roman worlds, from pre-Socratic fragments to the first Christian centuries.[59] Among these traditions, Hadot finds what he calls a "profound unity" within the "apparent diversity."[60] This unity is not so much located within a doctrinal universalism, though the schools could share much in common there. Instead, it is found in the formal contours of these forms of philosophical life and the spiritual exercises that co-constituted them. That resonance begins, of course, with the very idea of exercises taken up to bring about a transformation of the practitioner, however those terms are construed. But there is also another formal commonality evinced across Hadot's writings, if only ever a general and implicit one. In all cases, the diagnoses of human suffering proffered by different schools, the telos, or ideal state of wisdom that each presents as its resolution, and the specific exercises taken up to bridge them, all reciprocally determine one another (although not always exhaustively). Indeed, the intimate relationship between these three general poles is largely responsible for the great diversity within the unity that Hadot analyzes.

On its own, this observation is straightforward and uncontroversial. But it is often the case for Hadot that a simple premise leads to an intricate research program. In this case, a productive tension arises at the juncture of this formal relationship between diagnosis, telos, and exercise on the one hand, and what I have called Hadot's prescriptive project on the other. That tension illuminates certain implicit methodological and philosophical criteria that Hadot provides for understanding spiritual exercises beyond the ancient context, especially the problem of translating ancient spiritual exercises into new historical frames. Later, it will help provide a necessary basis for thinking through the politics of spiritual exercises and practices of the self. One goal of this chapter is thus to bring that tension and these implicit contours to light. And to do that, I must turn to the details of Hadot's treatments of ancient philosophical exercises.

Among the range of sources that Hadot engages, the philosophical schools that emerge and flourish in the Hellenistic period are often representative for him. This is in no small part because they evince both the diversity and unity of ancient philosophical practice, and due to their extended influence into the Roman period and beyond. Regarding their overlap, Hadot notes, "At first glance, in fact, one might wonder if the conceptions of wisdom were really all that different among the schools." He continues:

> Whether or not they laid claim to the Socratic heritage, all Hellenistic philosophers agreed with Socrates that human beings are plunged into misery, anguish, and evil because they exist in ignorance. Evil is to be found not within things, but in the value judgments which people bring to bear *upon* things. People can therefore be cured of their ills only if they are persuaded to change their judgements, and in this sense all these philosophies wanted to be therapeutic. In order to change our value judgements, however, we must make a radical choice to change our entire way of thinking and way of being.

Rooted together, one way or another, in the model of Socrates, they shared a commitment to philosophy "as a remedy for human worries, anguish, and misery."[61]

Of course, the doctors did not pronounce the same diagnoses or prescribe the same cures. The reasons for our unhappiness, the spiritual demands one seeks to address, the particular forms that our ignorance may take, all were understood in different terms. Thus "despite these apparent similarities, deep differences may be discerned." Within the Hellenistic context, our problems are brought about "for the Cynics, by social constraints and conventions; for the Epicureans, by the quest for false pleasures; for the Stoics, by the pursuit of pleasure and egoistic self-interest; and for the Skeptics, by false opinions."[62] Because the basic diagnoses of human disquiet differed from school to school, so too did the healing regimens they offered.

Take the Stoics and Epicureans, related but distinct traditions whose departures and resonances are instructive and arguably Hadot's most privileged examples. This latter attention, it is worth noting, is not only scholarly but personal, reflecting what Arnold I. Davidson calls Hadot's "subtle but significant displacement of his philosophical sympathies from Neoplatonism to Epicureanism and especially Stoicism." Indeed, this shift is the result of "Hadot's recognition of and increasing philosophical concern with the realities of everyday life," which dovetails with his concern to offer up philosophical perspectives that speak to contemporary needs.[63]

In *What Is Ancient Philosophy?* Hadot describes the Stoic outlook, which "consists in becoming sharply aware of the tragic situation of human beings, who are conditioned by fate." He continues:

> It would seem that we are not free at all, for it is not up to us to be beautiful, strong, healthy, or rich, to feel pleasure, or to escape suffering. All these things depend on causes which are external to us. A necessity which is inexorable and indifferent to our individual interest breaks our aspirations and our hopes; we are helpless and defenseless in the face of the accidents of life, the setbacks of fortune, illness, and death. [. . .] The result of this is that people are unhappy, because they passionately seek to acquire things which they cannot obtain and to flee evils which are inevitable. [. . .] There is thus a radical opposition between what depends on us and can therefore be either good or bad, since it is the object of our decision, and what depends not on us, but on external causes and fate and which is therefore indifferent.[64]

This last is the fundamental Stoic distinction between what does and what does not depend on us: our judgments on the one hand, and nature on the other. The "indifferent" or the "natural" comprises all that does not depend on us and "corresponds with the necessary linkage of cause and effect—in other words, to Fate, the course of nature, or the actions of other human beings. Thus, life and death, health and sickness, pleasure and suffering, beauty and ugliness, strength and weakness, wealth and poverty, nobility and baseness, political careers—all are indifferent, because they do not depend on us."[65] This is the world beyond our control, against which we can do nothing but prepare ourselves.

This distinction determines the Stoic injunction to "give up desiring that which does not depend on us and is beyond our control, so as to attach ourselves only to what depends on us: actions which are just and in conformity with reason."[66] The problem then is that we are ignorant and unable to distinguish between what does and does not depend upon us. We act as though we can impact events that are beyond our influence, and treat the things we can shape like unyielding laws of nature. We confuse fate and freedom, and that confusion is the source of our unhappiness. For the Stoics, the goal is thus a form of life that seeks "only the goods that [we] are able to attain, and [to] try to avoid only those evils which it is possible to avoid."[67] But to do so is the greatest challenge, as the task is not simply to understand such principles, but to live them as best we can.

It is not a matter of belief but of cultivating "a fundamental attitude, [which] consisted in a joyful 'Yes!' accorded at each instant to the movement of the world, directed by universal reason."[68] Even if unattainable, the telos of the Stoic life is "a complete reversal of our usual way of looking at things. We are to switch from our 'human' vision of reality, in which our values depend on our passions, to a 'natural' vision of things, which replaces each event within the perspective of universal nature."[69] As Hadot describes it, Stoic philosophical exercises meant nothing less than "practicing how to 'live;' that is, how to live freely and consciously." "Consciously," he continues, "in that we pass beyond the limits of individuality, to recognize ourselves as part of the reason-animated *cosmos*. Freely, in that we give up desiring that which does not depend on us and is beyond our control, so as to attach ourselves only to what depends on us: actions which are just and in conformity with reason."[70]

Epicurean principles both mirror and depart from those of the Stoics in instructive ways. Once again our unhappiness is rooted in ignorance and misjudgment, but in this case we confuse the nature of desire and pleasure.

The Epicurean principle consists in a threefold distinction, "between desires which are both natural and necessary, desires which are natural but not necessary, and desires which are neither natural nor necessary."[71] On this basis, people's unhappiness "comes from the fact that they are afraid of things which are not to be feared, and desire things which it is not necessary to desire, and which are beyond their control. Consequently, their life is consumed in worries over unjustified fears and unsatisfied desires."[72] This deprivation and the unhappy state it produces are again grounded in our ignorance and confusion. Rather than "seeking the only genuine pleasure, the pure pleasure of existing," which comes from both understanding and satisfying our true needs, we are "tortured by 'immense, hollow' desires, such as those for wealth, luxury, and domination."[73] Tortured, because to seek such pleasures is to attempt to sate desires that can never be fulfilled.

Like the Stoics, the Epicurean ideal was centered around a concept of nature, but in this case the practitioner sought to live according to natural and necessary desire: "Natural and necessary desires are those whose satisfaction delivers people from pain, and which correspond to the elementary needs or vital necessities. Natural but not necessary are, for example, desires for sumptuous foods and for sexual gratification. Neither natural nor necessary, but produced by empty opinions, are the limitless desires for wealth, glory, and immortality."[74] The sage understands that "it is enough to satisfy the first category of desires, and give up the last—and eventually the second as well—in order to ensure the absence of worries, and to reveal the sheer joy of existing."[75] Thus Epicurean philosophy "consists in knowing how to seek pleasure in a reasonable way" by seeking out only rational pleasures—those which are both natural and necessary.[76]

The Epicurean arrives at this state of wisdom through an askesis of desire, which "consists in limiting one's appetites—suppressing those desires which are neither natural nor necessary, and limiting as much as possible those which are natural but not necessary."[77] In this way, the askesis of desire brings about genuine, rational pleasure, wherein the body "is appeased and free of suffering; it consists in not being hungry, not being thirsty, and not being cold."[78] As the satisfaction of all natural and necessary desires, and the absence of any unnecessary desires, this rational pleasure is perfect. From this vantage point, "the Epicurean sage . . . like the gods, watches the infinity of the world arising out of atoms in the infinite void; nature is sufficient for his needs, and nothing ever disturbs the peace of his soul."[79]

Through this askesis, the Epicurean, like the Stoic, exercises a transformation of judgment, which is at once a transformation of oneself. Throughout his career, Hadot describes such efforts across traditions, historical periods, and locations in methodical detail: among Skeptics and Cynics, Platonists and Neoplatonists, Aristotelians and Christians, within the mystery religions, from Greek antiquity through imperial Rome, and further.[80] Regardless of time or place, these many and varied traditions all begin with the simple observation that human beings are unhappy and posit a reason why. That articulation of the origins of human suffering in turn informs a description of an ideal state of wisdom in which the suffering described would be either mitigated or defeated, and something like genuine happiness achieved. The latter is sometimes embodied in the figure of a sage, whether real or speculative, sometimes thought to be attainable, other times best understood as a model worth aspiring to. As Hadot puts it, again in the case of the Stoic trajectory: "The will to do good is an unbreachable fortress which everyone can construct within themselves. It is there that we can find freedom, independence, invulnerability, and that eminently Stoic value, coherence with ourselves."[81] The question then is one of the materials and methods by which this inner citadel constructed. It is here that spiritual exercises come in.

Ancient Spiritual Exercises

For all of the schools, and even for many of the more explicitly religious traditions that Hadot also engages, it is not simply a matter of understanding, but of training oneself toward the ideal. The fundamental distinctions of the varying schools are not so easily made within the course of daily life, certainly when attempting to control what seem like natural responses to the hardships that mark our days and nights. To suspend judgment altogether like the Skeptics, to understand that there is only one true pleasure like the Epicureans, to live "naturally" like the Cynics, or to abide by the rules of Christian monastic life: these traditions, among many others, recognized that any such choice of life is never easy. The changes in question must thus be cultivated, as a skill or trade is cultivated, through long and careful effort until it is second nature, part of oneself—whatever that "self" is taken to be, and however our "first nature" is described. The forms that this training takes, in terms of the specific spiritual exercises taken up and the overall form of life that they constitute, are tailored to deliver one from a particular understanding of disquiet to a corresponding model of wisdom.

Here we again see a great deal of diversity within the body of philosophical practice. In Hadot's terms, some of these practices could be "physical" and include things like dietary regimes, a range of physical exercises, or the choice of an ever-simplified ascetic existence, as we see most in the lives of the Cynics or the desert fathers. Others may be more strictly "discursive," such as philosophical dialogue, written practices like *hypomnemata* or epistolary exchanges, alongside reading or hearing the lectures of a master.[82] Finally, Hadot describes some exercises as "intuitive," such as practices of contemplation, reflection on the events of the day before sleep, and the like. In practice, given exercises would overlap some or all of these domains. Moreover, Hadot is clear that his view does not exclude the theoretical and discursive aspects of philosophy as we know it. It rather resituates them within the larger constellation of a full philosophical life.[83] And while different schools engaged in different practices, similar if not identical spiritual exercises are just as often taken up for different reasons and to different ends.

Returning to the dogmatic schools, Hadot argues that for the Stoics, the philosophical bridge from suffering to wisdom is built on the foundations of *prosokhē*, an ever-renewed attention to the present moment, which he describes as both the fundamental Stoic spiritual attitude and a spiritual exercise in its own right. This attention consists in "a continuous vigilance and presence of mind, self-consciousness which never sleeps, and a constant tension of the spirit."[84] It is through this "vigilance of the spirit" that the practitioner is able to keep the fundamental Stoic rule of life, "the distinction between what depends on us and what does not," among other core tenets ready to hand. It does so in part by taking our focus off of "the past and the future—two areas which do *not* depend on us."[85] Here, Hadot invokes a theme that runs throughout the ancient sources, and is especially highlighted in his own work, reflecting one of his core commitments: that worries directed toward the past and the future are among the basic causes of our troubles and that being fully present to the present is necessary for anything resembling happiness.

In his descriptions of *prosokhē*, Hadot ties this orientation to another of his favorite themes, the experience and perspective he calls "cosmic consciousness," the "view from above," "the contemplation of the Whole," the "spiritual exercise of the vision of totality," or sometimes "imaginative overflight."[86] It is here, moreover, that Hadot tends to see some of the most consistent overlap between the views he surveys,[87] though there is again diversity within the unity. In the case of the Stoics, the practice of attention to the present moment "allows us to accede to cosmic consciousness, by making us attentive to the infinite value of each instant, and causing us to accept each moment of existence from the viewpoint of the universal law of the *cosmos*."[88] This is the "natural" perspective from which we are able to distinguish what does and does not depend on us. That natural vantage entails a clear-eyed understanding of our own place in the universe, because this cosmic consciousness is at once a self-consciousness and a moral consciousness.[89] As the Stoic distinction between what is and what is not within our control is based on an understanding of nature, for one who has acceded to the perspective of the cosmos, this distinction is ever in view, because we have, in Hadot's terms, "assimilated" it to ourselves.[90] This process, perspective, and experience represent what Hadot calls a "lived physics."[91]

From our perspective, Hadot's invocation of physics may be counterintuitive, depending on how one already approaches any of these terms. Nonetheless, this idea of a lived physics or physics as a spiritual exercise overlays both the different classes of spiritual exercise that Hadot identifies and is taken up in diverse ways among different schools.[92] In the first place, physics serves a descriptive role, though one that has what Hadot calls an "ethical finality" insofar as "the rationality of human action is based on the rationality of nature."[93] Here, physics does not simply consist in a set of true or false claims about the cosmos. Instead, the understanding of the cosmos furnished by physical discourse serves to ground and justify the principles of the school, and in turn, the ethical prescriptions that are argued to follow from it. In this way, the shape of a philosophical life follows from the shape of nature itself.

The work of intellectual justification is also accompanied by physics as contemplative activity in its own right, one that cultivates a fundamental shift in perspective. On Hadot's account, the contemplation of nature is found in some form or another in traditions ranging from the Platonic dialogues, to the Aristotelians, to Plutarch and Seneca, and it is fundamental:

In the first place, physics can be a contemplative activity, which has its end in itself, providing joy and serenity to the soul, and liberating it from day-to-day worries. This is the spirit of Aristotelian physics: "nature, which fashioned creatures, gives amazing pleasure in their study to all who can trace links of causation, and are naturally philosophers." As we have seen, it was in the contemplation of nature that the Epicurean Lucretius found "a divine delight." For the Stoic Epictetus, the meaning of our existence resides in contemplation: we have been placed on earth in order to contemplate divine creation, and we must not die before we have witnessed its marvels and lived in harmony with nature.[94]

It is through just this kind of contemplative physics that one cultivates and experiences "the view from above," this imaginative overflight "which causes human affairs to be regarded as of little importance."[95] From this grander perspective, one stands in a newer, more ideal, relationship to the world, oneself, and the human community. At the same time, what is shared is again accompanied by what is not. Even from a cosmic perspective, we do not view the same thing or interpret similar experiences in comparable ways.[96] Indeed, the reasons for which one seeks a "view from above," what exactly it was taken to be a view "of," the particular "human affairs" that come into sharper view, and the nature of the viewer all vary. Even the ecstatic moment of "losing oneself" begins with a conception of the "self" to be lost, reasons for losing it, and the nature of the human being who emerges on the other side.

Of course, the contemplation of nature is only one form of meditative practice. Indeed, "meditation" is among the most recognizable and diverse forms of cultivation, such that it is better understood as a category or class of practices rather than a singular exercise. In the traditions that Hadot studies alone, practices of meditation differ in terms of object of contemplation, physical or material exercises that accompany them, the goals of the exercise, and much else. But within his work it is often in the context of discussing meditation that Hadot emphasizes the particularly important relationship to time, specifically to the present, that spiritual exercises are often meant to cultivate.[97] Following the ancient schools, Hadot argues that a given ideal can only be found within the present moment, which alone is our happiness. This is why Hadot was, after all, so moved by Friedmann's injunction to "step out of duration."

But as important as this emphasis on the timeless present is, it by no means excludes certain relationships with the past and the future, cultivated through meditative attention to both what has come before and what lies ahead. Among these are future-directed practices of anticipation and past-directed practices of memory, alongside forms of focused attention to the present moment and practices of self-examination, which weave together a complex temporality. Often meditation on past and future alike can direct and redirect one to the present, sometimes with the reciprocating goal of surer preparation for the fortunes and misfortunes that await us in the future.

Among the forms of future-directed meditation, the contemplation of death is so important that Hadot calls it "one of the most fundamental philosophical exercises" in general.[98] Across doctrinal or practical differences, the proper attention to death is a consistent prerequisite for the correct relationship to the present. As Hadot reminds us, Epicurus himself says, "the exercise of living well and the exercise of dying well are one and the same thing."[99] For the Epicureans, meditation on death allows us to understand that "death, qua non-being, is nothing for us," and that for that reason, "it also means rejoicing at each instant that we have acceded to being, and knowing that death cannot diminish the plenitude of the pleasure of being."[100] In this way, the contemplation of death serves the askesis of desire, cultivating the proper relationship to those desires that are both natural and necessary, in accord with Epicurean doctrine.

Within this general category of anticipatory contemplation, Hadot often returns to the example of the Stoic "premeditation of evils," in which "we are to represent to ourselves poverty, suffering, and death,"[101] in order to be ready in the face of even the most dramatic of life's possibilities. Although this exercise does not exclusively focus on death, the latter was one of its primary objects. As Hadot says, citing Philo of Alexandria, by focusing on potential future events and otherwise unexpected hardships, including our own eventual end, those who practice this exercise "do not flinch beneath the blows of Fate because they have calculated its attacks in advance; for of those things which happen against our will, even the most painful are lessened by foresight, when our thought no longer encounters anything unexpected in events but dulls the perception of them, as if they were old, worn-out things."[102] Premeditation thus prepared practitioners to respond to the inevitable difficulties of life through an askesis of judgment according to the fundamental Stoic principle of indifference to all that does not depend on us.

But meditation is not only a future-directed practice of anticipation. It also takes the form of past-directed practices of memory. The Stoics, Epicureans, and Skeptics, among others, practiced the memorization of the fundamental doctrines of the schools in the form of striking maxims that one kept ready at hand to repeat and recall in times of need.[103] Here, the practice of memorization and recall is not merely an example of what Hadot calls "conceptual construction." Rather, these maxims "had a psychagogic value: they were intended to produce an effect on the soul of the auditor or reader."[104] At the same time, the practice of memory was not limited to the recollection of maxims, but also included the contemplation of past events. The Epicureans endorsed the recollection and "re-actualization" of past pleasures—insofar as they were true pleasures at the time—through practices of memory in the present. Epicurus himself invokes the memory of philosophical conversations with his students, a representative case of genuine pleasure, to ameliorate his physical suffering.[105]

Alongside these practices of anticipation and memory, meditation also takes the form of contemplative self-examination, which requires both. In the Stoic case, meditative self-examination consisted in the daily anticipation and nightly reflection on oneself: "First thing in the morning, we should go over in advance what we have to do during the course of the day, and decide on the principles which will guide and inspire our actions. In the evening, we should examine ourselves again, so as to be aware of the faults we have committed or the progress we have made. We should also examine our dreams."[106] Such a practice, whether internal or through writing the self, serves as both preparation and correction. To such general forms of self-examination, we may add any number of practices, including contemplative or meditative practices within and far outside those that Hadot discusses. The same can be said of all of the examples I have rehearsed here, and this is arguably even more true for the concept of spiritual exercise as Hadot presents it in general.

I have only rehearsed a handful of the spiritual exercises from among the breadth of the philosophical traditions that Hadot works to conceptually reactualize. I have chosen these examples because I take them to be both representative of Hadot's approach in general, including cases he explores elsewhere, and because many of the themes described here will reappear in one form or another in this chapter or in those that follow. Further, if these examples are representative of his approach in general, they also provide a model and resources to further explore beyond the borders of Hadot's own research.[107] Above all, the cases glossed here illuminate the conceptual and practical coherence of spiritual exercises and the discourses that co-constitute them. The forms that spiritual exercises take are determined (though not always exhaustively) by the spiritual demands a given school or outlook seeks to address, as well as the ideal state wherein they are (possibly) ameliorated.[108] This relationship could be imperfect in many cases, or may appear incorrect or incoherent from a different philosophical or religious perspective, including our own. Not all schools or individuals practiced all of the same spiritual exercises, and in cases in which they did, they would do so in different ways to often quite different ends. So, while both the Stoics and Epicureans engaged in the anticipatory meditation on death in order to reshape the relationship to the present, they did so for different reasons, in order to create a different sort of person. What matters here is that it is from the perspective of this holistic understanding of ancient philosophy that Hadot argues that within the ancient schools even the recognizably discursive aspects of philosophy took their place within a complete form of life.[109]

Here, however, another challenge arises. If the goal of spiritual exercises is to produce a new person, to what extent does the specificity of the conditions that shape who one is at the outset determine this new "form of life" from the moment of that decision to the specification of a state of wisdom? If the problem of, say, poverty is among the classical objects of anticipatory meditation, is there not a profound difference between poverty as a possible future misfortune, rather than a genuine object of past memory, let alone the framing condition of one's present? While differing ancient schools and thinkers had different answers to the question of who can practice philosophy, there remains an assumed universalism in our reception of the ancient sources. The point is not that everyone can practice philosophy, that much is clear. I mean that in the diagnoses of human disquiet offered by the schools, including those that Hadot most endorses, there is a universalism of explanation. But even if our problems do come from the same ultimate sources, there is less attention to the particular modalities by which those general sources are either experienced or challenged in action. Hadot follows the texts in noting, for example, that women are certainly attested within the ranks of the philosophers.[110] But even then, the fact that so little is said about the particularity of those lives can be read as an implicit claim that such a life is not significantly different than those of our more familiar examples. And so, insofar as the details of the life from which we set out do not seem to matter, this problem of universalism is thus, in at least one major form, the problem of elitism. The latter in turn becomes the problem of politics.

III. ORDINARY PHILOSOPHY AND ORDINARY LIFE

For Hadot, "the essential part of philosophy is not discourse, but life and action," wherein discursive practices are re-situated in the service of broader philosophical life.[111] He further insists that this form of life is available to all, and he takes pains to distance his work from any explicit elitism.[112] Thus is it also clear that this concern with the possibility of philosophy as a universally approachable way of life is the foundation of his praise for ancient philosophy in general, though again, as Davidson notes, it also motivates the shift in Hadot's sympathies toward certain traditions.[113] In any case, and no matter the school or figure, Hadot's concern that "philosophy as a way of life" could, and indeed should, be an *everyday* way of life threads its way throughout his works. But Hadot is also under no illusion that to practice philosophy as an everyday way of life, at any time and place, is either easy or at times even possible. In the short but important piece "Is Philosophy a Luxury?," he demonstrates that the answer to the titular question will depend on just what we mean by both "luxury" and "philosophy." His answer comes in the form of a pointedly equivocal "yes and no."

Hadot's "no" is a consequence of his very idea of philosophy, and he says as much straightaway: "It will then become evident that the question raised obliges us to ask ourselves, necessarily, about the very definition of philosophy. And finally, even beyond the nature of philosophy, our reflection will lead us to the drama of the human condition."[114] Thus, in his approach to the ancients, Hadot wishes to "glimpse a type of philosophy that is, in a way, identical with a person's life, the life of a person aware of himself, ceaselessly rectifying his thought and his action, aware of his belonging to humanity and to the world." This understanding is at the heart of his first conclusion, that "philosophy cannot be a luxury, since it is linked to life itself. Instead, it would be an elementary need for human beings." Hadot argues that this understanding of philosophical reflection as an elementary human need is behind the universal impulse of schools like the Stoics and Epicureans, who "proposing to people the art of living as a human being, they addressed all human beings: slaves, women, and foreigners. They were missionary and sought to convert the masses."[115] Hadot endorses those ancient schools that not only held that philosophy was a way of life, but that it could be a way of life for anyone. Spiritual exercises, on this account, were not only the purview of those specialists who could "leave the world" to practice them.

And yet, just as Hadot rejects any kind of philosophy that would be a "luxury" of this sort, he is under no illusions regarding the economic, moral, political, and other factors that in the end do constitute philosophy as a luxury. This even includes those forms that fall under his own definition of philosophy as "part of life" and open to all. This is the heart of the semi-tragic "yes" that he offers:

> For we must not fool ourselves: this philosophy, conceived as a way of living, cannot, as always, be anything but a luxury. The drama of the human condition is that it is impossible not to philosophize, and at the same time it is impossible to philosophize. Philosophical consciousness opens up for people the profusion of the wonders of the cosmos and the earth, a more acute perception, an inexhaustible wealth of exchanges with other human beings, with other souls, an invitation to act with benevolence and justice. But worries, necessities, and the banalities of everyday life prevent us from acceding to this conscious life [in] all its possibilities. How can one harmoniously unite daily life with philosophical consciousness? It can only be a fragile conquest, always threatened. . . . And how could the billions of human beings crushed by poverty and suffering achieve this consciousness? Might not being a philosopher also mean to suffer from this isolation, this privilege, always bearing in mind this drama of the human condition?[116]

While philosophy writ large cannot be understood as the exclusive domain of elites, Hadot is clear that the conditions that produce such economic and social distinctions impede the practice of philosophy, even under his own definition. Indeed, certain ancient sources say as much themselves.[117] The banalities of everyday life, the large and small burdens of economic reality, access to education or other material needs: even under a description that assimilates philosophy to "part of life," the practical factors that make life itself difficult will also make philosophy difficult, and thus constitute it as a luxury. At the very same time, on Hadot's account, it is philosophy itself that can provide the tools we need to cope with and survive those difficulties. The irony is not lost on Hadot, and his equivocal answer is not a contradiction, but rather a problem, a question, and a knot to untie. On my reading, it is a political question just as much as it is a philosophical one, in several ways.

First, despite Hadot's efforts, most if not all of the examples of spiritual exercises that he analyses come from ancient religious or philosophical professionals, figures who fall squarely into the category of specialists. This is a result of a number of factors, from the problems presented by the preservation and persistence of ancient texts to consistent elite determination of the written record, not only in the ancient context, but in the intervening centuries and up to the present. Thus, while it is true, as Hadot insists, that some of the ancient schools were open to non-elite participation, it is less clear what a "lay philosophy" or a "philosophy from below" looked like. The philosophical cares and consequent insights of a Marcus Aurelius would certainly differ from those of the vast majority of his subjects, including the large number who were enslaved people. Even if women of any class, the enslaved, and common people in general participated in philosophical life, our picture of how they may have contributed to the shape of that life remains limited, and we are the worse off for that fact. The test case here would be someone like Epictetus, who began life a slave, but was yet a philosophical professional, a student of Musonius Rufus, and the doctor who operated the clinic.[118]

As I have argued already, if the spiritual exercises that one takes up are determined by the spiritual demands one faces, then the material or social conditions that create the divisions in question here also clearly constitute the troubles and worries that philosophy as a way of life is meant to address. And if that is the case, then either the exercises themselves or the modalities by which commonly accepted (and elite-determined) classes of practices are adapted would be determined by the specific and uniquely challenging conditions and demands of "ordinary" lives. Even if we think of philosophical specialists as "pattern-setters," it is clear that everyday philosophical life must be adaptive and creative—that is, philosophical—in its own right. And if so, even if the Stoics, Epicureans, or others "sought to convert the masses," we cannot be sure that the masses who did take up their doctrines, dogmas, and practices did so in the ways that appear in Hadot's studies. Indeed, on Hadot's very account, there is good reason to suspect, or rather to hope, otherwise.

Second, it is a political question insofar as any explicit politics that appear in Hadot's work almost always takes the form of the philosophical education of political elites or the role of philosophers as advisors to the elite. Hadot notes this in the case of Plato, whose fundamental intentions he argues were explicitly political, and took the form of a belief in "the possibility of changing political life by means of the philosophical education of those men who were influential in the city."[119] Hadot insists further that even during periods of political disaffection and seeming philosophical quietude, many persisted in their advisory and educational efforts, even at great personal risk. In general, Hadot says, "The philosophers never renounced their hope of changing society, even if only by the examples of their lives."[120]

But there is something disappointing and limited in this model of politics as the moral education or advisory suasion of an elite class, of those not simply in power, but those who by class or by wealth are in some sense born to govern others. This disappointment should be palpable from the perspective of any political outlook that founds itself in the interests and experiences of the dispossessed, the disinherited, the most vulnerable, those who labor, and so on. But it is also an internal tension, if not contradiction, to exclusively find this limited political conception of philosophy that, as Hadot insists again and again, is meant to be for all. And it is for this reason that we are justified in finding little sympathy for, say, a philosopher-emperor who Hadot reports: "Expressed feelings of impotence in the face of his subjects' inertia and lack of understanding."[121] Philosopher-kings, it turns out, are still kings.

Finally, the question of politics is even more significant, because it is this specific context within Hadot's work that one of the most consistent, if often implicit, questions within the overall body of literature on practices of the self emerges. It is, moreover, one of the major questions that guides the present work: How, under what conditions, and in what forms can the practice of caring for of oneself be identical or coterminous with caring for the other, for others, and in a genuinely political manner, for the city or community? Beginning as always with the model of Socrates, Hadot first insists that there is an ethical mutuality to be found in spiritual exercises in general, and in dialogue especially: "The intimate connection between dialogue with others and dialogue with oneself is profoundly significant. Only one who is capable of a genuine encounter with the other is capable of an authentic encounter with oneself, and the converse is equally true. Dialogue can be genuine only within the framework of presence to others and to oneself."[122] On that foundation, he further insists that spiritual exercises do not entail political quietism or a withdrawal from worldly life, as "the care of the self is thus not opposed to care for the city." In fact, and again on the Socratic model, "care for the self is . . . indissolubly, care for the city and care for others," or at least it can be in certain praiseworthy cases.[123] But Hadot does not elaborate this identity in much detail, and his formulation, one that unites the care of the self, the care of others, and the care of the city, is more complex than he implies in these fleeting comments. In fact, these brief remarks actually describe several different possible relationships, which may indeed be identical in some cases, or overlap to varying degrees in others, but are just as often distinguishable from one another.

First, there is an ideal wherein a practice or form of life in which the care of the self is identical or coterminous with the care of the singular other. In such cases, caring for another person is a spiritual exercise that brings about a transformation of oneself or vice versa. Sometimes the directionality may matter: I may start from a concern to change myself that in some way overlaps with a care for others. Or there may be an initially other-directed endeavor in which care of the second person brings about a fundamental change in the first. In other cases, the initial orientation will be indistinguishable. Hadot finds a version of this ideal evinced in the radical form of life embodied by Diogenes the Cynic, for whom, like Socrates, "care for himself was, indissolubly, care for others."[124] And yet a care of the self that is coterminous with the care of another or of others does not necessarily amount to a politics, as it may simply constitute an ethical relationship between individuals. Moreover, in the case of the care of *others*, such a relationship may also simply take the form of a moral or ethical effort directed toward the city as a whole. This kind of effort would seek to engender a more widespread moral or ethical revaluation among the community without, for example, addressing the formal structures or institutions that are politically constitutive of the city itself. Here we might distinguish between an ethics *within* the city and an ethics *of* the city.

Second, returning to Hadot's formulation, we can also delimit a care of the self that is coterminous with the care of others as a political project properly speaking. By the latter, I mean a form that intervenes on the level of both the existing governance or administration of the city or more pointedly on the level of determining the political constitution of the city itself. However, it is crucial to note that even a relationship in which the care of the self and the care of the city are coterminous does not inevitably produce any particular political form. It may simply replace the moral education or suasion of the elite previously marked by a Socratic smile with the grimace of the Cynic.[125] Similarly, there are many forms of political imagination that take the amassed moral lives of the population as the defining feature of the political. But any such view that does not take into account the ways in which political structures, institutions, or material conditions serve to shape the lives of the people, indeed "who the people are" on the level of both "I" and "we," would simply amount to the moralism discussed in the introduction. And so, the question becomes one of how, under what conditions, and in what form could we recognize a transformation of the self (or selves) that is coterminous with a transformation of those constitutive material and institutional features of the city that also shape the lives led within it? In other words, is there a form of the care of the self "from below" that is mutually indistinguishable from the care of the city via an intervention into its formal structures or institutions and thus does not amount to a form of reductive moralism?

Hadot does not conceive of the issue in these terms. As noted earlier, the political content of his work is relatively limited and somewhat outside his primary focus. He does, however, provide the basic groundwork for formulating the problems of both "ordinary" philosophy and the politics of spiritual exercises in the process of laying out many of the concepts required for thinking about spiritual exercises beyond his own direct analyses. On my reading, some of these same preliminary resources also speak to the problem with which this chapter began, the persistent question of practicing spiritual exercises in the present.

IV. SPIRITUAL EXERCISES IN THE PRESENT

Despite the many differences and distinctions among them, in Hadot's analyses ancient forms of philosophical life are characterized by mutually co-constituting relationships between philosophical diagnosis, telos, and practice. In some cases, identical spiritual exercises (or at least, practices belonging to the same larger class of exercises) could be taken up for different reasons and to different ends. In other cases, a given philosophical outlook would preclude the use of commensurate practices by differing schools (i.e., it would be very hard to imagine a Skeptic taking up a Cynic form of life). In all cases, for Hadot, such practices were the very body of ancient philosophy itself.

Here the prescriptive and descriptive threads within Hadot's research come together. Whereas Carlier saw a "discrepancy," I take it that the formal coherence of spiritual exercises excavated from Hadot's studies has direct consequences for any project that seeks to historically transpose ancient practices or identify new ones. From Hadot's initial invocation of Friedmann, through the analyses of ancient spiritual exercises that follow, further premises can be drawn out: First, that there is something called "spiritual demand," which motivates one's engagement in spiritual exercises. Second, that there are distinctly contemporary spiritual demands, and that as both Hadot and Friedmann refer to them, they are the product of some combination of economic, political, cultural, religious, and other conditions. Third, if that is the case, then constellations of spiritual demand are determined by the particular historical circumstances out of which they are generated, unique to different times and places. Finally, both the telos and the shape of the practices themselves must also be responsive to the conditions that motivate them. This means that properly contemporary spiritual demands should entail properly contemporary spiritual exercises. And for that reason, any discussion of spiritual exercises in the present requires a deep and rich understanding of the specificity of the consuming worries they are meant to assuage. On my reading, in all of their depth and care, Hadot's analyses of ancient philosophical life entail comparably rich analyses of the present, just as they furnish one model for such work.

For her part, Carlier is rather sanguine about the possibility of the historical transposition of ancient spiritual exercises on Hadot's account. In a brief itinerary in her introduction to *The Present Alone is Our Happiness*, she presents a series of ancient examples as self-evidently relevant:

> Was it known that the Scaevolas, adepts of Stoicism, proved themselves to be honest magistrates? Or that Mucius Scaevola, as governor of a province,

did not fill his pockets, as was customary, but paid for his trips with his own money, and demanded the same integrity from his subordinates? Or that when the Stoic emperor Marcus Aurelius, who was accountable for millions of subjects, learned of the deaths of child trapeze artists, he went to the trouble of commanding that these exercises should henceforth be protected by nets? Or that, defending the Roman borders against the Sarmatians somewhere in the Balkans, he asked himself about the legitimacy of that war?

Carlier concludes with the assertion that "these principles and examples would be useful in today's democracies, without there being any need to 'update' them."[126]

I am admittedly not as optimistic as Carlier here, and on my reading at least, neither is Hadot. Indeed, it is unclear what actual principles are being referred to, other than what seem like some general truisms. Do we really need ancient Stoicism to understand that civil servants should not take bribes or embezzle money? What does that tradition specifically offer us that we would not find elsewhere? And if it does offer something specific with regard to the honesty required of public figures, we would still need to understand the details of the life, work, and expectations of such figures at the time of the Scaevolas in order to see anything more than a general lesson. Similarly, it is easy to agree that rulers who are conducting war should interrogate the legitimacy of such action. But shouldn't the specifics of the kind of imperial (rather than, say, consular, monarchical, presidential, parliamentary, etc.) power that Marcus Aurelius was able to wield inform our understanding his reflections on his campaigns? Should we not also contextualize those reflections within what we know of the norms of war, diplomacy, and empire at the time, the experiences and lives of average soldiers then and now—and then recontextualize them against the hard-won lessons of war in the twentieth and twenty-first centuries?

It is also unclear what Carlier means by "updating" a given tradition, whether we agree that such an update is necessary or not. But if the working understanding of the kind of historical translation that I have attempted to excavate from Hadot's work is at all accurate, then I take it that there is no case in which any such practice can be simply transposed from one context to another. In fact, this is not even a prescriptive claim, but by Hadot's lights a descriptive one: any such attempt at transposition will entail translation, even in cases where we claim otherwise.

Indeed, Hadot himself is aware of these difficulties: "There can be no question, of course, of mechanically imitating stereotyped schemas. After all, did not Socrates and Plato urge their disciples to find the solutions they needed by themselves?" Still, Hadot strikes a critical balance, noting that "we cannot afford to ignore such a valuable quantity of experience, accumulated over millennia" in the "highly rich and varied Western tradition."[127] And so, while Hadot is not interested in the mechanical "imitation" of ancient spiritual exercises, his own methodology should commit him to the view that detailed historical, sociological, moral, and other forms of analysis of given conditions are required to bring ancient spiritual exercises into contemporary discourse.

In fact, Hadot's approach to the ancient texts, so meticulously developed and deployed throughout his oeuvre, evinces a model of detailed and methodical investigation necessary for the successful "translation" of ancient practices into a contemporary context. In *The Present Alone Is Our Happiness*, he describes these principles in more precise detail, in response to a question posed by Davidson regarding the interpretation of ancient texts:

> I feel like the first requirement of a scholar, not only for a scholar but also for anyone who reads an ancient text, is to aim for objectivity and, if possible, for truth. This is to say that there is no point in distorting the meaning of a text to adapt it to the demands of modern life, or to the aspirations of the soul, and so on. The first duty is above all the goal of objectivity.
>
> In addition, one must, whenever possible, always attempt to resituate the text under study within its historical perspective. It is extremely important not to commit anachronisms, in the rush to give the text a contemporary meaning. On this score, I would like to evoke briefly one of my constant concerns in the interpretation of texts, precisely to avoid anachronism. This is the effort to resituate, as much as possible, the works within the concrete conditions in which they were written. On the one hand, there are spiritual conditions, that is, philosophical, rhetorical, or poetic traditions. On the other hand, there are material conditions, school and social environment, constraints arising from the material support of writing, and historical circumstances. Every work should be resituated in the praxis from which it emanates.

Thus, he concludes: "In fact, the meaning intended by the ancient author is never contemporary. It is ancient, and that is all there is to it."[128]

Within the domain of his descriptive project, Hadot thus is adamant that in order to understand ancient texts, we must avoid anachronism and strive to understand the conditions under which a text was composed, the needs and demands it set out to meet. With regard to the prescriptive thread within his work, these principles speak directly to the problems of bringing those ancient practices into contemporary usage. In other words, if Hadot's project is a fundamentally historicist one, then that methodology and the principles that undergird it must go both ways.

And yet, within Hadot's own writing, we do not see anything approaching the depth and extent of his research into the ancient context in terms of what would, on that very model, be required to "update" or "translate" ancient spiritual exercises for another time and place. This is not so much a problem for Hadot, or with his work, but rather one that is suggested and framed by that work. At the very least, these lacunae in his own research are understandable. On the one hand, his primary goal remains the study and accurate recontextualization of ancient spiritual exercises. That project, the delineation of the methods required, was extensive enough to constitute a life's work. Understood in this way, the prescriptive project, while in many ways central to his own motivations, would always be secondary and dependent upon the descriptive. The former could never really get off the ground without the latter, certainly not without the rigor that Hadot would demand. On the other hand, if Carlier is correct that Hadot's work is meant to have an implicit prescriptive force, to "discreetly turn" his readers, then it would also make sense that he so seldom engages in explicitly prescriptive philosophical discourse. And so, as he says, this work is in fact ours to do, using the resources that Hadot provides, whether they be his readings of ancient texts or the methodological principles that produced them.

At the same time, Hadot does, in a handful of instances, indulge in commenting on the possibility of practicing spiritual exercises in the present, in ways that would be both "every day" and for anyone, layperson and specialist alike. However, even these few examples remain rather cursory and lack the depth and rigor with which he contextualizes ancient practices of the self. In other words, Hadot's body of work evinces little if any systematic exploration of the "contemporary spiritual demands" that he invokes via Friedmann in the first place. While both the logic of the ancient spiritual exercises that Hadot analyzes and the methodology he deploys in those analyses would together entail a comparably systematic study of the present, only the hint of such an approach appears in Hadot's work.

Instead, in the few instances that I have mentioned, Hadot rather consistently appeals to what appear to be a series of quasi-universalist generalizations, which can appear confusing given the depth and adamancy of his historicism. For that reason, it is worth being as clear as possible on just what Hadot is and is not saying in these instances. Take, for example, the question posed to him in the postscript interview at the end of *Philosophy as a Way of Life*, conducted from April to May 1992 by the translator Michael Chase during the course of the book's translation into English:

> MC: Are spiritual exercises still possible today? They were thought up in the very distant past, as responses to specific social structures and material conditions, but our current living conditions bear very little resemblance to those of antiquity. The spiritual exercises of the Stoics and the Epicureans, for example, are the consequences of the basic hypotheses of each school: on the one hand, faith in the providential Logos; on the other, atomism, belief in chance, and denial of post-mortem existence. Nowadays, however, we may no longer believe in these hypotheses. Is it still possible to practice the spiritual exercises of antiquity, separating them from the systems of which they were a part, and substituting our own basic hypotheses for the outmoded ones of antiquity?
>
> Let's take the example of injustice. One of the greatest sources of pain for modern man is, I would think, the suffering of innocent people. Every day, the media overwhelm us with images of this suffering, and we witness it every day in the streets of our cities. How can we avoid giving in to despair if we no longer believe, like Marcus Aurelius, in a divine providence, consubstantial with ourselves, which arranges everything for the best, and ensures that injustices are only apparent?[129]

Because Chase poses several questions here, and Hadot answers each of them, it is worth being as precise as possible in understanding his answers.

It is telling that Hadot's first response, to the initial question of whether or not spiritual exercises are still possible today, is again a reference back to the Friedmann quotation with which we began. In citing Friedmann, Hadot states, "I think this testimony suffices to prove that spiritual exercises are being practiced in our day and age." Strictly speaking, this seems quite true.

Hadot continues, remarking that "spiritual exercises do not correspond to specific social structures or material conditions. They have been, and continue to be, practiced in every age, in the most widely diverse milieus, and in widely different latitudes: China, Japan, India; among the Christians, Muslims and Jews."[130] And while this latter point could be taken to be a kind of vague universalism, there is no claim, at least not here, to a universal content or meaning to given practices, or even to shared practices. Rather, the point is that the practice of spiritual exercises is historically ubiquitous and is not excluded by any cultural conditions, even as the specific forms that these practices take and the goals toward which they work are shaped by those conditions. All that Hadot is claiming here is that it is always and everywhere possible to practice some form of spiritual exercise, within the strict definition of that concept that he provides.

The more precise, and more important, question that Chases poses to Hadot, even if only implicit in his own formulation, is that of *which* spiritual exercises are appropriate to any given context, and to contemporary life in particular. Further, how and by what standards do we evaluate an answer to such a question? What kind of work is required to determine that level of appropriateness or to determine the parameters of any attending "translation"? This is the force of the second part of Chase's question, with specific regard to the example of injustice. Hadot's answer is interesting, in that it tells us both a great deal and very little:

> You give the example of injustice and the suffering of innocent people. For Marcus Aurelius, the fact that there is a providence (that is, simply, that there is coherence in the world), does not mean that injustice is only an appearance. It is quite real, and in his *Meditations*, Marcus often expresses against liars and the unjust. For him, the discipline of action consists precisely in acting in the service of the human community; in other words, in practicing justice oneself and in correcting injustices. Such an attitude is independent of any theory of providence. Besides, Marcus himself says, "Whether or not the world is ruled by reason (and thus by providence), don't *you* act unreasonably." He then goes on to add that if we *do* act according to reason, that proves that there is also reason in the world. This is proof that it is one's choice of life which precedes metaphysical theories, and that we can make our choice of life, whether or not we justify it by improved or entirely new arguments.[131]

Following Hadot's response closely, he certainly answers the exegetical portion of Chase's question: we do not need to hold specific metaphysical commitments in order to address questions of suffering on the model of Marcus Aurelius. This point is important, because it is at least one of the conditions of the possibility of practicing spiritual exercises that are conceived of and delimited in one historical context, in some other time and place. However, this is about as far as Hadot's response goes.

Hadot's answer references Marcus Aurelius because Chase uses the emperor as his own example, but the question itself highlights an important contrast. We have on the one hand, those particularly "modern" sources of pain and injustice, and on the other, the ancient ideas and practices that Hadot describes throughout his work. I take Chase to be asking, even if only implicitly, not just if we can bridge ancient practices and contemporary conditions, but also how we would go about doing that. Something important, then, seems to have been lost in the space between question and answer here, which results in a kind of appeal to universalism in Hadot's answer.

The problem is that there is nothing contemporary about either injustice or suffering. Indeed, it seems safe enough to say that we can describe these as genuinely transhistorical features of human life—if only because these concepts are so profoundly general. My point is not that there is no value for us now in Marcus Aurelius's thought that "the discipline of action consists precisely in acting in the service of the human community . . . in practicing justice oneself and in correcting injustices."[132] Indeed, I agree with Hadot that this line of thinking and others like it remain quite compelling. The problem is that they remain insufficiently specified. If the term "contemporary" does not simply refer to any demand that exists in our time and place, but rather those that are rooted in the unique characteristics of our context, then Hadot's answer can at best provide a cautious and general first step. At worst, the better we understand the content of the term "contemporary" in a given instance, the more likely it is that we will uncover an entire range of issues that Hadot's vision may not be able to address.

Further still, Chase's question does seem to invoke the specificity of the present, and not just by asking if spiritual exercises are possible today. He makes mention of the fact that "every day, the media overwhelm us with images of this suffering," and this specific invocation of mass and electronic media is I think crucial.[133] It is not simply that there is suffering now as there always has been, that much is obvious. Rather, it is a particular problem for us that so much of the suffering in question is rooted in and mediated by technological and informational conditions that have never before existed—a theme that is in fact the beating heart of Friedmann's entire project, as we will see. And so, as much as Hadot gives us, it is significant that what he says in his response here about Marcus Aurelius does not, and without important work cannot, address this specific aspect of the question.

But again, this is not to say that to do so is impossible, or that examples do not already exist. Indeed, the invocation of Marcus Aurelius here is again suggestive. In "The View from Above," Hadot again returns to the *Meditations* and the practice of imaginative overflight. There, the emperor exhorts himself to "watch and see the courses of the stars as if you were running alongside them . . . for these imaginations wash away the foulness of life on earth. When you are reasoning about mankind, look upon earthly things below as if from above."[134] Compare these lines to the following breathless description of the cosmic vantage: "Trembling with excitement, I watched a world so new and unknown to me, trying to see and remember everything . . . Astonishingly bright cold stars could be seen . . . They were still far away—oh, how far away—but . . . they seemed closer than the Earth."[135] As Hadot first asked us of Friedmann, does this not sound like an exercise of the contemplation of the whole, if not by Marcus Aurelius, then by Ovid or Lucretius or any of a number of the other ancient sources? But this is not, in fact, a description of an "imaginative overflight," but rather of the first actual "view from above" on April 12, 1961, in the words of Soviet cosmonaut Yuri Gagarin, following his historic achievement as the first human being to inhabit the sky.

Gagarin's sentiments have been followed, in various forms and in a fantastic range of interpretations, by a significant number of the human beings who have thus far left Earth's atmosphere in spaceflight. This transformative experience has been termed "the overview effect" by Frank White, who has documented these experiences in numerous contexts, most prominently a book of the same title. White's work is detailed in its discussions of the different kinds of experiences reported from differing vantages (whether in orbit or from the moon), in the different interpretations given, and the differing kinds of personal transformation that occur for those who return to the ground following an overview experience. For some astronauts, he tells us, the grand perspective serves to refocus attention and effort into caring for others that takes the form of humanitarian or political work, where others have become artists, and so on.[136]

The reflections that White collects are distinct from Hadot's ancient sources, perhaps above all in that their descriptions of awe and transformation are consistently accompanied, or just as often fully interwoven, with detailed technical and scientific descriptions. While they do not have to include this feature, its persistence is a strong if implicit reminder that we cannot extract even such a recognizable experience from the technical, historical, and indeed political conditions that not only make it possible, but determine its very form. In Gagarin's case, the poetic and awed descriptions of the Earth referenced lead directly into a description of the fireproof glass and heat-shielding of the Vostok-1 capsule. One of White's interlocutors, the astronaut Ron Garan, gives a similar but more detailed account of his own experience outside the International Space Station in 2008:

> I clamped my feet to the end of the robotic Canadarm-2 on the International Space Station. The arm was then flown through a maneuver that astronauts call the "windshield wiper," which took me across a long arc above the space station and back. As I approached the top of this arc, it was as if time stood still, and I was flooded with emotion and awareness. Here I was, a hundred feet above the space station, looking down at this incredible manmade accomplishment against the backdrop of our indescribably beautiful Earth, 240 miles below. Witnessing the absolute beauty of the planet we have been given from this perspective was a deeply moving experience. But as I looked down at this stunning, fragile oasis—this island that protects all life from the harshness of space—a sadness came over me, and I was struck by an undeniable, sobering contradiction. In contrast to the indescribable beauty of the scene that I was witnessing, I couldn't help but think of the inequity that exists on our apparent paradise.[137]

Garan's description drives home the indistinguishable relationship between the ecstatic experience and its technological conditions. Here, the view from above is also the view from the end of a technological marvel in the form of the "grasp" of a robotic arm moving through a physical arc whose peak corresponds to and determines the dilation of time and the nature of the revelation.

It is certainly a challenge to fight the intuition to abstract such descriptions out into a generality that renders them commensurable with existing descriptions of other revelatory experiences. But this would be to lose the experience itself, which never happens in abstraction, and thus cannot be generalized out of the technological context that not only makes it possible, but determines its very form. Moreover, it is not simply a technical specificity, but a political one as well. Emmanuel Levinas, in a brief but pointed critique of Martin Heidegger via Gagarin's triumph, once described the latter in the following terms: "For one hour, man existed beyond any horizon—everything around him was sky or, more exactly, everything was geometrical space."[138] And yet, though suspended in a physically limitless horizon, Gagarin and those who followed him were still situated well within their technical and political horizons—even as such an event could perhaps constitute a glimpse over the very horizons that made it possible.

Indeed, that we begin with Gagarin the Soviet cosmonaut, that the very political condition of the birth of spaceflight was the Cold War itself, that so many of these overview experiences weave the marvel of the view from above into reflection on contemporary geopolitics, which are again the conditions of those experiences in the first place: none of these factors are ancillary to those experiences, but constitutive of them. Under different political and technical circumstances, recognizably comparable encounters will be experienced in radically different ways. The joy or sadness of the astronauts and cosmonauts of the past will not be the same as the ambivalent awe and melancholy of, say, possible future workers led to space by economic precarity or as climate refugees. Here, the smile of the overview becomes the grimace of a rather different vantage, as the very conditions that allow for the overview experience themselves become both a sight of political struggle and, for that very reason, the origin of the kinds of spiritual demands that spiritual exercises are meant to help ameliorate. The transformation of these conditions is at once the transformation of experience and practice: here, as in so many other cases, times, places, and needs, *the view from above must be a view from below.*

Friedmann, as we will see in chapter 2, calls vivid attention to just these tensions, the wages of the self between technological and political transformation.

V. IMPLICATIONS

There is at least one instance in which Hadot does address, in a negative way, some of the genuine differences between the ancient and contemporary contexts, by suggesting what might not be possible for us now. In *The Present Alone Is Our Happiness*, Davidson asks Hadot about the shift from a plurality of philosophical genres in the ancient world (dialogues, consolations, correspondences, and so on) to the relative homogeneity of contemporary academic writing. Regarding the practice of dialogue, Hadot says "Unfortunately, I think it is extremely difficult in our day to resurrect the dialogical character of ancient philosophy. It seems to me that this dialogical form of teaching can be realized only in communities of the type of the ancient schools, organized in order to live philosophy communally. [. . .] Perhaps it is possible in communities of the monastic type, but I believe that in everyday life and in university life, it would be very artificial."[139] Hadot's conclusion is surprisingly unequivocal: under the contemporary conditions that he describes, we cannot go back, and the possibility of dialogue as a way of life has been lost.

However, insofar as Hadot begins to specify those conditions here, to note the particular limitations and demands that they place on us, he also implicitly suggests just the kind of preliminary work required to formulate the sort of exercises that would be appropriate to them. But insofar as his "no" is itself, even implicitly, communicated in the terms that would eventually allow for a kind of "yes," then it is here that we again encounter the outer boundaries of Hadot's project. And yet, as I have insisted already, to identify the frontiers of any such project must be understood not as a limitation, but as the ground beneath the first steps into new conceptual and practical horizons. In practical terms, we still do not know what the historical translation of spiritual exercises would look like for Hadot. The handful of instances in which he speculates in this direction also lack anything beyond preliminary conjecture regarding the ways that ancient practices may be altered or augmented to meet contemporary needs. But if his work ends just as Hadot asks us to consider the practice of spiritual exercises in the present, it also provides a set of conceptual and practical resources, several important warnings, and perhaps most importantly, a series of positive criteria for either recognizing or cultivating properly contemporary practices of the self—including what we might call "practices of the other."

To re-invoke the shared language of Hadot and Friedmann with which this chapter began, spiritual exercises are shaped by what they call "spiritual demands," which are themselves shaped by historical conditions of various kinds. For that reason, as Hadot argues, the forms of life that may emerge from this constellation may evince a specificity and efficaciousness that can only be understood within the world from which they emerge. The details matter, and this is as true historically as it is politically. By Hadot's own reasoning, even when drawing on the resources provided by specialists, there may well be something about the experiences and needs of "average" persons that make them meaningfully distinct from those of the philosophical professional. But the space of those more humble, immediate, and local spiritual needs often falls outside those domains toward which Hadot and others have tended to direct their inquiries. And so, if we look again and get a more clear historical handle on what the demands are that we are concerned to address, if we then understand that practices come into being to treat those demands, and if our critical attention is not directed solely at specialists, then we may find uniquely "ordinary" and localized forms of practice that would have remained otherwise invisible. This goes equally for both genuinely new forms of practice and in the emergence and specification of new modes of recognizable categories of practice. In this way and by Hadot's own standards, the view from above must again begin with a view from below.

While these principles may seem clear, the work that they entail is rich and complex. Returning to the question of dialogue, rather than a kind of lament for something lost, we may reimagine Hadot's response to Davidson: if we have lost the ability to dialogue—or rather, the framework within which ancient forms of dialogue occur and flourish—how might a new modality of dialogue, perhaps a new genre, within new or even newly imagined social relations, be cultivated? This potentially new yet still unapproached relationship of dialogue would have to avoid the "mechanical imitation" Hadot warns us of by taking a rich and clear-eyed view of the kinds of problems it can and cannot address and that would reciprocally determine its form. Hadot does indeed hope that his readers will "hear a call," but the work of interpreting that call, and putting it into practice, is a project in itself, one that is beyond the bounds of his research, and which he must leave for others. We can, however, use the conceptual and methodological foundations that Hadot cultivates to further specify and pursue questions that his work helps to generate but does not ultimately pursue. And it is Georges Friedmann, with whom we began and to whom I now turn, in his meticulous attention to both the technological and political determination of spiritual demands and what he calls the "interior effort," who demonstrates at least one way of taking up the next stage of this work.

Chapter Two

GEORGES FRIEDMANN

From the Great Disequilibrium to the Interior Effort

I. AN UNQUIET WISDOM

In the introduction to his 1970 quasi-memoire *La puissance et la sagesse*, the French sociologist of labor and technology Georges Friedmann situates the collected reflections, field notes, and journal entries that constitute what he calls the "autobiography that I will never write,"[1] as follows:

> But gradually, as this work advanced, these events, these collective and personal experiences, necessitated a series of disruptive reassessments on my part, which profoundly changed my plan. In 1945, straining toward a humanism capable of "*genuinely* transforming the human condition," I had not forgotten the moral conditions upon which its realization depended, although I had indeed placed them in the third row, after economic and social conditions. Today, without denying the role of these latter—far from it, one will note—the observation of our world led me to affirm the essential role of these moral conditions. After having, during my period of "naïve Marxism," given a quasi-exclusive privilege to the "material" dimensions of things, I began to perceive with greater and greater clarity the *spiritual* dimension, which is so despised today; and yet, without it, there will never be a socialism with a human face.[2]

This work of reimagining the place of what Friedmann calls here the "spiritual" in general, and its relationship to the political in particular, emerges from a life and career dedicated to the investigation of human labor, our relationship to machines, the experience of war, and the question of revolution.[3] That its importance for him is tied directly to that life and that work cannot be overemphasized.

And yet, despite their deep significance, it remains unclear just what Friedmann means when he speaks of the "moral" and "spiritual" conditions that he is compelled to resituate, both in general and within political life in particular. What can it mean to speak of an ethics that we place neither in front of nor behind, but rather squarely alongside the political—let alone one that not only deserves, but on a certain understanding demands the appellation "spiritual"? That the language invoked here is not clear for Friedmann either and that at least one goal of the nearly five hundred pages of reflections and meditations that make up *La puissance et la sagesse* is to achieve some clarity on the very terms that he invokes at the outset is of course no coincidence.

La puissance traces and retraces the political, intellectual, and ethical concerns that marked Friedmann's life and career, from their initial emergence in his childhood and adolescence, to nearly the end of his life:

> And so here is a book that in no way hides its values, unbiased [*wertfrei*]. It navigates a counter-current, at a time when certain forces, whose historical determinations are evident, give rise on all sides to formal research whose point of departure is a de-valorization of all "human" content. After many years and many voyages on several continents, I began to feel the need for an "interior voyage." We will follow the steps of this development here, punctuated by the fragments of the autobiography I will never write. You will find here, communicated by a man who has sought to understand—and not to hide—his own weaknesses and failures, some responses called forth by the great questions that he has attempted to live. (Readers will judge for themselves the extent to which I have succeeded.)[4]

Indeed, in following both the "exterior journeys" and the "interior effort" of his life and career, *La puissance* can be recognized, by his own description, its contents, and its structure, as a kind of spiritual exercise in its own right.[5]

But if it is the substance of *La puissance* to chart the "internal" parallel of this journey—with all its difficulties, errors, insights and flaws—it cannot be divorced from those "exterior" conditions and experiences that shape and determine Friedmann's concern with what he calls the "spiritual dimension" in the first place. Here, Friedmann is again adamant, in ways that set several of the fundamental terms for his book, my reading of it, and my own project. Once again,

> its title, *Wisdom and Power*, is likely to bring about a misunderstanding, but one which should dissipate with this preface. The wisdom which is so necessary today is not a form of contemplation, a retreat from the unrest and abominations of the century. Far from being "rationalistic," in the restrictive sense of the term, I refer here to "reason" in the sense understood by Jaspers, which envelopes and includes a potential of intellect and love, everything in human beings that can aid us in *becoming human*, everything that can contribute to our "*humanization*." It is an unquiet wisdom, one that is active and audacious, and which, in the eyes of some, appears more or less ridiculous, but so be it.[6]

Friedmann's navigation across these pages is, as he insists, neither a spiritualism nor a moralism.

To understand Friedmann's concern with the "interior," the ways and reasons that he links it to the "exterior," and their resituation across *La puissance* and elsewhere, I follow both of these journeys over the course of this chapter. Through this reading, I attempt to delimit the practical and theoretical resources that Friedmann provides for articulating a conception of the care of the self that is coterminous with the care of the other and of others, of the community and the city. If a nascent form of this work begins to emerge with Hadot in chapter 1, it is the project that Friedmann more or less announces here. Whether he himself completes it or succeeds is another matter, though his contributions are decisive. In that direction, one of the primary goals of this chapter is to begin to draw out a conception of the relationship between "interior" and "exterior" that reflects Friedmann's desire to place the ethical and political neither in front of nor behind, but rather alongside one another, and thus avoids the forms of reductive moralism that he helps identify.

Friedmann was born in Paris in 1902 to German-Jewish émigrés. Despite, or perhaps thanks to, a comfortable urban upbringing and an elite education,[7] Friedmann tells us that in his youth he was somewhat enamored with rural life: "at sixteen," he says, "I wanted to become a farmer,"[8] but this was not to be. Following a series of intellectual adventures,[9] and at least one famous misadventure,[10] over the course of the late 1920s, Friedmann's lifework began in earnest at the opening of the new decade. Around 1930, his focus became the firsthand study of labor and *machinisme*[11] in both the socialist "East" and capitalist "West," or what he refers to as "the Technological Adventure of human beings in the twentieth century":

> I did not become a farmer. I chose instead (or did I choose?) to try and understand the Technological Adventure of human beings in the twentieth century. Over the course of 30 years, the lover of nature and solitude instead took to halls populated by machines, construction sites, the docks, mineshafts, and thermal power stations for his field of study. I passed a large part of the years of my youth and maturity in fumes, dust, and dins; in the middle of the thronging crowds of the cities and suburbs of the East and West, in the industrial zones of the "Old," "New," and "Third" worlds.[12]

The physical or "exterior" journeys described here constitute the substance and foundation of Friedmann's life and research. But this passage also names the central object of that work, "the Technological Adventure of human beings in the twentieth century." And its "external" pursuit, through the firsthand studies that Friedmann began during this period, is the foundation of his effort to resituate the "internal," the "spiritual dimension" within the constellation of moral, economic, and technological conditions.

This foundational concept, the "Technological Adventure of human beings in the twentieth century," he specifies, "corresponds to the acceleration of technological progress in the past century," although it does not simply denote the fact of the industrialized landscape and technological change.[13] It also refers to the consequences of those transformations in the experiences of human beings living and working amid social, economic, and technological change on a scale, at a pace, and in forms that he argues had never before been seen. It is thus under this heading that Friedmann gathers the new and varied forms of labor, mechanical innovations, daily stresses and satisfactions, the personal and lived experiences of workers, and the economic conditions that give rise to and shape all of these other factors—among so many other practices, places, and experiences—across his writings. And although Friedmann develops the idea of the Technological Adventure over several decades, it is a motivating concern from the very beginning of this period.[14]

Given the ways that Friedmann often talks about this "Technological Adventure," it is possible to read the concept as something that names a problem. It is used, however, as a strictly descriptive term, a technical phrase that does not necessarily entail a normative political or ethical judgment. Instead, the danger, the problem that Friedmann began to identify as early as the 1930s, emerges from but is not synonymous with the Technological Adventure, and is referred to in *La puissance* (indeed, it is the title of the book's first section) as "the Great Disequilibrium."[15] This "Disequilibrium" is characterized "by the increasing disproportion between, on the one hand, the multitudinous forms of power that technological progress confers on human beings, and on the other the moral forces that we have at our command to truly deploy them in the service of both the individual and society."[16] In other words, the Great Disequilibrium refers to a kind of political, economic, and ethical crisis of adaptation to the radical changes that constitute the Technological Adventure. In this way, as the name Friedmann gives to his diagnosis of the spiritual demands that mark life and work within the Technological Adventure, it determines both the telos and concrete forms that any "interior effort" that emerges in response to those conditions must take. These concepts are thus foundational for understanding not only his interest in spiritual exercises, but his understanding of what they are and what role they might play.

From the beginning of his career, Friedmann drew a close connection between the Technological Adventure and the Great Disequilibrium. In so doing, he also began articulating a view of the relationship between "interior" and "exterior" efforts; that is, of ethical practices of the self to political life and work. Friedmann's conception of that deep connection is reflected not only in the analyses he provides, but the methods he undertook in their pursuit. The latter included undergoing preparatory forms of technical training, including an early apprenticeship in machine-tooling from 1932 to 1933.[17] Direct experiences of this kind and the technical vocabulary they cultivated informed the depth and detail of his ongoing engagements with workers (as well as managers, engineers, and planners) on his ethnographic journeys. Here, a text like *Industrial Society: The Emergence of The Human Problems of Automation*, one of his doctoral theses and a founding text in the sociology of labor, is representative of Friedmann's sociological research in general, as well as the specific philosophical reflections centered in this chapter.[18]

At the same time, if Friedmann's commitment to direct engagement with workers is reflective of methodological and ethical concerns, it is equally informed by the explicit political commitments with which he opens *La puissance*. A committed Marxist and Russian speaker by 1930, Friedmann made the first of several research trips to the Soviet Union in September and October of 1932.[19] He returned to the USSR again in 1933 and 1936 to continue "his research into the organization of work in socialist countries and to facilitate further contacts . . . within Soviet intellectual circles."[20] Such visits allowed Friedmann to play the role of what Isabelle Gourné calls an intellectual "ferryman" between France and the USSR. The Soviet research resulted in the publication of numerous studies over the course of the 1930s, including a comparative study of factory work in the USSR, France, England, Poland, and Czechoslovakia in 1934, as well as seminal papers like "Machinisme et humanisme" and "Travail et communion en U.R.R.S"[21] in 1935. During this time, his research into labor and mechanization was supported in part by his involvement with numerous Marxist organizations, publications, and networks, both in France and abroad. All of this work accompanied Friedmann's decisive role in "the legitimation of Marxism in the French social sciences, even among Durkheimians who had proven resistant to the ideas of Karl Marx and Friedrich Engels since the end of the 19th century."[22]

Friedmann's time in the USSR was, of course, formative with regard to his relationship to the Soviet project, as well as his work and broader worldview. But these visits also laid the groundwork for his later disenchantment with certain trajectories within the Soviet state and with Stalin in particular. The editors of his *Journal de guerre* note that "in August of 1936, Friedmann found himself in Moscow during the first of Stalin's great show trials, the 'Trial of the Sixteen,'[23] in which Kamenev and Zinoviev were implicated. All of the defendants were executed the day after judgement was passed. In *La puissance et la sagesse*, Friedmann describes this event as having been a 'decisive shock.'"[24] Despite that shock, however, Friedmann, like many, remained hopeful for the future of the Soviet project. To that end, and as an explicit attempt at a productive contribution, he published *De la Sainte Russie à l'U.R.S.S. (From Holy Russia to the USSR)* in 1938.

In the preface, Friedmann describes it as "a book intended to serve the Soviet Union and the construction of socialism, without ignoring the errors and lacunae that are inseparable from such an immense effort."[25] In spite of these earnest intentions, the book caused a scandal within Communist circles for its retrospectively mild discussions of the "errors and lacunae"[26] of Soviet politics and culture in question.[27] In the ensuing "*affaire Friedmann*," and despite some support, Friedmann was abandoned and attacked by lifelong friends and former comrades, labeled a "Trotskyite apologist," a "traitor," and a "class enemy," among other repercussions.[28] The *affaire* led to a decisive break with the French Communist Party (PCF) in 1938.[29] But this break with the party was in no way a break with either Marx or the socialist vision, to which—despite many intellectual and political shifts, breaks, and transformations—he remained committed for the rest of his life. As he put it in 1970, "Even today, at the height of a great ebb of dashed hopes, I in no way renounce the socialist project. To use the greatest possible reason and justice in the organization of society, the production and redistribution of goods, to reduce from the very beginning the inequality of the chances for goodwill and accomplishing oneself, to aid human beings (who must also aid themselves), to penetrate—according to one's will and means—the universe of knowledge and beauty."[30]

In 1939, in the midst of the crisis around the publication of his book, France and Britain declared war on Germany, and another decisive experience began. In August of that year Friedmann was "mobilized as a lieutenant, an administrative officer within the Health Service, assigned to the Hospital Complementary Unit of Laon."[31] The Hospital Complementary Unit (HC) was a kind of mobile hospital unit and Friedmann spent the next year surrounded by the sick and the dying as the HC made its way south and west through France.[32] Friedmann's journey through war and death, beginning at Laon on August 26, 1939, and ending at Gontaud on June 28, 1940, is chronicled in his posthumously published *Journal de guerre, 1939–1940*.

The *Journal* is marked by concentric levels of reflection and observation: from observations of life during wartime, to a detailed description of the crisis of political and ethical faith provoked by the Molotov-Ribbentrop Pact, which was signed just over a week before Friedmann's first journal entry on September 6, 1939. Here, the political comes into direct dialogue with the "interior effort" for Friedmann. From the earliest entries, he describes the *Journal* as a form of "examination," an "effort to see clearly" that is familiar in its form to those exercises of written self-reflection described by Hadot.[33] Where Friedmann's "examination" is different, however, is its central focus on a spiritual self-evaluation prompted by the historical and political specificity of industrial automation and the future of state socialism. And if Molotov-Ribbentrop prompted a crisis of faith, Philippe Pétain's capitulation roughly a year later left Friedmann apoplectic, despondent, and Stoic in both senses, all in ways that would reengage and redouble his "interior–exterior," spiritual–political efforts. Most immediately, this meant taking refuge in Toulouse and joining the Resistance, which facilitated a range of formative intellectual encounters.[34]

Following the war and recognition of his service to the Resistance, Friedmann received the *Doctorat d'état* in 1946, with a major thesis entitled *Les problems humains du machinisme industriel*, and a minor thesis on *Leibniz et Spinoza*.[35] Although the minor thesis remains untranslated, the major thesis later appeared in English as *Industrial Society*.[36] At its publication, Friedmann placed *Industrial Society* as the second of a trilogy of works, the first being *La crise du progrès* (1936), though the final volume never appeared;[37] they are considered founding texts in the French sociology of labor. These texts helped inaugurate a career in which, as Edgar Morin puts it, Friedmann "never broke from his focus on human labor, and on the workers themselves,"[38] despite the many shifts and reassessments that mark his thought following the war.[39]

The sociological and philosophical approaches that Friedmann adopted as early as 1930, as well as many of the particular political commitments he held, naturally transformed over the next half century. And yet, on my reading, the ethical–political motivations that drove that method and his work overall remained quite consistent. Those commitments are also at the heart of his interest in and concern with spiritual exercises and the interior effort. It is for that reason I have devoted such attention to these biographical details: in a way that may or may not be unique among the figures that I address in this book, I take it that it is necessary to understand Friedmann's life in order to understand his thought. And I take that to be the case in no small part because my reading of Friedmann is grounded in and guided by two journals: *La puissance et la sagesse*, this philosophical semi-memoire, and to a lesser extent, the *Journal de guerre*, his philosophical–political "examination" of both the war and the crisis of political faith these circumstances precipitate for him.

On the one hand then, mine is in some sense a Hadotian reading of Friedmann, even as I find numerous problems within Hadot's brief but often-repeated comments on *La puissance*. I read these journals as philosophical works (and far richer ones than Friedmann's explicit philosophical commentaries) and as part of a philosophical genre, one with a long history as we have seen, though unique and particular to their time and context as well. On the other hand, I read Friedmann with Friedmann, from the perspective and vantage of *La puissance*, as he resurveys and re-theorizes his own life, experiences, and perhaps above all, his sociological output. Thus, and again in the spirit of Hadot and of Friedmann's own stated goals in the book, I take the shifts, ambiguities, and breaks in his work, especially Friedmann's reassessment of his earlier work in *La puissance*, as fertile ground proper to the genre in front of us. Finally, it is for all of these reasons that I will cite Friedmann often and in detail here, staying as close as possible to the texts, allowing them to speak for themselves in all of their complexity and not-infrequent confusion. It is not only the content that matters here, but the contours as well. What remains now, among the basic tasks of this chapter, is to understand just how the philosophy of the "interior" effort shapes and is shaped by the sociology and politics of the "exterior" in a way that aspires not to abandon one for the other.

The Material Present

Over the course of *La puissance*, Friedmann reflects upon the potential role for what he calls these previously ignored moral forces, this "spiritual dimension," in the work of ameliorating, and perhaps someday overturning, the dehumanization brought about by the Great Disequilibrium. Although the concepts that constitute his diagnosis of the spiritual demands that concern him are at least somewhat clear early on, this "spiritual dimension" that is meant to counter them is vague from the outset. This is in no small part because the specification of that category constitutes the task of the book as a whole, a text that both concerns itself with and stands as an example of the "interior effort." It is a book, much like the *Journal de guerre*, that "marks an effort to see clearly" and does so in a way that seeks to hide nothing of that effort itself, especially among those threads and themes for which his thought remains at its most unformed and vulnerable.

It is for this reason that Hadot was so drawn to *La puissance*, and why he references Friedmann's invocation of spiritual exercises there so frequently. But it is also here that Hadot and Friedmann diverge, though in ways that are both productive and complementary. As we have seen, Hadot's broader project, including his invocation of Friedmann, is motivated by the goal of "offering contemporary mankind a model of life" fit to address "contemporary spiritual demands," especially the everyday needs of those outside the ranks of the philosophical and religious specialists that populate his oeuvre.[40] But as we have seen, Hadot's analyses stop just shy of the translation work they themselves entail, even as they delimit some of the criteria necessary for any such translation to work. The latter includes the cultivation of a sense of what we mean when we speak of the "contemporary" and the "ordinary" in the first place. And so, if Friedmann differs from Hadot in both content and methodology, it also means that Friedmann can be read to pick up just where Hadot leaves off in at least two ways that are relevant here.

First, Friedmann's discussions of spiritual exercises and the "interior effort" are explicitly contemporary and primarily quotidian. His sociology of labor and his political–philosophical reflections are equally concerned with the lives and experiences of average people living and working in the midst of the Technological Adventure. In this way, a philosophical memoir like *La puissance et la sagesse* and a sociological work like *Industrial Society* share a fundamental and characteristic concern with the conditions of labor, technological change, education, war, and so on, in the mid-twentieth century. Similarly, his work engages but does not center philosophical specialists or economic and managerial elites. Rather, its fundamental concerns are the human wages of everyday life within the economic, technological, and political conditions that he describes. Within the context of his work, these two factors, the present and the everyday, are inextricably linked.

Taking *La puissance* as a guiding text, I thus read Friedmann's general oeuvre here as a detailed specification of the contemporary conditions—and contemporary dangers—against which his interest in spiritual exercises emerges and to which any interior effort must respond. Friedmann does not just show *that* contemporary spiritual exercises must respond to contemporary spiritual demands. Rather, he both demonstrates why they must and models the kind of work required to understand just what those demands might be in a given case. Perhaps most importantly, his rich descriptive and philosophical work demonstrates how and why the particular forms that such practices must take must be determined by the specificity of the demands to which they are meant to respond. In other words, in the face of a general tendency toward the universal in conversations around spiritual exercises, Friedmann helps show that given exercises must be tailored to the particular, immediate contours of the conditions against which they emerge. Once again, the view from above must be a view from below.

Second, where we can situate Hadot's concerns primarily within the domain of ethics and exegetical accuracy, Friedmann's overall project is fundamentally political from the outset. His concern with the "interior" is motivated by his observations of the large-scale effects of systemic technological change within given economic conditions on the everyday lives of workers on a mass scale. As we have also seen, although Hadot is concerned with the practice of spiritual exercises (and thus of philosophy) by nonspecialists, on the question of the role and nature of such practices within the particular material and economic conditions of the twentieth century, there is no parallel in Hadot's work (or in Foucault's, for that matter) for this aspect of Friedmann's work. Finally, and as he says at the outset of *La puissance*, among Friedmann's goals is that of bringing the "spiritual dimension" into alignment with certain economic and political concerns, a task far afield of Hadot's project.

This political concern also motivates his wariness regarding the charge of "spiritualism," itself a political category for Friedmann, for at least three reasons: First, certain "spiritualist" views amount to an abnegation of political responsibility, an unacceptable "retreat from the unrest and abominations of the century."[41] Even those forms of "contemplation" that would lay claim to an apolitical status have political consequences, whatever their own self-understanding. Second, a great deal of "spiritualist" doctrine is marked by a kind of nostalgia for romanticized and misrepresented forms of premodern or preindustrial forms of life. I return to the problem of nostalgia later, but in general, this impulse runs counter to Friedmann's ethical–political project, his Marxism, and his understanding of technological change more generally. Finally, the effort to distance himself from spiritualism is also a way of specifying that he does not seek to reduce politics to moralism. The integration of the "interior effort" into an analysis of "exterior conditions" is meant to reposition these domains alongside one another such that neither is prior or reducible to the other.

Regarding this question of moralism, however, recall that Friedmann also rejects its rough inverse, what he calls the "naïve Marxism" of his own youth—the problem being the naïveté, not the Marxism. It can be tentatively described as a view in which the ethical lives of individuals are simply taken to be causal effects of economic conditions or given political forms. Now, there is neither time, nor space, nor any need here to parse out Friedmann's reading of Marx or his relationship to various twentieth-century Marxisms, let alone to survey his views on the forms of state socialism and communism that he either engaged firsthand or observed during his lifetime. Suffice it to say that for Friedmann, this "naïve" view is not representative of Marx, of Friedmann's own Marxism past the 1930s, or of the Marxisms that he finds affinity with.[42] Moreover, Friedmann's explication of this worry is not treated in a comparably systematic fashion to his critiques of moralism, appearing more sporadically across his work. And as his central concern and my own target here are the problem of moralism, I will set aside his scattered attention to this question for now. I will return to it in brief later in the service of describing what I take to be one of Friedmann's core contributions to my own project here, on the relationship of human subjects to the "natural" and built environments. For my part, and again, it is moralism that concerns me overall, insofar as it is the critique to which the conceptions of ethical self-change that I explore are most vulnerable, Friedmann's included.

To be clear, although he does explicitly move away from what he calls the "quasi-exclusive privilege" he had given to "the 'material' dimension" or what he also calls the "exterior," Friedmann in no way rejects the importance of those conditions. Rather, the goal on this side is to situate a political philosophy of spiritual exercises somewhere between the extremes of moralism and a (real or imagined) material–economic determinism. It is thus equally clear Friedmann is in no way out to find a "perfect balance" at the center of the two: if Friedmann is no conservative, he is no moderate or liberal either, at least not in the period that concerns me. Rather, his goal is to offer a corrective, a rebalancing, from the inside of—and squarely on the side of—a left critique of the effects of rapid technological change under both Western capitalist modes of production and certain Soviet forms. This corrective operates within a general Marxist framework, though one grounded in the emerging conditions of life and work within the technological milieu that Friedmann observed.

And so Friedmann's political critique is already implicated in the ethical critique. The distinction between "the spiritual" and "spiritualism" is for him a political distinction, at very least insofar as it has political consequences. It is among my goals in this chapter to develop this distinction as he expresses it. But it is also here that I want to be both careful and clear: we cannot conflate the ethical and political critiques, we cannot assimilate these concepts to one another, and we cannot assume that a critique of the ethical status of egoist spiritualism is necessarily a political critique. We may, after all, criticize (or praise) "retreat" on purely ethical grounds, without engaging its consequences for political life. Moreover, it is after all possible to formulate a conception that posits a sharp distinction between these two domains, and in which, therefore, there are no political consequences for ethical choices and actions.

I insist on this distinction, or rather the possibility of such a distinction, in order to highlight the fact that Friedmann himself does not distinguish them, and indeed sees them as intimately linked. We cannot understand what is interesting or special about either the fact that he links the domains of ethics and politics or the way in which he does so without understanding that it is entirely possible not to do so or to do so in ways that are undesirable on his own account. And so it is not simply a question of identifying the fact that, for him, individual ethical retreat has social–political consequences. Rather, it is an issue of specifying the precise ways in which he conceives of that relationship, the reasons why the "interior" has political consequences, and vice versa. Perhaps above all, in order to argue that the way in which he links these two domains does not amount to what I have already referred to as the reduction of political life to the mere aggregation of the ethical lives of individuals, it is important to see that this linkage is an intentional one, rather than an uncritical or naïve assumption.

This chapter, then, concerns itself with specifying Friedmann's place in the development of the guiding questions of this study. First, Friedmann provides a productive model for the specification and analysis of contemporary spiritual demands, and thus the specification and recognition of what I have referred to as "properly contemporary" spiritual exercises. As I have already suggested, it is here that Friedmann picks up where Hadot leaves off on precisely this question. Hadot implicitly or explicitly lays out many of the criteria such an analysis would need to meet, even as he does not pursue them himself. Friedmann's analyses of "the Technological

Adventure of human beings in the twentieth century" and the "Great Disequilibrium" that emerges from it meet and expand upon many of those requirements. In turn, they further provide a model for determining the spiritual demands particular to any time and place, not just his own. Thus, even if the particular form the "contemporary" takes in his work remains particular to Friedmann and his mid-twentieth-century milieu, this model has concrete theoretical and methodological implications for future studies in differing historical and political conditions.

On the model that began to emerge in the previous chapter, we will need a more detailed sense of the diagnosis that Friedmann provides of the contemporary spiritual demands that emerge from the Great Disequilibrium and rapid pace of technological change. That reading in turn provides a foundation for understanding how the "spiritual dimension," spiritual exercises, or the "interior effort" fit into Friedmann's larger project. Above all, it is important to understand why the call to this "interior effort," as a complement but by no means a substitute for the "exterior" work he begins with, emerges for him as a consequence of the conditions he analyzes. Further, Friedmann provides the strongest case for the problem of nostalgia in this context, and in some sense demonstrates why forms of the care of the self that are marked by a romanticized notion of past practices or conditions tend to be tied up with moralism and reaction. He also demonstrates the urgency of recognizing spiritual exercises that are at once collective rather than individual, quotidian, and practiced every day, and that emerge from the conditions and experiences of average people rather than the more rarified instruction of specialists. In other words, Friedmann again demonstrates why the view from above must be a view from below. In so doing, he also shows why that perspective must further shift from an "I" to a "we," illuminating the importance of properly collective exercises and, in turn, the possibility of properly political practices of self-change. Finally, Friedmann begins to provide a kind of Second World perspective, which I take to be crucial to any future conversations in this general area, though much remains to be done in this regard.

However, much like Hadot, there are several further consequences that arise from these firmer foundations, consequences that mark the limits of Friedmann's project. These boundaries are arguably more ambiguous than Hadot's, though often productively so. First, there is the question of spiritual exercises themselves, especially the ways that any concrete iterations would be shaped by the conditions Friedmann so thoroughly explicates. Friedmann does not describe, analyze, or propose any particular spiritual exercises, let alone any particularly contemporary practices of the self. This absence is all the more stark, given that he lays out what I take to be a productive and necessary foundation for specifying and recognizing any such properly contemporary interior effort. But there is an ambiguity here: spiritual exercises do appear in Friedmann, especially in the form of texts like *La puissance* and the *Journal de guerre*, as well as in many of the moments and events described in those texts. Moreover, as I describe in further detail later, it is in these cases that this ambiguity becomes one of the most fertile grounds for thinking through the complex relationship between past conditions and practices and those that properly belong to the present. We can imagine "wholly new" spiritual exercises, unlike anything we have seen before. But in practical terms, we are more often faced with the far more complex cases of recognizable exercises taken up anew, in new ways, for new reasons, and under new conditions. This feature once again returns us to the rich ambiguity of the meaning of "new" in these contexts.

Another ambiguity arises then in turn: the question of whether, and if so how, Friedmann formulates a specific telos, a set of ideal principles, in response to the conditions he analyzes. But Friedmann is, at least in this sense, not a utopian. He does not look at the Technological Adventure and lay out an ideal future in which all of its worries and troubles have been ameliorated. This is, I think, a result of his attention to the present. What is possible for us is shaped by what is actual, and simply knowing what needs to be changed, and acting to bring about some change, will itself open up new possibilities for what we may build and cultivate later. This answer will always be unsatisfying for those who require that a system or plan be laid out before any action can be taken. But, with an instinct (and it seems to me only an intuition here, Friedmann is not explicit on this point) that resonates with the genealogical approach of someone like Foucault, it is enough for Friedmann to move away from certain conditions on the one hand, with a tentative and exploratory posture with regard to the future. There are of course certain principles, often enough Marxist principles in this case, that will guide that movement. But, as we will see further, his view of the relationship between the ongoing creation of ourselves and the creation of a world requires less an "exactitude in science" than an open door. This ambiguity is again productive in that it raises a set of questions that are only ever nascent, if present at all, in Hadot. Is it necessary or even desirable to specify a telos? What, further, do we mean when we talk about such a telos in the first place? Is it necessarily something strictly delimited and clearly articulated? Or can this trajectory itself be marked by productive ambiguity, by possibility rather than certitude? Can, and indeed should, a telos be a horizon?

Finally, Friedmann's work raises the question of the relationship between understanding the historical specificity of given spiritual exercises, whether existing or yet to emerge, and the political content and consequences of such practices. How do the tools that allow us to understand the applicability and intelligibility of a certain spiritual effort also allow us to understand the political efficacy of such practices? How are political demands and material conditions at once "spiritual demands," as I have begun to the define the latter, and vice versa? How can such political demands, if identified as in some way resonant with such "spiritual demands," be addressed through forms of ethical self-formation in ways that do not reduce the political to the ethical—that is, do not amount to moralism? What resources, if any, does Friedmann provide for identifying those possible cases in which the care of the self is coterminous with the care of the other, of the community, of the city?

II. THE TECHNOLOGICAL ADVENTURE OF HUMAN BEINGS IN THE TWENTIETH CENTURY

In *La puissance et la sagesse*, "the Technological Adventure of human beings in the twentieth century" is the general name Friedmann gives to the object of his research from the beginning of the 1930s until the end of his life. Even in the many cases in which the term itself is not explicitly invoked, it remains visible throughout Friedmann's sociological, philosophical, and personal writings. It is a phrase that specifies something that is at once precise and broad. It denotes the radical and ubiquitous technological changes specific to the early and mid-twentieth century in the industrialized and industrializing countries of the so-called socialist East and capitalist West. It further refers to the ways in which the penetration of these new technologies into all aspects of life, work, and leisure affect what Friedmann calls "human relations" in general.[43]

Friedmann argues that the changes that define the Technological Adventure are historically unique in both form and degree. The specific technologies themselves, the rapidity of their creation and dissemination, and the extent of their effect all contribute to a historical departure: "Human beings are now subjected to thousands of stresses, excitations, and stimulations never before known or seen. Every day, the ensemble of these technologies create, arrange, and further deepen, what I generally refer to as *the new milieu*."[44] For Friedmann, this is not simply a formal observation, but an affirmation that the specific content of that change matters, as it is unlike any previous upheaval. This does not mean that past technological and social revolutions were not comparably dramatic, but that this specific adventure is marked by its own unique challenges. It is not just that the world Friedmann finds himself thrown into is new—the world, after all, is always being made new—but that it is new in new ways and that he is able to observe technical, social, and environmental changes that had not been possible before industrialization and its consequences.

This thread is ubiquitous throughout his writings. In the early but representative 1939 article "L'homme et le milieu naturel" (Man and the natural milieu) Friedmann provides an overview of the changes brought about by a range of new industrial technologies. This "ensemble," which includes railroads, automobiles, airplanes, telephones and telegraphs, and nascent household technologies, "has transformed and continues, every day, to transform the conditions of human existence."[45] Within and beyond the workplace, "at every moment, life is further penetrated: it is a vast phenomenon which will not cease to advance, to further integrate itself into new areas of the life of work, home, the street, and leisure."[46] The worker departing the shop, field, or factory at shift's end "barely steps away from industrial mechanization when he is seized by the mechanization of transportation and leisure."[47] The Technological Adventure is thus not limited to certain geographic locations, cultures, technologies, forms of work, or times of day—and it transforms all of them.[48]

At the same time, Friedmann's attention to the Technological Adventure is not limited to his sociological researches and constitutes the core of his philosophical and personal writings. Indeed, over the course of 1939, the same year that "Man and the Natural Milieu" was published, Friedmann experienced a very different but commensurate incarnation of the Technological Adventure, recorded in detail in his *Journal de guerre*. And among the thematic diversity of the *Journal*'s widely ranging entries, Friedmann's sensitivity to that dynamic is viscerally represented in the passages that describe life and medical work in the HC. Take, for example, his third entry, dated September 10, 1939:

> Since my arrival here, in the course of helping to prepare this HC (six hundred beds), the talk has been almost exclusively devoted to the means of combatting the effects of these new technologies of death. They have progressed in leaps from the landmines that have already so effectively served to populate our cemeteries: new gases, incendiary "Elektron" bombs, air power, these concrete and metallic "lines" upon which thousands of young lives will be shattered.
>
> This fury has never yet ceased. Humanity is still so far from the moment in which we will become fully human.[49]

Here, he identifies both the presence and effects of "new technologies of death," as well as the endless work done to so much as learn how to mitigate their effects. It is against this backdrop that, roughly a week later, Friedmann soberly remarks, "I have known since this morning that we will be here for a long time—excepting those who will disappear before the end—for a very long time. This HC, which we have established, will see days filled with sadness, with wounded and poisoned flesh."[50]

But alongside the new forms of death and injury that Friedmann witnesses in the HC, the effects, the human wages, of these new forms inscribe themselves in places beyond the bodies of soldiers and the work of the medical staff. They also give rise to an endless need to adapt or discard old medical practices, all while creating new ones, in order to develop and deploy new methods capable of addressing these emerging and unique forms of brutality. Forms that are, in the very midst of the war, undergoing constant shifts and refinements: "The Germans have invented new engines, magnetic mines, etc. *Le Matin* wrote this morning that we must respond to them, we cannot indulge in a lazy optimism; to which they added, 'The war is a continuous creation.' "[51]

The *Journal*, however, does not simply reinforce or reiterate the descriptions and analyses of the Technological Adventure that populate Friedmann's sociological writings. The dire immediacy of the circumstances also demanded further theoretical reflection on the nature of the social and technical changes that already so concerned him. The looming machine and machinery of fascism that pursues the HC across France, filling its beds with these "continuous creations," hangs over the *Journal* and well beyond. It is in part for this reason that alongside those passages devoted to his medical work, the ongoing ruminations on the radical changes that so concern him are expressed with comparable depth in his descriptions of the landscape at the front. Perhaps above all, such passages illuminate the ways in which past and present are linked within the radical newness of the Technological Adventure.

In two early *Journal* entries, Friedmann documents the experience of traveling through the French countryside in order to retrieve supplies. In these missions, they would often pass several of the same cemeteries and monuments, all barely a generation old, dating from the First World War:

10 Sept. 1939

Coste[52] and I went to Reims by way of the national route: materials to recover, a lot of items "missing" from the bundles that we received. Raids at the Reims depots, complicating our ability to get the requisitioned goods. . . .

Traveling, back and forth, through all of these villages, shores, hills, and forts whose names I had read so often in my youth, in the reports of the previous war. Our driver, T., a farmer in the area, knows every last detail of the local terrain. Here, a group of fighter planes was destroyed by a nest of machine guns; there, an enormous, monstrous, and jagged-edged crater, recalls the two companies who fell upon a German mine in 1916; and along the route, here and there and there again, the great fields planted with neatly arranged crosses, draped with flags—the black and white crosses of enemies now so close; the monument to those killed in the tank brigades, those killed by trench mortars, the monument to riflemen. All of these names, which had until now only been names to me, now swell with images: Craonne, Berry-au-Bac, le Chemin des Dames. I want to hold myself back from considering this conflict from too great a universal perspective (*sub specie aeternitatis*), because although I (happily) find myself defending incontestable values and principles, in spite of all of their faults, I see the regimes and institutions of France and Britain with clear eyes. Nevertheless, how could I, returning from this "excursion," stop myself from thinking that 25 years later, humanity is yet again gripped by a new fury against itself? It is a truth that explains so many things: that fury never ceased. It was incubating.[53]

Roughly a month later, Friedmann again passed by some of the same monuments:

> 4 October 1939
>
> We are still making our way to Reims, through the long, narrow passes made up of cemeteries, mine craters, landscapes stripped and all the more sinister in the grey autumn morning. Here is a monument to the dead from the tank brigades, then the infantry, and the cemetery for marine riflemen; here again the famous mine that devoured an entire brigade; and there a battalion of *territoriaux* who were killed on sight.
>
> And here, once again, armies crawl across this dreadful landscape; the enormous machine of war has been stirred awake and made ready. We are here, and there, and among the occupants of this vehicle, I am the only one who was not here the *last time*... The car continues to traverse kilometers of these landscapes. I let myself go, the sadness is too powerful for me to respond to it: feeling of the uselessness of all of this, horror at both institutions and passions which, after a quarter-century, will reproduce and renew, worsen the destruction, and increase the slaughter.[54]

We see in passages like this a subtle, perhaps gentle, though striking awareness of a series of contrasts, the familiar, seemingly eternal, "machine of war" and its new iterations. In this way, we also glimpse the concentric layers through which Friedmann's insight passes. The remnants of the last war dot the countryside, and its technological legacy visible each day in the HC. And yet, in being so visible, Friedmann is able to gauge the changes that have come about since then, in new forms of warfare. Each day, he witnesses the effects of technologies that both emerge from and outstrip their predecessors, operating in overlaid circles that were not lost on Friedmann. These observations are important, because they allow us to further specify his understanding of the nature of the changes that, however subtle, constitute the Technological Adventure.

In *Journal* entries like these, Friedmann is aware of his place in a tragically ahistorical human experience—a fury that "never ceased," but was instead "incubating," and which, it seems, will always return. And yet, it was known even at the time, and certainly by an expert in machine culture like Friedmann, that the First World War had been in many ways a new experience. The "famous mine that devoured an entire brigade" or the chemical agents that had populated so many of the graves in question were as much proper citizens of the twentieth century as Friedmann himself, even as such technologies had origins in nineteenth-century conflicts.[55] Friedmann understood that these techniques could at once have roots in the past and perform new feats of destruction in the present. Indeed, he saw the present conflict in just this way: as a force that had not only reproduced but renewed itself as a "continuous creation." It had done so to destructive ends that had never before been seen—even as they emerge from a familiar recent past and take part in an unfortunately universal human experience. This "renewal" is thus representative of the Technological Adventure of human beings in the twentieth century. That is not simply because it is constituted by the introduction and use of new machines, but because their devastating novelty results in the political and spiritual crisis of adaptation that Friedmann calls "the Great Disequilibrium."

III. THE GREAT DISEQUILIBRIUM

If "the Technological Adventure of human beings in the twentieth century" is the name Friedmann gives to the central object of his research, the "Great Disequilibrium" is the name for the constellation of contemporary spiritual demands that he sets out to diagnose and address. From Friedmann's perspective, these would be the very demands to which Hadot poses the question of a potential role for the spiritual exercises of Greco-Roman antiquity. Much like the Technological Adventure, the constellation of symptoms that comprise the "Great Disequilibrium" are already visible in Friedmann's earliest work. Whether named or not, the Disequilibrium is always present in his studies of mechanization, automation, and the effects of rapid technological change on "human relations" in the twentieth century and their resulting dehumanization.

To be clear again, the Great Disequilibrium is not simply defined by technological change itself, but by the crisis that follows from our failure to adapt to those changes, and its effects on the linked spiritual and material well-being of the human subjects caught up in it. As he puts it in the preface to the 1956 American edition of *Industrial Society*:

> It is evident that, among the ills from which humanity suffers in the twentieth century, one of the most serious is the lack of understanding of the

structure and effects of the new environment into which men have been plunged during the last century and a half by the rapid development of a technical civilization. . . . The destiny of machine civilization, born of the application of science to society, everywhere provokes uneasy speculation, exacerbated by the material and moral chaos into which humanity has been plunged by two world wars.[56]

Here and elsewhere, Friedmann already speaks of the disequilibrium in terms of a material ill, one with "moral" consequences and "spiritual" wages. But Friedmann does not simply seek a diagnosis in such studies. His work is carried out in the service of discovering, or at least refining, and implementing a healing regimen. Thus, "the problems of mechanization must be grasped where they arise, observed and even experienced in their true nature. The various sciences from which they derive must be studied in order to judge the evils, and to define the remedies (if such exist) and the conditions under which the latter may operate."[57] There is perhaps no better summation of what Friedmann sets out to do across his career in general.

Labor and Dehumanization

The imbalance, the crisis of adaptation, that defines the Disequilibrium is marked first by what Friedmann refers to as the "dehumanization" of workers, alongside the attending concept of "despiritualization" (*Entseelung*), which I return to later.[58] Although *Industrial Society* is one of a number of investigations of these questions, its methods and conclusions are representative. There, Friedmann describes at least two forms of dehumanization: First, a general sense, reflecting the experiences of "the worker in mass-production workshops" who appears as "a raw material in the midst of other raw materials," or a "human ox,"[59] and for whom "the agonizing problems of the dehumanization of labor" are a central feature of daily life.[60] Second, a more specific form of dehumanization that has its origins in the "scientific management" whose dominant and then-ubiquitous form was developed by the American mechanical engineer F. W. Taylor. Taylorism pits the real worker against an impossible "composite" ideal and is among Friedmann's central targets in *Industrial Society* and elsewhere.

First, regarding the general sense of dehumanization, the text is blunt and unambiguous in its descriptive work, and Friedmann's concerns are apparent from chapter and heading titles like "Fatigue" and "The Working Environment." Indeed, the latter includes subsections on the problems of "Temperature, Humidity, and Ventilation," "Light," "Noise and Vibration," "Accidents," "Problems of Monotony," and so on.[61] These sections describe, in harrowing detail, the ways in which all of these conditions bring about forms of dehumanization particular to the Great Disequilibrium. He describes the phenomenon known as "industrial fatigue"[62] and the "stupefying" effects of noise on the factory floor[63] in comparable detail. Indeed, Friedmann cites an 1845 passage from Michelet describing the "spiritual" wages of the terrible problems of noise, which prefigure so many of the other elements which would be further amplified a century later:[64]

> Michelet, so acutely aware of the spiritual needs of the worker, eloquently voiced the sentiments of many of his contemporaries when, towards 1845, he wrote concerning the large spinning and weaving factories, that they are a "true inferno of tedium"; "*Forever, forever, forever,* is the word perpetually thundering in our ears from the rattling machines, which make the floors tremble. Never does one become accustomed to it. Tedium and vertigo and disgust are the same after twenty years as on the first day."[65]

Friedmann follows Michelet's description with Hyacinthe Dubreuil's observation in 1929 of the great love that Ford plant workers in Michigan had for attending silent films, as they presented a respite from the noise of the factory.[66]

These are just a few examples of the constellation of conditions and effects that Friedmann analyzes. In this general account of dehumanization, the worker becomes a kind of machine part or draft animal, tasked with stupefying and oversimplified labors under grueling physical and psychological conditions—conditions potentially unconducive even for the upkeep of machines themselves. And yet, alongside and in some sense within such inhuman conditions, there is the second complementary form of dehumanization, one that demands the superhuman accomplishment of given tasks. Friedmann's ongoing diagnosis of the Great Disequilibrium consists in the analysis not only of industrial conditions, but in existing attempts to adapt to new industrial transformations. Over the course of *Industrial Society*, Friedmann details the intersections of the work itself with the theories and practices of "rationalization" that marked industry between the late nineteenth and mid-twentieth centuries.[67] Some of the clearest examples of the reproduction and amplification of the Disequilibrium are thus to be found in the scientific management of Taylor, Ford, and others, which Friedmann identified as a direct cause of so much of the misery he observed.[68]

This second form of dehumanization has its origins in some of Taylor's central methods, such as the time and motion studies. In these practices, "the rationalizer breaks down a given operation into a certain number of parts and ascertains, from several workers, the minimal times for each part. Finally, he assembles the most rapid movements in a stereotyped series which will henceforth be imposed, as the standard and only method, on the workers."[69] The worker in this case is "dehumanized" by the creation of a nonexistent ideal "composite worker," against which the actual worker is measured, and thus always found insufficient. In this way, the product of the time study is at once the antithesis of the Marxist principle of "each according to their abilities" and a warped mask of Hadot's sage, as the ideal, attainable or not, toward which one cultivates oneself. Taylor's composite worker is thus one form, and a particularly challenging one, of what Friedmann later names the problem of "man inferior to his works,"[70] as it is this composite worker who represents the "human machine" meant to adapt "to the rate of the mechanical one."[71] And even in those cases, mythical or otherwise, where the real worker may compete with the output of the machine, such an inhuman pace can never be sustainable, let alone "humanizing."[72] As the legend goes, John Henry died with his hammer in his hand, and despite the near-mythic skill and strength that allowed for that deeply human victory, no other outcome was ever possible.[73] Moreover, where Taylor and his acolytes tried to establish these models "scientifically," such impossible ideals are still to this day fabricated on the caprice of bosses and managers who hold workers to imagined standards that may be less "exact" in some sense, but are for that very reason all the more exacting.

Friedmann's critiques of Taylorism's claims to the status of a science are as thorough as they are withering throughout *Industrial Society*. A central problem, as one critic put it, was the fact that "'Taylor was first of all an engineer; he knew the mechanism of the lifeless machine but not that of the living motor.'"[74] Or in the more blunt words of the American Federation of Labor, "'the inhuman and hideous system' called Taylorism . . . 'reduces human beings to the condition of mere machines.'"[75] Taylor's triumph is, of course, rivaled by that of Henry Ford, who "congratulates himself on the fact that the new technical means have 'eliminated human art from this operation.'"[76] And as Friedmann says, invoking Taylor's own language and echoing that of Ford, "The very expression, 'human motor' . . . suggested some confusion with certain tendencies of Scientific Management. In the industrial worker the latter had seen primarily the *motor* and very little of the *human*."[77] Thus despite Taylor's "sincere good-will"[78] and ambitions of bringing "harmony, not discord" through the "the application of science to industry,"[79] the most efficiently produced by-product of the system seemed to be the compounded misery of workers laboring in industrial conditions that were already inherently dangerous.[80]

Such attempts, Taylorist or otherwise, to "rationalize" industrial labor, or any form of work for that matter, only exacerbate the Great Disequilibrium. They do so by attempting to adapt the "human" to the "motor," rather than the inverse. They are thus dehumanizing in a strict and simple sense: to move toward the machine is to move away from our "humanization," reinforcing the status of human beings as "inferior to our works." However well intentioned these ensembles of industrial theory and practice may be, they emerge from and redouble the crisis of adaptation that marks the Great Disequilibrium. And on Friedmann's account, they cannot help but do so.

The Milieu and the Cycle of Adaptation

Friedmann targets Taylorism in *Industrial Society* not just because it is representative of the broader field of scientific management, but because it is representative of a ubiquitous and persistent constellation of impulses around labor and technology, and in turn the forms of life and work it served to further proliferate. He thereby also takes these concerns to reflect the situation within the general field of automated industrial labor: applying equally to the Fordist factory and, "without confusing situations and environments which are very different in character," to comparable problems observed in the USSR.[81] Thus, Friedmann argues that if the forms of dehumanization that emerge from machine labor are both symptoms and ongoing causes of the Great Disequilibrium, major attempts to adapt labor to the conditions in question instead tended only to reinforce them. Moreover, these effects are ubiquitous, extending well beyond the factory floor. Friedmann's criticisms of "rationalization" illustrate the cascade effect produced by the Disequilibrium: a set of conditions arise that are already disruptive in themselves, and insofar as the doctrines and practices meant to address those conditions are still determined by the forces which they seek to ameliorate, they will only continue to exacerbate the cycle of imbalance.

In *Industrial Society*, Friedmann argues that "the determining laws of an epoch sweep along the most powerful individuals in spite of themselves."[82] Or as he says in "Man and the Natural Milieu": "Human beings are not the same, we do not feel, behave, or think the same according to the epochs of our history, to the environment within which we live, and the technologies at our disposal. . . . In an ancient adventure in which causes and effects jumble together and reciprocally condition one another, human beings condition our environment, and through our environment, we modify ourselves, set forth toward new transformations."[83] Friedmann's assessment is rooted in a view of the reciprocal relationship between the effect of human labor upon the environment and the subsequent impact of those changes and that work back upon us. "The industrial milieu," he emphasizes, is a "complex reality which surrounds man at his work and which is created by and constantly reacts upon him."[84] In other words: when we labor upon the world, we labor upon ourselves.[85]

This fundamental insight and Friedmann's elaboration of that relationship are among his major contributions to the present work. It appears across his oeuvre in various places, though a brief and what might be called negative elaboration in *La puissance* is instructive. It is telling that the elaborations at issue appear within his reflections on "Marx, Marxisms, Communisms," including what he calls the "naïve" iterations of his own youth.[86] For Friedmann, the view he seeks to counter in fact begins correctly. From that perspective, "revolutionary action transforms the milieu, and the transformed milieu remodels the individual." So far, so good. But as much as Friedmann agrees with this claim, it remains only half right from his perspective. The initial premise is correct, that economic conditions, institutions, the built environment in general, or what he calls the "milieu" shape the individuals living and working within them, even "on the level of the self and being" as Hadot would put it. But this conception truncates the relationship between human beings and the milieu it begins to describe; it is a far too unidirectional and causal account for Friedmann. Here, there is simply a line from politics to ethics, in which the "new human being" emerges "automatically" from new institutions.

The former is the strict effect of an "operation of the outside upon the inside," a process in which "there is no place for an autonomous effort of governing the self, by the amelioration, the conscious development of spiritual forces, the strain toward the summit of oneself," which would in turn and again serve to shape the "external" forces in question.[87]

From Friedmann's perspective, this partial view is clearly superior to moralism, which misrecognizes or even ignores the roles of institutions, the "milieu," and material conditions in general in shaping who and what we are. At the same time, it still amounts to a mere counternarrative to the latter, trading in many of the same formal premises, though from another perspective, rather than offering a new way of looking at the relationship of the ethics of the individual to the political lives of institutions. If politics are not simply a product of ethics writ large, ethical life is not a wholly determined by-product of political conditions—even as those conditions matter a great deal.

For Friedmann, it is the cycle of change and adaptation that matters, the ongoing creation and maintenance of new institutions and practices, which in turn produce new people, who build new institutions, and so on. The problem then is that the radical content and pace of technological change have unbalanced the cycle of change and adaptation to those changes, creating the state of disequilibrium that concerns him:

> With the emergence of technological civilization, our environment has begun to constantly and profoundly evolve: a torrent of technological changes, world wars and social wars, the fever of everyday life. No possibility has the chance to truly clear a new path, or to fix itself in a stable set of behaviors—in instinct. The stimulations which issue from the technical milieu multiply themselves in a way that is superabundant, disordered, and chaotic. We can say the same thing for the reactions which correspond to them within the individual, on the level of sensibility and action. What had constituted the principal fabric of our psychic lives, in the natural milieu, has been diminished or even disappeared without having (not yet anyway) been replaced.[88]

It is for this reason that Friedmann is not only concerned with the exponential pace of technological change, but the political, social, and psychological effects of our ceaseless and often ill-equipped attempts to adapt to it. Indeed, it is the inexorable feedback loop of the effect that our labor has on the conditions under which we subsequently labor that is now marked by imbalance and has produced the condition diagnosed as the Great Disequilibrium. Thus, our failure to adapt—and to so much as know how to adapt—to the Technological Adventure results in a disequilibrium between "the power and non-control of technology, and the debility of moral forces," specifically the forces necessary for us to control the products of our labor and prevent them from controlling us.[89]

The overwhelming nature of the technological change that we ourselves have brought about has caused us to lose control over both our own works and the conditions under which they are produced. It is for this reason that dozens of pages of *La puissance* are devoted to innumerable examples of what he calls "the Power of Things over human beings"[90] or "man inferior to his works,"[91] which can be anything from the privileged example of nuclear weapons,[92] to automobiles,[93] to the effects of all of these technologies on human biology[94] and psychology, to any of the other "technological horrors" personally witnessed or reported to him during the war, in the postwar West, the USSR, and elsewhere.[95]

However, it must be just as clear that Friedmann's understanding of the relationship between human subjectivity, the natural–technological milieu, and the "cycle of adaptation" still constitutes a neutral analytic category:

> Human beings change. Our manner of thinking is no less variable, relative, tied to the ensemble of conditions of a civilization than our manner of sensing and perceiving. The logical processes of thinking among the contemporaries of Luther are not the same as those who visit the cinema or fly in airplanes. The natural environment which dominated Western Europe since the 16th century had a concurrent mentality, different from that of the inhabitants of the new milieu.[96]

For Friedmann, this claim has no necessary normative political or ethical content. I emphasize this neutrality because it is at once the cause of the Great Disequilibrium and the condition of the possibility of its resolution: "I do not believe, and I emphasize this here in order to avoid any misunderstanding, in an immutable human nature. In dominating the environment that we are given, human beings are able, reciprocally, to aid in our own transformations, our ascent towards our own heights—our humanization."[97] This view at once gives Friedmann an explanation for the physical and spiritual misery he has observed from the trenches, fields, and factory floors and gives him hope for the future. It is only insofar as this kind of relationship is the source of certain problems that it can also be a means of remedying them.

The question now becomes one of just what the treatment might look like, and why Friedmann comes to believe that the "interior effort" has some necessary role in the process of humanization that he hints can in some way counter the Great Disequilibrium.[98] But much like the question of spiritualism, and tied directly to it, in order to understand Friedmann's view and the reasons he comes to hold it, it is important to understand what that vision excludes.

IV. THE FUTILITY OF NOSTALGIA

The dehumanizing effects of labor under the Great Disequilibrium are sometimes accompanied by what Friedmann refers to as the "despiritualization" of work, which he invokes in *Industrial Society* alongside the dehumanization described earlier.[99] The great systems of "rationalization," whether Fordist, Taylorist, or otherwise, were at the time exacerbating this phenomenon: "Unfortunately, the trend of rationalized labor towards 'despiritualization' (*Entseelung*) takes a totally different course."[100] Where "dehumanization" roughly refers to the assimilation of the human being to a kind of machine, despiritualization seems to more specifically refer to a kind of disconnection of the workers from their work. Here, the machine becomes something other than an extension of oneself. Instead, the machine, the tool, becomes something that stands between us and the efforts and products of our labors: "In de-spiritualized work, the close bond between the worker and the task is loosened, sometimes even broken."[101]

In practice, despiritualization in part codes the shift from artisanal work to subdivided labor. In "Man and the Natural Milieu," Friedmann describes the model of artisanship in the following terms:

> Between human beings and the elements, nothing seems to interpose: it is close to them, things or beings, animals, tools, wind, land. The carpenter conceives and executes, plane in hand, sculpts, sands, varnishes, and finishes his work, all while, in so doing, debating with himself the merits of his own practice. Nothing separates him from his material, his work. Taking his tool

in hand, his hand is extended, he knows it, adapts it, fashions it to his grasp. The tool is an extension of his body, his skill, and his art."[102]

This kind of labor, in other words, "requires that man be present to his work. The work itself is still coextensive with human motion, technical efficacy with tools."[103] Although these descriptions can sound like romantic hindsight, the experience of despiritualization is born out in the firsthand testimonies Friedmann reports in *Industrial Society*: "Another worker, Watson, an old mechanic, reproaches Taylorism especially with having taken from the worker the responsibility for *his* tools, and *his* machine."[104]

However, the problem with the discourse of "despiritualization," tied as it is to a certain, perhaps romanticized, understanding of artisanal labor is that it is easy and intuitive to link a notion of "spiritualized" work to specific forms of labor. And to be clear, Friedmann does hold that at least certain forms of artisanal labor are characterized by a "spiritualization" that was in the process of disappearing: "Mechanization has once more deepened the opposition between work and culture, which, in certain of his activities, the medieval artisan had reconciled."[105] Friedmann is well aware of this tendency and works to avoid conflating the notion of "spiritualized" work with specific trades or economic relations. The problem is that such a reading can and very often does lead to a nostalgia for "the world which immediately preceded the technological civilization," or, even more typically, someone's romanticized idea of things like medieval artisanship and "pre-industrial" forms of life.[106] In other words: a romantic nostalgia for forms of life and ways of working that either no longer exist or never actually existed in the first place.[107]

However, Friedmann does see despiritualization as a problem, one that characterizes the Great Disequilibrium. Moreover, it is clear from his earliest works that it is a problem that he believes can and must be addressed. But he wants no part in any solution that is predicated on a nostalgic "return" to something, whether real or imagined. Here, Friedmann notes that even some proponents of rationalization lament the possibility that a movement away from artisanal trades amounts to the loss of "technical knowledge and human experience possessed by these true artists." These sentiments, sympathetically reported by François Simiand in his *Cours d'économie politique 1928–1929*, reflect the view of an interview subject that Friedmann describes as "a business leader who is highly devoted to propaganda for rationalization." In the latter's own words, "in these old trades there is 'to a certain degree and under certain circumstances not an inferiority but a superiority which should be preserved.'" Friedmann's response to all of this is unequivocal: "'Superiority?' Certainly. But is there anything more than a *pious wish* in this value judgement concerning the observable facts of modern large-scale industry?"[108] The problem here is again the association of a certain relationship to work to both certain forms of work and a vision of the past characterized by those forms of work.

In a short passage in "Signs," the first chapter of the first part of *La puissance*, and under the telling subheading of "An Irreversible March," Friedmann describes the critical valence of both the Technological Adventure and the Great Disequilibrium. Here he identifies the relationship between the two, and specifies the political and ethical consequences of each. It is telling that it is in this context that Friedmann specifies the critical and prescriptive goals of the book:

> Technological progress is irreversible. The stage of human history that we have entered, and whose pace increases in a rush before our eyes, is in no way comparable to any past age. It is an Adventure of wholly unique character. No technology is either good or evil in itself; all in fact contain *possible* benefits. How then, and under what conditions, can something which is not bad in itself, and which is even *potentially* good, become harmful to human beings? [. . .] Can we suppress, or at least reduce, the Disequilibrium which thus results for human beings? And if so, by what means? These are some of the questions to which this book will attempt to respond.[109]

Technological change, which includes changes in forms of work, is the basis for the Disequilibrium, but the latter is a contingent, historical consequence of the former. For Friedmann, industrialization and automation can either serve human beings or they can be sources of dehumanization. Both his ethics of the interior effort and his politics of "external conditions" rest on this understanding, as does his way of conceiving the relationship between the two.

In this way, despite the rather dire tone of his descriptions from *Industrial Society* in 1946 to *La puissance* in 1971, Friedmann is consistently clear that this is in no way a lament for something "lost," but rather a diagnosis of the present situation, and thus the exigencies particular to it:

> I do not believe, however, that we are now merely experiencing a new episode of the same grand misery that has trundled its way through history. This misery, this impoverishment, has always been profoundly embedded in *a society*, in *a culture*. Though a fact of civilization, it is not and cannot be the same, for example, in the United States in 1970 and in the medieval West. . . . Today, it is tied to the Great Disequilibrium, from which emerge the varying differences in its depth and extension, according to time and place. All told, the manifestation—which imposes itself with tragic evidence—of a moral under-development in industrially evolved societies corresponds to the acceleration of technological progress in the past century.[110]

These specific problems, these particular questions, could never have emerged before, because the conditions that produced them never existed before. Friedmann is neither a Luddite nor a romantic, and there is a clear answer in mind when he asks, "Doesn't the experience of the twentieth century confirm the responsibility for these evils which Marxism attributes to 'capitalist' modes of production?"[111] We cannot confuse this description of the problem with an endorsement of a nostalgic call back to some past form of life, no doubt suffused with its own particular troubles and dangers:

> Nostalgia for the past only merits a brief halt. Ineluctable technological progress, the universe that surrounds us, summon us to continue on our journey. The present is rich with possibilities, and in the tumult that comes with it, old virtues founder. An equilibrium—imperfect, and limited to certain privileged zones, but which had the virtue of existing—disappears, and another has not replaced it.[112]

We cannot go back, nor should we.

We cannot, because technological change is "An Irreversible March"—a telling subheading that appears in section I, "Signs," of part I, "The Great Disequilibrium," of *La puissance*. This is not a naïve teleological claim, nor is the important point here that change itself is inevitable (though he certainly thinks so).[113] Rather, one implication of the inevitability of change is the fact that all times and places carry with them their own particular problems, challenges, and dangers. A utopian nostalgia is not merely impractical and unrealistic, it is undesirable, because it amounts to trading one set of problems for another—and without the benefits that new forms of work, modes of production, and so on all carry with them.

Thus, Friedmann is unequivocal that we should not go back, because "technological progress is a good when it delivers human beings from pain and slavery."[114] In concrete terms, "despite all of the evils from which free time now suffers, there are today men, women, and even young people, who understand how to benefit from the new instruments that have been placed in their hands by technological progress: the latter being, I repeat, indifferent to the uses that one makes of it for better or for worse."[115] At the same time, he is under no illusion regarding the real problems and challenges that these changes bring with them. The point is that technological change is neither good nor bad, but rather at once inherently promising and inherently dangerous:

> Milling machine, transfer machine, cranes, digging machines, computers, Rolleiflex cameras, washing machines, transistors, submarines, automobiles, cars, spaceships—not a single one of these "machines" *can* now be used in the service of human beings, of our bodies and minds, without compromising our health, our freedom, our understanding of the world. And yet, at the same time, they all possess the capacity for aiding us, in the words of the sage, in passing from a lesser state of perfection to a superior one. Even assembly-line work (a form so passionately discussed in terms of the division of labor) can be beneficial in certain economic and social conditions, *if* they are combined with precautions which neutralize their dangers.[116]

For Friedmann, *even the assembly line*, perhaps the paradigmatic example of the tedium and stupefaction that has arisen through subdivided labor, may too, under the right conditions, be rendered a site of humanization.

Elsewhere, in the concluding remarks of *Industrial Society*, he describes the "magnificent possibilities" of both the humanization of industrial labor *and* of automation:

> The theory of automation gives hope to the total disappearance of unpleasant work, the relocating of workers driven from industry by technical progress in other skilled occupations, and the transformation of the man at work into a sort of demiurge or creator, making and minding machines. But these are technicians' abstractions which the actual evolution of capitalist

societies since the beginning of this century has cruelly contradicted. Complete automation is full of wonderful promises: freeing the worker from these subdivided tasks (in which he is half-absorbed by the machine), from assembly-line labor henceforth assigned to mechanical appliances, distributing consumption goods in great quantities, increasing comfort, shortening the working day for all, creating leisure for everybody, and consequently the means for attaining dignity and culture. But here again, technology and the suggestions of the human factor which tend to control its application in industry bring only a magnificent *possibility;* man, alone, through the social and economic organization in which techniques are integrated and oriented, can decide the degree to which this possibility may become actual.[117]

It is from this perspective that Friedmann asks, "Could we succeed, at a different stage of organization and wisdom, to overcome the physical, psychic, and social evils that [the Disequilibrium] has multiplied? For our species, the 'enthusiasm' of our Technological Adventure is hardly a century old; so very little time. Was Marx in fact more correct than the theoreticians of post-industrial society in situating his own époque within the prehistory of humanity?"[118]

The task is to identify the conditions under which that promise can be developed and the means to suppress those dangers. But it is a task that is possible: in maintaining that we are shaped by forces "outside" ourselves, Friedmann also maintains the possibility of actively engaging in that shaping. Indeed, such a conclusion follows from his understanding of human being, labor, and milieu. If in laboring upon the world, we labor upon ourselves, and if our goal is to alter the results of that labor in some way, we must first understand the particular dynamics of these processes within the specific conditions in which we find ourselves.

In other words, in order to respond to the problem in any meaningful way, we must not only describe it first, but do so continuously: "Here in the final third of the twentieth century, we engage in the Technological Adventure particular to us at a moment so fraught with dangers. How can we overcome those dangers without understanding them—without studying them?"[119] If indeed, "the Technological Adventure forces human beings to invent new forms of life, to discover a new sense of one's life: invention and discovery," what are the criteria, the standards, the values by which we can best pursue these forms of invention and discovery, in order to arrive at this "humanization," rather than reinforcing the cycle of Disequilibrium?[120] If appropriate "means" must be appropriate to these specific questions, problems, and conditions, how must we tailor those means and our tactics and strategies, in response?

V. THE LIMITS OF EXTERIORITY

Friedmann's first attempts at addressing the Great Disequilibrium were characterized by what he calls a certain "exteriority." Given his diagnosis of the origins of the situation in the material conditions of technological change, and the goal of achieving "the humanization of technology,"[121] in which "the machine is adapted to the person (and not the inverse, as has been and remains so often the case)," it was reasonable to assume that scientific, technological, and economic responses would suffice:

> In brief, I had accorded the social and biological sciences the power to work together toward the humanization of work, attacking—by way of external remedies—the evils which come from uncontrolled mechanization (un-dominated by human beings), which menace the physical and psychic equilibrium of human producers. I had faith in the ability of science to come to the aid of the body and spirit of working human beings, to defend them from the effects of anarchic and rapacious industrialization.[122]

As we have seen, however, Friedmann came to see the limits of such strictly "exterior" approaches: "The "exterior" remedies which have been recommended in order to humanize, insofar as is possible, both work and leisure time are, certainly, worthy of discussion. . . . I continue to think that they can, together, provide great benefits. But I see now the limits of their efficacy much more than I had at first."[123] Such means do have a role, but a specific one: "Exterior remedies constitute our defense against these dangers. But in this New Frontier, we must engage in an *offensive*, though quotidian, form of combat, an endless struggle within the indefinite field which calls to us: the mastery of technology, its humanization."[124]

Regarding this shift in perspective, Friedmann's emerging skepticism for strictly political and technological responses is rooted in part in his relationship with the USSR. The political and personal struggles of the era of Stalin "cast a crude light upon the disequilibrium between political power and the moral misery of those who have so atrociously abused it in the name of a doctrine of justice, proclaiming the reconciliation of human beings with ourselves."[125] But Friedmann is clear that the gulag or show trials in no way amount to an indictment of socialism itself. He neither abandons Marx nor recoils into moralism. The issue is rather that beyond the more spectacular political troubles of Soviet life, in its mundane, quotidian, goings-on, it became clear to Friedmann that "the dominant values of technological civilization exercise their corruptive force just as much in Moscow as in Washington, in Paris as in Beijing."[126] On his observation, the respective Technological Adventures of East and West in the twentieth century had more in common than many imagined.

The Great Disequilibrium was thus not only a Western problem. It was also evinced in many of the same ways, and for many of the same reasons, in the "socialist patrimony."[127] The political and technological aspects of the Soviet experiment he witnessed firsthand in the 1930s, and observed from abroad until his death in the 1970s, achieved neither the "human face" nor the *nouvelle morale socialiste* he sought.[128] And if the political domain that was founded upon the very principle of the rectification of the relationship of human beings to our labor within a modern, technological, and industrialized context could fail to achieve that balance, then Friedmann would conclude *not* that the socialist project was hopeless, but that there was something simplistic about his own reasoning:

> In light of these repeated shocks, I came to understand that my quasi-exclusive interest in "exterior" remedies had been the expression of a relatively simplistic scientific materialism. [. . .] This form of scientism is no more justified than any of the others. These "exterior" remedies are useful, certainly, and even necessary, but not sufficient. Bad institutions are not solely responsible for the "limits of the human factor." These limits are inscribed within human beings themselves. As with our physical, social and psychic environment, it is upon human beings and from human beings that we must reflect, and provoke action.[129]

This is not a naturalistic claim; if these limits are "inscribed within us," that inscription is itself the result of the complex and reciprocating relationship between laboring subjects, the work we do, and the work that is done to us in turn.[130] And if those conditions affect our responses to them, in the work that we do and the that way we do it, any work on our part to shift the terms will require somehow "stepping outside" and reapproaching the cycles and patterns within which we find ourselves, in even the smallest way: "In order to control our new milieu (that is, to "humanize" it), we are compelled to make choices. But in order to make those choices, we must rely upon values and the people who live them. How can we break from this circle?"[131] Thus, on this account, if "exterior" conditions (and "conditioning") produce "interior" effects, and vice versa, then to meet our material conditions only on the level of their "exteriority" is to misconstrue the nature of the dynamic in question, and to thereby impair the development of a response that is either effective or just.

In other words, insofar as any primarily "exterior" attempts to redress the effects of the Great Disequilibrium remain caught up within it and are shaped and reshaped by it, they will either fail or further exacerbate the imbalance. It is for this reason that attempts to adapt to the new landscape of the Technological Adventure of the twentieth century, attempts as wide-ranging as scientific management and the Soviet project, are on this reading subject to many of the same forces and problems. And it is why the goal of humanization requires an interior effort: "Our spiritual forces, save for some exceptional cases, are not yet in a state to address these conditions, and yet only they can save us, by aiding us in the mastery of our new milieu, and thus liberating us from it."[132]

What is required is a way of engaging and reshaping the subjects laboring under the Great Disequilibrium, such that the cycle itself is shifted not simply toward "humanization," but toward new *forms* of humanization appropriate to the technological milieu, and indeed beyond. For Friedmann, this means new and dynamic ways of cultivating subjects who, in laboring on themselves at once labor on the environment such that the newly produced conditions do not cycle back in an uncontrolled way that continues to reinforce and exacerbate our dehumanization. It is also for these reasons that the "interior effort" required to meet these demands must be tailored to them and cannot be uncritically imported from other cultures, great religions, or classical antiquity.

VI. THE INTERIOR EFFORT

It is for these reasons that Friedmann concludes that exterior solutions to the Disequilibrium, wrought by the kinds of technological, economic, and social change in contemporary life that he so assiduously describes, must be joined—neither in front of nor behind—by what he calls an "interior effort":

> In highlighting both the necessity and insufficiency of "exterior" remedies to the difficulties that have emerged in a technological society, both within work and outside of work, we have at the same time revealed the need for an *interior* effort in order to bring our own technical progress under control, and thus to ensure the moral and physical future of our species. It now becomes a question of studying the chances, the limits of such an effort, and, through these reflections, to discern the forces capable of reducing, and perhaps one day suppressing, the disequilibrium, of which we have already taken note of many signs.[133]

However, and as should be clear by now, he rejects any retreat into nostalgia, ethical spiritualism, or political moralism. The goal is to "resituate" the relationship between interior and exterior along new lines, not to fall back into the old terms by merely prioritizing one over the other: "In order to attenuate or suppress the Disequilibrium, we must call upon both 'interior' and 'exterior' remedies."[134] That is the challenge that emerges from Friedmann's work, and it is not an easy task.

It is in this way that *La puissance* is not so much a prescriptive text as it is a preliminary analysis and diagnosis, a kind of moral and philosophical companion to texts like *Industrial Society*: "I have no pretension however of providing a 'system' here, or of drawing up a structured and exhaustive list of values. Any such values would need to emerge from the critical observation of this new milieu and thus, in a manner of speaking, have directed my attention 'to the terrain.'"[135] Perhaps *La puissance* inaugurates a research program; perhaps it constitutes an avenue within the ongoing elaboration of one that has existed for some time. What matters is that there is no universal or trans-historical form of "interior effort." The internal work of differing times and places cannot be simply repurposed for the exigencies of another without a rigorous translation grounded in the kind of thoroughgoing assessment of "the terrain" he describes. If Hadot shows us why this work is necessary, Friedmann takes up the task with a care and attention to his terrain that mirrors Hadot's textual–historical approach to his own.

However, Friedmann takes it a step further. Among the dangers of proceeding without such rigor and attention, he identifies the specter of the very ethical spiritualism and its counterpart in political moralism and "retreat," from which he and others work to distance themselves:

> Some of course have sensed the need to cultivate new spiritual forces in contemporary man, but very few among even those are oriented in the only constructive direction: to search for these new forces in and through the recognition of the technological progress in question, through what Karl Jaspers calls a "loyalty" to the realities of the twentieth century. Lacking that loyalty, the denunciation of the dangers of technological progress so often devolves into a mythical nostalgia for the past, which in turn leads, as the case may be, to a global rejection of modernity, a negative and desperate attitude, an escape into *spiritualism* or mystical comforts, and religious or secular forms of retreat from the world.[136]

For Friedmann, we cannot simply exchange the exterior for the interior. To do so would be to continue to trade in a framework of mere opposition, which fails to understand the complexity of the relationship, or possible relationships, between these domains. This is especially true insofar as contemporary interior efforts, whether rooted in historical forms or not, require the work and attention he describes here to achieve this "loyalty" to the present.

It is here that Friedmann really sets out the task of *La puissance*, to discover a form of "interior effort" proper to contemporary life in its ability to address the Disequilibrium, without lapsing into a vapid spiritualism, useless nostalgia, or reactionary moralism by failing to understand the reciprocal relationship between material conditions and "spiritual" life. In the end, it is unclear to me whether *La puissance* achieves this or that such an achievement is at all its goal. What matters, however, is that its contributions are crucial in framing the problem and beginning to model the work required. Moreover, as undeveloped as it ultimately is in the text, Friedmann's negative specification of the set of terms that must be abandoned in order for a proper reformulation of the relationship of the ethical to the political is decisive: "Human beings are called today to undertake an interior conversion, one that is much more than a psychological adaptation to this new milieu. Only this conversion can allow us to take our own future in hand, to unlock it, at once on the level of the individual, of society, *and* of the species; a path of salvation, a new frontier, a long and decisive march."[137]

GEORGES FRIEDMANN

The question is, of course, just what this humanization should look like, and how it may be attained. For Friedmann, any real answer can only arrive on the other side of *La puissance* or the kind of work it represents.[138] But on my reading, beyond answers, the text is far richer when taken as an effort to detail the conditions under which such questions can and must be posed and the criteria that any such answers would have to meet.

Among the most important and extensive aspects of this task within *La puissance* is a kind of survey that Friedmann undertakes in part III of the book: "Où nous ressourcer?"[139] Here, Friedmann asks "In what way, from which religion, which doctrine, which social movement, can human beings today, draw upon for the moral forces that will aid us in balancing the material power with which we have been so endowed, in order to truly control the latter?" The work that follows from this central question takes the form of what he calls "a brief review, which claims to be neither thorough nor exhaustive."[140] It is a "review" of four traditions: Christianity, which means French Catholicism here;[141] Judaism;[142] "Hindu Spirituality;"[143] and "Marx, Marxisms, Communisms."[144] To each, Friedmann poses the question with which we began: that of the respective ability of each tradition to address what Hadot called "contemporary spiritual demands," which for Friedmann means in large part the Great Disequilibrium.

In fact, it is this section of *La puissance* that Hadot refers to in his invocation of Friedmann at the opening of "Spiritual Exercises." Recall that, after citing an important passage from part V of *La puissance*, Hadot refers to this section, part III, to tell us that Friedmann "comes to the conclusion that there is no tradition . . . compatible with contemporary spiritual demands." Hadot then goes on to ask why Friedmann did not include the philosophical traditions of Greco-Roman antiquity in his "review," and wonders aloud whether Friedmann was aware that his own reflections sounded a great deal like "a pastiche of Marcus Aurelius."[145] However, on the other side of *La puissance*, the *Journal*, and other texts, Hadot's conclusions here are somewhat off the mark, for at least two reasons.

On the one hand, Friedmann does not exactly exclude the traditions and figures that Hadot references, and it is clear that he was quite well versed in them. It is fascinating to note that in *La puissance*, Friedmann specifically invokes Marcus Aurelius, Plato, and Epicurus in the midst of his discussion of Marxism within the very section of *La puissance* that Hadot enquires about.[146] Admittedly, this passage is brief, and these figures do not receive the sustained attention that the major religious traditions do. Much more significantly, however, it is to Marcus Aurelius that Friedmann turns in the *Journal de guerre* in the midst of one the greatest spiritual–political crises of his life. In a series of entries between June 18 and 24, 1940, he frantically tries to make sense of Pétain's capitulation, just a few days before the *Journal* cuts off, and preceding the journey to Toulouse and the beginning of his time with the Resistance.[147]

On June 20, 1940, Friedmann opens the *Meditations*, which he describes as "a natural preview of the ordeals to come," noting, "If the world of Marcus Aurelius could seem insane to a sage, how much more must ours! The Barbarians are all around us, and the planetary spectacle of technologies turned against their creators is more tragic than that which offered itself to the philosopher-emperor at the edges of the Roman empire."[148] If the world and Friedmann himself were unprepared, spiritually and politically, for Molotov-Ribbentrop a year prior, the *Journal* makes it clear the armistice left him scrambling for the balance required to so much as make sense of these events, let alone take concrete actions against them. All of this while awaiting the Germans, to whom Friedmann—a French Jew—and his company had been surrendered. It is here that Friedmann answers Hadot's question, and in so doing begins to specify the questions that must be asked, the conditions that must be met, and the possibilities that are at least somewhat visible regarding the unique and properly contemporary demands of the Great Disequilibrium. And as Hadot later hoped, he begins to do so with the aid of the emperor's *Exhortations*, through a reading grounded in a clear-eyed view of the historical and technological distance between them.

Friedmann's relationship to the ancient sources in his *Journal* thus prefigures his "review" in *La puissance*. Contra Hadot's claim, it is not the case that Friedmann concludes that none of the religious traditions that he reviews in in part III are incapable of addressing contemporary spiritual demands *tout court*. His reviews are not concerned with determining whether the fundamental doctrines or practices of a given tradition are capable of responding to the demands in question. Indeed, it is clear that there is nothing inherently true of any of these traditions that would necessarily preclude them from addressing said demands—even as he remains consistent in warning that the lure of "mystical comforts" can be strong in the face of the "abominations" of the Great Disequilibrium.[149] Neither Friedmann's investigations nor his conclusions concern themselves with adjudicating the sufficiency of a given doctrine in itself; he does not take sides, nor does he "reject" any tradition or group.

Rather, part III does not so much come to any particular conclusions about Christianity, Judaism, Hinduism, or even Marxism. Instead, it poses certain difficult questions *to* them, and thus to any group, tradition, or party: How might we cultivate forms of "interior" effort integrated with the work of "exterior" transformation, which can help replace the cycle of the Great Disequilibrium with a cycle of humanization? Can such "interior efforts"—mass, collective efforts—operate such that they constitute the first steps in the creation of new human beings, whose material labors in turn contribute to the production of a new milieu, capable of again producing new human beings, and so on? How might we craft integrated efforts that will further cultivate a humanity that is no longer "inferior" to our own works, in which we control the technologies that we create and are not controlled by them? Despite the limits of his analyses, this is Friedmann's question, not simply to the traditions he discusses in part III, but in general. In this area, he and Hadot are in fact asking different questions.

And so, in a way that is consistent, for example, with the humanizing possibility of even certain industrial processes, Friedmann does not necessarily discount any of the traditions he invokes from serving to combat the Great Disequilibrium. What he does clearly discount is any "interior effort" that simply deploys existing beliefs and practices without both carefully tuning them to the exigencies of the new milieu *and* integrating them within a properly exterior, material effort. He also discounts any form of spiritualism, as egoistic practices and efforts cannot by definition intersect with the fundamentally political, social, and collective nature of the spiritual demands in question—at least, not for the better. Finally, he discounts any interior effort that is not substantively comprised of the spiritual–political efforts of average people, workers, the rank and file.

Returning then to Hadot's initial query, if the answer is not to be found in any existing regimen, individual practice, or tradition as it stands, it is because the contemporary spiritual demands of the Technological Adventure, as they manifest in the Great Disequilibrium are substantively new. The transformations in question are dynamic, chaotic, and dangerous. A stagnating insistence that things are not or will not be so different after all is itself constitutive of the Disequilibrium in some of its forms. Nostalgia, an active looking backward, is consistently tied to spiritualism, and thus at best amounts to retreat and abnegation of political and moral responsibility, and at worst further exacerbates the imbalance; typically, it contributes to both. The religious traditions he surveys in *La puissance* are thus substantively similar to the social and economic institutions he studies in texts like *Industrial Society*; with some singular exceptions, they too are caught up in the Disequilibrium. For Friedmann, the answer may either be found in new modes of spiritual exercise, in intentional "translations" of ancient spiritual exercises or familiar religious traditions, or in a careful interweaving of both, that is in turn integrated into a dedicated exterior effort. This means beginning with the Great Disequilibrium as it emerges from the Technological Adventure and arriving at states of "humanization" at once capable of breaking with the cycle of imbalance and representing that new relationship.

VII. HORIZONS AND LIMITATIONS

It is here that we encounter some of the major limitations of Friedmann's project, though much like Hadot, I take it to be an ambivalent and fertile boundary. Where Hadot provides exhaustive analyses of specific spiritual exercises, we see very little of that in Friedmann. At the same time, and as I have argued, Hadot's careful focus on things like ancient philosophical genre, language, and so on is itself a formal model for the necessary attention to the contemporary terrain that we see in Friedmann. In both his philosophical and sociological writing, Friedmann performs this second kind of analysis: a rich, fine-grained study of contemporary technological and political life, and thus the spiritual demands that emerge from that landscape. As I have argued, Hadot's own work necessitates the kind of study that Friedmann provides, but stops short of taking it up. In a complementary way, Friedmann's oeuvre models the kind of analysis required to determine the contours of any exercises taken up in the face of properly contemporary spiritual demands. However, Friedmann provides few if any concrete examples of such exercises—with at least two semi-exceptions in the texts of *La puissance et la sagesse* and the *Journal de guerre*. But to understand these books as spiritual exercises, they must be read in the context of his political and sociological engagements.

The first of these is the "interior voyage" at once constituted by and recorded in *La puissance et la sagesse*, a text whose depth I have most likely failed to do justice to here. Part of what grants the book this status is its recursive structure. Here, toward the end of his life, Friedmann engages in a kind of "writing the self" with previous instances of that same exercise as his source material. It is a series of meditations on previous meditations, ongoing reflections on old and at times scattered journal entries and notes from across his life and career. In this, it is already a somewhat unique document, in a way that can be said to speak to Friedmann's overall orientation toward the internal and external adventures of the twentieth century. It is, moreover, in and through this method of rewriting the self that *La puissance* is at once the kind of analysis of contemporary spiritual demands required for the practice of contemporary spiritual exercises, and a spiritual exercise in its own right. For Friedmann, the analysis of the Great Disequilibrium can itself contribute to the humanization required to inaugurate new cycles that may reach outside it.

In this way, the book is formally parallel to the larger goals that he articulates, in that it is a kind of horizon. We must first become "new"—in part, and as best we can—through an interior effort, though one that is integrated with "exterior" political struggles. Only then can such "new human beings" act upon the built and natural environment in order to begin to interrupt the cycle of the Disequilibrium, a disruption that in turn provides the conditions of possibility for newer "new human beings," who will again directly and indirectly labor on themselves in order to further humanize the "new milieu." It is a complex, ongoing process, a cycle of humanization, rather than a singular state of humanization. For Friedmann, writing *La puissance* can thus be understood as a formally similar process. The analysis of the Great Disequilibrium is itself an interior effort, of the sort required to further transform oneself in the ways necessary to further address, mitigate, and contribute to a break from within. Even as it is just one step in a process that does not and cannot stop there.

The second recognizable example of a concrete spiritual exercise in Friedmann's oeuvre is the "examination" that he takes up within the *Journal*. There, Friedmann's crisis speaks with an uncomfortable elegance, as he wrestles in real time with the fraught confluence of medical work in the face of new and overwhelming technologies of death and life, alongside the spiritual–political crisis of Molotov-Ribbentrop, shared as it was by so many at the time. His travels, whether on mission or in his peripatetic wanderings in the company of Dr. Coste, present him the living remnants of the last war: whether places of scattered memory, explicit memorials, or the "ruined" men and machines who populate the countryside. The text culminates in the devastating political echo of the armistice, after which the spiritual exercise that is the *Journal* itself fades so that another— one that is arguably among the paradigmatic spiritual–political exercises— may take its place in Toulouse. In the latter case, reflection and resistance and the relationship between them are thrown into sharp relief as forms of a political spirituality that must be further analyzed.

That an old copy of the *Meditations* partly guides the crisis of the *Journal* is again telling. Friedmann, the soldier, looks to the reflections of an emperor. The latter, as we know, seeks to provide a view from above, where that of the former is very much a view from below. That perspective, of the trenches and the hospital, or the fumes and dins of the factory floor, docks, mines, and fields, marks Friedmann's research and writing. Across his oeuvre, this persistent vantage demonstrates, in a way that we do not see in Hadot, that the question of spiritual exercises is also a political question. That demonstration alone is one of Friedmann's primary contributions here. And as a political–spiritual exercise, the *Journal de guerre*, precisely as a journal, speaks further to the role of differing kinds of exercises, their relationships to their respective contexts and demands, and in turn to one another.

If we read the *Journal* as a spiritual exercise in itself, it first provides detailed insight into the demands and conditions that practice is meant to address; it is an exercise of diagnosis. For that very reason, it can also be read as a practice of self-purification, a concept that I will return to in chapter 4. Making sense of the technological and political upheaval, especially the political crisis of the party and the USSR, alongside the situation of France in relation to Germany at the time of its writing, is a process not of quieting, but of transforming the "interior" dusts and dins of this landscape into something capable of acting "externally" on the political and technical environment. Here, the clarity, resolve, and so much else required for the next stage—in this case, the stage of active resistance—is cultivated.

At the same time, the nature of the *Journal* and so much of what it describes can be also understood to fall within the category of sustaining practices, exercises of political and spiritual survival, in the face of the very conditions it seeks to clarify and transform. Such practices of survival have much overlap with practices of transformation, but there is also a great deal that distinguishes them in ways that matter within the real lives that take them up. Among the major biographical threads of the *Journal*, I take it that Friedmann's work with patients in the HC becomes such an exercise, as do his explorations of the countryside behind the front in the company of his friend Coste. But beyond individual threads, across the text as a whole we can see that to at once diagnose a situation, sustain oneself in the face of it, act upon it, and prepare oneself for greater transformations may become indistinguishable. On my reading, this relationship is among the important recurring features of genuinely political–spiritual exercises.

It is clear that the *Journal*, like *La puissance*, performs some of the work that Friedmann's overall efforts entail, following from the requirements laid out with Hadot. In both cases, we see a familiar genre, writing the self in the form of meditation or exhortation, though one that combines a range of exercises. This combination is unique and significant, because the conditions that it responds to are themselves historically and politically unique and significant. This is further emphasized in that the focus of these exercises is the explication of the Technological Adventure and the Great Disequilibrium, especially the ways in which they both are and are not historically unique. These texts thus re-demonstrate the richness of the translation and recontextualization of recognizable practices, especially insofar as they themselves are concerned with the unique nature of contemporary technological conditions. But it is also for this very reason that I think these two texts, as recognizable spiritual–political exercises, might be understood to fall somewhat short of the full range of possibilities entailed by Friedmann's understanding of the interior effort—as those very texts themselves elaborate it—and as I have attempted to reconstruct it here.

However, the issue is not the articulation of spiritual exercises created out of whole cloth from materials bearing no relationship to the past. Friedmann demonstrates that when speaking of new practices, "new" can mean many things, including new versions of old technologies and forms of life, updated and translated for new purposes. The new always has a complex and organic relationship to what came before; past experience, practice, and shared frameworks of intelligibility are constitutive of improvisation itself, after all. At the same time, it all depends on which past we mean and our orientation toward it: there are clearly examples of spiritual exercises and experiences, insofar as they are mediated in some way by new technologies, which would have been impossible in the distant past, especially the ancient world that is Hadot's domain. There are also conceptual shifts that allow us to recognize certain exercises as both substantively identical and significantly different: either in who is practicing them, what their central concerns are, *how* they are shaped and reshaped in concrete practice by properly contemporary conditions, and any combination of the above. To belong to the same general category does not necessarily amount to a meaningful equivalence, certainly not in practice.

Here, the question becomes one of what exactly is at stake in the idea that an exercise or regimen is explicitly "new" under some definition. To be sure, there is room for such practices, and we may even identify given instances. But the fundamental question, which I have tried to draw out here, is one of the relationship of the forms that given practices take in response to the specific demands that they seek to address, and the goals, implicit or explicit, toward which they draw the engaged subject. A spiritual exercise is novel to the extent that the conditions that give rise to it are novel, though "novelty" has no value in and of itself.

With Friedmann, this means at least two things. First, that any interior effort emerging from the unique exterior technological conditions of a given time and place will be determined by those conditions. The interior effort can take many forms, however, including spiritualism, nostalgia, and retreat, among other forms of egoism and ethical–political abnegation. By definition, such moralistic efforts do not and cannot transform the self in any way that has any bearing on those initial conditions—save to possibly exacerbate them. This leads to the second point, that there must be forms of explicitly political–spiritual exercise, insofar as they can bring some transformative force to bear on the exterior conditions that produce the spiritual demands that motivate the practitioner in the first place. Recall that Friedmann never once abandons the view that the transformation of material conditions is fundamental to human flourishing, nor does he in any way reject the idea that technological change, properly controlled, is a boon to our humanization. At the same time, that humanization, through an interior effort somehow capable of transforming laboring subjects, is itself the foundation of our ability to become "superior to our works." In other words: our humanization is the condition of our further humanization, and the transformation of the technological milieu is the condition of its further transformation, because the "interior" and "exterior" efforts are the reciprocating conditions of one another. The question now becomes one of which practices are appropriate to that task, how they may be determined, according to what values, interests, and goals. How does the world that we find ourselves in shape the particular exercises we take up to reshape ourselves, in order to then reshape the world, and so on?

This formulation, and thus this question, are at the heart of Friedmann's political interiority, with several further consequences. First, it is a consequence of his overall account that such practices must move from the "I" to the "we"; they cannot simply be practices of the "self," but rather practices of "ourselves." The move from single to plural here is a challenging question, one that I believe must be at the heart of any discussion of spiritual exercises, practices of the self, or any related conceptions within this broader category. Arguably, much of the writing in this genre has been ambiguous at best on this issue. Friedmann does, however, begin to probe this question in ways that I find both productive and promising, if still preliminary.

Second, implicit in this formulation is a critique of any overreliance or overemphasis on religious or philosophical specialists, which emerges from this point about the "we." As he says in the section titled "Human Beings Superior to Our Works" in part IV, near the closing pages of *La puissance*:

> Hence the necessity of a quotidian combat, of an "everyday courage"—according to the fine title of the Czech film—for those great and most often small actions which require mastery of oneself, lucidity, and disinterestedness. This is the New Frontier, which is multiple, quotidian, prosaic, and glorious, in which men and women must struggle [...] struggling both with ourselves and with our technological objects. This is the boundless field open to human effort. It is the challenge launched toward human beings, to show ourselves, by ourselves, superior to our works.[150]

This interior effort must, on Friedmann's account, be both quotidian and popular; it cannot be the exclusive purview of figureheads, sages, or undemocratic and inorganic leaders. While it is never made explicit, this view also implicitly entails that the practices and efforts taken up by average people would have to be different in some fundamental ways than those of elites and specialists. And if, as Friedmann shows in detail throughout *La puissance* and elsewhere, the physical, economic, and material conditions within which average people engage in spiritual exercises are unique to that experience, then those exercises themselves must be shaped by that experience to some substantial degree. They must once again reflect a "view from below," rather than instruction received from above.

However, it is perhaps in these final two criteria, of collective and quotidian forms of the interior effort, neither in front of nor behind, but rather firmly alongside the exterior, that we again meet the limits of Friedmann's project. If he shows us the need for examples of properly contemporary, collective, and political practices of the self or regimes of interior effort, we do not yet see in his work any examples, even rough sketches, of practices that would meet all of these criteria in action. At the very least, however, Friedmann is in good company here. Hadot, as we have seen, does not provide such examples either, and as I will argue in the following chapter, Foucault unfortunately struggles with the same problem as well: a clear rejection of egoism within a body of research that consistently focuses on the individual subject.

VIII. IMPLICATIONS

Even as they remain somewhat incomplete, Friedmann's descriptions of the challenge of strictly exterior efforts to address certain conditions of distress and imbalance provides something fundamental that never quite appears in Hadot. The latter never provides the kind of rich description of the relationship between material conditions and spiritual exercises that we find in Friedmann, nor does Hadot speculate much about the ways that they might reciprocally impact one another. At the same time, as far as Friedmann's contributions go, it is possible to imagine further analyses arriving at new and differing conclusions regarding the fundamental conditions that give rise to the spiritual demands particular to the contemporary world, or any time and place for that matter. We are not obligated to adopt Friedmann's view that the rapid acceleration of technological change is the foundation for the most pressing demands of his time, or our own for that matter. For my part, I am sympathetic to the content of his claims regarding technological change and the specifics of both its possibilities and dangers, and I do believe that it holds great promise for the digital iteration of the technical milieu, "green" technologies, and perhaps its yet-unimaginable future forms.[151] But any debate regarding the continued accuracy of Friedmann's specific claims is tangential to my own goals. More importantly, his contributions are necessary to the broader understanding and elaboration of the idea of practices of the self that I hope to ground here, for the many reasons rehearsed over the course of this chapter.

Perhaps above all, it is the rich focus on "the terrain" that leads to so many of those core contributions. He furthers the importance of a genuine democratization of spiritual exercises, as a necessary consequence of any attempt to "resituate" the ethical and political and to collectively "re-source" ourselves. He again shows why the perspective of the everyday, that "view from below," must be an orienting point in any practices of this kind. Similarly, he shows how deeply material conditions inform spiritual demands, and therefore why there is always a politics to any regimen of practices of the self. He is even clearer that those politics may go in very different directions: either toward the cultivation of robust, just, and liberating relations to both oneself and to others, or an egoistic abnegation that amounts to ethical spiritualism, political moralism, or worse. In texts as seemingly different as *La puissance* and *Industrial Society*, we see the possibility of the theorization of a politics of self-overcoming, and in turn the necessity of aspiration to "resituate" the relationship between "exterior" material and political life on the one hand, and the "interior" effort of ethical self-change on the other, in a still-unarticulated governmentality in which neither is reducible to the other. If it is always true that in laboring on the world, we labor on ourselves, and so on, the interventions taken up on any of those fields of action must, on this view, be clear in the relations of self to self, other, and others that they will cultivate.

Parts of this work are firm and clear, and large swathes are ambiguous, as I have emphasized. This productive if frustrating ambiguity marks so much of Friedmann's writing, and we see it in the way that he revisits past reflections in *La puissance* or dwells in the fraught transitions of the *Journal*. Indeed, the *Journal* culminates in a transition, the necessary preparation for which is embodied in the text itself, among other works. It is for these reasons that I think it best to leave Friedmann here, amid one of these major transitions, tense with ambiguity, danger, and promise, in his own words, recorded at the end of the *Journal* on June 24, 1940, just two days after the armistice with Germany was signed. Here, Friedmann ends with a version of the famous question, "What is to be done?" It is likely that he was well familiar with the famous tract of that name. However, he poses the question in his own terms, in language particular to the moment in question, a moment that is especially telling from our outside perspective, prefiguring as it does all that is to come in Toulouse and elsewhere:

> Since the beginning of the war, and especially since the disgrace and chaos that have descended everywhere, I have sensed growing in me, corporeally, a new attitude with regard to life. New for me. An attitude which had been completely foreign to me until 1936, until I returned from my last and longest investigations in the USSR. There already, signs of an internal development.
>
> Today it is more than just signs. I feel as though the substance is not the same. It seems to be a question of maturation, of an experience in which the soul is steeped in pain without renouncing itself or renouncing its goals.
>
> Chaos in my country, the total chaos of the movement of human progress. Darkness hangs over this miserable species. Nothing but individuals. Working to govern ourselves, occupying ourselves with dear beings and of all the morsels of humanity that we encounter. Attaching ourselves to these little islands of goodwill, truth, and beauty.
>
> To at least sketch here, if I have the time to do it, what this attitude is (that is, without giving it more coherence than it actually has), this Stoicism, adapted to an era which I did not choose to be born into.
>
> Maybe these reflections will only be valuable to me. Maybe they will interest others who have been subjected to experiences analogous to my own.
>
> In the face of the agonies of all that which is false, erroneous, ignoble, in the face of all that which can shock one, grab one by the throat: What to do? What can I, me, what can I do?[152]

Chapter Three

MICHEL FOUCAULT

From the Analytics of Power to the Care of the Self

I. THE POLITICS OF ETHICS

In the first hour of the February 17 lecture of *The Hermeneutics of the Subject*, his 1981–1982 lecture course at the Collège de France, Michel Foucault makes the claim, almost in passing, that "there is no first or final point of resistance to political power other than in the relationship that one has to oneself."[1] This brief statement is perhaps Foucault's clearest affirmation that his concern with the relationship of the self to itself, a concern that serves as one of the guiding threads through his final lectures and publications and defines his notion of ethics, is "first and finally" a political one.

Foucault continues, elaborating in a way that could read as an overview of his work across the late 1970s and early 1980s, from the first volume of the *History of Sexuality* up to the *Hermeneutics* and beyond. "In other words," he says, "what I mean is this":

If we take the question of power, of political power, situating it in the more general question of governmentality understood as a strategic field of power relations in the broadest and not merely political sense of the term, if we understand by governmentality a strategic field of power relations in their mobility, transformability, and reversibility, then I do not think that reflection on this notion of governmentality can avoid passing through, theoretically and practically, the element of a subject defined by the relationship of self to self. Although the theory of political power as an institution usually refers to a juridical conception of the subject of right, it seems to me that the analysis of governmentality—that is to say, of power as a set of reversible relationships—must refer to an ethics defined by the relationship of self to self.[2]

By Foucault's own lights, however, the analysis of governmentality cannot merely "refer" to ethics as he construes it. It is further and "quite simply" that "in the type of analysis that I have been trying to advance for some time, you can see that power relations, governmentality, the government of the self and of others, and the relationship of self to self constitute a chain, a thread." It is thus "around these notions that we should be able to connect together the question of politics and the question of ethics."[3]

And yet, even within the *Hermeneutics* and the lecture in question, all of these statements can appear inscrutable. If it is his concern to "connect together the question of politics and the question of ethics," and if it is the case that "there is no first or last point of resistance to political power other than in the relationship one has to oneself," it is not clear, at least not from this brief aside, what the form, content, and consequences of that relationship really are or could be. Is this a formal and general claim, or does it entail some particular politics and some particular ethics? Here Foucault's succinctness obscures more than it reveals. Moreover, this passage in the *Hermeneutics* is one of the few places that Foucault explicitly identifies the goal of describing the link between the political and the ethical within his analyses, and a great deal is potentially at stake within his concise obscurity. And so, even as it constitutes one of the primary guiding threads of Foucault's late "ethical" period, the explication of the exact nature of the relationship between ethics and politics is rarely articulated and remains generally implicit within the lectures and later publications.

This is not to say that this claim simply appears without context. Foucault's point sits firmly within a deeper, though brief, discussion of "the possible historical importance of this prescriptive figure of the return to the self."[4] He notes first that this idea of a "return to the self" may not be the proper framework within which to understand the kinds of early Christian practices that he had just begun discussing in the February 17 lecture, in contrast and in tandem with the ancient, pre-Christian philosophical context. More immediately, however, Foucault points out that there is indeed something "modern" about this thread, describing the recurring theme of the "return to the self" in various forms from the sixteenth through nineteenth centuries.[5] Foucault does not, however, at least not here, provide much in the way of analysis regarding of this long list of varied figures and movements across the modern era: neither in their ability to "reconstitute an ethics and an aesthetics of the self," nor in their ability to offer us something in that direction today.

What he does note, however, is that these efforts have by no means disappeared. And while he does not pass too much judgment on the sixteenth- through nineteenth-century iterations of the ethics and aesthetics of the self, Foucault has some rare words for the twentieth-century forms current at the time of the lectures, forms that have no doubt persisted one way or another into the twenty-first century:

> What I would like to point out is that, after all, when today we see the meaning, or rather the almost total absence of meaning, given to some nonetheless very familiar expressions which continue to permeate our discourse—like getting back to oneself, freeing oneself, being oneself, being authentic, etcetera—when we see the absence of meaning and thought in all of these expressions we employ today, then I do not think we have anything to be proud of in our current efforts to reconstitute an ethic of the self.[6]

Foucault's comments here are as amusing as they are damning, though they are not without substantive content, and do not amount to a mere dismissal. Rather, they demonstrate that this problem has real stakes, both in general and for his own project, and represents a genuine challenge that must be taken seriously.

These passages from February 17 lecture of the *Hermeneutics* echo and develop Foucault's remarks in his opening lecture on January 6, as discussed in the introduction.[7] There, Foucault provides an exhaustive list of expressions by which the idea of a "care of the self" has been articulated and the contemporary and historical forms that it has taken. He does so in part to evoke a predictable discomfort on the part of his auditors at the sound of empty injunctions to do things like "exalt oneself, to devote oneself to oneself, to turn in on oneself," and so on. On the basis of these shared negative intuitions, Foucault notes that we are justifiably dissuaded from "giving any positive value to these expressions, precepts, and rules," let alone "making them the basis of a morality." As he says, these ideas and attending practices sound to us like forms of "moral dandyism," "either egoism or withdrawal," and worse. Above all, in political terms, they describe a "melancholy and sad expression of the withdrawal of the individual who is unable to hold on to and keep firmly before his eyes ... a collective morality (that of the city-state, for example), and who, faced with the disintegration of this collective morality, has naught to do but attend to himself."[8]

In these political critiques, it is hard not to hear an echo of another passing but damning comment, later on in the February 10 lecture of the *Hermeneutics*. There, in the midst of a long discussion of the idea of conversion, Foucault briefly invokes the intriguing notion of a "revolutionary subjectivity" and the idea of "schemas of individual and subjective experience of 'conversion to revolution.'" He suggests that a history of this concept should be written and then promptly drops it, though not before leaving some other rare and amusing words regarding his contemporary landscape: "And you know that these days, now, in our daily experience—I mean the perhaps somewhat bland experience of our immediate contemporaries—we only convert to renunciation of revolution. The great converts today are those who no longer believe in the revolution."[9]

Such critiques are not limited to the lectures. In the important 1983 interview "On the Genealogy of Ethics," Hubert Dreyfus and Paul Rabinow ask Foucault whether or not "the Greek concern with the self [isn't] just an early version of self-absorption, which many consider a central problem in our society?" In his response, Foucault offers more detail regarding the problems he sees in those forms of expression that "continue to permeate our discourse."

> You have a certain number of themes—and I don't say that you have to reutilize them in this way—which indicate to you that in a culture to which we owe a certain number of our most important constant moral elements, there was a practice of the self, a conception of the self, very different from our present culture of the self. In the Californian cult of the self, one is supposed to discover one's true self, to separate it from that which might obscure or alienate it, to decipher its truth thanks to psychological or psychoanalytic science, which is supposed to be able to tell you what your true self is. Therefore, not only do I not identify this ancient culture of the self with what you might call the Californian cult of the self, I think they are diametrically opposed.[10]

This "Californian cult of the self" is a paradigmatic iteration of the contemporary forms of the relationship to oneself that, according to Foucault, we have been encouraged to cultivate for some time. And it is representative, though by no means exhaustive, of the practical intersection those forms of ethical egoism (or spiritualism) and political withdrawal (or moralism) of which, he is clear, there is little for us to be proud.[11]

These remarks are fascinating for a number of reasons, though perhaps first and most generally because Foucault breaks form here in significant ways: for him, these are rare words indeed. That is to say, it is a well-known feature of Foucault's writing, frustrating to some, intelligible to others, and both to many readers, that he is what might be called normatively cagey.[12] There are, however, reasons for this. In an interview with François Ewald following the publication of the second and third volumes of the *History of Sexuality*, the former presciently asks Foucault: "Your last two books mark a sort of movement from politics to ethics. People are certainly now going to expect an answer from you to the question: What must one do? What must one want?" To this Foucault responds that "the role of an intellectual is not to tell others what they have to do. By what right would he do so? [...] The work of an intellectual is not to shape people's political will." It is rather "through the analyses that he carries out in his own field, to question over and over again what is postulated as self-evident, to disturb people's mental habits, the way they do and think things, to dissipate what is familiar and accepted, reexamine rules and institutions." It is then "on the basis of this re-problematization (in which he carries out his specific task as an intellectual) to participate in the formation of a political will (in which he has his role as a citizen to play)."[13] In other words, the work of defining, practicing, and inventing the good is not the work "of just some [intellectuals], but rather a collective work."[14] On this account, intellectuals have an important supporting role to play, but they are not, or should no longer be, history's main characters; that role is for the people.

Foucault's prescriptive reticence emerges from the nature of "critique," and the genealogical and archeological methods by which the critical endeavor proceeds.[15] His goal is not to detail prescriptive or polemical injunctions. It is rather, through historical and philosophical analysis, to de-naturalize not simply concepts and commitments, but the fundamental conceptual categories, implicit forms of thought, and invisible principles of sense that make those explicit concepts so much as possible.[16] Critique, and genealogy in particular, serves to dislodge the seeming necessity of given forms of life and forms of discourse through a method that demonstrates the depth and nature of their historicity, and thus contingency. This is not done in order to replace them with whatever it is we find in the recesses of that history; genealogy rejects the search for the "lofty origin."[17] It is rather an ultimately future-directed task that clears the conceptual and practical ground for new growth. On that preparatory foundation, the work of formulating and enacting positive political or ethical programs must be a democratic one, with the role of the intellectual in that stage being no greater or lesser than all of those others whose lives, and forms of life, are at stake.[18]

I raise all of this for several reasons. Most simply, Foucault's secondary outlook regarding the role of intellectuals speaks to one of my going concerns in this book, concerns that first emerge with Hadot and Friedmann: the problem of specialists and elites in determining the larger frame of practices of the self in their motivations, forms, goals, and so on. This role, as I have tried to show, stands in a variable tension with the necessity that all of these features, and especially a given regimen of spiritual or political practice, be determined in some significant measure by the immediate conditions, historical or otherwise, that mark a given landscape. This means that the everyday needs, perspectives, interests—that is, the *lives*—of human beings who inhabit and constitute given horizons of experience must not merely be taken into account, but must take an active role in their formulation, reformulation, and implementation. If, as I have insisted, the view from above must be a view from below, then the technologies of sight must be crafted in some significant way by those who are doing the looking.

Further, however, to clearly state that we "have nothing to be proud of" regarding a particularly "empty" form of the relation of the self to itself characterized by "egoism or withdrawal" is one of the clearest statements Foucault gives that this example, and the sort of thing it represents, is not just something that he does not want, but that we should not want, should not pursue, and against which should indeed cultivate alternatives according to different criteria and toward different goals.[19] This is much more than a matter of mere emphasis. Rather, on my reading, all of these disclaimers around egoism, withdrawal, or the "cult of the self" also betray genuine and substantive theoretical challenges and raise methodological questions regarding the constellation of concerns that characterize Foucault's late "ethical" work in general, the particular question of the relationship of ethics to politics, and thus to my own project.

First, there is what I have called the aesthetic problem, or guilt by an associated surface grammar, a guiding issue already described in the introduction.[20] It is clear enough that many of the expressions and particular practices of the self that Foucault disclaims evince an "absence of meaning and thought" and amount to empty platitudes. Others entail the abnegation of both liberatory political obligations, robust ethical relations, or both. For these and a range of other reasons, as terms containing the phrase "of the self" proliferate, "the immediate, initial connotations and overtones of all these expressions direct us away from thinking about these precepts in positive terms."[21] In the *Hermeneutics* and elsewhere, Foucault takes pains not only to describe what might be wrong with certain historical forms of the care of the self, but to remind us how intuitively and immediately awkward, uncomfortable, and unserious all of these terms sound to our ears, especially on the other side of the late twentieth and early twenty-first centuries. But he does so in part to demonstrate that these associations have also become ossified or naturalized. Thus, alongside the substantive critique of various cults of the self, there is the persistent interpretive curveball of misdirection and obfuscation that emerges from the very terms themselves.

To Hadot, Friedmann, Foucault himself, and indeed to us, the language "of the self" is often read to encode something either vapid or pernicious. It is in part for this reason that each in turn agonizes over using the term "spiritual." All are well aware that for many readers, to so much as speak of spiritual exercises is to invoke phenomena whose political and ethical content and consequences may only be understood in a wholly negative sense, which is taken to necessarily follow from these concepts themselves. These associations are accurate in many cases, hence the challenge here. If there is any substance to the aesthetic discomfort Foucault describes and that very much persists around all of these terms and injunctions "of the self," it is because certain historical iterations have betrayed a series of political consequences and commitments that are naïve at best and reactionary at worst. Conversely, however, there are also many practices that may appear to manifest self-absorption, political quietism, egoistic navel gazing, and so on, but which, when taken seriously and properly understood, ultimately may not. The problem is that upon simply hearing this language, some auditors will register a particular set of negative or unserious associations and immediately move on.

In this way, even to cautious ears, the notion of the care of the self in general may carry negative and uncomfortable connotations that are so immediate that no substantive analysis is likely to even get off the ground. The same is true for those "sympathetic" readers—committed spiritualists, self-identified egoists, and the like—who implicitly or explicitly endorse what we have all come to understand these terms, practices, and traditions to denote. The latter only compounds the certainty, and therefore the confusion, of the former. The danger that given trappings may distort an analysis thus remains a live one and a genuine concern, both for us and for Foucault. I take it that this is one of the primary reasons he so uncharacteristically disclaims the particular forms of the relationship of the self to itself that he does. If we already pre-reflectively think we understand what all of these terms and practices mean, any new interpretive or critical endeavors are already foreclosed.

Second, and beyond the question of surface trappings and misdirection, this issue of ossified associations and the problem of interpretive misdirection or foreclosure that may emerge from them leads in turn to a more fundamental formal question. Here we return to the themes of governmentality, the relationship of the self to itself, and the problem of linking ethics and politics with which we began. It is not an issue of showing *that* ethics and politics are tied together. Like the relationship of the self to itself, that these fundamental areas of human life and experience are always somehow linked should be self-evident. The problem is that this relationship, this chain of governmentality, can and has been historically formulated and deployed in many different ways, grounded in any number of practical or doctrinal orientations.

Moreover, some formulations may, for ideological or other reasons, obscure the actuality of an existing historical relationship between the ethical and political. Despite the implicit or explicit claims of the moralist, whether "liberal" or "conservative," it is simply the case that material conditions decisively shape us on the level of who we are and what we may do, even in political worlds constructed under some degree of illusion that they somehow do not. Foucault, like Friedmann, is as clear as possible on this; hence his central concern with the ways that given institutions—church, prison, school, clinic, and so on—constitute subjects, the guiding theme of his most famous works. This is one reason that there is something "politically indispensable" in general about the ways in which these domains are linked in both discourse and practice, *and* the way that they are actually linked in experience under given conditions. That the former may align with the latter to any given degree again makes such analysis, let alone action, all the more challenging.

The problem is that specific conceptions of the relationship of ethics and politics become so naturalized that it is only with critical scrutiny that we may glimpse other possibilities. Insofar as given expressions of the relationship of the self to itself amount to forms of "egoism and withdrawal," it is because they evince and emerge from a governmentality that links ethics and politics in a way that reduces the systemic, material conditions of political life to the aggregated moral self-constitution of individuals. But beyond and beneath particular claims or doctrines, this particular principle, if it can be called a principle, emerges from a *form* of thought that assumes certain *types* of relationship as given. In the form of governmental reasoning at issue, the relationship between ethics and politics is generally both reductive and causal, uncritically assuming that any relationship of this kind would take that form, even if it were to differ in prescriptive or descriptive content. For this reason, any mere counter-discourse, a view that implicitly or explicitly posits ethical life (including moral codes) as *merely* an effect of given political or economic conditions, would subsist within the same implicit reasoning. Recall that Friedmann's youthful naïveté fell within this second category, even as he shows how these inverted formulations abide within a shared conceptual economy.

Now, taking all of these parameters into account alongside my own overall concerns, what then is Foucault offering us here? And what, moreover, can all of this tell us about the nature of Foucault's ethics, especially in its political content and consequences? How are we to even go about understanding the claim that there is no first or final point of resistance to political power beyond the relationship of the self to itself, if it does not simply amount to a mere moralism? In this chapter, I make two forms of an argument. The first is a weaker critical-genealogical claim. This is that Foucault's work from the mid-1970s to the end of his life opens up a space for a revaluation of the relationship to ethics and politics that does not amount to a mere counter-discourse to the kinds of reductive and deterministic forms represented by political moralism, ethical spiritualism, or a naïve (that is, merely causal) materialism.

But there is a second, stronger and perhaps quasi-prescriptive claim, one that will constitute the central focus of this chapter. This same body of literature, when understood properly, may entail a specific revaluation of the relationship between ethics and politics, one that is determinative of the ethics of the care of the self. That revaluation emerges as a direct consequence of the positive analytics of power that initially appears in and around the first volume of the *History of Sexuality*, in the unique ways that the analytics of power determine, shape, and indeed produce the ethics of the care of the self. This revaluation at least allows for and at best entails a nonreductive governmentality in which the care of the self and the care of the other are coterminous and irreducible; in which to care for oneself is to care for the city on a level that is systemic rather than individual; in which an intervention on the level of "who one is"—or rather "who *we* are"—may also constitute an intervention into the material conditions that frame one's life; and wherein to care for the city in and through the material conditions that constitute political life is to most fully care for oneself.

This revaluation should also undermine any reading of Foucault's "ethical" period in terms of a "break" with the more recognizably political concerns of the mid-1970s. As should be clear, this exegetical claim has theoretical consequences. Foucault's ethics, specifically the political consequences of his ethics, will either appear incoherent or seem to evince a form of that egoistic withdrawal he himself explicitly criticizes, if it is not understood from the perspective of the revaluation in question. As I argue, Foucault's "turn" to ethics emerges from the analytics of power that precedes it on the one hand, and entails a reformulation of the relationship of ethics to politics on the other. Any reading that attempts to excavate the political consequences of his ethics that does not begin from that framework will misrepresent both the ethics and the analytics of power that preceded it. Foucault's ethics will thus appear as the very egoism, indeed the spiritualism, from which he, like Friedmann and Hadot before him, takes pains to distance himself—and that the positive formulation that I seek to excavate here should preclude.

On my view, to read Foucault's turn to ethics as a break from his earlier political work is not simply a problem of misinterpretation. It rather constitutes a genuine threat to the coherence of his later work as a whole, one that Foucault himself takes seriously, even if that gravity is often evinced implicitly.[22] Put differently, the condemnation of the "Californian cult of the self" is neither a simple disclaimer nor a dismissal founded on superficial aesthetic grounds. It is instead a substantive philosophical criticism of a certain form that one's relationship to oneself can take. And if the "cult of the self" is an especially ethically and politically pernicious historical iteration of that relationship, it is in part because it is formally representative of the kinds of self-constitution that Foucault must reject. That rejection, further, is a consequence of his very conception of power, as first articulated in the first volume of *The History of Sexuality* and developed through both the "ethical" writings and the elaboration of governmentality as a concept and methodological framework. It is thus a question of extracting and specifying those underlying criteria, and in turn reconstructing Foucault's positive vision here.

I will primarily focus on articulating the stronger claim, as doing so will also allow me to make the weaker *en passant* as it were. While Foucault might not use this language himself, I argue that by understanding the relationship of the positive analytics of power to the ethics of the care of the self, it is possible to articulate a formal relationship of ethics to politics that is, at least potentially and in certain special cases, mutually co-constituting rather than unidirectionally causal in form. This framing reflects something like what Frédéric Gros describes as the fundamental imbrication of *aletheia*, *politeia*, and *ethos* in Greek thought, and especially ancient Cynicism, in Foucault's *Courage of Truth* lectures. Of these, Gros says, "we should not hope for one of these dimensions to be consecrated as the fundamental dimension," characterized as they are by "two principles of necessary correlation and definitive irreducibility."[23] Still, Gros's description, while relevant and adjacent, reflects a set of concerns different from my own. A perhaps better comparison is to Friedmann's founding desire in *La puissance et la sagesse* to "resituate" the relationship between the moral and the material alongside one another.

However, where Friedmann provided a sociological and historical demonstration of the necessity to resituate and thus revaluate the spiritual and the political, he did not provide much in the way of theoretical detail. We know, for example, that the relationship to the environment, whether "natural" or "built," constitutes the subjects who labor upon it, which again and in turn impacts that labor, and thus the environment. But in his philosophical, sociological, and personal writings, Friedmann does not provide the kind of theoretical elaboration necessary to either understand how all of this is meant to "work." Nor can we find in those pages any substantive articulation of the reformulation of the relationship of ethics to politics with which he opens *La puissance et la sagesse*. Foucault, on the other hand, through the coherence of the analytics of power and the ethics of the care of the self, provides that necessary foundation, in the fine-grained detail necessary to theorize both that need, this revaluation, and their consequences.

In this way, Foucault begins to provide resources for filling in some of the theoretical gaps left in questions raised by Hadot and hinted at by Friedmann and to further refine and start to answer the guiding questions of this overall project: How exactly, under what circumstances and in what forms, can the care of the self necessarily constitute a care of the other? And conversely, how can the care of the other, of others, indeed the care of the city and of the community, constitute a form of the care of the self? How, in other words, can we understand the relationship between changing selves and changing material conditions?

At the same time, these standing questions also put pressure on Foucault's contributions, such that important new questions and ambiguities also arise here, related to both the strengths and gaps particular to his insights and methods. On the one hand, the firm theoretical foundation tends to dissipate in the face of the persistent question of collective subjectivity, the movement from "I" to "we." On the other, and in a way that in some sense follows from this first ambiguous horizon and is especially surprising given his standard methods, Foucault provides only limited historical resources for identifying cases in which the work of transforming oneself is at once the work of transforming one's world, and vice versa. However, like Hadot and Friedmann before him, both these foundations and ambiguities constitute a productive horizon.

II. THE HEAD OF THE KING REDUX

In the first volume of the *History of Sexuality*, *La volonté de savoir* (The Will to Know, or the *Introduction*, as it is inscrutably known in English), Foucault famously remarks that "at bottom, despite the differences in epochs and objectives, the representation of power has remained under the spell of monarchy. In political thought and analysis, we still have not cut off the head of the king."[24] In the time since its first appearance, this claim has become as familiar as it is interpretively well worn. But part of my overall goal here is to go back, look and look again, and take ethics and politics once more from the top, so it is worth dwelling on the head of the king once again for a moment. As is well known, this statement denotes several things. First and most simply, that when it comes to understanding power, the power of the state is only one form that power, even political power, may take. We cannot only locate our political concerns and analyses in the state, whatever its particular form. However important, the exercise of power is not simply or ultimately the purview of monarchs, aristocrats, or bureaucrats. Even as this point is clear enough, it often remains ignored, misunderstood, or abandoned in both unlikely and likely popular discourses.

Second and much more fundamentally, the model of power represented by the head of the king reflects a general conception of what power is and how it operates that Foucault terms the "repressive hypothesis" at the opening of *La volonté*.[25] When it comes to our received notions of power, the repressive hypothesis represents what is "self-evident," it is the "familiar and accepted" understanding, of which it is among the tasks of the genealogy of sexuality to decapitate (if by "decapitate" we mean "place back within a general economy of discourses,"[26] of course).

On this repressive view, power is a "negative relation"[27] whose characteristic model is that of the "juridical monarchy";[28] he also refers to it as a "juridico-discursive" conception.[29] Here, power in general takes the form of the king and the form of the law. It is a force that pushes down on autonomous subjects yearning to be free.[30] It consists in "rejection, refusal, blockage, concealment"; its effects "take the general form of limit and lack."[31] From "top to bottom, in its over-all decisions and its capillary interventions alike, whatever the devices or institutions on which it relies ... [it] operates according to the simple and endlessly reproduced mechanisms of law, taboo, and censorship." No matter the instance of its exercise, we find "a general form of power, varying in scale alone." Whether "one attributes to it the form of the prince who formulates rights, of the father who forbids, of the censor who enforces silence, or of the master who states the law, in any case one schematizes power in a juridical form, and one defines its effects as obedience."[32] According to the repressive hypothesis, whether explicitly argued or implicitly assumed, power is fundamentally something that says "no."

In contrast with this view, in describing his project at the outset of *La volonté*, Foucault offers three motivating doubts, the second of which is his "historical–theoretical question." "Do the workings of power," he asks "really belong primarily to the category of repression? Are prohibition, censorship, and denial truly the forms through which power is exercised in a general way?"[33] The answer, as should be clear, is "no." But Foucault is not offering a mere counter-discourse: "My purpose . . . is not merely to construct counter-arguments that are symmetrical and contrary."[34] It is rather to detail what he calls a positive, productive "analytics of power."[35] For Foucault, "relations of power are not in superstructural positions, with merely a role of prohibition or accompaniment; they have a directly productive role, wherever they come into play."[36] Power operates in ways that are fundamentally creative, productive, and thus "positive."[37]

To be sure, those very real "repressive" elements serve an important role in this productive framework, though one that serves to channel, redirect, and focus forms of power and relations of force. This is what Foucault means when he says that he wishes "to disengage my analysis from the privileges generally accorded the economy of scarcity and the principles of rarefaction, to search instead for instances of discursive production (which also administer silence, to be sure), the production of power (which sometimes have the function of prohibiting), of the propagation of knowledge (which often cause mistaken beliefs or systematic misconceptions to circulate)."[38] In the seeming repression of discourse around sex, for example, an entire range of social and moral forces were put in place to redirect that vocalization in particular directions, to particular ends. Sex found its way into the confessional, the analyst's couch, the witness stand, and the laboratory, and for all that, its importance and productive capacity are amplified rather than diminished.

But what do relations of power create then, if their effects are those of production and cultivation? They create forms of experience, possible subjectivities, and thereby, one way or another, people.[39] The "subjects" held back by the sovereign power of the law or the king are produced, cultivated in who or what they are, in those same relations of power whose role and work are far more capacious than the simple "no" with which one is first and immediately faced. The confessional (co-)creates the "sinner," the cell the "prisoner," medical–legal institutions and discourses bring about all sorts of new ways of being, and so on.[40] It is for these reasons that at the opening of the brief text "The Subject and Power," a late piece that in many ways summarizes the conclusions of *La volonté*, Foucault explains that it is his concern with "the different modes by which human beings are made subjects" that has led him to pay such close and careful attention to relations of power.[41] As he says, "It is not power, but the subject, that is the general theme of my research," and the analytics of power emerges from certain methodological exigencies generated by this line of inquiry.[42] For Foucault, if one wishes to understand the subject and the ways in which various forms of human subjectivity are constituted, their features and effects, one must look to the differing relationships of power within which we are implicated and necessarily participate.

In "The Subject and Power," Foucault is quite explicit that "what defines a relationship of power is that it is a mode of action that does not act directly and immediately on others. Instead, it acts upon their actions: an action upon an action, on possible or actual future or present actions."[43] In other words,

> Power operates on the field of possibilities in which the behavior of active subjects is able to inscribe itself. It is a set of actions on possible actions; it incites, it induces, it seduces, it makes easier or more difficult; it releases or contrives, makes more probable or less; in the extreme, it constrains or forbids absolutely, but it is always a way of acting upon one or more acting subjects by virtue of their acting or being capable of actions. A set of actions upon other actions.[44]

For Foucault, power is understood as "a 'conduct of conducts' and a management of possibilities," not because it can corral the "will" or "instincts" of an autonomous or transcendental subject.[45] Rather, relations of power operate as action on the possible actions of given subjects, because they are constitutive of those subjects themselves. In other words, "rather than asking ourselves what the subject looks like from on high, we should be trying to discover how multiple bodies, forces, energies, matters, desires, thoughts and so on are gradually, progressively, actually and materially constituted as subjects, or as the subject."[46] It is in this way that in shaping who one is through various institutional and practical forms, relations of power influence and direct what one may do.

With regard to the legal and punitive context explored in a text like *Discipline and Punish*, for example, "mechanisms of legal punishment" take hold "not only [of] offences, but [of] individuals; not only [of] what they do, but also what they are, will be, may be."[47] Punishment, like surveillance, confession, and so much else, "acts in depth on the heart, the thoughts, the will, the inclinations," what Foucault famously calls there the "soul."[48] In this way, we see that the very stakes of the give and take of relations of power are nothing less than "men's subjection: their constitution as subjects in both senses of the word,"[49] and the ability to exert influence over processes of subjection.[50] In this way, it is the subject that is at stake and the very site within which and over which relations of power engage in struggle. Foucault's goal is "To grasp the material agency of subjugation insofar as it constitutes subjects."[51] It is by managing the very constitution of subjects that human beings are subjected in the political sense.

And yet, the analytics of power do not end with this negative form of productive subjection. If "one of the first effects of power is that it allows bodies, gestures, discourses, and desires to be identified and constituted as something individual,"[52] and "[if] the individual is in fact a power-effect," then "at the same time, and to the extent that he is a power-effect, the individual is a relay: power passes through individuals that it has constituted."[53] Whether through confessional acts, practices of incarceration, or whatever other historical forms he takes up, it is perhaps Foucault's fundamental observation that we must begin to understand power not as a singular and totalizing force, but rather as a relationship, or indeed a series of relations.[54] Power is thus both productive and relational; it is not merely constitutive of subjects, but necessarily co-constitutive.

III. RELATIONS OF RESISTANCE

It is a consequence of Foucault's arguments thus far that where there are relations of power, there are also relations of resistance: "Where there is power, there is resistance, and yet, or rather consequently, this resistance is never in a position of exteriority in relation to power. Should it be said that one is always 'inside' power, there is no 'escaping' it, there is no absolute outside where it is concerned, because one is subject to the law in any case? [. . .] This would be to misunderstand the strictly relational character of power relationships."[55] Resistance, as understood here, is not something that is either ancillary or external to power. Rather it is entailed by the Foucauldian understanding of power itself; resistance is immanent in power, and power is immanent in resistance. Here, perhaps surprisingly and perhaps not, there is an echo of a conception of power that we find in mechanics and the physical sciences, defined as a "mechanical force applied to overcome a resisting force such as weight or friction."[56] This notion of "resisting force," of friction or gravity, intentionally or unintentionally translated into the domain of human life, very much captures the Foucauldian understanding of relations of power. Above all then, power is a kind of struggle, between unequal forces to be sure, but between mutually resisting forces, nonetheless.

Points of resistance are "present everywhere in the power network . . . [and] by definition, they can only exist in the strategic field of power relations. But this does not mean that they are only a reaction or rebound, forming with respect to the basic domination an underside that is in the end always passive, doomed to perpetual defeat." Rather, it is the multiple, mobile and above all strategic element that lends to resistance the possibility of efficacy as resistance, or transcendence into revolution:

> [Most often] one is dealing with mobile and transitory points of resistance, producing cleavages in a society that shift about, fracturing unities and effecting regroupings, furrowing across individuals themselves, cutting them up and remolding them, marking off irreducible regions in them, in their bodies and minds. Just as the network of power relations ends by forming a dense web that passes through apparatuses and institutions, without being exactly localized within them, so too the swarm of points of resistance traverses social stratifications and individual unities. And it is doubtless the strategic codification of these points of resistance that makes a revolution possible, somewhat similar to the way in which the state relies on the institutional integration of power relationships.[57]

Put differently, "power" and "resistance" are not exactly conflicting terms; rather, a relation of power is a situation in which different resisting forces, however unequal, engage and exert anything from raw force to tactical and strategic influence over one another.

This insistence on power and resistance as the varying poles of a relationship is the reason that Foucault can then say that "when one defines the exercise of power as a mode of action upon the actions of others, when one characterizes these actions as the government of men by other men— in the broadest sense of the term—one includes an important element:

freedom." He further insists that "power is exercised only over free subjects, and only insofar as they are 'free.' By this we mean individual or collective subjects who are faced with a field of possibilities in which several kinds of conduct, several ways of reacting and modes of behavior are available. Where the determining factors are exhaustive, there is no relationship of power." Indeed, "in this game, freedom may well appear as the condition for the exercise of power (at the same time its precondition, for freedom must exist for power to be exerted, and also its permanent support, since without the possibility of recalcitrance power would be equivalent to a physical determination)."[58] And so, if we understand resistance to be the deployment of force by one of these poles, we can also understand it to be synonymous with freedom—indeed, from a certain point of view we can understand "power" itself to be synonymous with both terms.

In this way, it is not simply that "power is exercised only *over* free subjects," but only *by* free subjects as well. "Freedom" is the capacity to exert resistance, but that capacity is the precondition for being engaged in relations of power in the first place. As Foucault further explains,

> The power relationship and freedom's refusal to submit cannot therefore be separated... At the very heart of the power relationship, and constantly provoking it, are the recalcitrance of the will and the intransigence of freedom. Rather than speaking of an essential antagonism, it would be better to speak of an "agonism"—of a relationship that is at the same time mutual incitement and struggle; less of a face-to-face confrontation that paralyzes both sides than a permanent provocation.[59]

Without this push and pull or give and take, without the fact of the resistance of one force to another, by definition we do not have a relation of power, but rather something else entirely, something that does not produce the sorts of effects that power does. Foucault has referred to such instances as "states of domination," a relationship of power so extreme that it can no longer be designated as either power or even a relation at all.[60]

What matters here, however, is that relations of power, in which the constitution of the subject is both the site and the stake, entail the possibility of acts of resistance on those same terms. The question now becomes one of just which historical forms resistance can take.

The Model of Counter-Conduct

In relations of power, constellations of force conduct subjects in given ways, taking on forms tailored to bring about given conducts. But as should be clear, the strategic fact necessarily cuts both ways: if the power that one meets takes on a certain form, the resistance with which one responds must take that form into account. In the corpus of Foucault's lectures and published materials, it is with the twinned notions of pastoral power and counter-conduct, as discussed in the lecture of March 1, 1978, in *Security, Territory, Population*, that we find arguably the best-articulated theoretical treatment of the strategic and agentive play of resistance that Foucault explicitly provides. Unfortunately, this idea of counter-conduct is not without its limits, and it is more or less never heard from again following the 1978 lectures.

In *Security, Territory, Population*, Foucault defines the idea of "conduct" as "the activity of conducting (*conduire*), of conduction (*la conduction*) . . . but it is equally the way in which one conducts oneself (*se conduire*), lets oneself be conducted (*se laisse conduire*), is conducted (*est conduit*), and finally, in which one behaves (*se comporter*) as an effect of a form of conduct (*un conduit*) as the action of conducting or conduction."[61] The power to conduct the conduct of others "takes as its instrument the methods that allow one to direct them (*les conduire*), and as its target the way in which they conduct themselves, the way in which they behave."[62] If this management or "government" of others by a "pastorate" of some kind is what is called conduct,[63] there are also those "equally specific movements of resistance and insubordination" that appear precisely "in correlation" with systems of conduct.[64] These are, as he says, "movements whose objective is a different form of conduct, that is to say: wanting to be conducted differently, by other leaders (*conducteurs*) and other shepherds, toward other objectives and forms of salvation, and through other procedures and methods. They are movements that also seek, possibly at any rate, to escape direction by others and to define the way for each to conduct himself."[65] Or, as he puts it a few pages later, counter-conduct occurs "always with an aspect of another form of conduct: to be led differently, by other men, and towards other objectives than those proposed by the apparent and visible official governmentality of society."[66] Such movements, without going into all of the detail Foucault does in the text regarding why he chooses this term, are referred to as forms of counter-conduct.

But Foucault is careful to specify that counter-conduct is not simply *any* response to a given political, economic, cultural, or religious situation. Such acts of resistance are "distinct from political revolts against power exercised by a form of sovereignty, and they are also distinct [from economic revolts against power] inasmuch as it maintains or guarantees exploitation." But if "they are distinct in their objective" they are also distinct in the forms that they take. This is because counter-conduct is by definition responsive to the forms of conduct against which it contrasts itself. This is one part, though an important part, of what he means when he says that there is "an immediate and founding correlation between conduct and counter-conduct,"[67] and also part of what he calls the "non-autonomous specificity of these resistances, these revolts of conduct";[68] that is, a specificity conditioned by precise goals and means, themselves conditioned by the conduct against which one reacts.

This relationship is evident in the historical cases that Foucault describes in *Security, Territory, Population*, all of which are of responses to Christian structures in recognizably Christian terms. Specifically, within the brief history of what Foucault calls the pastorate, he is not interested in what he refers to as "external blockages" or even those forms of resistance called heresies, let alone acts of full conversion, but rather "the forms of attack and counter attack that appeared *within* the field of the pastorate."[69] These forms of Christian counter-conduct "tended to," or at least intended to, "redistribute, reverse, nullify, and partially or totally discredit pastoral power in the systems of salvation, obedience, and truth . . . [within] the objective, the domain of intervention of pastoral power."[70] Thus "the struggle was not conducted in the form of absolute exteriority, but rather in the form of the permanent use of tactical elements that are pertinent in the anti-pastoral struggle, insofar as they fall within, in a marginal way, the general horizon of Christianity."[71]

In other words, Christian counter-conduct consisted in a struggle not over the ultimate doctrines of the faith in their broadest sense, but over how to understand and deploy them in real belief and practice. Christianity was the field of intelligibility for both pastoral conduct and (for example) ascetic or dissenting counter-conduct. Indeed, Foucault's examples in this case are in most, if not all, instances taken to gain their strength by claiming to be more "authentically Christian" than the pastoral structure against which they react—a stake with a long history of its own within that tradition.

It is for this reason that leaving Christianity altogether by converting to another religion, for example, would not constitute counter-conduct (although that possibility is worth exploring). Conversely, however, acting to redefine the nature and means of Christian salvation in the face of given structures, whose authority comes from their claim to mediating such salvation, is the formal model of what Foucault means by counter-conduct. The game, after all, has its rules, and while they may very well be bent, to break the constitutive rules of that field of intelligibility would be to depart from the form of resistance called counter-conduct altogether.

The example of the pastorate, from which the notions of conduct and counter-conduct emerge, remains a relation of power subject to the positive, relational analytics that Foucault introduces in *La volonté de savoir*. It is by "conducting the flock," through various practices, that its members are constituted as subjects—subjects whose actions are managed by that conduct. But if the constitution of the subject is both the site and stake of relations of power, and if power is only exerted over free, resisting subjects, then practices of counter-conduct must on some level address given forms of conduct once again on the level of subjectivity. It is in this way, at least primarily, that counter-conduct is representative of resistance within Foucault's understanding.

To be clear however, counter-conduct is not the paradigm of resistance: the two are not synonymous, nor is the former the general template for the latter. Counter-conduct is rather one historical form that resistance may take and does not exhaust the former category. But as a representative form, and indeed one of the few conceptual examples of resistance that Foucault ever really begins to elaborate, it does tell us quite a bit about the general idea of resistance and its status as a consequence of the productive, relational analytics of power that Foucault articulates in the years before *Security, Territory, Population*. And in so doing, it can be argued that the idea of counter-conduct implicates the more explicitly "ethical" conceptions that soon appeared in Foucault's work. Insofar as any act of resistance takes place on the level of the constitution of given subjects, in terms of who one is, then it is no longer an act of "subjection," but falls instead within the category of what are sometimes called practices of "subjectivation."[72] That notion is in turn tied to Foucault's conception of the "ethics of the care of the self" and indeed his definition of the "spiritual."

IV. "A KIND OF WORK": ETHICAL SUBJECTIVATION AND THE CARE OF THE SELF

In the opening lectures of *The Hermeneutics of the Subject*, Foucault defines "spirituality" in terms that are redolent of Friedmann and more or less directly reference Hadot. There, connecting "spirituality" to the ancient precept of the care of the self,[73] the former consists in "the search, practice, and experience through which the subject carries out the necessary transformations on himself in order to have access to the truth."[74] What Foucault calls "the spirituality of the subject's transformation of his own being"[75] consists in "the set of these researches, practices, and experiences, which may be purifications, ascetic exercises, renunciations, conversions of looking, modifications of existence, etc., which are, not for knowledge but for the subject, for the subject's very being, the price to be paid for access to the truth."[76] It is thus a "kind of work . . . of the self on the self," which is "an elaboration of the self by the self, a progressive transformation of the self by the self for which one takes responsibility in a long labor of ascesis (*askēsis*)."[77] Here, "ascesis" is understood "not in the sense of a morality of renunciation but as an exercise of the self on the self by which one attempts to develop and transform oneself, and to attain to a certain mode of being."[78] This ascesis "involves a series of practices" that are "a set of actions by which one takes responsibility for oneself and by which one changes, purifies, transforms, and transfigures oneself."[79] Foucault's conception of the spiritual here follows that of Hadot, and it is in this sense that I have used it across this book.

In texts like *The Use of Pleasure*, the second volume of *The History of Sexuality*, Foucault links his notion of "ethics" directly to "ascetics," and thus to spirituality, with their shared history "understood as a history of the forms of moral subjectivation and of the practices of the self that are meant to ensure it."[80] Here, "subjectivation" is described in terms "of the way in which individuals are urged to constitute themselves as subjects of moral conduct . . . the models proposed for setting up and developing relationships with the self, for self-reflection, self-knowledge, self-examination, for the decipherment of the self by itself, for the transformations that one seeks to accomplish with oneself as object."[81] Compared with the more "passive"—though even this framework is complex—idea of subjection to the larger institutions Foucault had previously explored, ethical subjectivation and the care of the self generally refer to the ways in which "the subject constitutes itself in an active fashion through practices of the self," in strategic relation to the constellations of power within which one finds oneself.[82]

In both *The Use of Pleasure* and the interview "On the Genealogy of Ethics," Foucault provides a kind of anatomy of the spiritual, describing four major aspects of the relationship of the self to itself. First, there is what he calls "the determination of the ethical substance," which "answers the question: Which is the aspect or the part of myself or my behavior which is concerned with moral conduct?" The "ethical substance" can be understood in terms of the general understanding of the "self" at issue in a given historical case, or the specific aspect of oneself that is being transformed or cultivated: *What* is being changed? *Who* is being converted? Second, there is what he calls the "mode of subjectivation [*mode d'assujettissement*]," understood as "the way in which the individual establishes his relation to the rule and recognizes himself as obliged to put it into practice." Third, there is what he calls the "self-forming activity [*pratique de soi*]" in "On the Genealogy of Ethics, or what he calls the "forms of elaboration" and of "ethical work [*travail éthique*]" in *The Use of Pleasure*. These are the practices themselves, the particular spiritual exercises that one takes up. Finally, there is the *telos*, a concept that I have used consistently across the previous chapters. This is the goal of a given relationship of the self to itself: "Which is the kind of being to which we aspire when we behave in a moral way?" In Hadot's terms, the telos includes the ideal models of sages and saints that model the particular "mode of being" that best accords with given ideal principles and toward which we should thus aspire.[83]

Against this taxonomy and the relationship of power and resistance in general, it should be clear that the forms that ethical practices of self-constitution take are variably codetermined by the telos toward which they are directed and the political or ethical demands one faces.[84] This means that practices of the care of the self can also carry with them the strategic, mobile, and responsive status characteristic of power relations more broadly. Indeed, in "The Ethics of the Concern for the Self as a Practice of Freedom," Foucault is asked whether or not "this care of the self, which possesses a positive ethical meaning, [can] be understood as a sort of conversion of power?" To this he replies unequivocally, "A conversion, yes. In fact, it is a way of limiting and controlling power."[85] And if all that I have said thus far has been coherent, then at least some of the reasons why this is the case, and at least some of the ethical–political implications of this broader insight should be increasingly clear.

We can say that (1) if "who one is," is implicated within and constitutive of the relations of power within which one finds oneself, and (2) if one's goal is to be governed and/or to govern oneself differently, and (3) if the fact of the possibility of freedom and resistance within relations of power means that one can participate differently—strategically—in one's own subjectivation, then (4) in certain cases, the strategic engagement in practices of the self that reshape who one is or who one may be can transform the relations of power within which one finds oneself—insofar as "who one is" is constitutive of those very relations. If one wants to be governed differently, then one may begin, in certain cases and contexts, by *being different* in a way that responds to or circumvents the apparatus of subjection within which one finds oneself. If relations of power constitute the subject, then the subject constitutes relations of power.

A further corollary follows from this conclusion, one that Foucault himself never really explores and that is generally absent in discussions of Foucault, power, and ethics. Here, it is important to remember that his entire oeuvre concerns itself with the ways that institutions mediate relations of power and in so doing produce subjects—church, prison, hospital, etc. The relationship of the self to itself is not immediate. Rather, it is a circuit that necessarily passes through countless institutions, discourses, practices, material and economic conditions, and much beyond. For that reason, if (5) given conditions of political or economic governance are a form of power relations that constitute the subjects living and working within them, then (6) explicitly political action on those forms of governance is also one form that practices of self-change can take. Even if only in a transitive sense, insofar as the transformation of material conditions entails the transformation of the subjects whose very lives are constituted by those conditions, then the work of political transformation is also—at certain times and in certain ways—a spiritual exercise. It is, finally, for this reason, that we must be clear: ethics cannot and does not replace politics on this view.[86] In fact, the way that their relationship to one another is conceived here makes any such "replacement" unintelligible.

What we have then is a nonreductive revaluation of the relationship between the ethical transformation of the self and the political transformation of the world. It is a way of understanding the claim with which this chapter began, that "there is no first or final point of resistance to political power other than in the relationship that one has to oneself," in which the political does not amount to the aggregation of individual morality. This perspective also reemphasizes the many and expansive ways the relationship of the self to itself may take form, recognizing the innumerable and circuitous practical, material, and discursive routes the self must take back to itself. Here, the political is not the "sum" of the ethical, nor is the ethical—understood as the active and intentional constitution of oneself as a subject through a relationship to oneself mediated by practices of self-change—simply a by-product of relations of power, given material conditions, or what Friedmann alternately called the milieu or environment. Instead, and as a consequence of the analytics of power and all that it entails for the ethics of the care of the self, ethics and politics are knit together and co-constituting; indissociable and irreducible, neither is absent from the other, at least not in the cases I am after here.

This relationship is further entangled insofar as one does not so much as try to transform the world without transforming oneself in the process, an implication Foucault only hints at. Whether who we become within that struggle remains or is further shaped and reshaped within the world whose horizon thus emerges is another vital question, though another one that Foucault himself does not explicitly raise.[87] Further, insofar as that work is never done alone, "we" do not transform *our* world without cultivating our*selves* in that process.[88] The fact of this plurality is vital and adds a dimension to the questions that Foucault raises that he, once again and for better or worse, does not address in any robust way. As Hadot puts it, Foucault's conception of the care of the self "is precisely focused far too much on the 'self,' or at least a specific conception of the self."[89] Despite some ambiguity, Foucault's focus ultimately remains on individual "selves," to what I take to be either the detriment or the promising limitation of the consequences of his own arguments and analyses.

Finally, and perhaps above all, the political implications of the care of the self are in the end never fully explored in classically Foucauldian historical analyses. With many caveats and complications, Foucault never really analyzes a mass movement. If it is a consequence of his arguments as I have reconstructed them that there are cases in which collective self-transformation is entailed by the transformation of material political conditions, and vice versa, he never really shows us what this would look like. What do genuinely political technologies of the self look like? What is the place of revolution in the history of subjectivity? Where is the "we" in all of this?

The Limits of Lost Concepts

It is here that we again arrive at the boundary waters of a project, though in this case it is a characteristically ambiguous horizon. If the limits that I have begun to outline here are meaningful as a consequence of Foucault's arguments as I have reconstructed them, they are all the more so insofar as Foucault himself does recognize them, after a fashion. This is because he leaves behind, almost in passing, a fascinating collection of what look like normative theoretical and historical resources that seem to at least circle the set of questions that emerge here. The set of notions and cases in question constitute what I call Foucault's "lost concepts," the most developed of which we have already seen in the notion of counter-conduct.[90] They are conceptually and historically rich, unique in Foucault's own work and in general, and full of analytic, and even liberatory, promise. But they are at the same time frustratingly brief, often only partially articulated, tangential to other lines of analysis, and always abandoned.

Here, I think of the notion of "biopoetics," relegated to a footnote, a beautiful, promising, and forgotten potential counterpart to the "biopolitics" and "biopower" that have taken on such lives and deaths of their own.[91] Such concepts are a horizon that comes into view from Foucault's own analyses, but that he never crosses himself. Even counter-conduct, which receives the most sustained treatment of any of this class of analyses, disappears with *Security, Territory, Population*, and finds no further analysis or elaboration. To be sure, many of these ideas have been or can be further elaborated in directions Foucault himself may have merely invoked in passing or would never have pursued himself. Still, to understand something about these ideas, even in brief, is to understand the limitations and promise of the politics of self-change and the ethics of political transformation.

We have for example the concept of "political spirituality," which only appears *once* in print initially, in the context of Foucault's famously vexed and controversial intervention into the movement that coalesced into the

Iranian Revolution.[92] At the very close of "À quoi rêvent les Iraniens?," published in *Le Nouvel Observateur*, October 16–22, 1978, Foucault concludes, "For the people who inhabit this land, what is the point of searching, even at the cost of their own lives, for this thing whose possibility we have forgotten since the Renaissance and the great crisis of Christianity, a *political spirituality*."[93] Even there, however, Foucault's invocation reads much more like the poetic culmination of a line of reflection than anything resembling a rigorous philosophical concept. It appears there undefined, and is never elaborated in the text. In fact, Foucault only repeats this language in interviews and contexts in which he is asked or challenged to clarify his meaning, and it is in contexts like these that we see both the promises and limitations of concepts like this.

In a 1979 interview with *Nouvel Observateur* recently uncovered in the archives, translated by Sabina Vaccarino Bremner, and published in *Critical Inquiry* in 2020, Foucault is asked about his use of this term.[94] As Bremner says, this interview is somewhat invaluable, as it contains arguably the most thorough definition of political spirituality, or at least of "spirituality," that Foucault provides. The interviewer notes how surprising this language was for many readers, insofar as it is "charged with so many connotations—especially the second word—in our traditions and in our minds."[95] On that count, and as I have noted often, I take it little has changed. The interviewer adds, I think tellingly, "Is this expression merely descriptive in nature?" The answer to that, on my reading, must of course be "yes," though we see in this interview and others what a challenge it is to maintain descriptive neutrality in the face of something like the Iranian Revolution.

Foucault responds by first defining "spirituality." It is telling that he does so in a way that is clearly resonant with Hadot's definition, and which I have followed over the course of this work. Moreover, Foucault's definition here is equally consistent with his articulations in texts like the *Hermeneutics*, which appear over the next several years following the interview. Strictly distinguishing it from religion, spirituality is "a certain practice by which the individual is displaced, transformed, disrupted, to the point of renouncing their own individuality, their own subject position. It's no longer being the subject that one had been up to that point, a subject in relation to a political power, but also the subject of a certain mode of knowledge [*savoir*], subject of an experience, or subject of a belief." It is a transformation, a "will for alterity" in contrast and relation, in this case, to given relations of subjection. He continues: "It seems to me that that possibility of rising up from the subject position that had been fixed for you by a political power, a religious power, a dogma, a belief, a habit, a social structure, and so on—that's spirituality, that is, becoming other than what one is, other than oneself." For that reason, "all of the great political, social, and cultural disruptions couldn't have taken place in history without originating in a movement of spirituality."[96]

And yet, just as many questions arise from these remarks, the concept of "political spirituality" and all that surrounds it quickly evaporate from Foucault's vocabulary. Due in no small part to the controversy around Foucault's invocation of the concept of "spirituality" and the overall outcome of the Iranian Revolution, political spirituality, Iran, and the concept of "philosophical journalism" that in part led him to report from Iran are not mentioned again in any public context after 1979.[97] The definition that he provides is exceptionally clear and productive for understanding Foucault's late "ethical" period in general, far beyond the brief conversation around Iran. And yet, while these brief comments may lend us something in terms of "spirituality," it is the challenging and potentially rich "political" qualifier that simply disappears.

A similar horizon appears with what is perhaps the most famous quasi-normative model that Foucault provides in the parrhesiastic "true life" of Diogenes the Cynic that Foucault explores, and indeed celebrates, in *The Courage of Truth*, his final lectures at the *Collège de France*, delivered just months before his death in 1984. Here, Foucault is not alone. For Pierre Hadot, Diogenes of Sinope is perhaps the only figure for whom "his care for himself was, indissolubly, care for others." Diogenes and the Cynics practiced a kind of audacious and confrontational asceticism that sought to radically confront and upend all manner of social norms. As Hadot describes it, "They did not fear the powerful, and always expressed themselves with provocative freedom of speech [*parrhesia*]."[98] It is this parrhesia, this unique form and practice not simply of "free speech, but of "true speech," integral to the Cynic's audacious form of life, that also captivated Foucault.

And yet, for all its attention and importance, Foucault's work on Diogenes is also profoundly ambiguous, above all in terms of any political lessons that we might glean. Perhaps first and foremost, while I think Foucault would agree with Hadot's formulation that the care of the self and the care of the other are indeed coterminous with Diogenes, I take this to be a description of a strictly or at least primarily ethical relationship in both treatments. It is a radical, exciting, and important ethical articulation to be sure, but on my reading it does not amount to a political form of the care of the city in its material and institutional basis. As I have argued earlier, the forms of life and ways of being toward which one turns and within which one transforms oneself must make direct and forceful contact with political relationships of power in order to transform those relations. How does the Cynic form of self-transformation, for all its admirable thoroughness, directly intervene on the level of political relations and conditions? I ask this with the clear understanding that there is political potential in Diogenes's intervention, but how to understand and articulate, let alone deploy, that possibility is not given to us by either Diogenes himself or, on my reading, Foucault.

In this way, I am not so sure that there really is a politics to Diogenes's mission, at least not as I understand it and have used the concept of the political across this book. To be clear, of course, I do not believe that there has to be in order for that mission to have great value. In a way, this limit on Diogenes provides the occasion to again stress a crucial distinction: not all forms of the care of the self, even when coterminous with the care of the other—or even plural others, in an ethical community—necessarily amount to a political intervention. Nor again should they in all cases. The ethical, indeed moral, care for others is vital in its own right and on its own terms. Its importance does not devolve from its reference to material and systemic transformations, though they are of course closely imbricated, as I have also maintained. Furthermore, some praiseworthy ethical relations may well turn pernicious or ineffectual on the political level.[99] On my reading, a large part of the value of Foucault's Diogenes in this context is that he demonstrates both particular forms of promise and the need to clearly specify certain limitations that emerge at the borders of ethics and politics, if we are to at all think and act beyond them.

To be sure, there is at least one area where clear possibilities for political analysis do open up, but Foucault once again quickly drops them. This promise comes in the moments that Foucault links up "the true life," the "other life" and the "other world," and then briefly links the latter to forms of nineteenth-century political action. For Foucault, the Cynic form of life serves to "manifest directly, by its visible form, its constant practice, and its immediate existence the concrete possibility and the evident value of an *other* life, which is the true life."¹⁰⁰ This idea of the true life as "other life" is certainly part of the appeal of Cynicism. This "other life," this new, irruptive form of life that the Cynics both evinced in themselves and encouraged in and for others, is for Foucault perhaps the deeper source of both Cynic scandal and promise.

However, if the "true life" transforms or leads us to "the other life,"¹⁰¹ it in turn stands in a complex relationship to something Foucault calls "the other world." As Foucault says, at least on some level and in some iterations, the Cynic "transposes anew the idea of *an other* life into the theme of a life whose otherness must lead to the change of the world. An *other* life for an *other* world."¹⁰² The political valence of this nexus of concepts is clear. While there is a long discussion of the religious nature of this claim, Foucault is certainly interested in the more worldly possibilities and iterations of the relationship between true life, other life, and other world. But how? It is here again that, I take it, we arrive at yet another cautious horizon. *That* there are political implications for the Cynic form of life seems uncontroversial, but also profoundly open-ended.

Indeed, this ambiguity is compounded because Foucault does invoke the political legacy, if not exactly the political possibility, of the Cynic true life, especially in the February and March 1984 lectures, before once again dropping the thread altogether. There his invocation of the connection between the other life and the other world emerges from a series of brief discussions of nineteenth-century "revolutionary militantism" and its link to the long political–religious traditions of "combative dirtiness" and revolutionary asceticism.¹⁰³ In the second hour of the February 29, 1984, lecture, he notes: "Revolution in the modern European world . . . was not just a political project; it was also a form of life. Or, more precisely, it functioned as a principle defining a certain mode of life."¹⁰⁴ Foucault claims that the revolutionary life in the West in this period took on three forms or "aspects": secret societies, organized movements such as "trade union organizations and political parties with a revolutionary function," and finally "bearing witness by one's life (bearing witness to the true life by one's life itself)."¹⁰⁵ It is this last, he claims, that has been overshadowed by the two former, and is perhaps the primary "support" of the Cynic life as "scandal of the truth" closer to our own time.¹⁰⁶

Foucault provides a handful of examples of this form of the "revolutionary life" as the Cynic "scandal of truth"; things like mid-nineteenth-century nihilism, terrorism, anarchism, and a scattering of other concepts. While interesting, it is important to be clear that these comments take up only a few pages and constitute an aside or a suggestion for further research at best. It is not clear, moreover, that these are the best examples to illuminate his own claims, though this is another question altogether. Much more importantly, they are not the kinds of examples that my own project seeks: cases in which some form of collective self-transformation, here in the form of "revolutionary lives," can be demonstrated to constitute an efficacious intervention on the level of material, economic, or systemic relations of power to bring about the "other world" that lingers just over the horizon.

What is interesting, however, is that Foucault does evoke the general form of such cases, declaring it a worthwhile research project, before moving on. Such a project would seek to understand the historical relationships between Foucault's second and third aspects of revolutionary life: the scandal of truth and organized movements. As he says, "It should not be thought that the dimension of the secret and style of life, or of life as scandal of the truth, completely disappears where revolutionism takes the form of organization in political parties." At the same time, he seems to limit the nature of such a hypothetical relationship to the possible clash between these two modes, rather than a space of possibility: "One can quite well imagine this analysis of the style of life in European revolutionary movements, and, however important it would be to make this analysis, so far as I know, it has never been done: how the idea of a cynicism of the revolutionary life as scandal of an unacceptable truth clashed with the definition of a conformity of existence as the condition of militantism in the so-called revolutionary parties."[107] He then simply concludes that "this would be another object of study," before moving on to discuss art for the rest of the lecture. The latter too presents a promising research program, though as it is specifically presented there, its limitations are comparable.

This is not to say that a political Cynicism is impossible, beyond the "conflict" with revolutionary discipline that Foucault notes. Certainly, the joy and audacity of the Cynics, cultivated carefully, and deployed strategically, may hold profound promise for mass organizing or the "strategic codification of points of resistance" that coalesce into revolution. This idea of "bearing witness with one's life" does not exhaust Cynicism after all, and its limited historical forms do not exhaust the potential of a political Cynicism. What further, generative roles or overlap could there be between it and the second aspect of "established organization" either in the historical cases he gives—trade unionism, political revolutions, and so on—or beyond them? Are there perhaps new, more efficacious, indeed more liberatory forms of the scandalous, audacious, and joyful "true life" that may intervene directly in the relations of power that constitute the current world and thus bring about an "other world?" Such possibilities may still be sought historically, then creatively and strategically determined in new forms within speculative practice, and identified and cultivated on the ground amid the rush of new and emerging movements, among many other possibilities. Here, Foucault leaves a rich series of suggestions and tools, but that constructive work again remains for others to take up.

I have dwelt a bit too long on this idea of a "revolutionary Cynicism," because if it were to be formulated and deployed well, it represents a potentially exciting and unique form of ethical–political life and action. But as in the case of political spirituality, Foucault only really lays the groundwork for what such a life could look like, and his investigations move on even before any genealogical interventions in this direction emerge. In some sense, his contributions in these areas are limited precisely according to his view of the role of intellectuals, whether intentionally or not. But there is one last concept, even more fleeting than the others, that I believe holds the greatest promise: what he calls "revolutionary subjectivity."

As I have already mentioned, in the first hour of the February 10, 1982, lecture of *The Hermeneutics of the Subject*, Foucault says, again in passing, that "one day the history of what could be called revolutionary subjectivity should be written."[108] This term itself appears only once in the *Hermeneutics*, but it is telling that it does so in the context of an analysis of conversion, itself within a longer engagement with a formative article by Hadot on ancient conceptions of conversion.[109] Foucault suggests that "from the nineteenth century the notion of conversion was introduced into thought, practice, experience, and political life in a spectacular and we can even say dramatic way"; that is, what he calls "conversion to the revolution."[110] It is with this example that he suggests his genealogy of revolutionary subjectivity, before lamenting the fact that the only political conversion many of his contemporaries experience is a conversion away from revolution and toward political quietism, and then quickly moving on to talk about ancient Greco-Roman and Christian conversion.

Later that same year, in a series of lectures in Toronto published as *Speaking the Truth About Oneself*, Foucault again invokes this idea of revolutionary subjectivity, though with slightly more detail. In this case, the concept appears within a discussion of asceticism and the relationship to the truth:

> After having studied the historical problem of subjectivity through the problem of madness, crime, sex, I would like to study the problem of revolutionary subjectivity. The time has come now to study revolution not only as social movement, or as political transformation; but also as a subjective experience, as a type of subjectivity. And I have the feeling that a certain light could be thrown on this revolutionary subjectivity by the interconnection and conflicts between the truth-oriented asceticism and the reality-oriented asceticism. I think that the fascination exercised by the idea of Revolution in the personal life of individuals was due [in] part to the promise that those two forms of asceticism could be practiced together: renouncing this reality, and moving towards another reality through the acquisition of truth and the constitution of oneself as a subject knowing the truth.[111]

From here, of course, Foucault moves on to a discussion of Musonius Rufus. Still, these passages are fascinating. There is certainly the resonance with the "will to alterity" that marked political spirituality. And this articulation resonates with his remarks earlier that year in the *Hermeneutics*.

Had Foucault carried out this project, a genealogy of revolutionary subjectivity, he could have clarified much that remains obscure even to this day. Perhaps under this umbrella, concepts like "political spirituality" would have been treated in more strictly historical terms, as one form that revolutionary subjectivity could take. Perhaps the brief discussions of Cynicism, ancient and modern, would have taken their place in that history. Perhaps the forms of life and experience cultivated by striking workers over several centuries; in cadre and party discipline; religiously articulated millenarian movements like the Diggers and Levellers; peasant uprisings and the like, could have been analyzed together in their concrete historical irruptions, demonstrating the breaks and continuities across them. What are, or what have been, the revolutionary "modes of subjectivation," and how have they been tied to a given political telos, in turn determining strictly political instances of "self-forming activity?" Such analyses could have further illuminated the link between who we are, who we wish to be, and the practices by which we may arrive at, if not cross, that horizon. In other words, the study of revolutionary subjectivity could have shown us the ways that revolution itself—the transformation of material conditions that is at once a necessary transformation of those living within them—constitutes one of the most vital historical forms of the relationship of the self to itself, and thus a form of spiritual exercise in its own right.

V. IMPLICATIONS

Over the course of this book so far, I have sought several things. Perhaps first among them, a theoretical frame within which the care of the self is coterminous with the care of the other and historical iterations of that form. To be clear, however, such a relationship is not necessarily a political one, as it can certainly subsist on the ethical level of individuals. This is the case for Foucault's ethics as it is for ethics in general: his late ethical works need not have political consequences at all and may simply stand as unique interventions within differing historical threads of philosophical ethics. This is not at all to the detriment of this or other projects, as ethical relations are fundamentally important on their own terms, without reference to politics. Moreover, I take it that given ethical relationships are all the better for taking the reciprocating form in question, though this intuition raises its own set of questions.

Beyond the singular ethical form, I have also raised the question of those relationships in which the care of the self amounts to the care of others, in the plural, and in which caring for others is at once care for oneself. To be clear again, however, this relationship, even in the plural, may still subsist on the ethical level; a care for a community, a family, a group of people of any kind may not necessarily be a form of political action, though it may well be. At the same time, such a relationship may also take on a political form, especially in those cases where the care of self and others occurs through interventions on the level of systemic and institutional political and social forms. It is this more explicitly political relationship of the self to itself, via both plural others and the material reality that constitutes us in who we are, that have centrally motivated my concerns here. In the reading that I have presented, from the analytics of power through the care of the self, Foucault provides a theoretical frame that allows for the possibility of both the ethical and political forms of this relationship.

And yet, the horizon of those resources has already appeared. As with Hadot and Friedmann, these are productive limits and provide an occasion to clarify certain terms and highlight the ways that given problems and ambiguities matter for this overall project. Both the ambiguity of Foucault's language and the critical (rather than explicitly constructive) nature of his project raise several issues that only really come into view when thinking through the negative inversions of Foucault's typical examples. In the case of ethical relations, we may have cases in which the care of the self is either ambiguous with regard to the other or even precludes genuine, robust ethical relations with others. This first problem is clear enough, and it is evinced in the majority of negative cases that populate the disclaimers of Hadot, Friedmann, Foucault himself, Lorde, and others in the introduction.

But there are also ideological cases in which a claim is made that caring for oneself in certain self-centered forms somehow amounts to caring for others, even as that claim itself is at once so ethically (or politically) frail as to fall apart under critical scrutiny and so stubborn as to persist in the face of even the most robust critique.[112] Such cases are so numerous and so dominant in our own world that they need not be rehearsed here, though I take them to be representative of both political moralism and ethical spiritualism. Insofar as they fall within those categories, they do not constitute forms of "care" in any meaningful sense, however they represent themselves. There are also those tragic cases in which "caring" for another somehow precludes the care of oneself, or is even to the detriment of oneself, whatever ideological cover is given for such coerced martyrdom. Whether or not a relationship of "care" exists at all in that direction is, of course, another issue altogether, though it seems clear enough that despite their own claims to the contrary, it would not.[113]

Similarly, there are certainly political cases in which "caring" for others or for the city amounts to self-abnegation at best, or forms of subjection, dehumanization, and states of domination at worst (and perhaps more typically). Such cases are often attended by ideological discourses that justify the claim that such states are in fact "good" for subjected peoples.[114] As in the ethical case, the inverse persists here as well: arguments that the care of elite selves, of whatever kind, have a positive universal political function are ubiquitous. There are, further and finally, those very clear cases of the "ethical" cultivation of oneself to ends that are clearly immoral, as noted in the introduction. Cases of religious or nationalist violence, in which the "spiritual" transformation of oneself is the very condition of murder, war, and other forms of destruction are ubiquitous. After all, whether individually or politically, we seem to spend a great deal of time turning ourselves into monsters.

These negative iterations demonstrate several further issues, some of which I have already touched upon. As noted earlier, there is ambiguity in some of Foucault's language: he can be read to run together terms like "the care of the self," "spiritual exercises," "technologies of the self," "subjectivation," the notion of the "spiritual" in general, and so on. This ambiguity can emerge for readers especially over the course of the *Collège* lectures, contemporary interviews, and so on, where Foucault is exploring all of these concepts out loud. Of course, it is possible and desirable to taxonomize all of these terms, and this work can be done by mining the texts. Here especially, it is important to distinguish the notion of "care" in the "care of the self" from, say, more neutral terms like "transformation" or "cultivation." In Foucault's work, it can be possible to take "the ethics of the care of the self" to be synonymous with "spiritual exercises" or "self-transformation," but as these negative concepts show, it is very much possible to "cultivate oneself" in ways that evince anything but forms of "care"—even in those ideological cases that I have mentioned that may insist that a relationship of "care" is somehow present in what are otherwise clear forms of dehumanization. If "the care of the self" is read as a direct synonym for self-transformation in general, then even cases that are ideologically false and morally and politically damnable would still, strictly speaking, fall within that category. It should also be noted that "to care" is a skill, and we often care for ourselves and others poorly, even to good ends and with the best of intentions.

At the same time, even if his usage is ambiguous, we can say that Foucault, like Hadot, generally associates the "care of the self" with particular ancient cultures of the self, and there is a historical specificity in his analyses that cannot be ignored. But again, there may be clear cases of the ancient care of the self that fit within and even historically define that category that we might still find morally or politically questionable—both in our own terms and those of the day. Further, it is also clear that like Hadot, Foucault is indeed interested in the historical translation of these categories. In this case, it seems to me that Hadot's language of spiritual exercises or Foucault's language of "technologies of the self," despite their own respective historicity, serve this general purpose far better. And yet, even those concepts tend to denote the specific domain of "self-forming activity" and lose some of the capaciousness of the full relationship of the self to itself that Foucault describes in places like *The Use of Pleasure*, "On the Genealogy of Ethics," and so on.

Following from this ambiguity, the critical and genealogical nature of Foucault's project means that he at least attempts to approach all of this with a kind of historical neutrality that can cause what might be called a normative obscurity. This issue is not particular to Foucault, of course. Insofar as something is a "spiritual exercise," it is a practice of self-transformation. This term, as I have insisted, is a formal description of a form of practice and has no *necessary* political or ethical consequences. To say that something is a spiritual exercise or a technology of the self is not to say that it is "good." Spiritual exercises as such do not produce the criteria of their own judgment, they do not generate moral codes, political values, or the like. That is the role of philosophy in its more recognizable discursive focus, as I have insisted—and as even Hadot understands. Of course, discursive philosophical (or religious) elaboration can very much constitute a spiritual exercise, depending on a range of criteria. However, the specification of a given telos or diagnosis or even regimen of practice is neither synonymous with nor a product of spiritual exercises as a form, and the form itself does not have an ethical or political value. Coupled with Foucault's reticence to lay out prescriptive claims, confusion arises about just what he is after when speaking of practices or technologies of the self.

I take the case of his notion of "political spirituality" as it applies to, say, Iran, to be both a good and bad example for this reason. Good in the sense that it demonstrates the nonnormative or analytic neutrality of these terms. "The spiritual," as I have noted, is not necessarily a good thing, and even those forms that tend to emerge in forms of religious violence or other ideological extremism are still very much forms of spirituality—a feature that is vital for understanding the very concept of the spiritual. It is a bad example in that the political and moral horrors that follow something like the Iranian Revolution are impossible to ignore. Without at least some kind of constructive distinction between politically and morally desirable forms of genuine care on the one hand, and strict analytic categories on the other, great confusion is perhaps inevitable.

Finally, and as I have already mentioned, for all of his concern with institutions and their political effects, Foucault's research from the analytics of power through the care of the self never really addresses the question of plural or collective subjectivity, at least not in a direct and substantive way. The constitution of the "we" and the "us" are not taken up in themselves and on their own terms. Recall the passage from the first hour of February 17, 1982, lecture of the *Hermeneutics* with which we began. Following his point that we have "nothing to be proud of" in contemporary efforts to reconstitute an ethic of the self, Foucault continues, culminating in that key passage that it has in some sense been my goal here to elaborate:

> In this series of undertakings to reconstitute an ethic of the self, in this series of more or less blocked and ossified efforts, and in the movement we now make to refer ourselves constantly to this ethic of the self without ever giving it any content, I think we may have to suspect that we find it impossible today to constitute an ethic of the self, even though it may be an urgent, fundamental, and politically indispensable task, if it is true after all that there is no first or final point of resistance to political power other than in the relationship that one has to oneself.[115]

And yet, if the ethics of the care of the self, as a constellation of practices of self-change and the cultivation of some intentional form of the relationship of the self to itself, is indeed a "politically necessary" practice, Foucault does not actually analyze in detail the forms of practice that could provide some of the most powerful historical elaborations of the political consequences of his ethics. Specifically, I mean to emphasize the fact that, whether millenarian or revolutionary, and with only the possible exception of that limited and equivocal intervention on Iran, Foucault never really analyzes a mass movement of any kind. More precisely, he does not analyze any historical instances of collective action in which "the strategic codification of . . . points of resistance that [make] a revolution possible," itself takes the form of spiritual exercises.[116]

It is in these last two gaps most of all that I wish Foucault had written that book on revolutionary subjectivity. Such a project could have addressed plural subjectivity, the constitution of "selves" rather than the self, a movement from the I to the we, and vice versa. It could have done so by analyzing historical forms of the political "will for alterity" through forms of collective self-transformation that attempt to intervene both directly in the self-constitution of the group and through interventions on the level of institutions, systemic political forms, and material conditions more generally. Such analyses could have placed cases like Iran, if Foucault insisted, both in its own richer historical and religious context and alongside those movements he insisted demonstrated something comparable: the Calvinists and Anabaptists to be sure, but the French, American, and even Russian Revolutions as well. Perhaps better, clearer examples could have emerged there.

Such a study could also have raised the question of whether, when, and how a "revolutionary subjectivity" remains when the revolution is over, and the historical attempts to maintain this form of life following given political transformations. Who must one become in order to bring about a political transformation, and is that initial transformation a condition of further transformation once the relations of power that are the revolutionary target are themselves radically altered? Is who one becomes in order to bring about political transformation who one remains following it? What forms of governmentality, and thus of subjectivity, persist across the revolutionary horizon and could some clarity on that relationship prove politically and ethically useful to future causes? Many more questions emerge and proliferate from this initial line of inquiry, and I cannot do them all justice here.

Now, all of this being understood it is worth again being clear that insofar as relations of power are in play, and for Foucault they always are, then political work has ethical effects at least, and may be a form of ethical subjectivation at most. In the same way, and for the same reasons, there may be cases in which forms of ethical subjectivation are themselves robust and nontrivial forms of political action. If, in order to create a different world, we must constitute ourselves differently through practices of subjectivation, then in order to be different on the level of who or what we are, we must create a different world on the level of the institutional and political structures that bind and constitute subjects in and through relations of power. While Foucault's genealogical work, including the models provided though his lost concepts, help demonstrate both the historical possibility and theoretical necessity of these criteria, it remains unclear within Foucault's researches what it would mean to constitute such interventions. It is only through the positive genealogy of mass organization, of political–spiritual exercise on a scale and in a form that are able to conterminously shape individuals, groups, and material conditions, that a genuine politics of self-overcoming can be evinced.

Building on the resources that Foucault—and Friedmann and Hadot—provide and with the limitations of those resources in view, I will begin to conclude this overall study with a preliminary form of the kind of analysis that I have begun to outline here. To do so, I turn to the heart of perhaps one of the most significant mass movements of the twentieth century, the Civil Rights era in the United States. This work centers the bus boycott of 1955–1956 in Montgomery, Alabama, and I take the work and thought of Martin Luther King Jr. as a theoretical, political, and practical anchor, without exclusively focusing on King or by any means reducing the movement to a single individual.

While this may seem like a jump from the French theorists I have engaged so far, there are several reasons for this choice. First, because the long Civil Rights era is co-constituted by an equally long, challenging, and rich intellectual tradition, one that speaks to the problem of the political nature of the "spiritual," understood as the constitution and transformation of oneself. We see this focus in King's invocation of "self-purification" as a necessary condition of political transformation. Indeed, I will argue that Howard Thurman, perhaps the most important theorist of nonviolence, civil resistance, and so much else of the generation preceding King and well into the Civil Rights era, is also one of the most powerful twentieth-century theorists of the subject and power, of the politics of the relationship of the self to itself in any context. Second, because the movement is both close and distant enough to give us some historical and theoretical purchase, while still carrying a sense of dynamic urgency. Its influence and importance persist: in the continuity of the endemic harms and forms of justice it pursues and in its role in shaping political strategy, including around the forms of life and practices of the self necessary to such a movement. Whether in positive forms that continue to augment theory and strategy, or in critical forms that chart dynamic new paths in new terms in contrast with the movement, or both, the long Civil Rights struggle still very much matters.

The movement is not an "example" of some theory presented in previous chapters—I have been as clear as I can in highlighting their limitations alongside their positive contributions. Rather, a range of questions, gaps, and challenges left open in previous chapters will be further specified, filled, and answered. If successful, it will provide critical resources that the others could not, and thus lend something substantive to our ability to read them. If really successful, of course, we will find ourselves with new questions and new problems. I begin with King, who will serve as our touchstone and guide, and his invocation of a political "self-purification."

Chapter Four

THE PRACTICE OF DIGNITY

Martin Luther King Jr., Self-Purification, and the Montgomery Bus Boycott

I. ONE EVENING IN NOVEMBER

Among the remarkable scenes recounted in *Stride Toward Freedom*, Martin Luther King Jr.'s historical reflections on the Montgomery bus boycott, cowritten with Bayard Rustin, is an encounter that occurred one night in November of 1956.[1] The news had just come down that the Supreme Court had ruled in favor of the boycotters, but there remained an interim period while the court's mandate made its way to Alabama and during which the boycott was maintained.[2] The predictable but no less terrifying response of the opposition was quick in coming, but it was the collective reply of the Montgomery community that King takes to be extraordinary. As he recounts it:

> That night the Ku Klux Klan rode. The radio had announced their plan to demonstrate throughout the Negro community, and threats of violence and new bombings were in the air. My mail was warning that "if you allow the n****** to go back on the buses and sit in the front seats we're going to burn down fifty houses in one night, including yours." Another letter cursed the Supreme Court and threatened "that damn Hugo Black": "When he comes to Alabama we're going to hang you and him from the same tree."

Ordinarily, threats of Klan action were a signal to the Negroes to go into their houses, close the doors, pull the shades, or turn off the lights. Fearing death, they played dead. But this time they had prepared a surprise. When the Klan arrived—according to the newspapers, "about forty carloads of robed and hooded members"—porch lights were on and doors open. As the Klan drove by, the Negroes behaved as though they were watching a circus parade. Concealing the effort it cost them, many walked about as usual; some simply watched from their steps; a few waved at the passing cars. After a few blocks, the Klan, nonplussed, turned off into a side street and disappeared into the night.[3]

From a strictly juridical perspective, King's account seems to describe the response of a community emboldened by a concrete political victory, with the behavior of community members in defiance of the Klan rooted in the Supreme Court decision. Indeed, it is both tempting and reasonable to say that what we have here, at its simplest and most extraordinary, is a group of people who are no longer afraid. And in the grammar of fear that frames such a view, one is "no longer afraid" or at least "fears less," because a cause for fear has been either removed or tempered. Here, a collective and personal transformation results from a legal transformation.

And yet, against the backdrop of King's overall reflections in *Stride Toward Freedom*, and in the context of the long nonviolent tradition within which King's lifework, Rustin's perspective, and the Montgomery movement are situated and co-constituted, any neatly causal account of these events is strained. And to take up that broader perspective, in its depth and complexity, is to consider all that must have gone into bringing such a moment about. No one, certainly not the now-seasoned activists of Montgomery in late 1956, was naïve enough to believe that a Supreme Court decision would have much bearing on Klan terrorism. Indeed, the very fact that the Klan took this action in the first place, coupled with the long history of retributive violence it invokes, justifies a perspective from which the court's decision is cause for greater concern, not lesser. Moreover, even if a cause were removed, its absence does not take away its status; a source of terror need not be present for its effects to persist. Further, even a Klan hypothetically constrained by the law—an idea that makes little historical sense—is still a dangerous institution.

To do justice to the courage and effort that King highlights in facing this particular threat in this particular way, it is more accurate to say that if this community had been justifiably afraid of the Klan before, that fear has undergone a kind of transformation. As King suggests, if the people were still reasonably afraid (or angry, or any of a range of appropriate emotions) of something that there are good and demonstrable reasons to fear, they now fear differently, and in a manner that is accompanied by a newly transformed courage. If we do not find of a simple lack of fear represented in this scene, King is clear that we do find the community in question with a new relationship not only to a threat and enemy, but to its own fear and thereby to itself. From this perspective, it is not that the victory in the court is the cause or origin of the courage evinced in the face of the Klan's threat, but rather something like the inverse. Instead, the complex relationship of courage, strategic insight, and so much else that we see in King's description of this late November action are in fact the conditions of the victory in *Browder v. Gale* and so much of what would follow. Here, for reasons that will be elaborated over the course of this chapter, a transformation "on the level of the self and of being," in both an individual and collective sense, is the condition of a legal and material transformation.

Recall Foucault's claim that "there is no first or final point of resistance to political power other than in the relationship one has to oneself." As we have seen, the confusion that may emerge from this claim is a real problem, evinced especially by the ease with which incautious readings may simply import to it a moralistic reduction of the political to an ethics "focused far too much on the self." However, as I have insisted, it is this reading that Foucault, like Friedmann, wishes to avoid, even as he does little in the way of the kinds of historical analyses that would clarify the generative depth so easily overlooked in the claim. And so it is not to Foucault that I look here for such a reading, even as he and others have done so much to show its import. Rather, to begin to approach the complexity and force of the events of that evening in November of 1956 and across a movement like Montgomery on the whole, to show how the transformation of individual and collective "selves" is the reciprocating condition of a political transformation may afford us some further insight into Foucault's under-elaborated statement in the *Hermeneutics*.

In other words, while I think that Foucault's theoretical insight is important to understanding the nature of the analysis of Montgomery that I elaborate here, the movement is not simply an "example." It rather challenges and contributes to a theoretical line that, though promising and I think vital, ultimately trails off into ambiguity in the thinkers that populate the previous chapters. I have taken pains across this work to show how Hadot, Friedmann, and Foucault help establish the stakes and contours of the some of the motivating questions that guide this book: First, how and under what conditions is the care of the self coterminous with the care of the other, of others, and of the city, such that none are simply reducible to the other? Second, how are such practices undertaken by average people, "nonspecialists," in ways that address the local ethical and political demands that frame everyday life? Despite the importance of those thinkers in framing and specifying these questions, they do not exactly answer them—nor do we need them to. Instead, in keeping with the particular historical concerns of this chapter, I approach this task primarily through theoretical and practical resources internal to the long Civil Rights era and the traditions that it draws on in its own self-constitution. These resources include but go far beyond King, engaging figures like Rustin, King's great mentor Howard Thurman, Rosa Parks, E. D. Nixon, Jo Ann Gibson Robinson and the Women's Political Council, the reflections of rank-and-file members of the movement, and many other voices, even as I cannot engage any of them to the depth and extent that I would like. All this is to say that the theory and practice of the politics of self-change do not by any means simply belong to European theorists, far from it.

In this way and with these resources, to understand the ways that Foucault's claim about the "first and final point of resistance" can be illuminated, for example, by events in Montgomery will be to finally address the practical and philosophical lacunae in the accounts of Hadot, Friedmann, and Foucault that I have worked to specify over the course of this project. It is Montgomery and King that allow us to understand these other projects, not (or not simply) the other way around. Among the primary reasons for this is that we are now, finally, speaking of the relationship of a community to itself, along and with the individual subjects or "selves" that constitute it—an analysis and a *practice* that is absent in the other thinkers that I have so far engaged in this book.

In this way, building on the tools and foundations established previously, this chapter makes at least three main arguments, reflecting the motivating questions of the book as a whole.

First, what we have in Montgomery and campaigns like it is a case in which the transformation of oneself is the condition of the transformation of the world—at the same time that the transformation of the world is at once the condition of the transformation of oneself. This includes but is not limited to the political, legal, economic, and other material conditions that frame one's life and experience, and thus who one is and might be. In other words, I aim to show that these respective transformations are co-constituting and mutually irreducible. One does not simply rest on the other, and one does not unilaterally determine the other. Here, finally, the care of the other and the care of the city are inherently forms of the care of the self, and vice versa. In such cases, we see that whether intentionally, consciously, or not, one does not bring about a political transformation without bringing about a transformation of oneself, or a community, on the level of "who one is." I take this dynamic to be a feature of liberatory organizing itself—at least at its best, when taken up to just ends and by just means. And for these reasons, it is ultimately my view that organizing itself, the mass movement, constitutes the paradigmatic form of genuinely political–spiritual exercise.

Second, highlighting the collective nature of the boycott and movements like it also draws out the "everyday" nature of the practices that constitute it. While major figures and thinkers like King figure heavily in this chapter, as they must, it is again important to understand, as Claudette Colvin herself points out in the *Browder v. Gayle* Supreme Court testimony that hangs above the door of the introduction to this book, this not simply a movement in which high-profile "leaders" directed the "masses," as it is typically portrayed in popular memory: "Did we have a leader? Our leaders is just we ourselves."[4] As important a figure as King is, it was not "his movement," as he too is clear. The perspective from Montgomery is a "view from below," from the vantage of the sidewalk as much if not more than from the pulpit, in which the daily practices and contributions of the rank and file constitute the substance of the movement. It is a movement of regular people standing in their own doorways and driveways and on their front lawns in defiance of the Klan, the same people who walked to overwhelmingly working-class jobs for more than a year. The practices that made up the movement were carried out by the mass of people harried each day by the political conditions in their own city.

Third, and tied directly to the everyday nature of the movement, the boycott was also a form of collective, communal, subjectivation. As King insists at the very opening of his preface to *Stride Toward Freedom*, "While the nature of this account causes me to make use of the pronoun 'I,' in every important part of the story it should be 'we.' This is not a drama with only one actor."[5] That Montgomery is a mass movement is clear enough. It is also on my reading a case in which the spiritual exercises that co-constitute the movement are themselves communal, and in which caring for others is at once caring for oneself, and vice versa. The counter-conduct we see here is necessarily collective, undertaken by something like fifty thousand people together, in forms that would either be meaningless or unintelligible on the level of the individual.

In sum: the boycott provides a historical model for a concrete politics of collective self-change, successfully undertaken within living memory by average people seeking to transform the material and legal conditions that framed their own everyday lives—taking into account the limitations and complications particular to the movement itself and what we might call its reception history in American culture. And while I could not articulate this model without the groundwork provided by Hadot, Friedmann, and Foucault up to this point, they themselves either could not, or simply did not, demonstrate anything like it. That is, they do not show a real case, in all of its complexity, of a care of the self that is at once a care of the other, of others, and of more than one community, such that no point in this constellation takes precedence, and none is prior or reducible to another.

I do not seek to make the quasi-moralist claim that the aspects of the boycott that I analyze here either exhaustively define the movement or approach a complete description of the conditions of its efficacy. Moreover, when I describe the boycott as politically successful, I mean that the movement accomplished its own stated political goal: the legal desegregation of the Montgomery bus system. At the same time, it is not my goal to somehow divorce the boycott from the larger history and context of the Civil Rights struggle, including the many forms of both protest and legal intervention that precede and frame both the movement itself and the *Browder v. Gale* decision.[6] But to simply tell the story of Montgomery along a neat causal–legal axis cannot do justice to the specificity of the movement, the experience of the participants, or the transformations that constitute the boycott and its consequences. Rather, my goal is to first and very simply draw attention to the status and indeed the necessity of collective practices of self-change in the ongoing transformation of the structural and legal, ethical and religious, and personal and cultural reality of this particular time, place, and struggle. Put differently, I make no attempt to explain why the boycott happened, but to instead say something about how it worked and to highlight some of its implications for the major questions that motivate me here. I make no claim to anything like an exhaustive account.

Finally, an important ethical and methodological point must be made at the outset: I have chosen to analyze a paradigmatic case of nonviolent resistance that I situate within the long history of nonviolent thought and practice. However, regardless of whatever sympathies I may have for that tradition, the goal of this chapter is not to endorse nonviolence as either a tactic or perspective. Instead, I focus on nonviolence because that tradition in general is especially thorough and explicit in articulating the role of practices of the self, forms of discipline, and "training in this mood," as well as the nature of the transformations they may engender. In other words, nonviolence brings certain formal criteria and relationships into productively sharp relief. It is entirely possible that other methods and outlooks, even violent ones, could meet these criteria. As I have said before, spiritual exercises are not necessarily "good," insofar as this concept simply describes a formal category of practice. However, my goal is to draw out those formal criteria and to show how they can indeed be employed toward liberatory ends, and the examples that I have chosen already operate within a conceptual tradition that itself highlights these very features. And so even as my aim is not to endorse nonviolence here, that tradition provides the kinds of examples that I think the body of literature around spiritual exercises requires to address the challenge of moralism and the question of politics in this context in general.

On that same note, and to be clear, I have done my best to represent the voices of figures involved in Montgomery and in the longer Civil Rights era in terms of their perspective on the role of nonviolence in those movements. However, I do not make any prescriptive universal claims regarding the efficacy or appropriateness of principled or practical nonviolence to circumstances to which I have no direct relationship. It is not, for that matter, the place of anyone outside a historic or contemporary movement to dictate strategy or outlook to any group of people pursuing justice for themselves and their community. This is especially important, as external claims regarding strategy and ethics are often used to undermine given movements and declare them illegitimate. As in Montgomery, only the community in question has the authority to decide what kind of approach can meet its own ethical and strategic standards in order to accomplish the political goals it has identified for itself. To be sure, those goals may evolve, and strategy and ethics are always the subject of dialogue and specification, both internally and with sympathetic outsiders and those in solidarity. That important and necessary relationship does not, however, amount to a license to dictate strategy or ethics from the outside—in some sense, this very issue is at the heart of King's "Letter from Birmingham Jail."

All this being established, I want to turn now from Hadot's spiritual exercises, Friedmann's interior effort, and Foucault's care of the self, to the theory and practice of political "self-purification" invoked by King in the "Letter from Birmingham Jail" and enacted in Montgomery and other campaigns. I believe that the analysis of the concept and practice of "self-purification" will also help articulate the potential role of the former three formulations in shaping and reshaping the "exterior" conditions within which subjects live and work, and vice versa.

However, to begin to address these questions and to demonstrate their relation to the broad threads of this project as a whole, we will need to first dwell a while with the insights of Howard Thurman, one of King's great mentors and on my reading one of the most important twentieth-century theorists of the subject and power, American or otherwise. It is Thurman's analysis of the politics of the disinherited self that will ground the analyses that follow, not, say, that of Foucault. In Thurman's 1949 landmark *Jesus and the Disinherited*, we find a conceptual framework that is not only internal to the nonviolent tradition but constitutive of that tradition, one that shaped strategy and practice across the long Civil Rights era, including Montgomery. It is thus a perspective that renders the politics of the self intelligible within that context, again in no small part because it carries some direct influence on the formulation and deployment of those very politics. Thurman's singular reflections on the relationship of the "inward center" to the politics of resistance, his analyses of the self and subjection orient the analysis of Montgomery that follows.

II. HOWARD THURMAN AND THE POLITICS OF THE "INWARD CENTER"

Born in 1899 and raised by his formerly enslaved grandmother, Howard Thurman was a kind of patron intellectual of the long Civil Rights era—though such a description does only minimal justice to his life, thought, or influence. Among much else, Thurman was a classmate of Martin Luther King Sr. at Morehouse College and later became one of King Jr.'s most formative mentors. Thurman was central in introducing Gandhian nonviolence to the American context, having met Gandhi in 1936 during a four-member "pilgrimage of friendship" alongside his wife, Sue Bailey Thurman.[7] Thurman had joined the National Council of the Fellowship of Reconciliation (FOR) in 1925, and this role, alongside his relationship to the Quaker mystic Rufus Jones, traces a line of influence directly to Bayard Rustin as well (I will return to FOR and Rustin in detail later).[8]

Thurman's 1949 *Jesus and the Disinherited* is a landmark, and its importance for King, among others, is equally decisive. The text can be read as a series of extended meditations on a set of political emotions. It opens with an introductory chapter that lays out his uniquely generative approach to Christianity and the figure of Jesus, to whom he generally attributes most of his insights. This is followed by a series of chapters that each address one of three "negative" emotions: "Fear," "Deception," and "Hate," respectively. The book culminates with the question of love. As it speaks directly to the example from King with which this chapter begins, and because I take it to be representative of Thurman's arguments overall, I will focus on the second chapter and the analysis of fear in particular.

Thurman describes fear as "one of the ever-present hounds of hell that dog the footsteps of the poor, the economically and socially insecure, the disinherited." This "ever-presence" is one of its primary features, a lingering unease "like a climate closing in." Fear, he continues "is like the fog in San Francisco or London. It is nowhere in particular and everywhere. It is a mood which one carries around with himself, distilled from the acrid conflict with which his days are surrounded." For Thurman, both the origin and nature of this experience are found in relations of power: "It has its roots deep in the heart of the relations between the weak and the strong, between the controllers of the environment and those who are controlled by it."[9] More specifically, it is rooted in relations of violence.

THE PRACTICE OF DIGNITY

Thurman links perpetual fear to the "varied dimensions" of perpetual violence to which the disinherited are constantly exposed, which produce what he calls a sense of "isolation and helplessness." As he says further, "Violence, precipitate and stark, is the sire of [fear]. It is spawned by the perpetual threat of violence everywhere."[10] A series of forces are at play here: "Always back of the threat is the rumor or the fact that somewhere, under some similar circumstances violence was used. That is all that is necessary. The threat becomes the effective instrument. . . . [The threat] is rooted in a past experience, actual or reported, which tends to guarantee the present reaction of fear."[11] Such is the terrorism of the powerful, even as this power is never solely exercised by some designated authority. Instead, "Every member of the controller's group is in a sense a special deputy, authorized . . . to enforce the pattern,"[12] even when any actual benefit to these "special deputies" is hard to discern. Even the built environment may play a role.[13] Real, concrete violence is enacted, which in turn produces a threat that need not be carried out again, or even persistently—though it often is—in order to produce the encroaching fog Thurman describes: "This anticipation of possible violence makes it very difficult for any escape from the pattern to be effective."[14]

However, among the interwoven themes of the book, Thurman also emphasizes the question of survival. As we will see, survival is also one of Audre Lorde's core themes. In Thurman's words: "There is one overmastering problem that the socially and politically disinherited always face: Under what terms is survival possible?"[15] The question of survival provides the foundation for his further arguments on liberatory political transformation, including the most important decision faced by the disinherited in all cases: "to resist or not to resist."[16] Thurman defines resistance as "the physical, overt expression of an inner attitude,"[17] and the text further considers the forms that real resistance may take, and the many reasons this "inner attitude" may or may not manifest in action at a given historical moment. Thurman links the problems of survival and resistance to the political emotions of fear, deception, and hate. However, and this is crucial, it is possible to easily misunderstand Thurman's project based on his chapter headings. This is because these negative terms are not critiques leveled at the disinherited, they are not meant to point out some kind of moral or political failing, and they are by no means considered unreasonable. They are instead the names and descriptions of "techniques by which the weak have protected themselves against the strong,"[18] and even fear itself is called "a form of life assurance."[19] In other words, even fear, deception, and hate are technologies of the self, and especially powerful technologies of survival.

On this picture, fear, like deception and hate later in the book, is at once a corrosive mechanism of power and a sensible form of "life assurance," a wholly reasonable response to those relations of power. As Thurman emphasizes again and again, the problem is not that one who experiences fear, deploys protective deception, or even feels hate against an oppressor has failed somehow, either morally or politically. The issue is rather that these particular political emotions are both personally and socially corrosive, as well as strategically limited. In Thurman's own words, "It is clear, then, that this fear which served originally as a safety device, a kind of protective mechanism for the weak, finally becomes death for the self. The power that saves turns executioner."[20]

Here, "death" refers to everything from physical death to a dehumanization and spiritual desiccation thorough enough to preclude active resistance. Of course, any discussion of death in this context must keep in mind Thurman's Christian commitments. The Resurrection is in many ways at the heart of his outlook, a perspective from which everything that dies, after all, someday comes back. Still, the position of the disinherited is always and in all cases precarious. The corrosive effects of fear, despair, and the like can eventually consume the subject, the death he describes here, and aside from providing the time needed to survive to engage in the work of liberatory political transformation, they cannot themselves transform an oppressive environment or the relations between "strong and weak." For Thurman, these techniques both reinforce those relations and allow one to survive within them.

The form that this corrosion takes is an integral part of the ways that the relations of power that Thurman and King describe are able to function and proliferate. For both figures, this dehumanization is not a by-product, but rather a strategic feature of the relations of power in question. On Thurman's picture, it is also necessary to understand this dynamic in order to understand and enact the conditions of its transformation. He argues that the experiences of the disinherited that produce these kinds of protective and corrosive fear (or hate, and so on), whether segregation, violence, poverty, or the like, operate on the level of the self, the soul, or the heart to condition what he calls the "inner life" of the disinherited, and thus determine the possible actions and responses of the disinherited to those very conditions. It is a process of ongoing dehumanization: "The whole experience attacks the fundamental sense of self-respect and personal dignity, without which a man is no man."[21]

Further, in an insight that he again attributes to Jesus, "anyone who permits another to determine the quality of his inner life gives into the hands of the other the keys to his destiny. If a man knows precisely what he can do to you or what epithet he can hurl against you in order to make you lose your temper, your equilibrium, then he can always keep you under subjection. It is a man's reaction to things that determines their ability to exercise power over him."[22] Here again, the conduct of conducts: the external, environmental production of fear, humiliation, the threat of violence, and so on, all serve to determine the "inner life" of the disinherited and thereby the "outer life" of possibility. This is among the core claims of *Jesus and the Disinherited*, and it is at once the center of his analysis of the material and spiritual degradation faced by the disinherited and, for that reason, the foundation of Thurman's understanding of practical resistance and political transformation.

It is perhaps no coincidence that we see something like this overall process within the November counteraction against Klan intimidation as King describes it in *Stride Toward Freedom*. There are strong historical reasons to fear Klan terrorism, and as King notes, displays of Klan aggression bring with them the shadow of past violence, and thus the production of fear, humiliation, and so on. On King's account, that fear tended to produce a certain response before the boycott, and for Thurman, that response itself is at once a reasonable one on the part of the community and a tactical goal on the part of Klan terrorism. As Thurman elaborates and King details, such acts of intimidation are constitutive of a larger strategy of dehumanization and material immiseration. King, like Thurman, Rustin, and so many others, elaborates his own experience with these kinds of experiences across his work. In Thurman's words, these practices of intimidation and dehumanization are meant to "determine the inner lives" of the community, in order to control and limit the kinds of reaction and response available to community members. All of that consequently determines the ability to maintain a relationship of economic, social, and "spiritual" subjection, with this last playing a necessary role in the former two.

The reason that the Klan chose to enact this display of intimidation following the Supreme Court decision is that, quite simply, it had worked before. In concert with an entire history of the kinds of tactics that Thurman describes, it was the kind of predictable action that had produced the kind of predictable reaction that served to reinforce a relationship of systemic oppression and exploitation.[23] The scene King recounts is striking, because on his account, something different enough now "determines the inner life" of the community, and informs this strategy of aggressive public indifference.

For Thurman, such resistance is possible because the inward center or inner life of the community has been protected enough in some way to survive until a greater transformation can come about. Although, again, I think that his account allows for even those who have experienced the spiritual death he describes to find their way home. Thurman's specific vision is again one he attributes to Jesus, whose message "focused on the urgency of a radical change in the inner attitude of the people. He recognized fully that out of the heart are the issues of life and that no external force, however great and overwhelming, can at long last destroy a people if it does not first win the victory of the spirit against them." In this way, "he placed his finger on the 'inward center' as the crucial area where the issues would determine the destiny of his people."[24] For Thurman, the process of transformation begins with what he calls the "stabilization of the ego," which "results in a new courage, fearlessness, and power."[25] This "stabilization" emerges through a fundamental recognition, or reminder, or reinforcement of one's dignity and value.

That recognition establishes "the ground of personal dignity, so that a profound sense of personal worth could absorb the fear reaction." This transformed relationship alone is of course not enough and must be built upon, but Thurman is clear that "without it, nothing else is of value." As he describes it, "The first task is to get the self immunized against the most radical results of the *threat* of violence. When this is accomplished, relaxation takes the place of churning fear."[26] In this way, the fear that determined one's "inner life" and prevented certain external actions is at least neutralized enough to pursue resistance of whatever kind against the conditions that are the initial source of that fear itself. The effect of this "immunization" on what he calls one's "inner equipment," the "inward center," "inner life," "the heart"—Thurman uses many terms here—is the first step toward active liberation. For Thurman, it is the "inward center" of the dispossessed that is targeted in relations of power, but is therefore the heart of the possibility of transformation and resistance.

On Thurman's general account in *Jesus and the Disinherited*, the source of this transformation is a religious realization: "the great affirmation of Jesus that man is a *child* of God," a point he develops across the book.[27] On this account, if one understands that the creator of the universe sees infinite value in one as an individual, that understanding serves as a kind of "inner armor" for one's dignity, staving off death just long enough for further transformation to emerge. Thurman reports having witnessed many transformations of just this kind in his many years as a preacher and educator. One may well agree with Thurman that this realization is the foundation of such a transformation, but it also seems clear from the text of *Jesus and the Disinherited*, and indeed from Thurman's lifelong devotion to interreligious and ecumenical dialogue, that even for him, particular religious commitments are not necessary for the liberatory process that he describes.

It is here that my reading begins to depart from Thurman, though not so much because of a religious disagreement, but rather for formal reasons, in part because his account becomes ambiguous around this point. Generally speaking, he describes the point of departure as a revelation through a realization, with the emphasis is on a kind of conversion experience. Of course, Thurman is clear that this realization alone is insufficient for further transformation, though it (or something like it) may be crucial to maintaining the armor of one's selfhood against the forces of dehumanization. What matters, I think, is that whatever the particular origin of this collective or self-recognition, Thurman does not claim that this moment of conversion is somehow self-sustaining or politically liberatory on its own. As he puts it, "Even though a man is convinced of his infinite worth as a child of God, this may not in itself give him the opportunity for self-realization and fulfillment that his spirit demands. Even though he may no longer feel himself threatened by violence . . . the individual must [still] reckon with the external facts of his environment, especially those that constrict his freedom."[28] It is one moment, however decisive, in an ongoing process. However, Thurman's point here is that following whatever inner transformation, the political task remains of transforming the external conditions that produce the need for that internal "immunization" in the first place.

In this section of the chapter on fear, Thurman goes on to very briefly reference a role for ongoing cultivation, contextualized in this way: "If a man's ego has been stabilized, resulting in a sure grounding of his sense of personal worth and dignity, then he is in a position to appraise his own intrinsic powers, gifts, talents, and abilities. He no longer views this [inner] equipment through the darkened lens of those who are largely responsible for his social predicament. He can think of himself with some measure of detachment from the shackles of his immediate world. If he equips himself in terms of training in this mood, his real ability is brought into play."[29] My question, indeed the question of this book, is one of what "training in this mood" consists in, or what it may become beyond the horizons currently visible to us? How is this "inner equipment" cultivated beyond the first decisive moment of the liberatory affirmation of the inward center?

Here we again find ourselves at the ambiguous horizons of a project, in this case Thurman's, even as the work in view is decisive for understanding what emerges beyond it. I say "ambiguous," because given his commitments across his life and written oeuvre, to engage someone like Thurman is to always engage in dialogue, even when exploring claims and dynamics that initially seem beyond that horizon. Still, new questions emerge here in terms that depart from Thurman's: Can we imagine this ongoing training, cultivation—and above all, collective struggle through mass organizing—as themselves constituting the ongoing process of immunization and stabilization, rather than seeing cultivation as something that proceeds from "immunization" understood more in terms of revelatory events? Is, say, Montgomery predicated on a moment of revelatory stabilization, or is it a process of ongoing collective cultivation, stabilization and restabilization, immunization and further immunization? Can we see what Thurman describes on the level of the self in terms of a perfectionism that is always ongoing and never quite complete, that is not, or at least not only, a foundation for further political work, but something that mutually develops with and within that work?

Jesus and the Disinherited provides a theoretical and political foundation for asking these questions, but Thurman does not directly link the political tasks that remain following a sufficient renewal of the relationship of the self to itself. I think this is perhaps tied to the fact that in this text, Thurman does not describe a training regimen, nor does he analyze particular forms that the cultivation of this liberatory "inner equipment" might or should take. It might be argued that, at least in this book, Thurman is much more concerned with revelation than cultivation, though there is again room for discussion on that point. Moreover, although it is very much implicit across this work and elsewhere, and much like all of the figures I have engaged thus far, the movement from the "I" to the "we" also remains ambiguous, as he does not address the contours of a transformation in the relationship of a collective self, a community, to itself. With the help of King and others, I will argue that the fortification of the "inward center" is cultivated in and through the collective political work of the mass movement and that these two stages are much more tightly bound together and at times coterminous. One consequence of this approach, I believe, is that we may more clearly see just how it is the "mass," the community, in the "mass movement" that matters most here. The courage and love required may well come from the divine, but they also come, very clearly, from one another.

All this is to say that even when these virtues are present, they must be cultivated; they require a "training in this mood," to again use Thurman's generative phrasing. I ground my reading of that underspecified training in the notion of "self-purification" invoked by King in his 1963 "Letter from Birmingham Jail."

III. FOUR BASIC STEPS

In the opening pages of the "Letter," King articulates the "four basic steps" that constitute any campaign of nonviolent direct action. They are: "collection of the facts to determine whether injustice exists; negotiation; self-purification; and direct-action."[30] While my focus is Montgomery, which predates the composition of the "Letter" by several years, it is clear that the same intellectual, ethical, political, and religious commitments articulated in Birmingham are very much at the heart of the earlier campaign. Although King invokes them in 1963, they were formulated and deployed well before. Indeed, the specific threads that I draw on in the letter predate King himself, and can be found in Rustin's notes, to which I will return below, as well as even earlier documents in the Gandhian tradition.[31] Of course, King gives these concepts his own tenor and contours in Birmingham, garnered and refined in concrete experience across several campaigns, including Montgomery.

With regard to Jim Crow, as one iteration in a long history of institutional racism, it can be argued that the first step, the "collection of facts," had been ongoing for lifetimes, even as it is taken up in other forms at the outset of the campaign. This raises an important point in relation to someone like Friedmann. Certainly, the nature of the investigation and its theorization is also specific to the landscape of the problem. The question of technological change is of a different form than that of, say, de jure segregation, insofar as King, Thurman, Rustin, and others whose lives were shaped by the latter understood its spiritual wages with a unique intimacy. However, no matter the case, none of these figures hold that such experience on its own naturally generates productive or liberatory perspectives or strategies. As Friedmann points out, our instincts in such cases are typically caught up and determined one way or another by the forces we seek to address; a similar point grounds much of Foucault's research, as is well known. For Friedmann as for King then, an intentional, redoubled investigation is required, one that indispensably includes rich and challenging reflection on first-person experiences, all of which further requires ongoing theorization—even using "outside" conceptual resources. The careers and writing of King, Rustin, and Thurman themselves are ample proof of that. In the cases of Birmingham, Montgomery, and so many other places, King concludes that "there can be no gainsaying the fact that racial injustice engulfs this community . . . Its ugly record of brutality is widely known."[32] And the precise forms by which that injustice operated are central to understanding both legal victories in the courts and the ethical transformations that concern me here.

As in any campaign of the Civil Rights era, the second stage in Birmingham, the stage of attempted negotiation, bore little fruit, as even the minor concessions were short-lived. Thus, "as in so many past experiences, our hopes had been blasted, and the shadow of deep disappointment settled on us. We had no alternative but to prepare for direct action, whereby we would present our very bodies as a means of laying our case before the conscience of the local and national community."[33] For this reason, we can see the second stage, negotiation, is an extension of "the collection of facts," the initial investigative stage. Through these two preliminary exercises, the community in Birmingham, as in Montgomery, assessed and articulated the clear but sometimes implicit constellation of injustices at issue, their individual and collective effects, and some of the forms of resistance they could expect to face.

In this way, even failed negotiation can serve as a form of the necessary work of assessment and articulation: a critical specification of what is possible, what is necessary, and what to expect from the opposition. This even included the specific form and extent of that resistance from different figures and groups within the city: even the white power structure was not entirely monolithic, and different responses could be expected from clergy and merchants, police and councilmen, Klansmen and bored liberals. All of this information mattered in the ongoing articulation, preparation, and refinement of the concrete forms of action required to address the conditions in question. In this way, both the collection of facts and the stage of attempted negotiation can be understood to build on previous lived experience to jointly constitute a methodical diagnosis of the spiritual demands particular to the crisis of legal segregation. This diagnostic work not only catalyzes those forms of experience into political action, but specifies the possible forms that recognizing oneself as the subject of an ethical–political call to action can and must take.

In the "Letter," following these first two stages, King describes the third, that of "self-purification." Here, self-purification is articulated as a form of preparation for direct action, a constellation of practices of the self, of work on oneself—not alone, but necessarily in the company of others—required for ongoing direct action. In Birmingham, like Montgomery before, the latter took the form of "sit-ins, marches, and so-forth,"[34] among many other practices. For King and others, however, those actions would only be possible, let alone successful, on the condition of an entire range of practices that constitute the process of self-purification. Following the failure of the white merchants in Birmingham to negotiate, King reports: "We had no alternative except to prepare for direct action, whereby we would present our very bodies as a means of laying our case before the conscience of the local and national community. Mindful of the difficulties involved, we decided to undertake a process of self-purification." King continues, describing, albeit briefly, the forms that the process of self-purification took: "We began a series of workshops on nonviolence, and we repeatedly asked ourselves: 'Are you able to accept blows without retaliation?' 'Are you able to endure the ordeal of jail?'"[35]

In the movements in question, the work of preparatory self-purification takes the form of training and workshops in nonviolent techniques, skills that allow one to undergo specific, and familiar, forms of physical and emotional hardship. But what exactly is being "purified?" What is being removed or exorcised from the individuals and communities participating in direct action through these practices? How do such practices "purify" one, exactly? And perhaps above all: is such "purification," with its clear ethical and religious associations, in fact a necessary condition of the explicitly political work of sit-ins, marches, economic boycotts, and direct action more generally? Is King correct, and if so how, that direct action requires self-purification? Or is this simply a laudable but unnecessary ritual? A morale boost at best, and a moralistic distraction at worst? The answers to these questions, as I have argued in the preceding chapters, are to be found in the spiritual demands to which the boycotters in Montgomery were responding and by which they were motivated, and the telos toward which their work aimed. As the November action against the Klan begins to demonstrate, legal segregation understood primarily in terms of juridical repression can account for neither its historical operation nor the efficacy of the tactics deployed in Montgomery.

I thus argue that based on King's account, the conditions of segregation are not primarily conditions of repression, nor even what Foucault calls *partage* or "dividing practices," but instead what he calls subjection, refracted here through Thurman's articulation of the relationship of the self to itself.[36] They are conditions within which repression and division are singular aspects within a web of constructive power relations. And in that way, they comprise one aspect of the relations of power within which the constitution of subjects is tied to the emergence, proliferation, and maintenance of a set of juridical–legal conditions. I follow King and Thurman in exploring two of the central axes of subjection by which de jure segregation operated: the closely linked production of fear and dehumanization. These axes do not exhaust either legal segregation in Montgomery in the 1950s or individual and systemic racism in the United States more broadly. They exist alongside economic privation and other forms of exploitation and immiseration and reciprocally operate in their service. My argument here, again following King and Thurman, is that these are representative examples among the central forms of constructive disciplinary power, operating on the level of the collective self and being of the community in question, which were among the conditions for the maintenance and operation of a set of legal and economic relations.

I thus argue in turn that for King, Thurman, and others, the spiritual–political demands produced by de jure segregation required the strategic articulation and deployment of practices of collective subjectivation in order to shift legal and political conditions in Montgomery.[37] In other words, the situation required and gave rise to a genuine politics of self-change, the framework and model that it has been my goal to articulate over the course of this book. Here, it takes concrete form in the third and fourth aspects of King' schema: self-purification and direct action itself. Indeed, just as I have already suggested that both "fact collecting" and "negotiation" in King's terms already complicate and further specify the diagnostic work of identifying spiritual demands, I argue that both self-purification and direct action here constitute closely linked but not identical subcategories of spiritual exercise. The concrete historical case of Montgomery allows us to see a necessarily reciprocal relationship between the care of the self and the care of the other, self-change and political transformation, and above all, the ethical labor of constituting new forms of dignity that operate directly on the conditions under which both individual and community further co-constitute one another. And it will, I hope to demonstrate, tell us even more about the care of the self, spiritual exercises, the interior effort, and what King and others call self-purification. It will finally articulate their necessary role in shaping and reshaping the "exterior" conditions within which subjects live, work, and practice.

IV. SEGREGATION AND SUBJECTION

Following the brief autobiographical account in *Stride Toward Freedom* of how he came to be minister of the Dexter Avenue Baptist Church in Montgomery in 1955, King surveys the range of institutional practices constitutive of legal segregation in that city, by which "the two communities moved, as it were, along separate channels."[38] The system was exhaustive, and included outright segregation in cases such as educational institutions and taxi services, extending into a massive disparity in income and domestic material conditions, a lack of legal recourse for Black citizens and "the unequal justice of Southern courts,"[39] and the plague of voter disenfranchisement.[40]

Each of these examples is in its own way representative of the wider system of segregation in its forms, tactics, and effects, just as each helps illuminate what is at stake ethically and politically in situations of this kind. This is in no small part because in discussing each, however briefly, King consistently insists that questions of dignity versus indignity, fear versus courage, trust versus suspicion, weariness versus peace are at the very heart of the situation as a whole and are present in each of its instantiations. He is clear that the emotional and personal wages of the practices that accompany the material custom of demanding that two groups of people stand, shop, live, commute, etc., in two different places are an integral part of the maintenance of the larger constellation of political and economic relations.

King finds particular significance in those insidious forms of segregation by which people could physically inhabit the same space, but would be treated in different ways. Although the Black and white citizens of Montgomery "used the same shopping centers . . . Negroes were sometimes forced to wait until all the whites had been served, and they were seldom given the dignity of courtesy titles."[41] Among many other examples of this kind of practice, the bus system is, of course, among the most infamous. There "Negroes and whites . . . rode to work together at either ends of the same buses, with a sharp line of separation between the two."[42] That "sharp line" was far more than a physical division and was reinforced by practices and habits whose symbolic potency was equal to that of the material aspect of the division that these two poles served to co-constitute. King reminds us that it was in this context that "the Negro was daily reminded of the indignities of segregation," describing, for example, the "abusive and vituperative" speech and actions of white bus drivers who hurled repulsive and dehumanizing language and threats toward Black passengers.[43] Further, "Negro passengers [frequently] paid their fares at the front door, and then were forced to get off and re-board the bus at the rear. Often the bus pulled off with the Negro's dime in the box before he had time to reach the rear door."[44]

It is significant that what he describes as "an even more humiliating practice" became the point from which the historic events of the year following King's arrival in Montgomery were set into motion. It was the ostensibly simple question of seating that produced such customs as forcing Black riders to stand over empty seats in the white section:

THE PRACTICE OF DIGNITY

Even if the bus had no white passengers, and Negroes were packed throughout, they were prohibited from sitting in the first four seats (which held ten persons). But the practice went further. If white passengers were already occupying all of their reserved seats and additional white people boarded the bus, Negroes sitting in the unreserved section immediately behind the whites were asked to stand so that the whites could be seated. If the Negroes refused to stand and move back, they were arrested. In most instances the Negroes submitted without protest.[45]

Even on those occasions when some individual would attempt to protest this situation, as in the case of the Reverend Vernon Johns, they would sometimes find themselves quite literally standing alone:

One day [Johns] boarded a bus and sat in one of the front seats reserved for whites only. The bus driver demanded that he move back. Mr. Johns refused. The operator then ordered him off the bus. Again Mr. Johns refused, until the driver agreed to return his fare. Before leaving, Mr. Johns stood in the aisle and asked how many of his people would follow him off the bus in protest. Not a single person responded.

King reports that Johns was told a few days later when speaking with another passenger present during his protest that he simply ought to have known better.[46]

For King, the case of Reverend Johns is not simply an example of a by-product of the system, but one of the underlying tactics by which such a system operates at all. In such cases, forcing someone off of a bus or even having them arrested are not simply mechanistic responses to breaches in given rules, and do not function alone.[47] Rather, on King's account, practices of humiliation and personal degradation necessarily accompany such a legal apparatus and work to preemptively command or control behavior and potential responses of subjected peoples—again, a conduct of conducts. Even acts like arresting someone or forcing them off the bus, which we take to act upon a purely juridical subject, to again use Foucault's terms, carry with them a productive force whose efficacy is of a piece with that of name-calling and making people stand over empty seats.

Like Thurman, King never blames or locates the causes of injustice within the community itself. And again like Thurman, he pays meticulous attention to the dehumanizing effects that segregation had on the soul of the community and that, on both of their accounts, "needed to be remedied before any real social progress could be effected."[48] Insofar as such problems are not only the result of given conditions, but serve a role in maintaining them, the stakes of addressing them are clear to King. On his account, a persistent indifference that "expressed itself in a lack of participation in any move toward better racial conditions and a sort of tacit acceptance of things as they were," as well as fears that any action would jeopardize the relative economic security of certain community members, and finally what he describes as a "sheer apathy," all needed to be addressed.[49]

For King, this situation and these problems were rooted in what he calls, again echoing Thurman, "a far more basic force" in the form of a "corroding sense of inferiority, which often expresses itself in a lack of self-respect." As he describes it,

> Many unconsciously wondered whether they actually deserved any better conditions. Their minds and souls were so conditioned to the system of segregation that they submissively adjusted themselves to things as they were. This is the ultimate tragedy of segregation. It not only harms one physically but injures one spiritually. It scars the soul and degrades the personality, while confirming the segregator in a false estimate of his own superiority. It is a system which forever stares the segregated in the face, saying: "You are less than . . ." "You are not equal too . . ." The system of segregation itself was responsible for much of the passivity of the Negroes of Montgomery.[50]

On this reading, the system of exclusion is at once a system of productive subjection.

King himself was no stranger to what this looked and felt like. Indeed, this theme appears almost immediately in the book when he recounts early memories of his father's encounters with segregation or his own experiences as a young man.[51] In language again redolent of Thurman, King describes the effects of systemic dehumanization on his own inward center: "As a teenager I had never been able to accept the fact of having to go to the back of the bus or sit in the segregated section of a train. The first time that I had been seated behind a curtain in a dining car, I felt as if the curtain had been dropped on my selfhood . . . the very idea of separation did something to my sense of dignity and self-respect."[52] King echoes this in the "Letter," when he describes the experience of articulating the realities of systemic racism to his daughter. There, he shares the experience of seeing "the "ominous clouds of inferiority beginning to form in her little mental sky, and [seeing] her beginning to distort her personality by developing an unconscious bitterness toward white people." This "curtain" that he describes falling upon his own selfhood, that of his children, and of so many others found King forever battling what he calls a "degenerating sense of 'nobodiness.'"[53] For King, as for Thurman, this "curtain" was not merely an effect of segregation, but the condition on which such a system is possible. It is for this reason that so many of the slogans of the long Civil Rights era joined language to practices that demanded the recognition of selfhood, humanity, and dignity. Here, one need look no further than the iconic signs carried by Memphis sanitation workers in 1968 that simply read "I Am A Man."

Now, there is another side to this overall picture, one that is as important as it is false, and that must be carefully distinguished from the historical picture that King and Thurman describe. In both designing policy and responding to the movement, whether rhetorically or in many of the brutal actions taken against protesters, the city of Montgomery, the police, and any unofficial white "deputies" operated according to well-known and long-standing racialized assumptions regarding the Black community.[54] Such views and accompanying practices significantly predate Jim Crow and persisted as ideological weaponry in the maintenance of white supremacy in its various iterations. They thus came naturally to twentieth-century segregationists. In cases like Montgomery, racist commitments accompanied and justified strategic assumptions regarding the tactical efficacy of intimidation, humiliation, and anti-solidaristic appeals to individual well-being over collective good.

However, and to be as clear as possible: as King, Rustin, Thurman, and others are adamant, it is not the case that these assumptions were ever in fact true, even as the production of fear and humiliation were integral to the maintenance of the system of segregation. The point is rather more complex and is dependent upon the claims that I have built over the preceding chapters. Relations of power, of subjection, are both dynamic and uneven by definition. The assumptions that the powerful hold about an oppressed group as subjects need not necessarily be *correct* in order to operate effectively. This is especially the case if claims regarding the ontological status of a given group are naturalized, and thus understood to describe the "truth" of the transcendental nature of the other. A tactic may "work" well enough (however "working" is understood in a given case), even as those who deploy it are overconfidently incorrect about the reasons for its operation. As King and others knew well, this gap presents a strategic opening, allowing them to take tactical advantage of the assumptions in question.

At what I take to be an important level, then, part of this ideological chasm entails conflicting notions of the self in general, beyond just the nature of particular subjects, though that is a discussion for another time. What matters is that historical claims about the "nature" of subjected peoples do not need to be the case for tactics of intimidation, violence, humiliation, and economic deprivation to work. To put it more bluntly: it is eminently and profoundly sensible to be afraid of a group like the Klan, and even to endure certain privations of dignity when, for example, one simply needs to get to work. Indeed, the very simple reason that the scene in November with which we opened is so remarkable is that, regardless of any legal protection, no one could possibly be blamed for hiding at the presence of the one of the most violent terrorist organizations in American history. Racist claims about the ontological nature of a given group are certainly not necessary to understand that rather simple point, regardless of the views held by the Klan, White Citizens Council (WCC), or a Montgomery city bus driver. Here, it goes without saying that any claims thus made on my part in this chapter reflect the account given by King and Thurman.

All this is to say that if in Montgomery, "While there were always some who struck out against segregation, the largest number accepted it without apparent protest," and if they seemed "resigned to segregation . . . [and] accepted the abuses and indignities that came with it," King and others saw an intimate relationship between those abuses and that resignation.[55] And as uneven as the production of that relationship may have been, if King is correct, under certain conditions and in certain ways, it "functioned," at least for a time.

V. THE EMERGENCE OF THE MOVEMENT

In *Stride Toward Freedom*, King notes that it is perhaps impossible to provide a comprehensive explanation for why the movement emerged as it did, when it did: "Every rational explanation breaks down at some point. There is something about the protest that is suprarational; it cannot be explained without a divine dimension."[56] Indeed, by 1955, the idea for a boycott had already been circulating among the veteran activists of several important Montgomery organizations, though such an action had not yet been taken up. And yet, for whatever reason, some constellation of factors came into alignment with the arrest of local NAACP secretary Rosa Parks on December 1, 1955.

Despite popular assumptions, "the charismatic leader—Dr. Martin Luther King Jr.—did not formulate the plan for a mass boycott in Montgomery." Its origins are rather more complex and communal: "E. D. Nixon, a longtime resident of the city, who had only a grammar school education, and members of the Women's Political Council [WPC] led by Jo Ann Robinson, an English teacher at Alabama State College, were the ones primarily responsible for planning the boycott."[57] Nor did the idea for the boycott emerge spontaneously from Mrs. Parks's refusal to move and subsequent arrest, which was itself, by her own account, something with which she (and others) already had a great deal of experience. "Indeed, in the 1940s Mrs. Parks had refused several times to comply with segregation rules on buses" and had in those years already been "ejected from a bus for failing to comply."[58] As she put it to Aldon Morris in a 1981 interview, "My resistance to being mistreated on the buses and anywhere else was just a regular thing with me and not just that day."[59] Further still, as the adult advisor to the NAACP Youth Council from 1954 to 1955, Parks served as a mentor to young people who "took rides and sat in the front seats of segregated buses, then returned to the Youth Council to discuss their acts of defiance with Mrs. Parks."[60] Finally, Parks had also attended a series of nonviolent training workshops at the famous Highlander Folk School in New Market, Tennessee, in the summer of 1955, just a few months before her action on the bus.[61]

By the time of Parks's arrest at the end of 1955, she and Nixon had already had a working relationship dating back at least a decade: "During most of the years that Mrs. Parks worked as secretary for the NAACP, Nixon served as its president." It was Nixon who posted Parks's bond and that evening sought her consent for "the use of her case to challenge the Jim Crow laws on the buses. She agreed." That same evening, Nixon, using a map of Montgomery and a slide rule, did a few calculations, and "discovered that there wasn't a single spot in Montgomery a man couldn't walk to work if he really wanted to. I said it ain't no reason in the world why we should lose the boycott because people couldn't get to work."[62]

Nixon and Parks were not the only people in Montgomery considering a boycott. On the day of Parks's arrest, the WPC was also discussing and planning such an action. This important group of professional Black women had already confronted the City Commission twice in 1954 over issues related to bus segregation, and in 1955 over hiring Black police and the condition of parks and playgrounds in the Black community. Indeed, the WPC had already begun to plan a boycott several months before the Parks arrest, on the occasion of the arrest of Claudette Colvin on March 2, 1955.[63] Nixon and the WPC began the mobilization together, bringing in students and teachers from Alabama State University, and key Montgomery ministers like E. N. French and Ralph Abernathy, who all played central roles over the following year.

On December 5, 1955, four days after Parks's arrest, Nixon, Abernathy, and others met to formulate the demands to present to the bus company. They also agreed to form an "organization of organizations," so as to avoid both the bureaucracy of larger organizations like the NAACP and the internal politics among local organizations. That evening, the Montgomery Improvement Association (MIA) was formed, with the young Martin Luther King Jr. as its first president. Abernathy had originally asked Nixon to serve as president, but Nixon felt that a minister "would be more appropriate" from numerous organizational standpoints.[64] King fit the bill in a number of ways.

King was only twenty-five years old when he became the minister at Dexter Avenue, and twenty-six when the Montgomery movement began.[65] And while his collected writings evince a lifelong interest in nonviolence, he was not exactly versed in nonviolent traditions, nor was he yet an organizer. Indeed, on some accounts he was chosen as the figurehead and president of the newly formed MIA for at least two reasons, though they are by no means exhaustive.

First, for his clear charisma and rhetorical skills: "A few months before Mrs. Parks' arrest, Nixon had heard King give a guest lecture for the NAACP. Nixon remembers that he was so impressed with King's speaking abilities that he told a friend who attended the lecture, 'I don't know how I am going to do it but someday I am going to hang him to the stars. On December 5, 1955, I hung him there.'"[66]

Second, King was also an attractive leader thanks to his youth and what Morris calls his "newcomer status." King had few or no commitments among the various organizations that might be at odds with one another. Nor was he beholden to the white power structure, which Morris argues attempted to "co-opt and control black leaders by giving them personal rewards." Thus "the newcomer status enabled ministers to be independent of the white power structure in actuality and in the eyes of the community."[67] In other words, it was in part King's *inexperience* that placed him in such a central position within the movement. As Rustin put it much later, driving home the point about the relationship between struggle and preparation:

> I do not believe that one does honor to Dr. King by assuming that, somehow, he had been prepared for this job. He had not been prepared for it: either tactically, strategically, or [in] his understanding of nonviolence. The glorious thing is that he came to a profoundly deep understanding of nonviolence through the struggle itself, and through reading and discussions which he had in the process of carrying on the protest, and not that in some way, college professors who had read Gandhi had prepared him in advance. This is just a hoax.[68]

But it was not just King who was inexperienced, or who would come to that deeper knowledge that Rustin mentions.

Despite some crucial past organizing, not even the WPC, or Parks and Nixon, or Abernathy and the other ministers had ever actually organized a boycott, let alone a nonviolent mass movement—arguably no one in the United States had. Indeed, this combination of past experience, *inexperience*, skill, and a new set of conditions in a particular political moment could be said to characterize the birth of the Montgomery movement in general. Even the movement's inaugural action, Parks's arrest on December 1 itself, both *was* and *was not* a unique event. It was an act that she (and many others) had been arrested for numerous times before, an experience familiar enough for her to later describe it as "a regular thing." Nor was the idea of a boycott new: the example of the eight-day Baton Rouge boycott of 1953 loomed large, and the idea of organizing a mass action had already been proposed and attempted, albeit unsuccessfully.

Thus despite the prior experience of many participants, and even framing political events from *Brown v. Board of Education* to Baton Rouge,

Montgomery was "the watershed of the modern civil rights movement."[69] And while speculation as to just what had changed may be unproductive, it is clear that Parks, King, Nixon, the WPC, and others in Montgomery were experienced enough to know that in order for this moment to bear fruit, they would need to be further prepared. And that preparation, including the self-purification that took concrete form in training workshops for nonviolent direct action, required help. Specifically, the nascent movement knew that it required help from experienced activists, seasoned in nonviolent action in ways that neither the relatively young leadership in Montgomery nor the rank and file of the movement had yet experienced.

VI. DIRECT ACTION AND SELF-PURIFICATION

As Morris describes it, "The Montgomery movement introduced the nonviolent approach to social change to the black masses." Indeed, while nonviolent techniques had been practiced and developed in the United States for decades, including among Black activists, nothing of the kind had ever been undertaken on this scale before: "Until this bus boycott, most blacks were unfamiliar with the techniques and principles of nonviolent direct action. The Montgomery movement served as a training ground where nonviolent direct action was systematically introduced and developed among the masses and the local leadership of the boycott." Regardless of role or experience, everyone participating in the movement would learn together. One of the first venues for this collective training was the "Nonviolent Workshop," which "was introduced to the civil rights movement" in Montgomery. From the beginning of the campaign, "a block of time was specifically set aside at the weekly mass meetings to train blacks in how to use nonviolence as a tool of social change."[70] This was a time of self-purification, in King's sense, and a time of training the inward center, in Thurman's. But like all spiritual exercise, the Nonviolent Workshop was just that: a workshop, a space of practice, and one that did not spring fully formed from Montgomery, but rather required both ongoing work and expert knowledge.

This expertise and training first arrived in Montgomery with two individuals whose contributions, for varying reasons, have been underemphasized in popular discourse: Bayard Rustin (1912–1987) and the Reverend Glenn Smiley (1910–1993), who often, at least initially, conducted the workshops.

Both were "experts on nonviolent protest, having received extensive training through their long affiliations with pacifist organizations,"[71] especially the Fellowship of Reconciliation—an organization whose national council Thurman had begun serving on in 1925.[72] Rustin, whose influence on the Civil Rights era is inversely proportional to the historical lack of public knowledge on his life and work, served as a mentor to Smiley throughout their early years at FOR.[73] By 1956 and their respective arrivals in Montgomery, Rustin and Smiley had become "skilled colleagues who shared similar movement halfway house experiences, and both were equipped with a theoretical and practical understanding of nonviolent direct action."[74]

Despite their long personal and professional relationship, Rustin and Smiley came from different backgrounds and experiences. Rustin was Black, openly gay, a Quaker, a former member of the Young Communist League, a confidant of A. Philip Randolph, and a consummate organizer and practitioner of nonviolence with years of experience. Rustin's relationship with FOR was strained by the time of Montgomery, as he had been unjustly forced to resign several years prior.[75] He had, however, "previously worked with FOR for twelve years, serving first as a field secretary and later as Race Relations Secretary, and he helped FOR organize the Congress of Racial Equality (CORE). By the time of the Montgomery movement, Rustin was Executive Secretary of the War Resisters League, another movement halfway house closely associated with FOR."[76] In fact, Rustin's long experience and reputation within the movement are evinced by an anecdote from his first visit to the King household: "Coretta Scott King, who met him at the front door, recognized him instantly as a former lecturer for the Fellowship of Reconciliation; she remembered his speaking at her high school in Marion, Alabama, during the early 1940s. Waving aside the letter of introduction he was handing her . . . she said, 'I know you, Mr. Rustin.'"[77]

Glenn Smiley, on the other hand, was a white Methodist minister, who was at the time serving as FOR's national field secretary. Smiley "began assisting in training Montgomery blacks in the methods of nonviolent protest action in February of 1956" and formed an enduring bond with King.[78] Smiley "was to be of considerable assistance, especially because, in addition to his knowledge of nonviolence, he was a minister and a Southerner. He knew the language of Southerners and was comfortable in the Black churches where the mass meetings were held."[79] That Smiley was white actually turned out to be an asset to the MIA, as it allowed him to liaise with the white community, both sympathetic and hostile, as well as gather information: "I would try to build bridges and connections with the white community in Montgomery, as well as serve as an open and above-board intelligence by which Dr. King could be kept informed about white thinking. Where possible, I would also keep watch on the White Citizens Council, and in some cases, even the Ku Klux Klan."[80]

Despite their differences, both Rustin and Smiley brought something unique to the table, and "their roles in the Montgomery movement were complementary."[81] Both were older than King, lifelong pacifists steeped in Christian and Gandhian traditions of nonviolence and were considered by many to be among the most qualified individuals to advise the Montgomery movement. Along with their collective experience, both brought a kind of creative energy to the religious and political situation on the ground. While Smiley came to Montgomery as FOR's official representative, Rustin came at the behest of A. Philip Randolph and Lillian E. Smith, and was the first northern political and organizational advisor to arrive in late February of 1956.[82] His visit was short-lived, though his impact there and subsequent working relationship with King were both extensive.[83] Despite his commitment and experience, Rustin was dogged in Montgomery, as he was elsewhere, by what John D'Emilio calls "the triple jeopardy that Bayard's identity and beliefs created—leftist, black, homosexual."[84]

These factors, coupled with the fact that he was clearly a Northerner, curtailed his stay in Montgomery. Although "Rustin had already disclosed his 'personal problem' to King, who felt that the value of Rustin's political acumen, not to mention his access to financial resources in the North, outweighed any threat his gayness or radical past posed to the boycott," others did not agree.[85] Less than two weeks after arriving in Montgomery, a reporter "threatened to expose him as a homosexual and ex-Communist, [and] Rustin was unceremoniously smuggled out of town in the trunk of a car."[86] Although this combination of factors led to the brevity of Rustin's visit to Montgomery, it seems clear that the insights garnered through a life on the "two crosses" of being Black and queer contributed to his organizational capabilities.[87] The skill and empathy he brought to the work were the result of the very factors that drove him out of Montgomery.

Upon their respective arrivals, Rustin and Smiley got to work in arranging the nonviolent workshops and contributing in other ways. One of Rustin's first interventions in Montgomery encapsulated the spirit of creative protest as a kind of tactical subjectivation and helped set the tone for actions deployed over the course of the next year. Rustin arrived in Montgomery on Tuesday, February 21, 1956, "the day a grand jury delivered indictments against more than a hundred leaders of the protest, charging them with violating the state's laws against boycotts." The threat of arrest was a standard form of personal and economic intimidation, carrying with it well-known consequences:

> The indictments were meant to disrupt the boycott by stoking fear into the hearts of leaders and participants alike and by consuming the community's scarce resources of time and money. Any encounter with the white South's criminal justice system was a fearful prospect for a black man or woman; it was especially so in the heated atmosphere of the boycott.[88]

Beyond the threat of arrest, the idea of putting out warrants for one hundred people at a time seems to reflect both a kind of shock and awe display of power on the part of the city, as well as an attempt at fully decapitating the movement.

King was away in Nashville when Rustin arrived, and they had not yet met in person. Rustin instead met with Nixon and Abernathy, with whom he "turned his attention to the daunting challenge of the indictments." Rustin "proposed a classic Gandhian tactic" to the two leaders. "Rather than wait at home for the sheriff to arrive and be taken like common criminals, all of the indicted should don their Sunday best and present themselves in groups to the authorities. There was no reason to cower, Rustin told them. They should wear the indictment with pride."[89] Rustin reports the scene at the courthouse the next morning as follows:

> One hundred leaders of the protest received word that they had been indicted. Many of them did not wait for the police to come but walked to the police station and surrendered. E.D. Nixon was the first. He walked into the station and said, "You are looking for me? Here I am." This procedure had a startling effect on both the Negro and white communities. White community leaders, politicians, and police were flabbergasted. Negroes were thrilled to see their leaders surrender without being hunted down. Soon hundreds of Negroes gathered outside the police station and applauded the leaders as they entered, one by one. Later those who had been arrested were released on $300 bail.

They gathered at the Dexter Avenue Baptist Church for a prayer meeting and sang for the first time a song which had been adopted that morning as the theme song for the movement. The four stanzas proclaim the essential elements of a passive struggle—protest, unity, nonviolence, and equality.[90]

Much like the Klansman on that November night almost a year later, the city expected the threat of arrest to provoke fear, intimidation, and docility in what it took to be an inherently "cowed" community. Instead, they were met with a carnival atmosphere, which both bolstered collective dignity and faith in the movement, and set the city back on its strategic heels. As one speaker at the February 27 mass meeting noted to the crowd:

> It used to be that the white man could toe us along. The white man has discovered that Negroes are no longer afraid to go to jail. I spent Wednesday night in jail. Remember this day, the year of our lord, 1956. I stayed home all day waiting for them. They tried to finger-print me and were all thumbs. When they finished they couldn't tell what it was. They tried to do it again and I said "Don't bother, Mr., I'll do it myself." We don't mind going to jail, giving our lives. All we want is to make this contribution for you and yours.[91]

These events shifted Rustin's view of the boycott, and his plans. Indeed, "by his second day in Montgomery, Rustin was rethinking his original plan to offer formal training on Gandhian nonviolence. Opportunities to teach were occurring organically, as each new situation unfolded."[92]

Rustin's approach made sense not just for the pragmatic reasons we have already seen with regard to the only seemingly preparatory activities of negotiation and collecting information, but was also in accord with nonviolent principles. Again, however, those immediate opportunities were cut short for Rustin himself. On February 27, five days after the arrests, Rustin penned the last entry in his "Montgomery Diary." Following an afternoon meeting of the working committee, he noted: "As I watched the people walk away, I had feeling that no force on earth can stop this movement. It has all the elements to touch the hearts of men."[93] Following his departure from Montgomery, Rustin continued to marshal financial resources and public opinion from afar, and he and King remained in close contact, with Rustin serving as a mentor and advisor to King off and on for the rest of the latter's life. As Jervis Anderson puts it, "King and Rustin formed one of the most creative alliances in the civil rights movement."[94] During and after Rustin's brief time in Montgomery, Smiley began and continued to hold nonviolent workshops.

It is not possible here to provide the kind of thoroughgoing analysis of the workshops that I would like, first for lack of space in this chapter. There are also some challenges around sources. The Montgomery workshops are referenced throughout both the primary and secondary literature as having taken place for a set amount of time during each of the mass meetings, even as that literature is sometimes short on detail regarding practical exercises.[95] Most importantly, however, such an analysis would find a more appropriate venue in a dedicated study. Instead, for the purposes of a methodological trajectory that emerges more directly from the goals of this chapter and the book as a whole, I will turn now to a series of three analyses that should complement one another and develop all that has been said thus far.

First, taking a step back from Montgomery itself, I begin the home stretch of this chapter with an often-referenced but rarely analyzed archival document from 1941, Rustin's "Lesson Plan on Non-violent Action."[96] Because both he and Smiley were primarily active through FOR from the late 1930s up until the boycott, it is productive to revisit the models of the countless workshops given in the preceding decade and a half, especially as Rustin's outline here is so rich and thorough. Moreover, the "Lesson Plan" is uncanny in its echoes of later philosophical and organizational texts across the Civil Rights era, especially King's "Letter." Further, despite important contextual differences, there is no indication that either Rustin or Smiley was fully reinventing the wheel in Montgomery.[97] A document like this thus provides a systematic view of both the theoretical context and content of the practices and perspectives that would have informed the community going into the movement and that would have been adapted over the course of the year. Following this discussion of Rustin's framework and some of the practices that it includes, I turn to Smiley and his description of one of the large-scale exercises he helped facilitate. In this case, a "sociodrama" undertaken toward the end of the boycott, in which Montgomery residents prepared for riding the desegregated buses. Finally, this line of analysis culminates with what is perhaps the consummate political–spiritual exercise of the boycott, the iconic practice that is most recognizably constitutive of the movement: the daily walk to work.

Rustin's "Lesson Plan on Non-violent Action"

There are at least two extant versions (two and four pages respectively) of Rustin's "Lesson Plan," each divided into the same twelve sections.[98] Part I, "Orientation," states: "Struggle and conflict are present in all phases of life and nature. Man has largely used violence to solve his problems. Non-violent direct action is not an attempt to do away with conflict, but a technique for peacefully solving it. The real choice then is between violent and non-violent method." But it is Part II, "Motivation," that begins to reveal consistent themes regarding the relationship of self- and collective transformation to changes in what Rustin calls, in language redolent of Friedmann and Thurman, "man's environment." Rustin elaborates: "There are two fundamental ideas on which faith in non-violent direct action is based: A.) Belief that goodwill is the most powerful and constructive force at work in human relationships. B.) Belief that progress depends on changes in man's attitude and environment at the same time."[99]

In the four-page version of the "Lesson Plan" archived by the Denver FOR chapter, there are some additional notes that immediately follow these two points, which may be cause for some confusion. The text states:

> There is power in non-cooperation with evil in bringing about the disintegration of evil. To cooperate with an evil is to help perpetuate that evil.
>
> Non-violent direct action, when used to dissolve discrimination against persons of color, involves non-cooperation with existing patterns of segregation and discrimination, and the use of active goodwill toward persons who have been practicing discrimination.
>
> Participants in non-violent direct action know that the hope of changing unjust practices lies in changing the hearts of those who have been doing wrong.[100]

It is this last comment, on "changing the hearts of those who have been doing wrong," that may appear confusing. That is, it may seem like the sort of naïvely moralistic injunction in which systemic change (in this case, ending legal segregation) is taken to be the causal result of an aggregation of individual ethical reformation.[101]

It is interesting to note that the fourth section, "Application,"[102] states: "This technique can be used wherever there is an area of social or economic tension, as in cases of: A.) Racial discrimination and prejudice."[103] Rustin then carefully distinguishes these two terms:

> Racial discrimination is a policy, often based on business or economic reasons, or mere tradition, and something that can be broken suddenly by a change in policy. Non-violent direct action is most effectively used in breaking discrimination of this kind.
>
> Racial prejudice is something that lies deeper within the self, an abnormal scar on the subconscious mind impressed there by unfortunate conditioning and miseducation. A racial neurosis can never be healed through coercion, but can be dissolved only through time by normal personal contacts, absolute goodwill, kindness and understanding. However, the momentary shock to an individual of the challenge of non-cooperation with his discriminatory policy, which may be a product of his prejudice, can be a positive initial stimulation toward his eventual change of mind.[104]

In more contemporary terms, the former references the political, systemic, and economic forms of racial oppression, and the latter the moral and subjective aspects of it. Rustin points out that the purpose of nonviolent noncooperation is not to change hearts and minds, which it cannot do, even as it may eventually contribute to such a change. Moreover, this is not how, on Rustin's view, nonviolence is actually meant to work, and that "eventual shift" is not the primary strategic goal. The goal instead, and as King is also clear, is to create and foster a state of productive crisis—and not merely an "interior" or moral crisis on the part of the oppressor.[105]

But Rustin concludes in a way that is again reminiscent of Friedmann's reciprocating formulation of the relationship of the "interior" to the "exterior," arguing that "it is a scientific fact that racial discrimination breeds prejudice, and that racial prejudice causes discrimination."[106] Here we see that "non-cooperation" is not only an ethical term, but a political one as well. Moreover, we see that in this schema—as would be true in the boycott roughly fourteen years later—the two concepts cannot be distinguished, either in their social–economic operation *or* in the forms of political action taken up to end them. This view does not reduce "discrimination" to "prejudice," and thereby entails forms of direct action that target at least three axes in concert: the ethical status of members of the oppressing group, the individuals taking part in direct action, and the structural and environmental conditions that frame and inform all of these factors.

This fundamental attitude is further reflected in the two sections that follow. It is fascinating to note that this document precedes King's 1963 "Letter" by twenty-two years, though its resonance with the later text, whether the result of direct or indirect influence, seems quite clear. This is because Section V details what Rustin calls the "five necessary steps preceeding [sic] direct action," which both mirror and depart from King's four stages in important ways.[107] The first two steps are nearly identical to King's:

A. Investigation—The exploited must be aware of and thoroughly examine all the factors involved and the degree to which they affect the total community.
B. Negotiation and Arbitration—Re-examination of these same factors in light of justice and community life by <u>all concerned</u> in the conflict, exploited and exploiters, and the attempt peacefully to reach justice.[108]

In some sense, the "Lesson Plan" is even clearer than the "Letter" with regard to these preparatory steps in the specification of the spiritual demands in question. Indeed, the Denver version includes further practical details regarding the practice of investigation, specifically with regard to an exercise labeled "The Test":

<u>The Test</u>—Steps in a typical CORE project, e.g., in a restaurant:
Purpose: To determine whether discrimination exists and, if so, to what degree it exists.
A small group, including one or two persons of color, together enter a restaurant normally with the attitude of expectancy of being served. If service is granted it is known that discrimination, if it exists at all, at least is not complete. A few days later a small Negro group preceded and followed by separate white groups is a good pattern, and finally a visit is made by one or more Negroes alone.
Participation in these projects not only affords fellowship between the participants, but also is good visual education for others in their seeing people of varied complexional colors associating naturally and in harmony.
Note: An effective technique to be used by both Whites and people of color when confronted with discrimination, is the "Why?" method. Here the victim of discrimination proceeds as though equality existed. Upon being

told to move to the balcony of a theater, for example, or that he cannot be served in a given restaurant, he simply asks, "Why?" His response to the obvious answer is also, "Why?" Although finally he may be forced to accept the consequences of his position such as being arrested or being moved into a segregated area, he has raised a vital issue. One reason why racial discrimination and prejudice have flourished in the North as well as in the South has been the docile acceptance by Negroes of segregation in principle. Another reason is the consequent conditioning of white people since childhood to be unaware of segregation as an issue.[109]

"The test" is neither a passive act of consideration, nor is it merely a form of "reconnaissance." The investigation itself is an active practice of ongoing confrontation, which gathers and confirms information through the cultivation of skills and attitudes necessary for further action. It reflects a relentlessness that is necessary in cases where the nexus of discrimination and prejudice is encountered. Even the seemingly simple "Why?" method does important work here: in a context wherein oppressed and oppressor have been conditioned to accept and avoid questioning their circumstances, that form of relentless questioning serves to create the kind of creative tension that Rustin and King both describe as one necessary component of large-scale change.[110]

Rustin's five steps continue with two more that can be seen as expansions on the previous two: "C. Education and awakening of 'cause consciousness;'" and "D. Demonstration and Ultimatum," which I will bracket here for lack of space. The final step, however, is near to King's "self-purification," in ways that not only illuminate King's later formulation, but in some sense the spirit and strategy of nonviolent direct action throughout this period:

E. Self-examination—Realization by the oppressed of their own guilt and demonstration of their willingness to make sacrifices in order to achieve their ends.

Note: Negotiation and self-examination must be established before and maintained during the entire period of conflict. Once the conflict has taken on any aspects of violence, application of these factors becomes impossible.[111]

In other words, this form of nonviolent protest, on both King's account in 1963 and Rustin's in 1941, requires not simply ongoing and persistent action directed toward oppressive structures and individuals, but ongoing self-examination, and indeed self-purification, by those engaged in direct action. Neither practice, even if we are to distinguish them, can thus remain within the framework of "preparation," as they must be consistently taken up and renewed at all times. This does not mean that one is already practicing direct action even in the preparatory phase, as we have already seen with "Investigation" and "Negotiation." It means that the political struggle itself is also, always, an ongoing form of preparation for that very struggle.

The implications of self-examination extend further, however, as the sections of the "Lesson Plan" that follow reciprocally integrate the role of such forms of subjectivation within the political struggle. Section VI, "Psychological factors in non-violent direct action" states that

> To achieve necessary unity for a program of direct action, the basic behavior pattern must permit the exploited to: 1. Have no fear, 2. Tell the truth, 3. Admit their guilt, 4. Behave creatively at all times in a completely non-violent manner, even in the case of physical attack, and 5. Raise the struggle from a physical to a moral plane.[112]

This is immediately followed by Section VII, which emphasizes the nature and role of "Discipline":

> While personal and group disciplines are essential requisites of this technique, there is not discipline for discipline's sake. On the contrary, the discipline must grow out of the demands of the actual situation. Where suffering is involved, participants in non-violent direct action try to assume it themselves rather than imposing it on the wrong-doer.

The discipline described here is needed to fulfill the requirements described in each section of the "Lesson Plan." As Rustin says, this discipline is not for its own sake, but is cultivated in its specificity based on the conditions to which one responds and the goals that one articulates.

Further, as in the case of ongoing self-examination, the "psychological factors" that Rustin describes here are cultivated as they are enacted. To "have no fear" under conditions that are calibrated to cultivate fear. To "tell the truth" under conditions that are born in bad faith, maintained through tactics like fear and humiliation, and within which no spoken dissent may be openly brooked, under pain of violence in its varied forms: it is neither simple nor easy to act in ways that contravene such relations of power, and resistance is not simply conjured from sheer force of will. "The Test" then becomes a methodical practice not only of fact-finding but of cultivating the antithesis of fear; the apparently simple "Why?" method an exercise in parrhesiastic questioning, of engaging the truth when one's oppression is tied to the violent obscuration of the truth.

It is the same in "admitting one's guilt," when one is not "guilty" of anything, certainly not of any apparent injustice. This item may well be read as a kind of moralistic self-flagellation, and it certainly warrants further critical exploration. But from Rustin's perspective, it constitutes a form of disciplined introspection and thus of self-purification. Such a practice allows participants in nonviolent direct action to "assume [suffering] themselves, rather than imposing it on the wrong-doer," and to do so not out of guilt, but rather free of guilt. Finally, the cultivation of what Rustin here and others elsewhere simply call creativity (number 4 above), serves as the primary attitude through which both the smaller tactics and larger strategies of the boycott took some of their most effective forms—including the ways that the boycotters came to understand themselves.

Smiley and the Sociodrama

Smiley put many of these principles into direct practice in Montgomery in the nonviolent workshops. In his rare and brief pamphlet, *Nonviolence: The Gentle Persuader*,[113] Smiley describes what he calls "the most interesting one," which included an exercise in the form a large-scale "sociodrama." These meetings took place at Reverend Abernathy's church, beginning on December 21, 1956, just after *Browder v. Gale* was announced, in preparation for the first integrated bus rides. This particular workshop was probably "the most interesting" in part because it was the largest he had ever been involved in: "It was the biggest nonviolent workshop, I guess, in history because it involved about five thousand people and people had said that you cannot hold a workshop with five thousand people." Morris adds that "they did; in fact, they were held on four consecutive days before the buses were desegregated in Montgomery." [114] Smiley reports that "notable among the many activities was the erection of a simulated bus in the place where the pulpit would normally be," which served as the setting for the sociodrama. Here, participants would "'get on the bus' to represent various problems they would face on bus-riding day,"[115] especially the inevitable encounters with resistant white drivers and riders.

This practice of sociodrama was for Smiley "nothing new, as it has been used in one form or another in many teaching situations," and it exercised the principles and techniques seen in the "Lesson Plan." Smiley explains that all of the characters "had to be played by black actors, as there were only about five white people in the audience, all of them observers from the north." He continues:

> A black minister played the part of the white driver, and other members of the movement had the unique experience of trying to understand how a white person felt as they acted out their version of the problem; that is part of the value of the device.
>
> One was a white woman sitting alone in a seat for two, having said that she "would never sit by one of them." Another . . . was a woman who kept saying "Now come on back here where you belong, honey, and don't cause us no trouble."
>
> Then I asked a volunteer to get on the bus and try to solve the problem of the white woman sitting in the seat for two. She boarded the bus, pretended to deposit her dime in the till, and approached the seat, whereupon the "white" woman put her package in the seat to try to prevent the occupation. This surprise move confounded the bus boarder for a moment and I asked, "Now, what if she won't remove it for you?" "Then I would pick it up and throw it on the floor," she said.
>
> There were shouts of "No" from the audience, so I asked the attorney, Mr. Gray, to speak to the problem. He explained how the woman had no legal right to the seat and could not take the seat as her own just by putting a small package on it. Nevertheless, in the present circumstances, if the bus boarder touched the package, she might well be arrested and charged with theft, and many nodded their heads in agreement, having had embarrassing experiences with white people in homes where they had worked.
>
> Another woman got on the bus when the first had withdrawn. She looked at the package, then said in a friendly tone, "May I carry your package for you while we ride along together?" The woman refused to accept her presence and just looked out the window. A third woman said this: "I like the idea of asking the woman if I could carry her package and, since she didn't

yield, I would get as close to the seat as I could, bow my head and pray silently that God would bless me and the white woman, and help us both to realize that all we wanted was to get this awful load off our feet." At that, there was a chorus of "amens," for no one could think of anything better to get at the woman's conscience.

And so we went through the problems that had been outlined.[116]

Smiley led this exercise again and again for the next four days, including a session of the same workshop with seventy sympathetic white Montgomery residents.[117] He emphasizes even at this late stage of the boycott, after the Supreme Court victory, that the required discipline still needed ongoing cultivation. King corroborates this in *Stride Toward Freedom*, noting that "sometimes the person playing a white man put so much zeal into his performance that he had to be gently reproved from the sidelines. Often a Negro forgot his nonviolent role and struck back with vigor; whenever this happened, we worked to re-channel his words and deeds in a nonviolent direction."[118]

Here we may see an affinity between the core aims of the sociodrama and the ancient practices of anticipation discussed in chapter 1. In both cases, one imagines a future in terms of both the evils that one will face, and the passions that will shape one's reaction to those circumstances. It is through practice that one first identifies the conditions one will face, then learns to creatively adapt oneself in order to adapt to them in a way that is both politically efficacious and ethically resonant. At the same time, this is a practice of anticipation, meditation, and self-examination that the ancients are unlikely to have ever imagined, either in its content, its reasons for being, technological conditions, political ends, or its status as a genuine view from below.

The affinities and differences are further refracted back through the principles and tactics outlined in Rustin's "Lesson Plan" and King's "Letter." This practice of anticipation is also a practice of self-examination. And in turn, the self-examination that one undergoes on the stage, here with the help of a sympathetic audience of comrades, is also a form of self-purification. Indeed, with the help of the other participants, even, or perhaps especially, in the form of shouts from the audience, one can come to see and "admit one's own guilt," in terms of the very natural impulses that may not correlate with the nonviolent telos of the exercise, for one example. In this way, it is also the purification of a community of political subjects, wherein that which must be purified is tied to conditions of political subjection through historically unique technological conditions around mass transit. Indeed, the modern intersection of "race" itself and the physical machinery of city buses produce subjective conditions that must be addressed by forms of discipline that, as Rustin says, "grow out of the demands of the actual situation" in all of its specificity and detail.[119]

The sociodrama also reinforces the point, central to the "Lesson Plan," that the work of preparation for direct action, indeed of self-purification, is an ongoing process, always present and always necessary throughout the duration of the political engagement. Even at such a late stage in the boycott, there was still work to be done, the kind of work on oneself and on the community that seeks to undo sustained forms of subjection, which cannot happen overnight. As Smiley says,

> If segregation had been stopped in Montgomery after a couple of weeks of boycott, we would probably have never heard of the protest again, except perhaps for a footnote in history. The fact that it took 381 days of walking, of inconvenience, of being jailed. And the expenditure of mountains of energy and money gave nonviolence time to mature and to be refined into a marvelously effective illustration of the power of love and nonviolence to achieve some historic changes in America.[120]

Or as Morris so clearly puts it, "It took time to create the nonviolent protestor."[121]

But if all agree that "it was a difficult task requiring intense preparation," both the "Lesson Plan" and Smiley's sociodrama demonstrate that the lines between self-purification and direct action itself are much more blurred. Rather than a kind of two-stage program, preparatory exercises and sustained direct action are better understood as aspects of a more general practice. The distinction between the two is an analytic one, not a practical or even historic one; their relationship is mutual and co-constituting. Even the stages of fact-finding and negotiation continued up to the very end of the boycott, as exercises that could not let up for a moment. This is because, as Lillian Smith notes in a letter to King, "You can't be an expert in nonviolence; it is like being a saint or an artist; each person grows his own skill and expertness."[122]

One cannot be an expert, in other words, because that growth has no endpoint; nonviolence, on this view, is a way of life and a form of perfectionism, rather than a status achieved after sufficient work. It is for this reason that the ongoing cultivation of necessary self-discipline, examination, and purification began the moment the idea of a boycott emerged. And as these documents show, it is for this same reason that these forms of discipline characterized the very act of boycotting the buses, above all in the daily pilgrimage to work.

The Pilgrimage to Work

Through the help of figures like Smiley and Rustin, organizations like FOR and CORE brought a great deal of experience and expertise to Montgomery. In the same way, seasoned local activists and organizers like Nixon, Parks, and the WPC, as well as new leaders like King and Abernathy, contributed equally crucial efforts to the organization of the boycott. Even A. Philip Randolph "indicated that the Montgomery leaders had managed thus far [more] successfully than 'any of our so-called non-violence experts' a mass resistance campaign and we should learn from them rather than assume that we know it all."[123]

And yet, it was the city of Montgomery and the movement as a whole that arguably did the most teaching. This is in no small part because "until the Montgomery movement nonviolent protest methods had never been used in America on a mass scale by any of the pacifist organizations, including FOR."[124] Montgomery was a historic collective effort, constituted by a committed rank and file. Thus when Abernathy addressed the February 27 mass meeting at Holt Street Baptist, he reminded the crowd: "This is your movement; we don't have any leaders in the movement; you are the leaders. Someone asked me yesterday—'Who are the leaders?'" Before he could answer, "the congregation answered for him, saying at one time—'We are;' or 'There ain't no leaders,' etc."[125] This was not a rhetorical flourish, but a truth that contributed to the conditions of the movement's success and influence.

In a memo to King following the end of the boycott, Rustin identifies several features of the Montgomery movement "not found in other movements or efforts":

> It was organized; used existing institutions as foundations so that all social strata of the community were involved. It thus had the strength of unity which the school integration efforts have lacked, thereby leaving the fight to heroic but isolated individuals. Montgomery could plan tactics, seek advice and support, develop financial resources and encompass a whole community in a crusade dominating all other issues. The reason there were those who did not want to give up the boycott is due in part to the consciousness that this welding of a comprehensive, unified group had a quality not to be lost. The fellowship, the ideals, the joy of sacrifice for others and other varied features of the movement have given people something to belong to.[126]

Thus, he continues, "Montgomery was unique in that it relied upon the active participation of people who had a *daily* task of action and dedication. The movement did not rely exclusively on a handful of leaders to carry through such fundamental change."[127]

The Montgomery community accomplished these changes in various ways, including through practices by which the strategic balance was significantly altered and a new set of rules constituted. This is why it was not just the fact of "daily action and dedication" in general on the part of the boycotters, but rather the precise forms of that action that made all the difference. It is a case in which the creation of another world entailed the creation of new, other selves. Although one must do so in precise ways that do not simply reflect some abstract value, these new selves cannot simply amount to the embodied form of some "pious wish," in Friedmann's terms. It must instead be the kind of self—whether as a first-person "I" or a third-person "we"—capable of bringing a strategic weight to bear on existing conditions, a force powerful enough to establish new subjective and political horizons. And if the world one wishes to alter or abandon functions through an economy of violence (physical, legal, symbolic, etc.) and its attending fear, then one must, through strategic means that are parallel and responsive but in no way equivalent, work toward rendering neutral and passing beyond those methods of violence and sources of fear.

It is for this reason that we may take the simple practice of walking to work rather than riding the bus as representative of the forms of collective spiritual–political exercise most characteristic of the movement. It is the best example here of just what I mean by a strategic practice that is responsively parallel but not formally equivalent. It is no accident that it was the simple act of walking that demonstrated to King that "[the] community was now fully awake."[128] Further, because it was sustained by many participants for the better part of a year or more, it is also the practice that best embodies the ongoing, dialectical, and perfectionist trajectory of the movement. This practice of walking to work is also significant in that while it may seem an individual activity, its political syntax is necessarily collective. As the case, say, of Vernon Johns demonstrates, such action is only effective, intelligible, and indeed transformative insofar as it is constitutive of a genuine mass movement. Finally, the walk to work was a practice born of political circumstances that brought about clear changes among practicing subjects "on the level of the self and of being" in ways that produced the most clear and direct tactical results with regard to the political and economic "environment," to use the language of King, Thurman, Rustin, and Friedmann.

At a special meeting of the MIA executive board on January 30, 1956—the day that King's home was bombed—he and the other ministers had met to discuss the strange incident of several ministers unaffiliated with the MIA who had met with city officials and agreed to a "compromise" that would end the boycott. It is clear from the minutes of the meeting, however, that it was the commitment of the rank and file that kept the boycott going, rather than instruction from the leadership. Some of the latter were, at least at this juncture, amenable to entertaining a "compromise," though one that Nixon and others pointed out was no compromise at all. At the meeting, King reports "I've seen along the way where some of the ministers are getting weary . . . If you have that impression (that N. should go back under the same conditions to the buses), we won't ostracize you. We should iron it out here (exec. Meetings) and show wherein we shouldn't go back."[129]

It was clear to several people at the meeting, however, that those walking to work would not accept any concessions short of victory. Indeed, it had been raining heavily that morning, a difficulty that only demonstrated the already robust commitment of the boycotters regardless of—or in part thanks to—any personal hardship. As one member put it, "'This morning was the test.' The rain was pouring and 'they still walked.' 'If they don't want to go back, I don't see why we should decide otherwise. Folk just made too much sacrifice. I hold that we should go on to the end. I think we should stay just where we're at.'"[130] Because of this commitment, no compromise would be made in January. The executive board knew that the rank and file would simply not allow it. As King put it:

> From my limited contact, if we went tonight and asked the people to get back on the buses, we would be ostracized. They wouldn't get back. We shouldn't give people the illusion that there are no sacrifices involved, that it could be ended soon. My intimidations are a small price to pay if victory can be won. We should make the illusion that they won't have to walk. I believe to the bottom of my heart that the majority of Negroes would ostracize us. They are willing to walk.[131]

Nixon was more concise: "If we accept it, we are going to 'run into trouble.' . . . 'If that's what you're going to do, I don't want to be here when you tell the people.' "[132]

No compromise was sought or accepted. However, the boycott did not simply persist, it became a way of life. At the February 27 mass meeting, one speaker reflected the collective experience thus far: "For the past 84 days many of us have sacrificed, suffered, and been put in jail. In spite of our previous experiences, the fact remains, the end is not here yet. The novelty has worn away, and we're down to the deep roots of the situation we find ourselves in. We've emptied ourselves of pent-up emotions. Something will fill that vacuum—what it is remains up to you."[133] Something had changed by February, but it had begun months earlier. As Jo Ann Robinson put it, "After December 5, 1955, the people were able to release their suppressed emotions through the boycott movement, which allowed them to retaliate directly for the pain, humiliation, and embarrassment that they had endured over the years at the hands of drivers and policemen while riding on the buses."[134] The practices of walking and organizing allowed participants an ongoing form of self-purification. To empty oneself of pent-up emotions, and to "retaliate directly" to the system of legal segregation through direct action, were not simply by-products of the boycott. Instead, they were the reciprocating conditions and effects of its success. One had to "empty oneself" in order to effectively engage in the various actions that constituted the boycott, but those actions, like walking, or even driving others, constituted some of those practices of self-purification.

King, Abernathy, and others saw this connection directly. As King said in his remarks to the March 1 mass meeting:

God is using Montgomery as a proving ground. He will cause democratic conditions to stand where they should stand. We have now new dignity and awareness. We are God's children. We're walking because we're tired of being suppressed politically. We're walking because we're tired of being suppressed economically. We're walking because we're tired of having [been] segregated and discriminated. Freedom is the just claim of all men. As we walk we're going to walk with love in our hearts. Somebody has to have sense enough to cut off the hate. The power of love is very strong; love your enemies. The whole armor of God is the weapon of love and the breastplate of righteousness. There is something about love that transforms; we're going to keep on in the same spirit.[135]

Abernathy's dialogue with the crowd that same evening reflects a similar understanding:

Are you tired? [*Response*:] "No-o-o!" Are you weary? R. "No-o-o!" Do you feel like turning around? R. "No-o-o!" Are you still with the movement? R. "Yes-s-s-s-s!!" "If all the cars break down and go to the garage, what are you going to do? R. "Walk!" Are you still praying? R. "Yes-s-s-s!" We must keep God at the forefront. It takes strength to walk to and from work, and only God can give us that strength. We aren't going to leave Montgomery, we're going to enjoy freedom right here in Montgomery.[136]

In a similar exchange about a month later, Abernathy and the crowd collectively affirm "If we can't walk, we'll crawl."[137] Walking in this case was not merely symbolic, nor did it simply amount to an act of economic resistance. It was instead a practice of collective self-purification in which ethical transformation was tied directly to political transformation. It was not just a show of what Abernathy calls strength, but one of the primary ways in which that necessary strength was cultivated.

Indeed, from the first day of the boycott, but on many others to come as well, the pilgrimage to and from work demonstrated to King that in this practice a change was taking place: "They knew why they walked, and the knowledge was evident in the way they carried themselves. And as I watched them I knew that there is nothing more majestic than the determined courage of individuals willing to suffer and sacrifice for their freedom and dignity."[138] Indeed, "so profoundly had the spirit of the protest become a part of the people's lives that sometimes they even preferred to walk when a ride was available. The act of walking, for many had become of symbolic importance." For King, this is best evinced by the case of a driver who "stopped beside an elderly woman who was trudging along with obvious difficulty. 'Jump in, grandmother,' he said. 'You don't need to walk.'" However, "she waved him on. 'I'm not walking for myself,' she explained. 'I'm walking for my children and grandchildren.'"[139] King, Jo Ann Robinson, and others recount a similarly representative story; in Robinson's telling: "Yet another woman 'who had walked halfway across town' was given a ride by a minister who asked if she was tired. She replied, 'Well, my body may be a bit tired, but for many years now my soul has been tired. Now my soul is resting. So I don't mind if my body is tired, because my soul is free.'"[140]

It was the production of weary souls by the system of legal segregation, a weariness that was meant to sustain it, that the overarching strategy had to target. One had to trade a weary soul for weary feet, and many in the white community believed that the physical burden would prove harder to bear than the spiritual one with which people had already been living and that the boycott would fail. But like the discipline required to sustain them, rested souls and weary feet must also be cultivated, and there were certainly times in which it seemed to some like the latter would win out over the former. This proved incorrect, but hindsight must not obscure the fact of just how obvious or self-evident it must have seemed from a vantage point within a relationship of power for which weary souls were among the very conditions. Although that apparatus was complex, made up of more and more insidious components than a series of laws, it still operated through means clear enough and identifiable enough to make crucial forms of response and resistance possible.

The movement as a whole was incredibly complex to be sure, addressing the question of legal segregation on numerous levels and with an entire array of methods, many which have not been discussed here. However, even within such a dynamic and multivalent movement of resistance, simply to *walk*, to do so far enough, long enough, and with a certain kind of determination, could and did produce the kind of deep and sustainable dignity King, Thurman, and others held to be a condition for the neutralization of the fear and violence integral to the system. As Robinson reports, even early on in the movement, the work of the boycott caused people to "[feel] reborn, important for the first time. . . . Many were themselves surprised at the response of the masses, and could not explain, if they had wanted to, what had changed them overnight into fearless, courageous, proud people, standing together for human dignity, civil rights, and, yes, self-respect! [. . .] They were really free—free inside! They felt it! Acted it! Manifested it in their entire beings!"[141]

In this way, we can see that it was not the Supreme Court decision of November 13, 1956, that altered the community's relationship to its own fear that evening in November with which we began. Rather, that legal victory and a courageously indifferent response to a well-known threat were themselves rooted in a new relationship of the community to itself, marked by the cultivation of new and newly refined forms of courage, dignity, and so much else, of which the act of walking to and from work constituted a crucial element.

VII. IMPLICATIONS

There is a moment during the first meeting of the newly formed MIA (on the day of Rosa Parks's trial and the first day of the boycott) that, for King, demonstrates one of the core tensions faced by the movement. As he describes it:

> Several people, not wanting the reporters to know our future moves, suggested that we just sing and pray; if there were specific recommendations to be made to the people, these could be mimeographed and passed out secretly during the meeting. This, they felt, would leave the reporters in the dark. Others urged that something should be done to conceal the true identity of the leaders, feeling that if no particular name was revealed it would be safer for all involved.[142]

From the strategic perspective of King, Rustin, Thurman, and indeed many of the rank and file, it could seem that urging secrecy would mean stepping back into the economy of power and the dynamic of fear that the community is trying to escape.

E. D. Nixon saw this tension as well, and as King reports, "After a rather lengthy discussion, [Nixon] rose impatiently" to address the meeting:

> "Somebody's name will have to be known, and if we are afraid we might just as well fold up right now. We must also be men enough to discuss

our recommendations in the open; this idea of secretly passing something around on paper is a lot of bunk. The white folks are eventually going to find out anyway. We'd better decide now if we are going to be fearless men or scared boys."

With this forthright statement the air was cleared. Nobody would again suggest that we try to conceal our identity or avoid facing the issue head on. Nixon's courageous affirmation had given new heart to those who were about to be crippled by fear.[143]

If one of the goals is to no longer be afraid in general, then a collective practice of bravery, fostered by Nixon's parrhesiastic intervention, would contribute to the work of countering one of the key features by which the system of segregation functioned. For King, this same point is also central to the question of violence and its potential use by the movement.

As the movement progressed, King and others continued to stress the vision and strategy of nonviolence, and "from the beginning the people responded to this philosophy with amazing ardor." Naturally, this outlook was not universal:

To be sure, there were some who were slow to concur. Occasionally members of the executive board would say to me in private that we needed a more militant approach. They looked upon nonviolence as weak and uncompromising. Others felt that at least a modicum of violence would convince the white people that the Negroes meant business and were not afraid. A member of my church came to me one day and solemnly suggested that it would be to our advantage to "kill off" eight or ten white people. "This is the only language these white folks understand," he said. "If we fail to do this they will think we're afraid. We must show them we're not afraid any longer."[144]

Now, as clarified at the beginning of this chapter, my goal here is not to claim that these possible approaches are clearly wrong—it is not my place or goal to pass those kinds of judgments or to endorse either violent or nonviolent resistance. For King, however, it is clear that he is in fact in agreement with this last sentiment regarding fear. But from his perspective, these kinds of arguments still operate within the economy of power that the movement sought to undo. From this vantage, even if only strategically, to respond to the current system with that kind of violence would be to give the city of Montgomery not only what it wanted, but what it expected. Instead, the strategies deployed to escape this dynamic would have to meet the forces arrayed against the movement in ways that were parallel though asymmetrical.

For King, "the use of violence in our struggle would be both impractical and immoral" for all of the reasons we have been discussing here. "To meet hate with retaliatory hate would do nothing but intensify the existence of evil in the universe. Hate begets hate; violence begets violence; toughness begets a greater toughness. We must meet the forces of hate with the power of love; we must meet physical force with soul force."[145] Thus, if King's interlocutor here was indeed correct that violence was the only language by which the system of segregation could communicate, then from King's perspective to respond violently would be to continue to play by the rules of a game written by that system on its own behalf. It would be exactly the sort of response the city expected. On this view, to play by the rules that the system has constituted, to speak the language of fear and violence, is to at very least cede it the advantage, and to at most ensure its continued victory.

King speaks explicitly of the "miscalculation of the white leaders" in precisely these terms. The latter continued to operate not simply according to the tactics they had always deployed, but out of a fundamental misunderstanding of who the Black community in Montgomery was. Thus, as King and Rustin say together in an early piece for *Liberation*: "Because the mayor and city authorities cannot admit to themselves that we have changed, every move they have made has inadvertently increased the protest and united the Negro community."[146] King and Rustin then go on to list fourteen separate attempts to intimidate and harass boycotters to abandon the movement between December 1, 1955, and February 22, 1956, alone. Each item in the list notes exactly how each tactic backfired, from printing the call to boycott on the front page of the newspaper, to bombing the homes of King, Nixon, and others: "Every attempt to end the protest by intimidation, by encouraging Negroes to inform, by force and violence, further cemented the Negro community."[147] Each is a case, in other words, of becoming someone for whom these effects may no longer take hold, even just long enough to transform the conditions of their origin. Here, changing oneself allows one to change the world, which becomes the condition of further transformations of oneself, and so on.

In Montgomery, in practice, the self-purification and direct action that King and Rustin describe together constituted an ongoing form of explicitly political self-change. If direct action is itself a practice of purification, and if its success depends precisely on rested souls, then even the preparatory training exercises so crucial to the mass movement are themselves forms of direct action. This is because in *acting directly* on one of the primary and necessary sites of contestation—the subjectivity and dignity of acting participants—one also *acts directly* on the economic and political relations of power that rely on the endless production of tired feet and weary souls.

CONCLUSION

Audre Lorde: Survival, Immediacy, and Poetry as a Way of Life

I. CARING FOR ONESELF

Consider the following passage:

> What have I had to leave behind? Old life habits, outgrown defenses put aside lest they siphon off energies to no useful purposes?
> One of the hardest things to accept is learning to live with uncertainty and neither deny it nor hide behind it. Most of all, to listen to the messages of uncertainty without allowing them to immobilize me, nor keep me from the certainties of those truths in which I believe. I turn away from any need to justify the future—to live in what has not yet been. Believing, working for what has not yet been while living fully in the present now.
> This is my life. Each hour is a possibility not to be banked. These days are not a preparation for living, some necessary but essentially extraneous divergence from the main course of my living. They are my life. [. . .] I am living my life every particular day no matter where I am, nor in what pursuit. It is the consciousness of this that gives a marvelous breadth to everything I do consciously.[1]

With the exception of the more contemporary tone and texture of the prose, doesn't this text read like an excerpt from one of Friedmann's philosophical journals? Might it not be found among his wartime meditations from the trenches in the face of the German advance or his late reflections on power and wisdom through the retrospective view of a life and life's work? Alternately, may it not read like a pastiche of any of a range of Hadot's favored ancient sources, though with something of a modern voice emerging in the process of linguistic and philosophical translation? It is neither, of course, but rather a passage from the epilogue of Audre Lorde's "A Burst of Light: Living With Cancer," her famous bio-poetic account of fighting cancer for the second time (the first, of course, recounted in the landmark *Cancer Journals*), dated August 1987, about five years before her death in 1992.

Whether Lorde would have been "aware of the resemblance" to either set of sources, as Hadot once asked of Friedmann,[2] is a less interesting question, at least in the terms in which Hadot posed it. And yet, there is no doubt that some form of that question speaks to this text, though in ways and with implications that would diverge from and invert many of Hadot's standing concerns. Those resonant departures and inversions would, in their own ways and in the unique forms we already see in this passage, reflect the political, ethical, and indeed spiritual challenges that constantly presented themselves to Lorde and that her poetry, prose, and autobiographical publications all conversely present to anyone who takes them up and reads them.

Perhaps the greatest accompanying resonance may be felt in the ongoing task of understanding how to meet the "contemporary spiritual demands" of oneself and one's community in ways that meet the specificity of those demands, the various conditions from which they emerge, and the very "self" in question. In all such cases, it is not, as it has not been over the course of this book, an issue of identifying such resonances on the level of mere similarity and moving on. This question of specificity, in contrast to any easy universality, has been one of many guiding threads here, in ways that lead to texts like Lorde's late reflections in "A Burst of Light" and elsewhere. The problem, its implications, and the ways in which they can help us are especially apparent, on my reading anyway, in such texts and their reception history.

The passage that opens this chapter follows one of the most famous sentiments in "A Burst of Light," and one that has, for better or worse, found itself among the most recognizable of Lorde's career. She concludes the first

CONCLUSION

paragraph of the epilogue by telling her readers that "caring for myself is not self-indulgence, it is self-preservation, and that is an act of political warfare."[3] Lorde's claim here is a rich and complex one, implicating almost every aspect of her life and career as a poet, speaker, philosopher, activist, and so much else. Read against the backdrop of that life and that work, it is a statement that contains multitudes, even as those multitudes once again reflect the specificity of that life, work, and the particular conditions that shaped them. It is, of course, at the same time that very particularity, the fine-grained detail of a life and a work as they are reflected here, that in no small part generates its ability to speak beyond its own context, if not its universality.

Like so many others, this statement has taken on something of a life of its own in popular discourse. That is not necessarily a bad thing: Lorde's place in and across numerous scholarly fields and in popular political and ethical life has been vital in the years since her passing. Conversely, however, in many popular invocations of Lorde's sentiment, her echoed language may appear denuded of its context, indeed of its very politics. There is universality, and there is universality, after all. The latter problem has served as one of the guiding threads of this work, and it remains a core question for any study of practices of the self, especially where the forms of "translation" and the emergence of new practices invoked in previous chapters are concerned. Among many other ideas and exercises, Lorde's language of caring for herself and its status as a political practice in direct opposition to any form of self-indulgence are sometimes associated with something called "self-care," even as Lorde, someone for whom language matters profoundly, does not use that nominalization.

Any quick search will return an entire range of such invocations, far too numerous and diverse to catalog or treat here, especially as that process of reception and reinterpretation is also incredibly dynamic. Within that set, moreover, the proximity and distance of given references and forms of inspiration to Lorde's work and the particular challenges of "A Burst of Light" vary greatly. To be sure, a study of the popular reception history of this quote alone, from its role in shaping radical politics to its invocation as an endorsement of the very self-indulgence and political abnegation that Lorde herself disclaims, is an important and worthwhile task in its own right. However, the history of those invocations, whether memetic, journalistic, or scholarly, and within concrete political struggle, vital artistic practice, or otherwise, is well outside my task here.

In the same way, the concept and practice of self-care in its twentieth- and twenty-first-century popular forms denotes a range of concepts and practices that is so large, complex, and diverse that it too very clearly merits ongoing attention within religious studies and adjacent fields, that much is clear. As I emphasized in the introduction, it is my hope that much like other popular practices of the self, some of the theoretical tools developed across this work may contribute to more careful insight into the concepts and practices that fall under the broad category of contemporary self-care. As in so many other cases, it seems to me that various aesthetic trappings and explicit political claims on the part of practitioners can serve to obscure much of what is rich and interesting—including what may be understood as politically liberating or ethically and politically damaging—within given forms of self-identified self-care.

When, for example, do forms of self-care that might be assimilated to the idea of, say, "treating oneself" constitute genuine political action, if ever? When is self-care simply a nice thing to do, and how and under what circumstances may it constitute an abnegation of one's ethical and political duties to others or even intersect with conditions of injustice toward the other? Building on existing engagements with these questions and posing them in new terms and contexts requires that we continuously disentangle rigorous and appropriate uses—especially in their creative forms—from politically denuded misappropriations of both the concept of "self-care" and the vexed invocations of figures like Lorde within such contexts.[4]

At the same time, something as seemingly apolitical or self-indulgent as, say, taking a warm bath can have any number of implications based on context or description. If one needs to care directly for one's joints and muscles in the midst of the physically and emotionally taxing work of participating in a mass movement, marked by days and nights and months of marching and protesting, then to care for oneself physically constitutes a nurturing condition for ongoing political effort. Lorde herself insists on this perspective in a number of ways. From this vantage, even the most seemingly innocuous forms of the care of the self take on the status of the care of the other, of others, of the city, family, community, planet, and whatever else falls within an ethical–political horizon. A meal, a drink, a game, new shoes, a new shirt, etc.—in the context of concrete, organized political work, all of these may take on a not-insignificant political valence, one that is wholly necessary, even if never wholly sufficient. Such questions

CONCLUSION

are worth asking, and such analyses are worth taking up, both for scholars and those working on the ground, especially insofar as the latter have so much to teach the former, as always. But once again, while I hope to lend some perspective and resources to such analyses, and as they are very much worth highlighting here in reference to everything I have attempted to explore in the preceding chapters, this is not my task here.

What I would like to do, by way of concluding this book, is to briefly return to Lorde's claim that caring for herself constitutes a form of political action and then just as briefly place it in the context of her life and work. On that foundation, my goal is to pose some new questions and highlight new directions for analysis against the background of all that I have attempted to establish. These further questions are resonant with the central threads of this project, yet constitute a trajectory that is slightly oblique to the core concepts and arguments thus far. That is, they emerge from and address some of the same core themes—above all, the politics of self-transformation and self-overcoming—though they do so through different enough terms and from a different enough perspective and archive and, above all, different forms of life and experience to constitute a distinguishable enough line of reading and research.

Unfortunately, or perhaps fortunately, I cannot offer the kind of analysis of Lorde here that I have for the other subjects of this book. First and foremost, for reasons of space. Further, and again unfortunately, because even after a great deal of time spent with her work, I must admit, in the spirit of this book overall, that I am no expert in Lorde. I simply do not feel textually equipped to produce the kind of analysis that would engage that work with the breadth, detail, and sense of finality that I would find satisfying and that her work warrants, at least not yet. There is a classic and emerging body of literature on Lorde that can speak to so many of these themes in ways that I cannot at this juncture, even as I hope to reapproach her body of work through the lens I have tried to polish here.[5] It is, conversely, for that very reason that these limits constitute a fortunate horizon, as it means there is more to do. Indeed, most importantly and most substantively, Lorde presents a rich and challenging, though branching, trajectory from the core themes that I have sought to develop so far. She leads the concepts and practices that concern me here in new directions that I think are better served as the beginning of an entire series of conversations, rather than the end of one.

My goal then is to conclude by briefly engaging Lorde's work as a jumping-off point, a place to raise questions and suggest areas of research and dialogue that I believe will take the study of spiritual exercises, the care of the self, the politics of self-change, and so on, in necessary theoretical and practical directions. That work will, if successful, open up a space to reread all that I have claimed and attempted to formulate in the preceding chapters against those new questions, resources, and perspectives.

For these reasons, my invocation of Lorde here is in no way meant to be something that is simply tacked on to the end of a discussion. It is not an afterthought, but is instead very much a forethought. It is meant to begin conversations that both build on and challenge what I have developed here, and to most simply and I think most productively reapproach those same themes from different though related perspectives. It is also, finally, for all of these reasons that these final thoughts cannot emerge through anything close to the exhaustive or thoroughgoing reading of Lorde that I would prefer. Rather, these next steps will focus on a particular set of texts and illustrative themes: above all, the central question of *survival*, which constitutes a vital throughline at the core of all of Lorde's work. I will explore that theme through two other themes that will serve as suggestions for future research: First, noting that there are fundamental ways in which someone like Lorde, and indeed someone like Thurman before her, demonstrates a necessary urgency that challenges and develops notions of contemplation and "premeditation" that tend to be associated with philosophy as a way of life, spiritual exercises, and the like. Second, by addressing the ways in which she presents a more direct or immediate conception of the relationship of the self to itself as a political intervention, through a notion of poetry as a way of life, itself understood in dialogue with notions of discursive and lived parrhesia.

II. SURVIVAL, PREMEDITATION, AND THE IMMEDIACY OF EVILS

Over the course of this book, I have made certain central claims and held to certain core principles with the goal of elaborating the possibility of particular forms of political self-transformation, or of political transformation as a form of self-change, or of a care of the self that is reciprocal and coterminous with the care for others. Among them, I have described the relationship of the self to itself as a circuit that passes through any number of material conditions, institutions, and forms of social reality. This framing was primarily developed in chapter 3. Although this is my own language, I think that this formulation is helpful in understanding someone like Lorde, and that again in rather different language, she herself understood something like this dynamic.

By this I mean that when Lorde says that caring for herself is an act of political warfare, she is speaking from the perspective, as she so often reminds her readers, of a Black woman, lesbian, feminist, mother, poet, and daughter of immigrants, someone who grew up poor in the New York of the early and mid-twentieth century, and so much else.[6] That is, her life and work sit at the intersection—in the strict sense of that term[7]—of a dynamic set of conditions, forms of experience, classes of identity, and through them, forms of disinheritance, immiseration, and dehumanization. At the same time, through all of these, that life also sits at the center of forms of radical flourishing, care, hope, *kinds of work*, and so much else. Perhaps above all however, it cannot be emphasized enough that when she records this famous line about caring for herself, it emerges from and is given its meaning by the conditions of its utterance: cancer of the liver, metastasized from the breast cancer for which she had already undergone the harrowing treatment and postmastectomy traumas recounted, for the sake of herself and others, in *The Cancer Journals* several years before "A Burst of Light."[8] Ultimately, we can only understand Lorde's "caring for herself" in relation to another of her most famous texts, the landmark poem "A Litany for Survival," as the care of those selves who, like her, "were never meant to survive."[9]

Lorde herself makes this point, again in the epilogue of "A Burst of Light," invoking the ways that the experience of cancer, especially in its physicality, is linked to an entire life lived under threat: "But those of us who live our battles in the flesh must know ourselves as our strongest weapon in the most gallant struggle of our lives."[10] To add the many well-known ways in which individuals, let alone individuals who share any of the forms of life and experience Lorde notes, find themselves encountering the medical systems in question and whose challenges Lorde too documents, is to only further emphasize the political gravity of the work of care and survival. Against all this, the very idea of "caring" accrues dimensions of meaning that require careful and ongoing rereading.[11]

CONCLUSION

Among the most generative ways that we can read Lorde's conception of "caring for herself" here is through the lens of what is arguably one of the most important, frequently invoked, and challenging notions in all of her work: the concept of *survival*. This term and concept appear constantly across Lorde's oeuvre, though she also uses the language of *self-preservation*, as we have already seen. These usages are complex and dynamic: the terms sometimes appear synonymous, sometimes they do not, and each can shift in meaning across iterations and context. For these reasons, Lorde's rich use of these terms warrants further reading and elaboration. It is also in these cases that Lorde reminds me most of Thurman, the thinker in this text with whom I believe she has the greatest affinity, a resonance that again presents exciting avenues of investigation.

This theme of survival is everywhere in Lorde's work. She opens *Zami*, her autobiographical "bio-mythography," with the question: "To whom do I owe the symbols of my survival?"[12] Lorde's rich celebration of the many people in her life who answer that question are everywhere in her work, often with all of the complexity that anyone who may play such a role can bring to our lives. In the early chapters of *Zami*, she devotes a great deal of description to the ways that her mother navigated the dangers of her life in New York, and the things that she took from those lessons, as well as those tactics that Lorde developed on her own.[13] Much of this complexity and urgency are captured in her account of leaving home at seventeen, which she describes in contrast to her mother's experience, as a process by which she "began to fashion some different relationship to this country of our sojourn. I began to seek some more fruitful return than simple bitterness from this place of my mother's exile." For all of the challenge and complexity of her relationship to her mother, she is clear that "thanks to what she did know and could teach me, I survived in them better than I could have imagined. I made an adolescent's wild and powerful commitment to battling in my own full eye, closer to my own strength."[14] Here we begin to see the distinction that Lorde makes between the rich concepts of "survival" or "self-preservation"—which denote something much closer to self-flourishing—and mere *safety*.

This distinction between safety and survival is a vital one, and there is already generative writing on these concepts and their tensions.[15] In dialogue with that existing literature, it is very much worth exploring and developing these concepts within ongoing analyses of spiritual exercises

CONCLUSION

and the care of the self, especially in their political valence. Lorde draws out this fissure in many places, though it is made especially powerfully in her account of having an abortion at eighteen and coming through the other side of the procedure and its aftereffects: "Even more than my leaving home, this action which was tearing my guts apart and from which I could die except I wasn't going to—this action was a kind of shift from safety towards self-preservation. It was a choice of pains. That's what living was all about."[16] In a world of inevitable pains—evils that are so aggressively present that they need not be premeditated—the ability to choose them is here a difference between safety and a survival that is something much more than *mere* survival. In Lorde's oeuvre, one of the most powerful articulations of this tension can again be found in "A Litany for Survival." In her words:

> For those of us
> who were imprinted with fear
> like a faint line in the center of our foreheads
> learning to be afraid with our mother's milk
> for by this weapon
> this illusion of some safety to be found
> the heavy-footed hoped to silence us
> For all of us
> this instant and this triumph
> We were never meant to survive.[17]

This illusion of safety is no safety at all, and survival is many things at once, though all of them something more than bare life.

Here, we might read, even if roughly, Lorde's idea of "safety" with King's concept of passive or "negative peace," and her ideas of survival, self-preservation, and "caring for herself," with King's positive, active peace, that is itself "a kind of work" in many forms.[18] This comparison, and Lorde's own language, help us see that this "safety" is no safety at all, as it is by no means a state of genuine peace. We may also read her criticisms of the idea of "looking on the bright side," a vacant concept that doctors and nurses assail her with following her mastectomy, in line with this notion of "safety" and its illusions. In *The Cancer Journals* she tellingly links these concepts to what she calls "superficial spirituality," which like this idea of "looking on the bright side," is in fact "a euphemism used for obscuring certain realities of life, the open consideration of which might prove threatening or dangerous to the status quo."[19] Here again, Lorde has much to contribute to our understanding of the ways that spiritualism, especially but not exclusively as an egoism, has the ability to obscure questions of justice and liberation by an obfuscating orientation toward the self. There is even more to gain, I think, by further and fully extrapolating this notion of survival and its opposition to mere "safety" and then reapproaching the questions of the politics of caring for oneself with those tools in hand.

It is just here that another question arises, one that puts productive pressure on standing conceptions of philosophy as a way of life, spiritual exercises, and the care of the self more broadly, and that is in line with several of my core concerns across this book. Much like Thurman in chapter 4, and perhaps even Friedmann in chapter 2, Lorde's concept of survival and her general approach introduce a vivid urgency to all of the questions she raises, and indeed all of the questions I have sought to raise in this book. Hadot too helped open the question of elites in chapter 1, and asks us "Is Philosophy a Luxury?," answering with a challenging "yes and no."[20] Even if his answer to that question seems to clash with Lorde's insistence that poetry is absolutely not a luxury, the productive tension created between these two answers is all the more fascinating and worth further exploration. Indeed, I suspect that, with many qualifications, they are not so far apart as they may seem.

All this is to say that we might see a contrast here between someone like Lorde or Thurman and many of the features of more familiar forms of philosophy as a way of life, especially but by no means exclusively in ancient forms of philosophical exercise (let alone the complexities of contemporary academic life). Specifically, we may read this urgency, the focus on survival, as in conflict with historical conceptions of "the good life" or an "ideal" life as a life of theoretical contemplation in many ancient sources. Here, we might think of certain historic readings of Plato and Aristotle, even as all such texts and tensions remain subject to interpretation and debate.[21] Thankfully, exegetical challenges around ancient texts are well outside my concern here, and it merely suffices that these challenges and questions emerge in the first place, especially as they are by no means particular to classical antiquity. We equally see this tension in contemplative and especially monastic or ascetic religious practice, lives intentionally lived apart from the world by intellectual and religious specialists. We may also see it in cases like those Hadot begins with in answering his own question, noting that we "shall have to evoke, very briefly, what might be called the economic aspect of this problem, that is, the financial conditions indispensable for doing philosophy in our modern world."[22]

The point here is simply that it can and has been assumed that there is an inherent value in a life of purer contemplation, one that has the time to think, to dialogue, to refine, and so on at leisure. From that perspective, there is something that the life of immediacy and crisis, the life devoted to survival, is necessarily missing or cannot achieve, tragically or not. Such a life, it is assumed, simply lacks the time and resources for forms of sufficiently undisturbed contemplation. Here, let us consider an example that has served a number of roles across this work already and should thus be familiar: the imagination or "premeditation" of future evils. As we have seen, Hadot rehearses this example often, and it figures prominently in Marcus Aurelius, Seneca, the other Stoics, and beyond.[23] One imagines future misfortune, war, death, poverty, exile, and so on, in order to be prepared if and when these things befall us.

And yet, thinking with Thurman, Lorde, and others, whose work is so often and so importantly autobiographical, we must ask: What does the premeditation of evils look like when the evils need not be "premeditated" or imagined, as they mediate almost every aspect of one's existence? What is the premeditation of death and war when death and war stalk one's life from the first moment to the last? When one was never meant to survive or lives with one's back against the wall, does this immediacy not lend something real and indeed profoundly valuable that is at once incomprehensible for those for whom such circumstances remain within the realm of contemplative imagination, however refined and well-intentioned? As Lorde so gravely puts it, "Unless one lives and loves in the trenches it is difficult to remember that the war against dehumanization is ceaseless."[24] Is this not, at least in part, because the specificity of so many of the misfortunes—specifically, the *injustices*—that so many face are so often unimaginable in the strictest sense?

Furthermore, for Lorde, these realities, as inexcusably tragic and dehumanizing as they are, are at once a source of *clarity*. Here, we find another of her most challenging insights, even as it is one that is not always front and center. As a child, Lorde's family took a vacation to Washington, D.C., and in the midst of the summer heat, they were denied counter service at an ice cream fountain near their hotel. The experience left Lorde bewildered and furious, though it was formative. As she put it later in *Zami*, for her in the summer of 1948 and against the backdrop of the end of the war, the transformations in China, Indian independence, and so much else, "My revolutionary fervor that had begun with a white waitress refusing to serve my family ice cream in the nation's capital was becoming a clearer and clearer position, a lens through which to view the world."[25] These experiences, in other words, did not obscure reality, nor did they prevent in any way, her political, philosophical, and poetic contemplation, let alone its transformation into language and action. Instead, by her own account, they sharpened her insight, attention, and language into a fine and effective set of tools for survival and transformation—with nothing of the tragedy of those circumstances lost or glossed over.

Across Lorde's life and work, that focus, the sharpness in the reflection, comes from the demands of survival. Those demands, at once spiritual and material, refine a form of clarity that may not appear without something so profound at stake as one's dignity or future or life. It may well be something that the "contemplative life" misses, not just in a set of facts or concepts, but in a refined theoretical, contemplative, and indeed artistic precision that emerges first through such a crucible. Whether, when, and how it can be translated to others who do not share those experiences is of course another question entirely. For some, philosophy begins in wonder. But does it not also, for so many, begin and persist in crisis? And may not that state sharpen and clarify not only our actions, but our concepts? Does not the immediacy of interlocking injustices provide a vital lens through which to imagine and pursue the genuinely good life, not just individually, but collectively and systemically? These core questions challenge and complicate much that is taken for granted in the study of spiritual exercises and philosophy as a way of life. And for all that, they raise further questions for any such life in real practice. This is especially the case if, as I have pursued across this book, we want to understand the forms of political life that emerge from and seek to transform those very conditions.

III. POETRY AS A WAY OF LIFE

On the basis of the claim developed in chapter 3, regarding the ways in which the relationship of the self to itself is materially and institutionally mediated,

CONCLUSION

I argued in chapter 4 that insofar as organizing within mass movements that work toward material transformation and collective liberation are an intervention on the level of crucial nodes in that circuit, such practices thus constitute a paradigmatic form of political self-transformation. Such work is all the more exemplary insofar as the ongoing forms of practice that together constitute a larger movement are themselves self-transformative in ways that reciprocally co-constitute the larger political intervention. In a movement, one's very form of life is transformed, in order to further transform the conditions that brought it about, and thus the future conditions of life in general, and the new, perhaps more liberatory, relationships that we may have with ourselves and others. The question of how the forms of life and experience that emerge within such movements—so often described as liberatory, beautiful, and nourishing themselves—can (or should) model forms of life following any success is a rich and fascinating one, and well worth pursuing in future studies.

Lorde herself was not known, at least not generally, as an organizer, even as she engaged in a number of significant movements over the course of her life, perhaps especially but not exclusively in efforts against apartheid.[26] However, while these cases are important, much of Lorde's work and what she sometimes calls a "self-conscious life" evince what are in some ways more "immediate" forms of intervention—though all of these terms require further specification.[27] She is, after all, first and foremost a poet, though one who takes poetry to be something beyond the discursive and, rather, a fundamental and necessary way of being. As she so famously puts it in the landmark "Poetry Is Not a Luxury," "I speak here of poetry as a revelatory distillation of experience, not the sterile wordplay that, too often, the white fathers distorted the word *poetry* to mean." It is for this reason, defined as a "revelatory distillation of experience," that "poetry is not a luxury." It is, rather, "a vital necessity of our existence. It forms the quality of the light within which we predicate our hopes and dreams toward survival and change, first made into language, then into idea, then into more tangible action." For Lorde, "this is poetry as illumination," and in that way, beyond a merely discursive practice, I think we can also say that it is poetry as a way of life.[28]

Now, taking all of the complexity and ambiguity within this vision seriously, it may be argued that Lorde's very form of life, what we might call her "poetics of existence," operates more directly on the level of the self and of the immediate community than those organizing-based forms of intervention that target given systemic conditions. At the same time, of course, any research program that takes up an analysis of Lorde's life and lifework from this perspective would need to much more thoroughly and subtly parse out these distinctions and clarify how and when they ultimately do us no good, when they elide and produce even more complex dynamics. (Indeed, the need for just that kind of reading is my point here.) All of that being said, and much more centrally on my reading and based on all that I have claimed here, I see the kind of relationship of the self to itself that we see in the life and work of someone like Lorde as much more challenging to understand as a political exercise than those rehearsed in chapter 4. This is once again precisely because if we read this work well and wade into these rich ambiguities, any strict distinctions quickly dissipate into generative clouds of theoretical and practical possibility.

This claim will no doubt appear counterintuitive to many, as standard conceptions of the politics of the self tend to center the kind of immediacy that I am thinking of here. The challenge, I think, is that while the kind of work Lorde presents in no way slides into the "self-indulgence" she mentions, the distinction between such a life and the political moralism or ethical spiritualism that have concerned me over the course of this book can be much harder to disentangle. That challenge is the result of a number of factors, including many of the forms of aesthetic or other misdirection discussed in the introduction and chapter 3. There are also the much greater challenges of understanding, carefully and in context, when, how, and under what conditions practices that seek to directly transform the self may also constitute a genuine political intervention, understood collectively, systemically, or materially. And although I argue in chapter 3 that Foucault provides a framework for understanding just such interventions, historically and theoretically pinning down genuine and robust cases remains a challenge.

I cannot perform such analyses here, of course, as my goal is to conclude by proposing avenues for further work. However, one fascinating and I believe fertile approach would be to read Lorde's poetry, autobiographical writing, and the life captured by that work through the lens of parrhesia as Foucault explores it in *The Courage of Truth* and related texts. Indeed, in chapter 3, I briefly express my standing misgivings about whether or not the life and mission of someone like Diogenes the Cynic, Foucault's favorite

CONCLUSION

ancient parrhesiast, can really be understood or elaborated in terms of a political intervention.[29] Lorde, I think, is another matter entirely, and the possibilities for such a reading are potentially riveting. Parrhesia here is not just fearless or audacious true speech, nor is it only a courageousness of the "true life as life of truth." Rather, I think we can in fact read it as a reciprocal form of the *transformation of silence into language and action*, in the form of a body of poetry and prose produced by and co-constitutive of a courageous and bio-poetic life of truth. Here, the discursive and lived modes of parrhesia that Foucault praised do, I think, find a politics in a meteoric poetics of existence that evinces at once the beautiful life, life as art form, and the life of truth that Foucault began to sketch and that goes beyond what he had begun to imagine.

This idea of "the transformation of silence into language and action" is among Lorde's most powerful terms of art, and the title of another landmark text. That "The Transformation of Silence Into Language and Action" first appeared as a talk, a public address given at a Modern Language Association panel in Chicago on December 28, 1977, is significant. We may, I think, take this term and concept as a kind of road map for reading Lorde as parrhesiast, work I look forward to taking up in a future project (ideally in the company of others). Such a reading could begin with Lorde's true speech, which is at once solemn, audacious, and full of joy in the act of transmuting silence into language, while at the same time sorrowful and trepidatious at the conditions that demand it. As she asks her audience in late 1977, "What are the words you do not yet have? What do you need to say? What are the tyrannies that you swallow day by day and attempt to make your own, until you sicken and die of them, still in silence?"[30] Of course, parrhesia carries an inherent risk, by definition.[31] And as we have seen through the core theme of survival, by simply being who she is, Lorde was fundamentally attuned to that risk. It is something she marks again in this same speech, with a careful vulnerability that is at once a challenge: "And of course I am afraid, because the transformation of silence into language and action is an act of self-revelation, and that always seems fraught with danger."[32]

Here, we may see an initial resonance with the ancient parrhesiasts, those who put themselves at risk to advise the prince or challenge the powerful. At the same time, I read Lorde against several of the problems of class and power and so much else explored in chapters 1 and 2, not to mention all of the themes that shape her own work. While many of the parrhesiasts Foucault describes in texts like *The Courage of Truth* were in a position of subordination to the powerful, we cannot assimilate their positionality to that of someone like Lorde, or to members of what Thurman called the disinherited community, those who live with their backs against the wall. For Lorde, as someone who "lived her battles in the flesh" in almost every aspect of her life, that difference is fundamental. A distinction then with the ancient parrhesiasts, one worth reading more deeply: risk here does not simply emerge in the act of speech or as a part of one's position as advisor to the powerful. Rather, that risk is an intimate one, as to simply be who she is, let alone to speak, is marked by risks of death, physical, harm, deadly negligence, and so much else. In texts like "The Transformation of Silence" and "A Burst of Light," all of this is again amplified by her cancer diagnosis.

This risk and the reasons for it open up the next step in a possible reading of Lorde as parrhesiast, in this case as *lived* parrhesia, the true life as the life of truth, the expression of truth in action, beyond just the discursive. It is this model of lived parrhesia that Foucault sought in the ancient Cynics, in Diogenes especially. Of course, as in the case of Diogenes, the lived parrhesia practiced by Lorde is in part discursive, bringing together speech, writing, and action in forms that are delightfully and productively confrontational. These effects are again compounded and complicated when we understand, as Lorde consistently emphasizes, the way that her life and position as a subject is already a site of contestation and danger. As she again says to her audience in 1977, "Perhaps for some of you here today, I am the face of one of your fears. Because I am woman, because I am Black, because I am lesbian, because I am myself—a Black woman warrior poet doing my work—come to ask you, are you doing yours?"[33] Here, spoken language is a revelatory distillation of respective experiences and a parrhesiastic practice of truth grounded in but not limited to the discursive.

Other cases can be found across Lorde's work. These include the excoriations in "The Language of Difference," that she lays against a group of white Australian feminists who invited her to speak at an August 1985 conference commemorating the 150th anniversary of the founding of the State of Victoria, a conference at which Indigenous Aboriginal women were neither present nor acknowledged. A similar case may be found the previous year, when she was accused of "brutalizing" the organizers of the First International Feminist Bookfair in London for "simply asking why Black

CONCLUSION

women were absent." In that case, however, as she puts it, "if my yelling and 'jumping up and down' got dirty looks and made white women cry and say all kinds of outrageous nonsense about me, I know it also reinforced other Black women's perceptions about racism here in the women's movement, and contributed to further solidarity among Black women of different communities."[34]

These cases are powerful and generative moments of parrhesia, of a relationship of the self to itself that passes through truth and through others to return to itself, grounded in the discursive, in speech, and in poetry. There is one final step in thinking through the transformation of silence into language and action as a form of parrhesia, one that mirrors Foucault's final interest in figures like Diogenes, in which the truth is most forcefully and most fundamentally *enacted* and *lived*, rather than primarily spoken or written. On my reading, one of the most generative and indeed moving instances of parrhesiastic action on Lorde's part once again emerges from the challenge of cancer. One powerful example is found in Lorde's defiant refusal to wear a prosthesis following her mastectomy, recounted in the third and final section of *The Cancer Journals*, titled "Breast Cancer: Power vs. Prosthesis." I cannot, again, give these passages the attention they deserve here, but it is for that reason that I think they are among the best places to leave this current conversation as we mark out areas for new dialogues.

Lorde discovered what turned out to be a malignant tumor in her right breast on Labor Day (September 4) 1978, and underwent a mastectomy just a few weeks later, at the end of September. The passages in *The Cancer Journals* that recount this experience are as harrowing as they are moving. Early on in the piece, Lorde describes her first visit to the doctor's office following surgery, and the profound importance she placed on dressing for the visit in a way that made her feel like herself and that affirmed and reinforced a sense of power and agency. In her words:

> This was my first journey out since coming home from the hospital, and I was truly looking forward to it. A friend had washed my hair for me and it was black and shining, with my new grey hairs glistening in the sun. Color was starting to come back into my face and around my eyes. I wore the most opalescent of my moonstones, and a single floating bird dangling from my right ear in the name of grand asymmetry. With an African Kente cloth tunic and new leather boots, I knew I looked fine, with that brave new-born

security of a beautiful woman having come through a very hard time and being very glad to be alive. I felt really good.

As she walked into the doctor's office, she reports, "I was really rather pleased with myself, all things considered, pleased with the way I felt, with my own flair, with my own style."[35] Here, this act of dressing, of presenting herself to the world in a way that stood as a kind of defiance to the surgery and to the cancer, mattered enormously.

And yet, to the doctors, nurses, and others in the office, all that mattered was the shock and worry that Lorde was not wearing the lambswool prosthesis she had been given. Despite her clear statement that it just did not feel right, the nurse and others kept insisting that Lorde would "feel better with it on" and that it was, of all things, "bad for the morale of the office." As Lorde says, however, "this was to be only the first such assault on my right to define and to claim my own body."[36] The rest of the piece discusses the politics and economics of breast cancer and mastectomy, the uses of prostheses, and the ways that the medical literature Lorde encountered reflected what she saw in practice, an almost total focus on what for her are superficial cosmetic concerns. Now, to be as clear as possible, Lorde's point is not to pass judgment on anyone who would choose to wear a prosthesis. The issue for her is fundamentally one of agency and the freedom to genuinely relate to one's own body and experience in ways that one needs and wishes to: "There is nothing wrong, per se, with the use of prostheses, if they can be chosen freely, for whatever reason, after a woman has had a chance to accept her new body."[37] The problem, of course, is that in the circumstances she describes, whatever one's ultimate choice might be, there is no time or space for that process.

Needless to say, knowing the social, personal, and other risks involved, Lorde does not wear the prosthesis. I think we can read this choice, generatively, as an act of lived parrhesia. Here, it is worth citing her, in her own words, in full:

Prosthesis offers the empty comfort of "Nobody will know the difference." But it is that very difference which I wish to affirm, because I have lived it, and survived it, and wish to share that strength with other women. If we are to translate the silence surrounding breast cancer into language and action against this scourge, then the first step is that women with mastectomies

> must become visible to each other. For silence and invisibility go hand in hand with powerlessness. By accepting the mask of prosthesis, one-breasted women proclaim ourselves as insufficients dependent upon pretense. We reinforce our own isolation and invisibility from each other, as well as the false complacency of a society which would rather not face the results of its own insanities. In addition, we withhold that visibility and support from one another which is such an aid to perspective and self-acceptance. Surrounded by other women day by day, all of whom appear to have two breasts, it is very difficult sometimes to remember that I AM NOT ALONE. Yet once I face death as a life process, what is there possibly left for me to fear? Who can ever really have power over me again?[38]

Here, on these terms, Lorde lives in a way that establishes a relationship of the self to itself in order to intervene, in a liberatory manner, in the possible relationships that others may have to themselves. That transformation comes about through the translation of silence into action, and action into language, and into the language and action of others. This idea, which provides a way of seeing the "translation of action into language," also allows us to rethink and develop the notion of parrhesia itself. We can, I think, read this parrhesia not only in terms of the relationship of oneself to oneself, but as an intervention into the circuit that constitutes the relationships of others to themselves. And here, as always, the parrhesiastic act is not an end in itself, but is rather in the service of truer principles and forms of life. If these choices make others uncomfortable, it is only so that others, even and perhaps especially those who may choose other than she did, would have the chance to genuinely make such a decision, rather than having it preemptively made for them.

Perhaps then, like the immediacy that clarifies in ways that imaginative premeditation may not, the parrhesia of the cancer survivor lends us something that the ancient models may well point us toward, but do not themselves articulate or demonstrate. One of the reasons that I conclude with Lorde, indeed, is to bring us back to our own present and to thus point up the proliferation in our time and under our conditions of spiritual demands that are at once political demands. The question here, at its most basic, is one of what kinds of people we must become, based on how those conditions have already shaped us, in order to transform them and, in so doing, further transform ourselves. There is very clearly no one answer to such a question, and I have only scratched the surface in thinking about how to articulate the question, let alone to begin to answer it. It is clear, however, that a body of work like Lorde's has a role in all of these tasks, for reasons well beyond the brief suggestions I have noted here.

IV. IMPLICATIONS

I end with Lorde, as I have said, because I would like to begin with Lorde. On my reading, Lorde's work, poetry and prose, very much collectively constitutes a landmark in the history of writing the self and, indeed, of the care of the self. It does so in a way that is very clearly an intervention into the constitution of the very self that writes—rather, the selves that write—and as a further intervention into the political conditions and relations of power within which that self is co-constituted. For this reason, to read Lorde following the trajectory of this book and then to reread that trajectory against Lorde and her legacy is to necessarily recomplicate and challenge the literature and guiding concepts that I have centered. On my reading, and in the spirit of this book as a whole, "that effort is necessary, that ambition is just," to again paraphrase Friedmann as invoked by Hadot.

Further contributions, which I have not been able to address here, would be found in Lorde's powerful discussions and mobilization of a range of political emotions. I am thinking here in particular of her rich reflections on anger, in texts like her 1981 piece "The Uses of Anger: Women Responding to Racism" especially, but across her writing as well.[39] Lorde richly develops a thread that appears in nascent forms in earlier movements within Black and other radical traditions, including the nonviolent tradition, regarding the complex relationship to anger, and the work of transforming and deploying this maligned but powerful and deeply human emotion toward liberatory ends. This work and all that it entails very much present a challenge to liberal conceptions in general, but perhaps especially to some of the more sanitized liberal reconstructions of nonviolent practice. It is also, I think, a vital intervention in the study of the relationship of the self to itself via transformative practice that occludes any distinction between "interior" and "exterior." If after all, "controlling" or "letting go" of one's passions, including anger, is among the standard examples of self-transformation that someone like Hadot invokes, how much more so is the transformation of anger into action within the crucible of the self?

CONCLUSION

A comparably productive intervention emerges from Lorde's conception of the erotic. Here, like the notion of "survival," she elaborates a capacious concept that works its meaning well beyond existing conceptions. The erotic is not some "confused, trivial . . . plasticized sensation." It is instead something at once less concrete and more powerfully productive, a "measure between the beginnings of our sense of self and chaos of our strongest feelings."[40] This open space is full of possibility, but for Lorde, it has been reduced in order to, among so much else, reduce what is possible, crucially for women. There is much more to say about this articulation, but for now these brief descriptions suffice to note just how much they have to offer the study of practices of the self, spiritual exercises, philosophy as a way of life, and much more within the constellation of themes and questions that I have sought to open in this book. It also goes without saying that figures like Lorde, among many other feminists and queer theorists, present a necessary set of challenges to everything I have claimed here, especially insofar as I have insisted that the specificity of the demands and conditions that one faces always and necessarily matter.

I emphasize the readings I have proposed here and many that I have not as a challenge to as much as an extension of anything I have established. Indeed, we can already see how the very gravity of Lorde's work commands a transformation in the categories that I have been thinking through. Whether in terms of how to care for oneself, how to live, how and under what conditions the care of the self may be coterminous with the care of the other, of others, of the community—these productive tensions are already apparent and need only to be further specified and cultivated. How does the emphasis on survival, linked as it is so closely to that poetry that is not a luxury present us with the possibility of a radically new and perhaps radically more vital conception of the premeditation of death? How does training for death, which is at once training to live, including in the biological sense, sharpen and transform itself when one's life is stalked by death at every turn? How does training for death in this more vital and immediate form move beyond contemplation into necessary action? It is with Lorde, I think, that we see how the persistent precarity of one's life lends such gravity to the work of transformation that one takes up, whether alone or in the company of others.

As she put it in a journal entry dated December 9, 1985, again in the context of facing cancer, "I am going to write fire until it comes out my ears, my eyes, my noseholes—everywhere. Until it's every breath I breathe. I'm going to go out like a fucking meteor!"[41] Those trails are very much still with us, constantly falling to earth and settling in new places. But if Lorde spoke of "[going] out like a fucking meteor," among the many things we can learn from her and from this orientation toward death, in ways that are resonant with the long history of the care of the self and fundamentally challenge and transform that history, is how to live like one. In closing this work and looking toward further research and conversation, I want to leave the last word to Lorde and some language that I think, against the backdrop and on the foundation of everything I have sought to establish here, may serve us well. Indeed, in many ways, these sentiments or some version of them motivate my entire project here, and they are worth keeping in mind in any rereading of the politics of self-transformation that may be taken up. As Lorde says:

> The only really happy people I have ever met are those of us who work against these deaths with all the energy of our living, recognizing the deep and fundamental unhappiness with which we are surrounded, at the same time as we fight to keep from being submerged by it.[42]

NOTES

INTRODUCTION

1. See Isabelle Gourné, "'Philosoviet' Commitments and a Sociological Stance Between the Two World Wars: Georges Friedmann's Political and Intellectual Role," *Sociologie du travail* 54 (2012): 356–374.
2. See Georges Friedmann, *La puissance et la sagesse* (Paris: Gallimard, 1970); Georges Friedmann, *Journal de guerre, 1939–1940* (Paris: Gallimard, 1987).
3. See Michel Foucault, "On the Genealogy of Ethics: An Overview of a Work in Progress," in *Essential Works of Michel Foucault, 1954–1984*, ed. Paul Rabinow, vol. 1, *Ethics: Subjectivity and Truth* (New York: New Press, 1997), 263.
4. It also appears in major nonviolent landmarks like Krishnalal Shridharani's (1911–1960) *War Without Violence: A Study of Gandhi's Method and Its Accomplishments* (New York: Harcourt, Brace, 1939). Shridharani's major contemporary, Richard Bartlett Gregg, speaks briefly of a related "social purification" in the context of mass nonviolence, through militant training. Admittedly, this turn of phrase can sound somewhat chilling to our ears out of context, but writing in 1934, Gregg describes this concept in the following positive terms: "Still another way in which mass nonviolent resistance operates is to end and clear away social defects, economic mistakes and political errors. The semi-military discipline of the resisters, the getting rid of bad habits, the learning to struggle without anger, the social unity developed, the emphasis on moral factors, the appeal to the finest spirit of the opponents and onlookers, the generosity and kindness required—all these constitute a social purification, a creation of truer values and actions among all concerned." Richard Bartlett Gregg, *The Power of Non-violence* (New York: Fellowship Publications, 1944), 93.

INTRODUCTION

5. Audre Lorde, "A Burst of Light: Living with Cancer," in *A Burst of Light: Essays by Audre Lorde* (Ithaca, N.Y.: Firebrand, 1988), 131.
6. See Jan Patočka, *Plato and Europe*, trans. Peter Lom (Stanford, Calif.: Stanford University Press 2002). Patočka was a student of Husserl, and his unique philosophical background certainly differs from those of the other figures I engage here. He is engaged by figures like Jacques Derrida (1930–2004) and Paul Ricoeur (1913–2005), and Foucault does mention him from time to time. His political situation is also unique, as his life and work took place in Czechoslovakia in the mid-twentieth century, on the other side of the so-called Iron Curtain, with all of the added complexity and importance of the Czech experience, especially between 1968 and 1977. Patočka was a primary author, signatory, and spokesperson of Charta 77, lending further depth and interest to the political implications of his work. He died at the age of 69 in March of 1977, one week after falling ill following ten hours in the custody of Czech police. It is my hope to one day engage Patočka's "care of the soul" in the context of a study like this. There are a number of parallels to the life and work of Friedmann, beyond having died in the same year. And I believe that it is extremely important to engage the question of practice of the self in general and in a political sense through the lens of life and experience within the so-called Second World.
7. See Stanley Cavell, *Cities of Words: Pedagogical Letters on a Register of the Moral Life* (Cambridge, Mass.: Belknap Press of Harvard University Press, 2004), 13. See also chapter 1, section I, "Consumed by Worries, Torn by Passions," note 46.
8. "The coincidence of the changing of circumstances and of human activity of self-change [*Selbstveränderung*] can be conceived only as *revolutionary practice*." Karl Marx, "Theses on Feuerbach," trans. Clemens Dutt, in *German Socialist Philosophy*, ed. Wolfgang Shirmacher, The German Library (New York: Continuum, 1997), 105. It is very interesting to note that the *Marx-Engels* reader, edited by Robert Tucker and published by Norton in 1978, which is arguably the most ubiquitous collection of Marx's work found on Anglophone, or at least American, bookshelves and university syllabi, omits the term "self-change" or *Selbstveränderung* from its translation of the "Theses." There, it is simply reads "The coincidence of the changing of circumstances and of human activity can be conceived and rationally understood only as revolutionizing practice." See Karl Marx, "Theses on Feuerbach," in *The Marx-Engels Reader*, ed. Robert C. Tucker (New York: Norton, 1978), 144.
9. See Pierre Hadot, "Spiritual Exercises," in *Philosophy as a Way of Life: Spiritual Exercises from Socrates to Foucault* (Oxford: Blackwell, 1995), 101.
10. Pierre Hadot, "My Books and My Research," trans. Matthew Sharpe and Federico Testa, in *The Selected Writings of Pierre Hadot: Philosophy as Practice* (London: Bloomsbury Academic, 2020), 34.
11. Pierre Hadot, Jeannie Carlier, Arnold I. Davidson, Marc Djaballah, and Michael Chase, *The Present Alone Is Our Happiness: Conversations with Jeannie Carlier and Arnold I. Davidson*, 2nd ed. (Stanford, Calif.: Stanford University Press, 2011), 87. Elsewhere, in "My Books and My Research," Hadot elaborates, speaking of "certain procedures or endeavors which we can more precisely call spiritual exercises: that is, practices aimed at a modification, an improvement, and a transformation of the self." Hadot, "My Books and My Research," 36. See also chapter 1, section I, "Consumed by Worries, Torn by Passions," note 3.

INTRODUCTION

12. Pierre Hadot, *What Is Ancient Philosophy?* (Cambridge, Mass.: Belknap Press of Harvard University Press, 2002), 6. Hadot again elaborates elsewhere: "At the origin of these exercises, there is an act of choice, a fundamental option for a certain way of life. One then actualizes this option in the order of inner discourse and spiritual activity: that is, in meditation, dialogue with oneself, examination of conscience or exercises of imagination such as the view from above on the cosmos or the earth. One also embodies this option at the level of action and everyday conduct." Hadot, "My Books and My Research," 36.
13. See Michel Foucault, *The History of Sexuality*, vol. 2, *The Use of Pleasure*, trans. Robert Hurley (New York: Pantheon, 1985), 26–28; Foucault, "On the Genealogy of Ethics," 263–265.
14. Foucault, "On The Genealogy of Ethics," 256.
15. Foucault, *The Use of Pleasure*, 28.
16. See chapter 1, section III, "Ordinary Philosophy and Ordinary Life. See also William James, *The Varieties of Religious Experience* (New York: Penguin, 1985), 6.
17. See chapter 1, section IV, "Spiritual Exercises in the Present" and section V, "Implications."
18. Hadot for example, likely inspired by Foucault's use of the language of the "care of the self," speaks of Diogenes the Cynic in just these terms: "His care for himself was, indissolubly, care for others." Hadot, *What Is Ancient Philosophy?*, 111.
19. Friedmann, *La puissance et la sagesse*, 10.
20. Michel Foucault, *The Hermeneutics of the Subject: Lectures at the Collège de France, 1981–1982* (New York: Palgrave-Macmillan, 2005), 252.
21. Pierre Hadot, *Philosophy as a Way of Life: Spiritual Exercises from Socrates to Foucault*, ed. Arnold I. Davidson (New York: Blackwell, 1995), 81.
22. Friedmann, *La puissance et la sagesse*, 10.
23. That this point is rather urgent for Friedmann might be read into the fact that in the text itself, there is actually a footnote at the bottom of the page directing the reader to this endnote. Friedmann, *La puissance et la sagesse*, 10.
24. Friedmann, *La puissance et la sagesse*, 443.
25. See Robert Wuthnow, *After Heaven: Spirituality in America Since the 1950s* (Berkeley: University of California Press, 1998), 115, 52, 2, 1, respectively.
26. Foucault, "On the Genealogy of Ethics," 271.
27. Foucault, *The Hermeneutics of the Subject*, 12. Interestingly, it is of Foucault's own work that Hadot poses the question of whether or not what we have in the former's notion of "the care of the self" is nothing more than "a new form of Dandyism, late twentieth century style." Hadot, "Spiritual Exercises," 211.
28. Foucault, *The Hermeneutics of the Subject*, 12.
29. Foucault, *The Hermeneutics of the Subject*, 13.
30. Hadot, "Reflections on the Idea of the 'Cultivation of the Self,'" in *Philosophy as a Way of Life: Spiritual Exercises from Socrates to Foucault*, ed. Arnold I. Davidson (Oxford: Blackwell, 1995), 207.
31. Friedmann, *La puissance et la sagesse*, 132.
32. Friedmann, *La puissance et la sagesse*, 119.
33. Friedmann, *La puissance et la sagesse*, 11.
34. Friedmann, *La puissance et la sagesse*, 151.
35. Friedmann, *La puissance et la sagesse*, 151.

INTRODUCTION

36. See Ronald Turner, "The Way to Stop Discriminaton on the Basis of Race . . . ," *Stanford Journal of Civil Rights and Civil Liberties* 11, no. 45 (April 9, 2015): 45–88, https://ssrn.com/abstract=2592570.
37. Briefly, I take it that either something really is a genuine quietism or actually amounts to a moralism in practice. I am skeptical of the claim that such an impulse or practice is ever genuinely apolitical. Such views and their attending forms of life are also fascinating in terms of the kinds of ethical relationships they have historically produced.
38. Friedmann, *La puissance et la sagesse*, 10.
39. Michel Foucault, *The History of Sexuality*, vol. 1, *An Introduction*, trans. Robert Hurley (New York: Random House, 1978), 10.
40. Friedmann, *La puissance et la sagesse*, 57–60.
41. See chapter 2, section I, "An Unquiet Wisdom."
42. If known to English audiences, it is often through his writings on Judaism. However, I do not engage this material in this text, as it raises far too many questions that are well outside my concerns here.
43. See Friedmann, *La puissance et la sagesse*, foreword and part 1, "The Great Disequilibrium."

1. PIERRE HADOT: ANCIENT SPIRITUAL EXERCISES AND CONTEMPORARY SPIRITUAL DEMANDS

1. Georges Friedmann, *La puissance et la sagesse* (Paris: Gallimard, 1970), 359–360 (my translation). Despite his importance in France as a sociologist of labor, his expertise on and work within the Soviet Union, the publication of his war journals and his engagement with the philosophical tradition (cf. his *Leibniz et Spinoza* [Paris: Gallimard, 1946]), Friedmann remains little known in the Anglophone world, with little of his work translated since his death in 1977. For that reason, all translations of Friedmann are my own, unless otherwise specified. This particular passage seems to be something of a favorite of Hadot's, as it appears several times in the English collection *Philosophy as a Way of Life*, as well as in his book *What Is Ancient Philosophy?* and in conversation with Arnold I. Davidson in the interview "Philosophical Discourse as a Spiritual Exercise," among other instances. However, the translation differs between the English versions, and I have retranslated it for consistency in both the language and my reading of Friedmann. See Pierre Hadot, "Forms of Life and Forms of Discourse in Ancient Philosophy," in *Philosophy as a Way of Life: Spiritual Exercises from Socrates to Foucault*, ed. Arnold I. Davidson (Oxford: Blackwell, 1995), 70; Pierre Hadot, "Spiritual Exercises," in *Philosophy as a Way of Life: Spiritual Exercises from Socrates to Foucault* (Oxford: Blackwell, 1995), 81; Pierre Hadot, *What Is Ancient Philosophy?* (Cambridge, Mass.: Belknap Press of Harvard University Press, 2002), 276; Pierre Hadot, Jeannie Carlier, Arnold I. Davidson, Marc Djaballah, and Michael Chase, "Philosophical Discourse as a Spiritual Exercise," in *The Present Alone Is Our Happiness: Conversations with Jeannie Carlier and Arnold I. Davidson* (Stanford, Calif.: Stanford University Press, 2011), 93.
2. Hadot, "Spiritual Exercises," 81. I will bracket the many questions and problems that arise around the generalized language that Hadot uses to describe the latter

1. PIERRE HADOT

grouping of traditions. It is also worth noting that Hadot's characterization of Friedmann in *La puissance et la sagesse* is not entirely accurate, as Friedmann was very familiar with the work of Marcus Aurelius. See Georges Friedmann, *Journal de guerre, 1939–1940* (Paris: Gallimard, 1987), especially the entry of June 20, 1940, p. 280. Further, Friedmann's particular critiques of certain contemporary religious movements are not at all general ones. Rather, they are specifically tied to the problems around rapid technological change and what he calls "the Great Disequilibrium." Nor does he refer to "Oriental" traditions, but instead engages in a sustained conversation about Hinduism that reflects a surprising familiarity with both Indian politics and the anti-colonial struggle, as well as a direct knowledge of influential Indian popularizing movements like the Ramakrishna Mission and Sri Aurobindo Ghose. If Friedmann's reflections in *La puissance et la sagesse* seem at all dated from our perspective, they remain surprisingly thorough in context.

3. Hadot, "My Books and My Research," 35. See also Hadot et al., "Philosophical Discourse as a Spiritual Exercise," 87. Note that, regarding this definition of spiritual exercises, in his own invocation and elaboration across *La puissance et la sagesse*, Friedmann clearly means something quite similar.
4. Hadot, "Spiritual Exercises," 82.
5. Pierre Hadot was born in Paris on February 21, 1922, to a pious mother and a father who became disillusioned with the church. Nonetheless, Hadot had what he refers to as a "holy water childhood" in Reims, educated by priests in varying religious institutions. Pierre Hadot, Jeannie Carlier, Arnold I. Davidson, Marc Djaballah, and Michael Chase, *The Present Alone Is Our Happiness: Conversations with Jeannie Carlier and Arnold I. Davidson*, 2nd ed. (Stanford, Calif.: Stanford University Press, 2011), 4–5. According to the wishes of his mother, Hadot followed his two older brothers into the seminary in 1937 and was ordained in 1944. Due to an increasing philosophical gap between his own views and church dogma (especially the publication of Humani Generis by Pope Pius XII on August 12, 1950, and the proclamation of the Dogma of Assumption on November 1 of that year), and a desire to marry, Hadot left the priesthood in June of 1952. Hadot et al., *The Present Alone Is Our Happiness*, 22. Although his relationship with the church is complex, Hadot is clear about the central role that his religious education played in the philosophical and philological development that served as the foundations of his career. See "Tied to the Apron Strings of the Church" in Hadot et al., *The Present Alone Is Our Happiness*, chap. 1, for a more detailed description of Hadot's intellectual autobiography.)
6. As he puts it, "even Loyola's *Exercitia spiritualia* were deeply rooted in the exercises of ancient philosophy." Pierre Hadot, "Ancient Spiritual Exercises and 'Christian Philosophy,'" in *Philosophy as a Way of Life: Spiritual Exercises from Socrates to Foucault* (Oxford: Blackwell, 1995),126. Elsewhere, Hadot uses rather stronger language: "Ignatius' *Exercitia spiritualia* are nothing but a Christian version of a Greco-Roman tradition," Hadot, "Spiritual Exercises," 82.
7. Hadot, "Spiritual Exercises," 82.
8. Hadot, "Spiritual Exercises," 82.
9. It is worth noting that Hadot uses much stronger language in some places, arguing that within his works, "one finds the idea that philosophy should be defined as a spiritual exercise." Pierre Hadot, "My Books and My Research," trans. Matthew Sharpe and Federico Testa, in *The Selected Writings of Pierre Hadot: Philosophy as*

1. PIERRE HADOT

Practice (London: Bloomsbury Academic, 2020), 34. Statements of this kind are misleading, however, as they may suggest that there is no place for familiar forms of systematic or discursive philosophical practice, when it is clear that far from dismissing such practice, Hadot instead re-situates those familiar forms within a broader framework centered on spiritual exercises.

10. In *What Is Ancient Philosophy?*, Hadot immediately notes that there is "nothing wrong" with the way that students learn philosophy in contemporary academic contexts. And yet, "the history of 'philosophy' is not the same as the history of philosophies, if what we understand by 'philosophies' are theoretical discourses and philosopher's systems. In addition to this history . . . there is room for the study of philosophical modes of life." Thus, he seeks "to show that a profound difference exists between the representations which the ancients made of *philosophia* and the representation which is usually made of philosophy today" in the university. Hadot, *What Is Ancient Philosophy?*, 1–2. In an epigraph to the same book, Hadot invokes Henry David Thoreau's quip from *Walden* that "there are nowadays professors of philosophy, but not philosophers" and explores Thoreau's claim in further detail in an article of the same title; see Pierre Hadot, "There Are Nowadays Professors of Philosophy, But Not Philosophers," *Journal of Speculative Philosophy* 19, no. 3 (2005): 229–237.

11. Pierre Hadot, "Ancient Philosophy: An Ethics or a Practice?," trans. Matthew Sharpe and Federico Testa, in *The Selected Writings of Pierre Hadot: Philosophy as Practice* (London: Bloomsbury Academic, 2020), 55.

12. Hadot, "My Books and My Research," 34. Elsewhere, he elaborates the issue in greater detail: "It must be recognized that generally speaking the philosophical works of Greco-Roman antiquity almost always perplex the contemporary reader. I do not refer only to the general public, but even to specialists in the field. One could compile a whole anthology of complaints made against ancient authors by modern commentators, who reproach them for their bad writing, contradictions, and lack of rigor and coherence. Indeed, it is my astonishment both at these critics and at the universality and persistence of the phenomenon they condemn that inspires the reflections I have just presented, as well as those I wish to turn to now." Hadot, "Forms of Life and Forms of Discourse," 61.

13. Hadot, "My Books and My Research," 34. To be sure, many current scholars may argue with Hadot's claim here regarding this phenomenon of "deploring inconsistencies," as it may not reflect their own methods or reading, though it will certainly reflect readings of ancient texts in any number of contemporary cases. That is, of course, all well and good, as Hadot is describing a historical exegetical stasis in French philology, classical studies, and philosophy that motivates not just his insight but his later methodological approach.

14. Pierre Hadot, "Marcus Aurelius," in *Philosophy as a Way of Life: Spiritual Exercises from Socrates to Foucault* (Oxford: Blackwell, 1995), 179. Indeed, several of Hadot's major exegetical and philosophical works are devoted to the *Meditations*; see, e.g., Pierre Hadot, *The Inner Citadel: The Meditations of Marcus Aurelius*, trans. Michael Chase (Cambridge, Mass.: Harvard University Press, 2001); Pierre Hadot, *Introduction aux "Pensées" de Marc Aurèle* (Paris: Librairie Arthème Fayard, 1997). Regarding the title, it is worth noting that despite the tradition of referring to the text as *The Meditations* in English, the 1916 Loeb edition translates the Greek title as *The Communings with Himself of Marcus Aurelius Antonius*, in line with Hadot's

1. PIERRE HADOT

point here. See Marcus Aurelius, *The Communings with Himself of Marcus Aurelius Antonius, Emperor of Rome, Together with His Speeches and Sayings*, ed. and trans. C. R. Haines (Cambridge, Mass.: Harvard University Press, 1916).
15. Hadot, "My Books and My Research," 38.
16. Hadot et al., *The Present Alone Is Our Happiness*, 57.
17. See Hadot, "Marcus Aurelius," 179.
18. Hadot, "My Books and My Research," 38.
19. Marcus Aurelius, *Meditations, with Selected Correspondence*, trans. Robin Hard (Oxford: Oxford University Press, 2011), 7.13.47.
20. Hadot, "My Books and My Research," 38.
21. Hadot details these physiological and psychological accounts in Hadot, "Marcus Aurelius," 179–181. See also his brief remarks to Davidson on these questions in Hadot et al., *The Present Alone is Our Happiness*, 57.
22. Ilsetraut Hadot (née Marten, b. 1928) is a pathbreaking classical philologist and philosopher, whose work remains relatively poorly known in the Anglophone world. Pierre Hadot speaks of the central importance of texts like her *Seneca und die Griechisch-Römische Tradition der Seelenleitung* [Seneca and the Greco-Roman Tradition of Spiritual Guidance] (Berlin, Walter de Gruyter, 1969), in the development of his thought in *What Is Ancient Philosophy?*, ix, and on numerous other occasions.
23. See Pierre Hadot, "Jeux de langage et philosophie," *Revue de Métaphysique et de Morale* 67, no. 3 (July–October 1962): 330–343. In *The Present Alone Is Our Happiness*, Davidson notes: "It is not insignificant . . . that you [Hadot] were the first in France to have discovered Wittgenstein." Hadot responds here and elsewhere with several points on Wittgenstein, regarding both the charges of "inconsistency" leveled early on at the latter's work and the ways that Wittgenstein helps frame and motivate Hadot's studies, among other related points. However, Hadot himself does not take credit for discovering Wittgenstein in France, noting that "Jean Wahl certainly knew him as early as 1946," though Hadot's early engagement was a decisive contribution. In conversation with Davidson, Hadot provides some fascinating history regarding the introduction and reception of Wittgenstein in France, and it is clear that he was indeed one of the earliest readers and popularizers of the latter's work, even attempting an early (never published) translation of the *Tractatus*. Although brief, this conversation with Davidson illuminates a great deal about Hadot's reading of Wittgenstein, and the ways that it frames his research in general. See Hadot et al., *The Present Alone Is Our Happiness*, 132–135. For a closer reading of Hadot's philosophical relationship to Wittgenstein, see Sandra Laugier, "Pierre Hadot as a Reader of Wittgenstein," *Paragraph* 34, no. 3 (November 2011): 322–337, https://doi.org/10.3366/para.2011.0028.
24. Hadot, "My Books and My Research," 34.
25. Hadot, "Forms of Life and Forms of Discourse," 61.
26. See Pierre Hadot, Jeannie Carlier, Arnold I. Davidson, Marc Djaballah, and Michael Chase, "Interpretation, Objectivity, and Mistakes," in *The Present Alone Is Our Happiness: Conversations with Jeannie Carlier and Arnold I. Davidson* (Stanford, Calif.: Stanford University Press, 2011), 63.
27. Hadot, "Forms of Life and Forms of Discourse," 50–52. Hadot provides this summation in reference to the work of Pierre Courcelle (1912–1980), and the ways it reflected his own approach. Courcelle was a scholar of Latin patristics and a

specialist in Augustine. A friend and colleague to Hadot at the École Pratique des Hautes Études, he held the chair in Latin literature at the Collège de France until his death in 1980. Hadot dedicates his inaugural remarks at the Collège de France to Courcelle and includes a detailed description of both Courcelle's reading of Augustine and the scandal it provoked at the time.

28. Hadot, "My Books and My Research," 34.
29. He continues: "On cannot read an ancient author the way one does a contemporary author (which does not mean that contemporary authors are easier to understand than those of antiquity). In fact, the works of antiquity are produced under entirely different conditions." Hadot, "Forms of Life and Forms of Discourse," 61. Or, as he puts it elsewhere, "In order to explain this phenomenon, I gradually came to observe that it is always necessary to explain the text in light of the living context in which it was born: that is to say, the concrete conditions of life in the philosophical schools, in the institutional sense of the word." Hadot, "My Books and My Research," 34. This methodological attention to contextual detail is the hallmark of Hadot's oeuvre. As Andrew Irvine puts it in his introduction to a 2021 translation of one of Hadot's earliest articles: "The firm basis of Hadot's creativity was intensely thoughtful engagement with ancient texts in their original languages." Pierre Hadot, "Epistrophe and Metanoia in the History of Philosophy," *Philosophy Today* 65, no. 1 (Winter 2021): 202. Of course, it is worth remembering that even with all the scholarly care, skill, and attention one can muster, Hadot insists that it is still "very easy to fall into anachronism, because we are not aware of many of the historical conditions under which it was written—who it is aimed at, who it copies, perhaps." Often enough, we simply do not know what we do not know. Hadot et al., "Interpretation, Objectivity, and Mistakes," 63.
30. Hadot, "Marcus Aurelius," 179.
31. Regarding these particular examples, see Hadot, "Marcus Aurelius," 183–191. See also Hadot, "My Books and My Research," 38.
32. On the influence of Epictetus and the Stoic tradition on the emperor, see Hadot, "Marcus Aurelius," 191–202; see also chap. 4, "The Philosopher-Slave and the Emperor-Philosopher," in Hadot, *The Inner Citadel*.
33. Hadot, "Marcus Aurelius," 195, 201.
34. More even than for Hadot, the concept of "humanization" is foundational for Friedmann; see chapter 2, section I, "An Unquiet Wisdom."
35. Hadot, "Spiritual Exercises," 85.
36. Hadot, "Spiritual Exercises," 82. Just before this passage, Hadot lists in the detail the many possible substitutes for the language of the spiritual, and the reasons why none of them will ultimately suffice to articulate his vision.
37. Hadot, "Spiritual Exercises," 83, 91. Hadot analyses this notion of "conversion" and the differing forms that it may take in a number of places. See also Pierre Hadot, "Conversion," trans. Matthew Sharpe and Federico Testa, in *The Selected Writings of Pierre Hadot: Philosophy as Practice* (London: Bloomsbury Academic, 2020), 93–104; Hadot, "Epistrophe and Metanoia."
38. Hadot, "Spiritual Exercises," 101.
39. Hadot, "Spiritual Exercises," 102.
40. Hadot, "Spiritual Exercises," 83.
41. Hadot, "Spiritual Exercises," 83.

1. PIERRE HADOT

42. Hadot, *What Is Ancient Philosophy?*, 135. Note that for Hadot, the ancient schools were "ways of life" *insofar as they were organized as schools* or, even in the case of the Cynics, by virtue of *rejecting* the organizational structure of the schools and choosing to live philosophically in plain sight.
43. Hadot, "Forms of Life and Forms of Discourse," 57.
44. Hadot, *What Is Ancient Philosophy?*, 49.
45. Hadot, "Forms of Life and Forms of Discourse," 57. In *What is Ancient Philosophy?*, Hadot describes the unattainability of the sage in similar terms, noting, however, that "the only universally recognized sage was Socrates—that disconcerting sage who did not know he was a sage." Hadot, *What Is Ancient Philosophy?*, 224.
46. Hadot, "Forms of Life and Forms of Discourse," 58–59. The idea that ideal state is at once always unreachable and always pursuable may be read in resonance with Stanley Cavell's conception of "Emersonian perfectionism" and the "unattained but attainable self" at the heart of his elaboration. In Cavell's words: "In Emerson's and Thoreau's sense of human existence, there is no question of reaching a final state of the soul but only and endlessly taking the next step to what Emerson calls 'an unattained but attainable self'—a self that is always and never ours—a step that turns us not from bad to good, or wrong to right, but from confusion and constriction toward self-knowledge and sociability. Plato's idea of a path to one goal (the one sought by the sage) does not exactly fit Emerson's idea of how to live. In both, the idea of philosophy as a way of life plays a role in assessing your life now, but Emerson is less interested in holding up the life of the sage as a model for ours than in reminding us that the power of questioning our lives, in, say, our judgment of what we call their necessities, and their rights and goods, is within the scope of every human being (of those, at any rate, free to talk about their lives and to modify them)." Stanley Cavell, *Cities of Words, Cities of Words: Pedagogical Letters on a Register of the Moral Life* (Cambridge, Mass.: Belknap Press of Harvard University Press, 2004), 13. At the same time, it strikes me that Cavell's notion of a particularly Emersonian perfectionism and the "unattained but attainable self" at its heart both do and do not feature in the differing schools Hadot analyzes or Hadot's own philosophical commitments. Although this concept and the literature around it are near to this project in many ways, they are complex enough on their own terms that I simply cannot do justice to them here, let alone situate them in dialogue with Hadot. The best I can do is a passing footnote for now. For more extensive and insightful discussions of the overlap between Hadot, Cavell, and others, see Daniele Lorenzini, "La vie comme 'réel' de la philosophie. Cavell, Foucault, Hadot et les techniques de l'ordinaire" in *La voix et la vertu. Variétés du perfectionnisme moral*, ed. Sandra Laugier (Paris: Presses Universitaires de France, 2010), 469–487; Daniele Lorenzini, "Must We Do What We Say? Truth, Responsibility and the Ordinary in Ancient and Modern Perfectionism," *European Journal of Pragmatism and American Philosophy* 2, no. 2 (2010): 16–34; Daniele Lorenzini, "Ethics as Politics: Foucault, Hadot, Cavell and the Critique of Our Present," in *Foucault and the History of Our Present*, ed. Sophie Fuggle, Yari Lanci, and Martina Tazzioli (London: Palgrave Macmillan UK, 2015), 223–235.
47. Hadot, *What Is Ancient Philosophy?*, 36.
48. See Michel Foucault, "On The Genealogy of Ethics: An Overview of a Work in Progress," in *Essential Works of Michel Foucault, 1954–1984*, ed. Paul Rabinow, vol. 1,

1. PIERRE HADOT

Ethics: Subjectivity and Truth (New York: New Press, 1997), 265; Michel Foucault, *The History of Sexuality*, vol. 2, *The Use of Pleasure*, trans. Robert Hurley (New York: Pantheon, 1985), 28. I follow Foucault in using the term *telos* throughout the present work to simply refer to whatever ideals one works toward when working upon oneself through practices of ethical self-change, though I will sometimes simply refer to the telos in the simple language of "goals" or "aims." In this case, the figure of the sage is a personification of the philosophical telos of the school, though a set of un-personified ideal principles can serve the same role, as can the idea of the next life in varying religious contexts, etc.

49. Hadot, "Forms of Life and Forms of Discourse," 59.
50. Hadot et al., "Philosophical Discourse as a Spiritual Exercise," 93.
51. Hadot, "Forms of Life and Forms of Discourse," 59.
52. Hadot, "Spiritual Exercises," 87.
53. Hadot, "Spiritual Exercises," 108.
54. Hadot, "Reflections on the Idea of the 'Cultivation of the Self,'" in *Philosophy as a Way of Life: Spiritual Exercises from Socrates to Foucault*, ed. Arnold I. Davidson (Oxford: Blackwell, 1995), 208.
55. Jeannie Carlier, introduction to Hadot et al., *The Present Alone Is Our Happiness*, xv.
56. Goldschmidt describes the Platonic dialogues in these terms, but Hadot often borrows it for broader purposes. See Victor Goldschmidt, *Les "Dialogues" de Platon: structure et méthode dialectique* (Paris: Presses universitaires de France, 1947) in Hadot, *What Is Ancient Philosophy?*, 73; Hadot, "My Books and My Research," 35; Hadot, "Ancient Philosophy," 56.
57. Carlier is paraphrasing Hadot here, who says "For my part, I would say that it is a matter of what Kierkegaard called the method of indirect communication. [. . .] Thanks to the description of spiritual experience lived by another, one can give a glimpse of and suggest a spiritual attitude; one allows a call to be heard that the reader has the freedom to accept or to refuse. It's up to the reader to decide." Hadot et al., *The Present Alone Is Our Happiness*, 147.
58. The unironic presence of this text on the innumerable and ubiquitous reading lists compiled by neoliberal spiritualists, especially those spiritual-capitalists who anachronistically look to books like the *Meditations* in search of nuggets of wisdom regarding amorphous concepts like "leadership" or "entrepreneurship" would, on a surface reading, seem to evince that ease. Conversely, there is arguably nothing that makes Hadot's point about the uncritical projection of contemporary prejudices back onto ancient texts as the anachronistic readings (if, indeed, the texts in question are ever actually read at all in these contexts) of ancient figures like Marcus Aurelius or Sunzi by the cottage industry of "entrepreneurial" and "management" literature. The airport bookstore is about as far as you can get from the clinic of Epictetus.
59. Hadot wrestles with the problem of the textual record in almost all of his writing. For just a few examples, see Hadot, "Spiritual Exercises," 84; Hadot, *What Is Ancient Philosophy?*, 95, 135.
60. Hadot, "Spiritual Exercises," 101.
61. Hadot, *What Is Ancient Philosophy?*, 102.
62. Hadot, *What Is Ancient Philosophy?*, 102–103.

1. PIERRE HADOT

63. Arnold I. Davidson, preface to Hadot et al., *The Present Alone Is Our Happiness*, xi.
64. Hadot, *What Is Ancient Philosophy?*, 127.
65. Hadot, *What Is Ancient Philosophy?*, 132–133.
66. Hadot, "Spiritual Exercises," 86.
67. Thus "mankind's woes derive from the fact that he seeks to acquire or to keep possessions that he may either lose or fail to obtain, and from the fact that he tries to avoid misfortunes which are often inevitable." Hadot, "Spiritual Exercises," 83. See also Hadot, *What Is Ancient Philosophy?*, 126–139.
68. Pierre Hadot, "The Sage and the World," in *Philosophy as a Way of Life: Spiritual Exercises from Socrates to Foucault* (Oxford: Blackwell, 1995), 251.
69. Hadot, "Spiritual Exercises," 83. On Hadot's reading, it is this task that motivates the *Meditations* of Marcus Aurelius
70. Hadot, "Spiritual Exercises," 86.
71. Hadot, "Spiritual Exercises," 87.
72. Hadot, "Spiritual Exercises," 87.
73. Hadot, *What Is Ancient Philosophy?*, 117.
74. Hadot, *What Is Ancient Philosophy?*, 117. As Hadot notes on the same page, this attitude is reflected in an Epicurean saying: "Thanks be to blessed Nature, who has made necessary things easy to obtain, and who has made things difficult to obtain unnecessary."
75. Hadot, "Spiritual Exercises," 87.
76. Hadot, *What Is Ancient Philosophy?*, 115.
77. Hadot, *What Is Ancient Philosophy?*, 117.
78. "It cannot be increased, and no new pleasure can be added to it." Hadot, *What Is Ancient Philosophy?*, 116.
79. Hadot, "Forms of Life and Forms of Discourse," 58.
80. It is interesting to note that Philo of Alexandria is perhaps the only, and certainly the primary, Jewish philosopher whom Hadot discusses. It is unfortunate, however, that while many of those readings include Philo in the cannon of ancient philosophy, few, if any, describe the *Jewish* nature of his work. He briefly remarks in "Ancient Spiritual Exercises and 'Christian Philosophy'" that "Philo portrayed Judaism as the *patrios philosophia*: the traditional philosophy of the Jewish people. The same terminology was used by Flavius Josephus." Hadot, "Ancient Spiritual Exercises and 'Christian Philosophy,'" 129. And yet, as in this case, Philo's Judaism only tends to arise in conversations about Christianity and is often otherwise absent. Indeed, even in arguing for the "traces" of the Eleusinian Mysteries in Philo's outlook, his Judaism goes unremarked. See Hadot, *What Is Ancient Philosophy?*, 162. Similarly, Hadot rarely, if ever, mentions Islam and the profound history of Islamic philosophical discourse and practice in any substantive way. In this he again joins Friedmann, as Islamic traditions of any kind are glaringly absent in the section of *La puissance et la sagesse* in which he surveys various religious and political views while undertaking the spiritual exercise of "re-sourcing" himself. I find this absent presence troubling, though for reasons to be explored elsewhere.
81. Hadot, *What Is Ancient Philosophy?*, 127.
82. As noted in the introduction, Hadot makes this threefold distinction at the beginning of *What Is Ancient Philosophy?* in the course of defining spiritual exercises: "By this term, I mean practices which could be physical, as in dietary regimes,

1. PIERRE HADOT

or discursive, as in dialogue and meditation, or intuitive, as in contemplation, but which were all intended to effect a modification and a transformation in the subject who practiced them. The philosophy teacher's discourse could also assume the form of a spiritual exercise, if the discourse were presented in such a way that the disciple, as auditor, reader, or interlocutor, could make spiritual progress and transform himself within." Hadot, *What Is Ancient Philosophy?*, 6.

83. As he says of certain Stoics, in their response to Ariston of Chios, "who sought to eliminate the physical and logical parts of philosophy and allowed only ethics to remain," in fact "the logical and physical parts of philosophy were not purely theoretical. They too corresponded to a lived philosophy." Hadot, *What Is Ancient Philosophy?*, 137–138.
84. Hadot, "Spiritual Exercises," 84. For a similar but more detailed elaboration of *prosokhē* in Hadot's terms, see Hadot, *What Is Ancient Philosophy?*, 136–138.
85. Hadot, "Spiritual Exercises," 84–85.
86. Hadot, "Spiritual Exercises," 97–98. Hadot's most thorough comparative discussion of this practice of "the view from above" can be found in the text of that title; see Pierre Hadot, "The View from Above," in *Philosophy as a Way of Life: Spiritual Exercises from Socrates to Foucault* (Oxford: Blackwell, 1995), 238–250.
87. Indeed, because the grand perspective is central to his own commitments and so clearly captures his fascination, there is potentially a case to be made that Hadot overemphasizes its ubiquity and can only do so through a kind of anachronism that betrays the care and precision that otherwise marks his research. At the same time, there is also strong textual case for Hadot's emphasis on both its ubiquity and universality.
88. Hadot, "Spiritual Exercises," 85.
89. "Such self-consciousness is, above all, moral consciousness, which seeks at every moment to purify and rectify our intentions. At every instant, it is careful to allow no other motive for action than the will to do good. Yet such self-consciousness is not merely moral; it is also a cosmic and rational consciousness. Attentive people live in the constant presence of universal Reason which is immanent within the cosmos. They see all things from the perspective of Reason, and consent joyfully to its will." Hadot, *What Is Ancient Philosophy?*, 138.
90. "It is not just an act of cognition, but one of "[steeping] ourselves in the rule of life (*kanon*), by mentally applying it to all of life's possible different situations, just as we assimilate a grammatical or mathematical rule through practice, by applying it to individual cases." Hadot, "Spiritual Exercises," 85.
91. Hadot, *What Is Ancient Philosophy?*, 138.
92. Hadot, "Ancient Philosophy," 67.
93. In sum, "Philosophical discourse about physics aimed to justify the choice of life we have just mentioned, and to make explicit the way of being-in-the-world that it implies." Hadot, *What Is Ancient Philosophy?*, 129. On Hadot's account, this orientation informed Stoic, Epicurean, and even Cynic forms of life, among many others from antiquity to the present.
94. See Hadot, "Spiritual Exercises," 96–98.
95. Hadot, "Spiritual Exercises," 98. As he says of the Stoic perspective, "Putting theory into practice begins with an exercise that consists in recognizing oneself as part of the Whole, elevating oneself to cosmic consciousness, or immersing oneself within

1. PIERRE HADOT

the totality of the cosmos. While meditating on Stoic physics, we are to try to see all things within the perspective of universal Reason. To achieve this, we must practice the imaginative exercise which consists in seeing all human things from above." Hadot, *What Is Ancient Philosophy?*, 136. Or, as he notes regarding the *Meditations* of Marcus Aurelius: "The philosopher must abandon his partial, egoistic vision of reality, in order, by way of physics, to rise to the point of seeing things as universal Reason sees them. Above all, the philosopher must intensely wish the common good of the universe and of society, by discovering that a part can possess no other proper good than the common good of the All." Hadot, *The Inner Citadel*, 99. See also chapter 7 in the same text for Hadot's discussion of the "discipline of desire" in the *Meditations*, where Hadot argues that the askesis of desire is tied directly to the practice of physics in the text. Regarding the contemplative practice of physics in the Epicurean school, see Hadot, "Spiritual Exercises," 87–88. For further discussion of ancient physics as a spiritual exercise, note Hadot's remarks in Hadot, "Ancient Philosophy," 65–67.

96. See Hadot, "Spiritual Exercises," 97.
97. Hadot, *What Is Ancient Philosophy?*, 197.
98. Hadot, *What Is Ancient Philosophy?*, 198. Here he continues, speaking to the widespread understanding of this orientation, noting that we would be wrong "to oppose meditation on death and meditation on life. They are fundamentally identical, and both are an indispensable condition for becoming self-aware."
99. Epicurus, "Letter to Menoeceus," in *The Art of Happiness*, ed. Daniel Klein (London: Penguin, 2012), 157.
100. Hadot, *What Is Ancient Philosophy?*, 197.
101. Hadot, "Spiritual Exercises," 85.
102. See Philo, *On the Special Laws* 2.46, in Hadot, *What Is Ancient Philosophy?*, 137.
103. As a "dogmatic" tradition, the Stoics "tried to present their doctrine in accordance with a rigorously systematic logical sequence" that supported the Stoic requirement to "keep the school's essential dogmas present in their minds, by dint of a constant effort of memory." Hadot, *What Is Ancient Philosophy?*, 106–107. By thus "engraving striking maxims in our memory . . . when the time comes, they can help us accept such events, which are, after all, part of the course of nature." With these maxims and rules "at hand," we can "check moments of fear, anger, or sadness." Hadot, "Spiritual Exercises," 85. Like their Stoic counterparts, the Epicureans and Skeptics practiced similar exercises of memorization. Hadot, *What Is Ancient Philosophy?*, 106, 145.
104. Hadot, *What Is Ancient Philosophy?*, 106–107.
105. Hadot, *What Is Ancient Philosophy?*, 195.
106. Hadot, "Spiritual Exercises," 85.
107. While Hadot does engage certain threads within Christian traditions, especially those that he takes to be in continuity with ancient philosophical culture, the class of more recognizably religious exercises comprises perhaps the largest field of possibility. From theistic prayer and contemplation, to practices of confession and spiritual guidance, to acts of pilgrimage, musical and aesthetic practices of all kinds, forms of religious and spiritual community-making, and the innumerably different meditative practices we find across traditions, the relevant possibilities are far too numerous to simply list. Hadot himself only gradually came around to

1. PIERRE HADOT

engaging Asian traditions, e.g., even as great scholarship continues to emerge in dialogue with his work. See, e.g., the posthumously published *Wisdom as a Way of Life: Theravāda Buddhism Reimagined*, ed. Justin McDaniel (New York: Columbia University Press, 2018), by the great scholar of Buddhism Steve Collins, to whom I owe a debt of gratitude in this work, as described in greater detail later.

108. There is a complex semi-affinity between the set of relationships that I outline here as necessary to the constitution of a full or proper "form of life" in Hadot's terms, and what Foucault calls a "unified moral conduct" constituted by the fourfold distinction the latter makes between "ethical substance," "mode of subjectivation," "ethical work," and "telos." See Foucault, *The Use of Pleasure*, 28. See also chapter 3, section IV, "A Kind of Work."

109. As Hadot puts it, "The logical and physical parts of philosophy were not purely theoretical. Rather, they too corresponded to a lived philosophy." Moreover, "in a philosophy that is put into practice, the limits between the parts of philosophy became indistinct." Hadot, *What Is Ancient Philosophy?*, 137–138, 172–173.

110. For just a few examples, see his remarks on the Platonist Axiothea of Phlius, the Cynic Hipparchia, as well as Hadot's account of the Epicurean "life in common, which did not disdain to allow slaves and women to participate in it," in Hadot, *What Is Ancient Philosophy?*, 72, 109, 125. The problem in all of these cases is not the extent to which women could participate in philosophical life, but rather the extent to which are now able to see how deeply they helped fashion that life.

111. Pierre Hadot, Jeannie Carlier, Arnold I. Davidson, Marc Djaballah, and Michael Chase, "Is Philosophy a Luxury?," in *The Present Alone Is Our Happiness: Conversations with Jeannie Carlier and Arnold I. Davidson*, ed. Jeannie Carlier, Arnold I. Davidson, Marc Djaballah, and Michael Chase (Stanford, Calif.: Stanford University Press, 2011), 188.

112. Hence his criticism of contemporary academic practice as something that "by contrast . . . appears above all as the construction of a technical jargon reserved for specialists." Hadot, "Spiritual Exercises," 272. We know for certain that when Hadot speaks of philosophy, he does not mean the academic career of the contemporary philosophy professor, of which he is clearly quite critical, as we have already seen. But I am indebted to the late Professor Steve Collins for the most illuminating conversation I have ever had on this question, at the University of Chicago Divinity School coffee shop one afternoon in the fall of 2016. Professor Collins's generosity, grace, and insight are well missed and cherished, as are our too-brief and infrequent discussions of Ornette Coleman and the trajectory of free improvisation. As Professor Collins noted to me, Hadot's vision does not necessarily exclude the particular form of academic philosophical life as economic vocation. This is perhaps especially true for the role of teacher and mentor, of which our conversation that afternoon was an example. At the same time, even such an exchange, and this overall contemporary form, no matter how we approach or understand it, is very much an academic and economic luxury, and we must bear in mind the many economic, political, and cultural resources that make it so much as possible. Conversely, and to directly and intentionally undermine my own initial claim, it is certain that equally rich, perhaps richer, conversations with far greater stakes are occurring at this very moment in contexts of profound economic, political, and other forms of hardship and danger. Perhaps these are the models we should look

to, rather than those of ancient autocrats. At very least, Hadot's "yes and no" to the question of whether philosophy is a luxury may even be found in some instances of one of his own favorite counterexamples. In some cases, times, and places, the professor of philosophy may yet be a philosopher after all.

113. In Hadot's terms: "This was why dogmatic philosophies like Stoicism and Epicureanism had a popular missionary character: since technical and theoretical discussions were matters for specialists, they could be summed up—for the benefit of beginners and students who were making progress—in a number of formulas which were tightly linked together, and which were essentially rules for practical life. In this respect, such philosophies coincided with the 'missionary' and 'popular' spirit of Socrates. Whereas Platonism and Aristotelianism were reserved for an elite which had the 'leisure' to study, carry out research, and contemplate, Epicureanism and Stoicism were addressed to everyone: rich and poor, male and female, free citizens and slaves. Whoever adopted the Epicurean or Stoic way of life and put it into practice would be considered a philosopher, even if he or she did not develop a philosophical discourse, either written or oral." Hadot, *What Is Ancient Philosophy?*, 108. See also Davidson, preface to Hadot et al., *The Present Alone Is Our Happiness*, xi.
114. Hadot et al., "Is Philosophy a Luxury?," 186.
115. Hadot et al., "Is Philosophy a Luxury?," 189.
116. Hadot et al., "Is Philosophy a Luxury?," 189–190.
117. E.g., Hadot references Porphyry's remarks in *On Abstinence*, describing them as follows: "Porphyry was perfectly aware that such a way of life was radically different from that of the rest of humanity. He is addressing, he says, not people who 'practiced manual trades or who are athletes, soldiers, sailors, orators, or politicians, . . . but people who have reflected on the questions, 'Who am I?' Where do I come from? Where must I go?' and who, in their diet and in other areas, have established for themselves principles different from those which rule other ways of life." Hadot, *What Is Ancient Philosophy?*, 158. We see this attitude elsewhere as well, and in all cases, it should force us to ask ourselves what, if anything, is it that necessarily excludes the practice of the manual trades from reflecting on the question "Who am I?" The answer, of course, is absolutely nothing. And while on paper all of this may seem clear, it very much remains a tension and an assumption in popular discourse in our own time: the idea that such reflection is the purview of certain people by virtue of not just education, but of certain forms of work, and thus of economics. This is especially tragic when, e.g., it is an assumption made without question by educated individuals claiming commitment to a more just world. For my part, I cannot but repeat that experience shows otherwise. It is a fact that philosophical reflection, debate, argument, and so on do not simply happen on a jobsite, but that those conversations are—with their own humorous, sometimes dark, sometimes strange, sometimes brilliant voices—a constitutive feature of work in common of this kind. The claim, implicit or explicit, that complex ideas or forms of argumentation are the purview of some but not others is unequivocally false. The same experiences that shape my outlook on this issue in general directly inform my approach in this book, including my hostility to any top-down view of intellectual life, or life in general for that matter. I am much more interested, as I hope is reflected throughout this project, in the contours of so-called ordinary lives.

1. PIERRE HADOT

118. A further and crucial point of analysis here would be the well-documented influence of Epictetus on the great Haitian revolutionary Toussaint Louverture, though the questions this raises are well outside of anything Hadot references and sit much more squarely in my own space of interest.
119. Later, in reference to the Stoics, he notes that Stoicism followed the Socratic tradition of a teaching that sought "to mold citizens—political leaders, if possible, but also philosophers." Hadot, *What Is Ancient Philosophy?*, 58, 103.
120. Hadot, *What Is Ancient Philosophy?*, 94–95.
121. Hadot, *What Is Ancient Philosophy?*, 94.
122. Hadot, "Spiritual Exercises," 91.
123. Hadot, *What Is Ancient Philosophy?*, 37; and see the section titled "Care of the Self and Care of Others" (36–38).
124. Hadot, *What Is Ancient Philosophy?*, 111.
125. As Hadot puts the comparison between them: "Although Socratic care of the self, by making people attain inner freedom, dissolved the illusions of the appearances and phantoms linked to social conventions, it nevertheless retained a kind of smiling urbanity, which disappeared with Diogenes and the Cynics." Hadot, *What Is Ancient Philosophy?*, 111.
126. Carlier, introduction to Hadot et al., *The Present Alone Is Our Happiness*, xix.
127. Hadot, "Spiritual Exercises," 108.
128. Hadot et al., "Interpretation, Objectivity, and Mistakes," 67–68.
129. Pierre Hadot, "Postscript," trans. Michael Chase, in *Philosophy as a Way of Life: Spiritual Exercises from Socrates to Foucault* (Oxford: Blackwell, 1995), 282; see also 285.
130. Hadot, "Postscript," 282.
131. Hadot, "Postscript," 283.
132. Hadot, "Postscript," 283.
133. Hadot, "Postscript," 282.
134. Marcus Aurelius, *Meditations* 7, in Hadot, "The View from Above," 244.
135. Yuri Gagarin and Vladimir Lebedev, *Survival in Space*, trans. Gabriella Azrael (New York: Bantam, 1969), 3–4. Gagarin is the first to have seen the Earth itself from orbit, an experience that is uniquely resonant with philosophical-historical conceptions of the view from above, especially, on my account, when its technological specificity is understood. The latter is a point that Friedmann consistently emphasizes, as I discuss in chapter 2. Of course, as Friedmann also emphasizes, and as Gagarin and his co-author Lebedev are clear, to make this claim—and to highlight it as a technological feat—is to also understand it as something that is in continuity with others who have come before. Lebedev and Gagarin include many examples from the history of human attempts to leave the ground and the experiences of awe that accompanied them. For them, as for Friedmann, that an experience or a technology has a history is a given, and this fact does nothing to diminish its specificity. Gagarin had reverence for previous aviators, and knew well that he had accomplished—and experienced—something no one else had before. I return to these themes in chapter 2, where this dynamic represents something of a core hermeneutic, moral, and indeed political for Friedmann.
136. Frank White, "Episode 107: The Overview Effect," interview by Gary Jordan, *Houston We Have a Podcast*, 2019, https://www.nasa.gov/johnson/HWHAP/the

-overview-effect. See also Frank White, *The Overview Effect: Space Exploration and Human Evolution*, 4th ed. (Reston, Va.: American Institute of Aeronautics and Astronautics, 2021).
137. Ron Garan, foreword to the 3rd edition, in White, *The Overview Effect*, ix
138. Emmanuel Levinas, "Heidegger, Gagarin and Us," trans. Seán Hand, in *Difficult Freedom: Essays on Judaism* (Baltimore, Md.: Johns Hopkins University Press, 1990), 233.
139. Hadot et al., "Philosophical Discourse," 56.

2. GEORGES FRIEDMANN: FROM THE GREAT DISEQUILIBRIUM TO THE INTERIOR EFFORT

1. Georges Friedmann, *La puissance et la sagesse* (Paris: Gallimard, 1970), 11.
2. Friedmann, *La puissance et la sagesse*, 10. Regarding the notion of "socialism with a human face," Friedmann often references this phrase, most famously associated with the Czechoslovakian Communist Party of Alexander Dubček and the events leading up to the Prague Spring of 1968, and later to the Charta 77 movement in which Jan Patočka played an important part. For lack of space in the present work, I do not engage Friedmann's understanding of this concept.
3. See Georges Friedmann, *Journal de guerre, 1939–1940* (Paris: Gallimard, 1987).
4. Friedmann, *La puissance et la sagesse*, 11.
5. See Friedmann, *La puissance et la sagesse*, 119.
6. Friedmann, *La puissance et la sagesse*, 11.
7. Friedmann was "doté de diplômes socialement valorisé," as Isabelle Gourné puts it. Isabelle Gourné, "'Philosoviet' Commitments and a Sociological Stance Between the Two World Wars: Georges Friedmann's Political and Intellectual Role," *Sociologie du travail* 54 (2012): 359. See also Friedmann, *La puissance et la sagesse*, 378. See also the biographical preface entitled "Georges Friedmann (1902–1977): ses œuvres, ses engagements, 1920–1939" by Edgar Morin, in Friedmann, *Journal de guerre*, 25.
8. Friedmann, *La puissance et la sagesse*, 32.
9. During the period from about 1924 to 1930, Friedmann cofounded the *Groupe Philosophies*, named for a journal he coedited with the poet Pierre Morhange (1902–1972) and the philosophers Georges Politzer (1903–1942), Norbert Guterman (1900–1984), and Henri Lefebvre (1901–1991). This core group of five friends came together at the École normale, and was, he says, "Closely knit by their trenchant views, their enthusiasms, their arrogant refusals, their revolts: one of them rich, the rest not at all." Friedmann, *Journal de guerre*, 25–26; see also Elisabeth Roudinesco, *Jacques Lacan & Co: A History of Psychoanalysis in France, 1925–1985* (Chicago: University of Chicago Press, 1990), 56–71; Stuart Elden, *Understanding Henri Lefebvre: Theory and the Possible* (London: Continuum, 2004), 2. Friedmann himself was "the rich one," and would attempt to use his inherited wealth to support the group's various endeavors. Over the last half the 1920s, the friends published four short-lived journals. The first of these, *Philosophies*, for which the group is still known, was on Friedmann's account, "a review whose tendencies were 'epic, mystical, metaphysical.' " Friedmann, *Journal de guerre*, 26. The six issues of *Philosophies* appeared between March 1924 and March 1925. *Philosophies* folded after only six

2. GEORGES FRIEDMANN

issues, to be replaced by the shorter-lived *L'esprit*, which saw only two issues in May 1926 and January 1927. Roudinesco, *Jacques Lacan & Co.*, 61. Although "no member of the group adhered to Marxism" (Roudinesco, *Jacques Lacan & Co.*, 56), by the time *L'esprit* closed down at the end of 1926, "the adventurers joined the ranks of the Communist Party" (Roudinesco, *Jacques Lacan & Co.*, 61) and in turn founded a new publication project, "la société d'édition Les Revues," in 1929. Continuing the quintet's previous activities, the société published two short-lived journals: *La revue de psychologie concrète* and *La revue marxiste*. Friedmann, *Journal de guerre*, 26.

10. The group's final attempt at publishing was again short-lived: both of the latter two journals were forced to cease publication for financial reasons, following the "tragico-bouffounne" events of the "roulette affair." Friedmann, *Journal de guerre*, 26n9. In 1929, Friedmann and Pierre Morhange lost a large portion of Friedmann's inherited fortune, and thus the group's funding, at the Monte Carlo casino, to a con artist claiming to be a fellow Marxist who would double their finances at the roulette table. The twenty-seven-year-old idealists, waiting outside because their new acquaintance claimed he could not properly concentrate with them present, never saw the man or Friedmann's inheritance ever again. This absurd series of events remains the subject of speculation as to whether the man, "Spektor," was a "run-of-the-mill swindler" or an agent of "the Parisian corridors of the Comintern." For more details regarding "the affair," its aftermath, and the subsequent history of its interpretation, see Roudinesco, Jacques Lacan & Co, 61–62.; Friedmann, *Journal de guerre*, 26n9; and M. Trebitsch, "Les mésaventures du groupe Philosophies (1924–1933)," *La Revue des reviews* no. 3 (Spring 1987).
11. For greater detail on the notion of *machinisme*, its translation into English as "mechanization," and Friedmann's usage overall, see François Vatin, "'Machinisme,' Marxism, Humanism: Georges Friedmann Before and After WWII," *Sociologie du travail* 49 (2007): e16–e33, http://france.elsevier.com/direct/SOCTRA.
12. Friedmann, *La puissance et la sagesse*, 32.
13. Friedmann, *La puissance et la sagesse*, 108. It is important to note that in articulating this problem, Friedmann thought that the coming digital society, which he foresaw in the 1970s, would arise as a kind of extension of industrialization and carry with it, magnify, and renew many of the same problems in new and perhaps even more consequential terms. This seems to be the case, especially insofar as the former cannot not be separated from the industrial means, forms of labor, and environmental and ecological wages that accompany the production (including the mining of rare materials), disposal, and "recycling" of digital technologies. Thus, as he says, in a way that remains resonant: "We are still living in this age, and it is unclear when it will end," or as he more succinctly puts it, "The game is not over." (Friedmann, *La puissance et la sagesse*, 108, 109.)
14. "Interest in these problems, which have always seemed to me among the most important and disquieting of our epoch, concerning as they do humanity's moral as well as its material future, had begun to engage my attention as early as 1930." Georges Friedmann, *Industrial Society: The Emergence of the Human Problems of Automation*, 2nd ed. (New York: Free Press, 1967), 21.
15. See Friedmann, *La puissance et la sagesse*, 15.
16. Friedmann, *La puissance et la sagesse*, 23.

2. GEORGES FRIEDMANN

17. Friedmann, *Industrial Society*, 21, 11.
18. "The facts employed here are almost exclusively direct testimony coming from workmen, foremen, engineers, and from the studies of industrial psychologists specializing in the human problems of industry, [of the latter,] frequently men who have themselves practiced the mechanized trades which they were studying." Friedmann, *Industrial Society*, 21.
19. Isabelle Gourné, "'Philosoviet' Commitments," 359. All translations from Gourné's paper are my own. As Gourné describes it, a result of his "repeated visits to the USSR and the ethnographic work that his mastery of Russian and political connections allowed him to conduct there, Friedmann became, within the universe of the French social sciences in the 1930s, one of the principal intermediaries with the USSR." Gourné, "'Philosoviet' Commitments," 360.
20. Gourné, "'Philosoviet' Commitments," 359–360.
21. Georges Friedmann, *Problèmes du machinisme en U.R.R.S. et dans les pays capitalistes* (Paris: Éditions sociales internationales, 1934); Georges Friedmann, "Machinisme et humanisme," *Europe*, no. 151 (June 1935): 437–444; Georges Friedmann, "Travail et communion en U.R.R.S.," *Europe*, no. 153 (September 1935): 58–80.
22. Gourné, "'Philosoviet' Commitments," 360.
23. This "Trial of the Sixteen" was held from August 19 to 24, 1936, and is also called "the Trial of the Trotskyite-Zinovievite Terrorist Center." See Friedmann, *La puissance et la sagesse*, 249n.
24. Friedmann, *Journal de guerre*, 60. See also Friedmann, *La puissance et la sagesse*, 249, 272n, 362–363. Note that Vatin, citing Melnik-Duhamel, argues that at the time (in 1938, with the publication of *De la sainte Russie*), Friedmann was much more sympathetic to Stalin, and even to the trials. While this can be debated, it is absolutely clear that the shift that culminated in a firm anti-Stalinism within just two to three years began around or even before this time. There is no trace of any form of apologetic to be found in the *Journal*, and Vatin admits that Friedmann sensed "the 'leaden cover' that was being clapped down on the Russian intelligentsia." See Vatin, "'Machinisme,' Marxism, Humanism," e25fn34.
25. Friedmann, *Journal de guerre*, 56n1.
26. As he writes a year later in his war journals, "There is an immense critical work to be done, a critique completely stripped of all passion, by people who know both Marxism and the USSR well. On what points and in which ways has the latter departed from the socialism of Marx and Engels. Only such a critique will allow us to draw real lessons from the Soviet experience." Friedmann, *Journal de guerre*, 81. Friedmann had taken himself to be doing just that work in *From Holy Russia*, and following not only the Affaire, but the Molotov-Ribbentrop Pact, he worried that such work would never be done, at least not in good faith, and not in his own lifetime.
27. For a fuller account, see §2.3, "The Academic Reception of *From Holy Russia to the USSR*," and §3, "The Georges Friedmann Affair: The Closing of the Space of Possibilities in the Communist World," in Gourné, "'Philosoviet' Commitments," 366–372. See also Catherine Melnik-Duhamel, "L'affaire Georges Friedmann: à propos de la publication de *De La Sainte Russie à l'URSS*," Mémoire de diplôme d'études approfondies (DEA), Institut d'études politiques (Sciences Po), 1986. Friedmann argues, as Vatin notes in "'Machinisme,' Marxism, Humanism" (e25fn34), that

2. GEORGES FRIEDMANN

many of the problems of the USSR were rooted in various "survivals" from the Russian Empire, although Vatin seems to express skepticism. On this understanding of Friedmann's argument, that the problems of the USSR are problems inherited, knowingly or not, from "Holy Russia," it is clear given the politics of the time how such a view could be seen as both relatively mild from one perspective and scandalous from another. Whether or not Friedmann was correct in these particular analyses, the genealogy of Soviet governmentality remains a vital project.

28. "Recensions of the book appeared not only in Commune, the PCF's cultural review, but in the political journals and organs as well (*Cahiers du Bolchevisme, L'humanité, Russie d'aujourd'hui*). This diversity of publications attests to the attention that Friedmann's book drew from communist leadership, above all from Maurice Thorez, whose archives include an entire dossier on the episode." Gourné, "'Philosoviet' Commitments," 368. On the polemic that ensued with André Gide and the "virulent criticism" of Friedmann by his friend Georges Politzer, see Vatin, "'Machinisme,' Marxism, Humanism," e25.

29. Friedmann, *La puissance et la sagesse*, 272. See Friedmann's full note here for a more detailed description of his relationship to the CPF from 1930 to 1936, and a first-person account of the "affair" following the publication of *De la sainte Russie* in 1938.

30. Friedmann, *La puissance et la sagesse*, 280. On this point, Friedmann is adamant in several places in *La puissance* and elsewhere. Compare this statement in 1970 to the following entry from the *Journal*, dated September 13, 1939: "And because I believe that socialism remains, in one way or another, necessary to our future, because now more than ever I believe that a new civilization can only achieve a modern humanism on a technological foundation, and that the latter entails the rational organization of the resources of the globe, a material and moral solidarity of nations, a solution to class conflict, I want to try, with a clear head (and a beating heart), to understand the attitude, the methods, and the intentions of the USSR. I am going to try and understand and to judge Stalin's 'realism,' the mental attitude, the diverse mental attitudes of those who have undertaken their 'turning point,' one more time, with him—after him." Friedmann, *Journal de guerre*, 47.

31. Friedmann, *Journal de guerre*, 29.

32. The editors of Friedmann's journals describe the HC as follows: "Beginning in 1939, the mobile Hospital Complementary Unit (HC) operated within the general organization of the health service, at an intermediate level between the ambulances [cf. notes on pp. 207, 218] and the evacuation hospitals [cf. 218n2]. They were either assigned to an army corps, or, as was the case for Friedmann, to a communications hub—in this case, a regulation station (temporary railroad stations used to dispatch men and goods to combat areas). The HC comprised 6 doctors (possibly including specialists), two pharmacists, two administrative officers, and 130 nurses. It had a mixed function, both surgical and medical, with a capacity of 500 to 700 beds." Friedmann, *Journal de guerre*, 37n1.

33. On this theme of the "examination" and what he calls its several "grand themes," see Friedmann, *Journal de guerre*, 57, 65, 67, ff. Note this "examination" itself, while not always explicitly identified as such in given entries, clearly marks the bulk of the *Journal*. On the idea of an "effort to see clearly," see Friedmann, *Journal de guerre*, 46–47.

2. GEORGES FRIEDMANN

34. Following the Armistice with Germany on June 22, 1940, Friedmann maintained his *Journal* for roughly another week, until June 28, where the final entry cuts off abruptly. On June 24, 1940, he writes: "my emotions have been given over, since yesterday, to alterations of indignation, revolt, inspiration, sadness." Friedmann, *Journal de guerre*, 292. On that same day, he notes that "I . . . believed in this army, into which I was mobilized, and which I gave my full support (these notebooks carry the trace of that belief), right up until the disaster of the 15–17 of May. Following that, I have continued to do my duty, at my post, but without faith and without hope." Friedmann, *Journal de guerre*, 290. Soon after, he "took refuge in Toulouse, in the unoccupied territory, the Pétainist portion of France; finally, he engaged himself in the Resistance alongside his friend Jean Cassou." Edgar Morin, "Préface: Il était minuit dans le siècle," in *La puissance et la sagesse*, by Georges Friedmann (Paris: Gallimard, 1970), 13. During this time in Toulouse, through what he called "the somber winter of 1940–1941," Friedmann made a number of important acquaintances. See Friedmann, *La puissance et la sagesse*, 229. Through Cassou, Friedmann first met Violette Chapellaubeau and her future husband, the influential philosopher and sociologist Edgar Morin, as well as her close friend Vladimir Jankélévitch. Morin, "Préface: Il était minuit dans le siècle," 15. See also Françoise Schwab, "Vladimir Jankélévitch à Toulouse, 1940–1945, Une parenthèse inoubliable, La guerre," *Cités* 2, no. 70 (2017): 110, https://www.cairn.info/revue-cites-2017-2-page-105.htm. It was also during this time that Friedmann first met Swami Siddeswarananda (1879–1957) of the Ramakrishna Mission, through whom "India first crossed my path." Friedmann, *La puissance et la sagesse*, 229.
35. Friedmann was awarded the Médaille de la Résistance, with rosette; see Reynaud Jean-Daniel, "Friedmann, Georges (1902–1977), Professeur d'histoire du travail (1946–1959)," in *Les professeurs du Conservatoire national des arts et métiers, dictionnaire biographique 1794–1955, A-K*, ed. C. Fontanon and A. Grelon (Paris: Institut national de recherche pédagogique, 1994), 545.
36. Friedmann, *Industrial Society*.
37. See Vatin, "'Machinisme,' Marxism, Humanism," e21. See also Georges Friedmann, *La Crise du progrès: Esquisse d'histoire des idées: 1895–1935. 6e éd.* (Paris: Gallimard, 1936).
38. Morin, "Préface: Il était minuit dans le siècle," 16.
39. In "'Machinisme,' Marxism, Humanism," Vatin sketches this trajectory through a reading of Friedmann's use of the term *machinisme*. However, due to his ongoing self-critique, I take Friedmann's oeuvre to be somewhat more coherent than other readers may. At least on my reading, the shifts and changes are kind of the point.
40. Pierre Hadot, "Reflections on the Idea of the 'Cultivation of the Self,'" in *Philosophy as a Way of Life: Spiritual Exercises from Socrates to Foucault*, ed. Arnold I. Davidson (Oxford: Blackwell, 1995), 208; Pierre Hadot, "Spiritual Exercises," in *Philosophy as a Way of Life: Spiritual Exercises from Socrates to Foucault*, ed. Arnold I. Davidson (Oxford: Blackwell, 1995), 81.
41. Friedmann, *La puissance et la sagesse*, 11.
42. For any reader eager to point out that whatever I have just described is not Marxism, rest assured, that point is clear enough. However, to fully address Friedmann's relationship to Marx would constitute a project in itself, one that I simply cannot take up here. Despite that, I will track and note the major affinities with Marxist

2. GEORGES FRIEDMANN

concepts and clear references to Marx's texts as diligently as possible in the notes over the course of this chapter, clarifying as I can in limited space and time.

43. See Georges Friedmann, "L'homme et le milieu naturel: Panorama du nouveau milieu (1939)," in *Annales d'histoire sociale (1945), Hommages à Marc Bloch II* (Cambridge: Cambridge University Press, 1945), 104.
44. Friedmann, "L'homme et le milieu naturel," 105.
45. Friedmann, "L'homme et le milieu naturel," 103–104. His remarks on the mechanization of leisure time on p. 104 on are particularly interesting.
46. Friedmann, "L'homme et le milieu naturel," 105.
47. Friedmann, "L'homme et le milieu naturel," 105.
48. Regarding time, our relationship to night and day, and each to the other, Friedmann notes that "along with the hours absorbed by productive work, machines have penetrated every second of the day, and even sometimes, in the great urban centers, the heart of the night as well." Friedmann, "L'homme et le milieu naturel," 103.
49. Friedmann, *Journal de guerre*, 41, entry of September 10, 1939. Note that in this passage, Friedmann specifically refers to "bombes à électrons," but this is not a reference to some kind of atomic power, which would be anachronistic at the time of this journal entry in 1939. Rather, he is speaking of Elektron, the registered trademark name for a class of magnesium alloys first created in Germany in 1908 and later trademarked and manufactured by the British company Magnesium Elektron Limited beginning around 1934 or 1935. Both Great Britain and Germany used Elektron-based incendiary devices extensively in the Second World War. The magnesium casing could burn hot enough to penetrate armor plating. Dousing the fires produced from the device with water would only intensify the reaction, and the ordinance could, of course, be deployed by air. In fact, Elektron incendiaries were used in the infamous destruction of the city of Gernika, Spain on April 26, 1937. See Richard Rhodes, "Guernica: Horror and Inspiration," *Bulletin of the Atomic Scientists* 69, no. 6 (November 1, 2013): 19–25. See also Horst E. Friedrich and Barry L. Mordike, *Magnesium Technology: Metallurgy, Design Data, Applications* (Berlin: Springer Science & Business Media, 2006), 2–5. That Elektron is at once a brand-name and the substance used in one of the most resounding acts of destruction of the twentieth century is extremely telling from Friedmann's perspective. This single substance is thus representative of the "new technologies of death" that he references here and that so decisively contribute to the Great Disequilibrium.
50. Friedmann, *Journal de guerre*, 49, entry of September 18, 1939.
51. Friedmann, *Journal de guerre*, 103, entry of November 23, 1939.
52. Dr. Florent Coste (1896–1973); see the biographical note in Friedmann, *Journal de guerre*, 39. Friedmann spent a great deal of time with Coste during this period of the war.
53. Friedmann, *Journal de guerre*, 39–40.
54. Friedmann, *Journal de guerre*, 65.
55. These technological precursors, as is well known, range from the American Civil War to the suppression of colonial subjects by European powers, among so many other forms of directed brutality.
56. Friedmann, *Industrial Society*, 17–19.
57. Friedmann, *Industrial Society*, 19.

2. GEORGES FRIEDMANN

58. In Friedmann's use of the terms "dehumanization" and "despiritualization" (*Entseelung*), there is a clear resonance between these concepts and the "estrangement" and "alienation" (*Entfremdung* and *Entäusserung*) described by Karl Marx in the "Economic and Philosophical Manuscripts of 1844" (*The Marx-Engels Reader*, ed. Robert C. Tucker, 66–125 [New York: Norton, 1978]). It is also clear, given Friedmann's familiarity with Marx and Friedrich Engels, as well as his work in the USSR, that any such resonance with the manuscripts is likely no coincidence. In fact, David Ryazanov (1870–1938), the Soviet editor of the manuscripts, sent a package containing at least some part of the manuscripts to the *Revue marxiste* in 1928—one of the short-lived publication projects of Friedmann and his friends in the *Groupe Philosophies*. Guterman, one of the members of the group, published a translation of a few fragments from the manuscripts in 1929, the first translation of these texts in any language. See Elden, *Understanding Henri Lefebvre*, 16, 48n1. Guterman and Lefebvre then published the first complete French translation of the manuscripts in 1933. See Perry Anderson, *Considerations on Western Marxism* (New York: Verso, 1979), 51. However, recall that Friedmann himself was a speaker of both German and Russian, making frequent trips to Moscow, and had been in the city in 1932, the year the manuscripts were initially published. The fate of Ryazanov, executed in January 1938 during the *Yezhovshchina* (the "Great Purge" or "Great Terror" of 1937), is certainly of a piece with many of the other excesses that contributed to the "decisive shock" felt by Friedmann in the 1930s. There are thus several possible historical reasons for the recurring resonance of Friedmann's work and that of both the early and mature Marx.

However, even despite all of this rich context, it is also clear from Friedmann's explication in *Industrial Society* and other sources that neither "dehumanization" nor "despiritualization," are synonyms rough or exact, for alienation. My very preliminary view of these concepts, especially the technical use of "dehumanization" tied to Taylor and scientific management (as specified later), and the concept of "despiritualization," related in part to "de-skilling" but an arguably subtler concept, is that they can be read indeed as descriptions of particular forms of experience, a kind of phenomenology of life and work within the Great Disequilibrium and the economic and technical conditions that define it. On my reading, if these concepts have a clear affinity with Marx, whether as point of departure or touchstone or as original concepts in a kind of Marxian spirit, they do not amount to a simple recapitulation of Marxist categories. Most importantly, to even begin to explore these resonances requires a dedicated reading of the already ambiguous concepts of estrangement and alienation, which are themselves highly ambiguous both in the early Marx and in attempting to read them against or with the late Marx. Such tasks must unfortunately be added to the analyses of Marx and Friedmann that I have already identified as being well outside the goals of my work here, part of the greater undertaking than I cannot responsibly take up in this context. (My thanks to Claudia Hogg-Blake and Matthias Hasse at the University of Chicago for exploring these themes with me.)
59. Friedmann, *Industrial Society*, 55, 61.
60. Friedmann, *Industrial Society*, 54.
61. See Friedmann, *Industrial Society*, 77, 93, 94, 97, 108, 129. The resonances of these descriptions with those of workers in, say, contemporary mass-shipping warehouses are uncanny.

2. GEORGES FRIEDMANN

62. See Friedmann, *Industrial Society*, 84–85.
63. See Friedmann, *Industrial Society*, 100.
64. For a commendable though brief explication of Michelet's influence on Friedmann, especially with regard to the concept of *machinisme*, see Vatin, "'Machinisme,' Marxism, Humanism," e17.
65. Friedmann, *Industrial Society*, 97.
66. The context for this observation regarding silent films is Dubreuil's observation that "if one can speak of the crushing of the worker's intellectual life, the noise of machinery should perhaps be considered its cause above anything else." Friedmann, *Industrial Society*, 97–98. Film has a longstanding and important place in the history of the "self-care" of the exhausted and overworked, coinciding directly with the emergence of the "machine culture" from which the medium itself also arises. That Charlie Chaplin's 1936 landmark *Modern Times* was inspired by exactly those same Michigan autoworkers could not have been lost on those audiences.
67. See Friedmann, *Industrial Society*, 30.
68. See Friedmann, *Industrial Society*, 37, 261, 274.
69. Friedmann, *Industrial Society*, 53.
70. Friedmann, *La puissance et la sagesse*, 39.
71. Friedmann, *Industrial Society*, 42.
72. "The increased productivity sought by Taylorism is obtained less by rationalization than by intensification of work. The performances achieved by exceptional workers are, with very slight reductions, demanded of the mass of their comrades with no guarantee that the latter can maintain this effort for any length of time." Friedmann, *Industrial Society*, 55.
73. In "Mississippi" John Hurt's 1928 version of "Spike Driver Blues," the unnamed narrator speaks of the legendary railroad spike-driver John Henry with an intimate reverence and trepidation, solemnly vowing to us, his fellows, and his captain that "This is the hammer that killed John Henry / But it won't kill me, but it won't kill me, but it won't kill me." John Smith Hurt, "Spike Driver Blues (1928)," in *Avalon Blues: The Complete 1928 Okeh Recordings* (New York: Columbia Records, 1996). Hurt's is only one among hundreds of recorded versions of the legend of John Henry, who despite his victory against the steam-powered spike-driving machine, famously "died with his hammer in his hand." In a recording of the more traditional lyrics by Williamson Brothers & Curry for Okeh records in 1927, we hear John Henry himself lay out the stakes of the contest: "John Henry told his captain, 'Man ain't nothin' but a man,' Before I'll be beaten by this old steam drill, Gonna die with my hammer in my hands." Williamson Brothers & Curry, "Gonna Die with My Hammer In My Hand (1927)," in *Anthology of American Folk Music*, Vol.1, *Ballads* (Washington, D.C.: Folkways Records, 1952). In Hurt's version, the speaker will do anything to avoid that fate, abandoning his own hammer, lest it be found, as John Henry's was, "layin' side the road . . . all covered in red / That's why I'm gone." The enduring persistence of the figure of John Henry, in these countless songs and retellings, is a testament to the deep resonance of a figure who embodies the human wages of the contest of labor and automation. See Scott Reynolds Nelson, *Steel Drivin' Man: John Henry, The Untold Story of an American Legend* (New York: Oxford University Press, 2008); "John Henry," Library of Congress, https://www.loc.gov/item/ihas.200196572.

2. GEORGES FRIEDMANN

74. Edgar Atzler, in Friedmann, *Industrial Society*, 55. Atzler (1887–1938) was a German physiologist who wrote on what he called *Arbeitsphysiologie* or "Industrial Physiology." In 1927, Atzler published a text called *Body and Work. Handbook of Industrial Physiology*. See Edgar Atzler, *Körper und Arbeit. Handbuch der Arbeitsphysiologie* (Leipzig: G. Thieme, 1927).
75. Friedmann, *Industrial Society*, 262. Others simply referred to Taylorism as "organized overwork," which produced nothing more than "the loss of all initiative in the worker who was turned into an automaton and a moron by the Taylor system." Friedmann, *Industrial Society*, 42–43, 53.
76. Friedmann, *Industrial Society*, 201.
77. Friedmann, *Industrial Society*, 67.
78. Friedmann, *Industrial Society*, 31.
79. Friedmann, *Industrial Society*, 40–41.
80. As Friedmann dryly notes, "'the science of machine labor' perfected by Taylor was in any case, apart from any other assessment of it, not winning the approval and gratitude of those whom it directly concerned and to whom it claimed to bring easier work and financial satisfaction." Friedmann, *Industrial Society*, 43.
81. As Friedmann puts it in a note toward the conclusion of *Industrial Society*, "Without confusing situations and environments which are very different in character, it is important to observe here that similar problems arise within the present framework of Soviet industry. In the words of the journal of the Young Communists of the USSR (*Komsomolskaia Pravda*, July 17, 1935): 'There are in our country many students for whom there is a gulf separating the work of an engineer from that of an ordinary worker, and who have nothing but contempt for those who are engaged in production. In their opinion it is the exclusive task of the engineer to make plans and that of the worker to carry them out.'" Friedmann, *Industrial Society*, 372n.
82. Friedmann, *Industrial Society*, 31.
83. Friedmann, "L'homme et le milieu naturel," 106.
84. Friedmann, *Industrial Society*, 373.
85. Here again, the echo of Marx, this time from the opening of chapter 7 of *Capital*, "The Labor Process," where he notes, albeit briefly, that in labor man "acts upon external nature and changes it, and in this way he simultaneously changes his own nature." Karl Marx, *Capital*, Vol. I (New York: Penguin, 1990), 283.
86. "Marx, Marxisms, and Communisms" is the title of part 3, chapter 4 of *La puissance et la sagesse* (pp. 248–281), and it is a fascinating section for a number of reasons. As the title suggests, the plurality of these "Marxisms" is important for Friedmann. His explorations here follow the general structure of *La puissance*, consisting of texts and notes that were initially written in 1943 and revisited in 1970. This source material comes from a time before so many of the key events that constitute the adventure of twentieth-century communism, events that are so crucial for him, as for so many others on the left in both "East" and "West." In his own words, the passages he rereads here were written "after the Moscow trials and the Germano-Soviet pact of 1939, but—it is important to remember—before the revelation of the crimes of Stalin, before Budapest, the Sino-Soviet confrontation, the recognition of the challenges of central planning, the retreat of new administrative systems into the methods of liberal economics, the political disaffection of the population and especially the youth in 'socialist countries,' before Prague 1968–1970, before the

2. GEORGES FRIEDMANN

grand planetary crisis of communism and, simultaneously, the calling into question of the theoretical and practical value of Marxism, its desacralization, and within the tumult and the conflict among so many who identify themselves, today, as Marxists." It is against all of this, nearly three decades of challenges and transformation, that he asks, "How, in 1970, can we speak of *a* Marxism?" Friedmann, *La puissance et la sagesse*, 254. Again, I leave the question of Friedmann's relationship to Marx's work and to his place in and relationship to twentieth-century Marxism for another venue.

It should be noted however that this overall section is fascinating for another reason: it appears within the larger section of the book in which he surveys a range of traditions, primarily religious traditions, in order to "re-source himself." Indeed, it is the same section that Hadot invokes in his initial query to Friedmann. In asking Friedmann why he does not look to Greco-Roman antiquity, Hadot only references Friedmann's engagements here with religious traditions, not the chapter on Marxism—even as it is actually within this discussion that Friedmann does indeed engage figures like Plato, Marcus Aurelius, and others, even if only in passing.

87. Friedmann, *La puissance et la sagesse*, 251.
88. Friedmann, *La puissance et la sagesse*, 41.
89. Friedmann, *La puissance et la sagesse*, 65.
90. Friedmann, *La puissance et la sagesse*, 44.
91. Friedmann, *La puissance et la sagesse*, 39. Note that this term corresponds with the spiritual-political quasi-telos he identifies in the title of part 5, section 7, of *La puissance*, "Man Superior to His Works." Friedmann, *La puissance et la sagesse*, 406.
92. "The most convincing proof of the Power of Things over human beings today is to be found in our attitude with regard to the nuclear menace." Friedmann, *La puissance et la sagesse*, 44.
93. See Friedmann, *La puissance et la sagesse*, 59–60.
94. "The progress of scientific and technical knowledge (each so effected by the other) has brought about for us, as living organisms, a number of consequences, though there is no need to enumerate them all here. I will content myself to highlight the variety of biological transformations which can be observed in the new milieu of industrialized societies." Friedmann, *La puissance et la sagesse*, 39. He then goes on to speak about birth and death rates, infant mortality, life expectancy, changes in age of puberty and menopause—all phenomena which are, tellingly, either identical to or reminiscent of those which Foucault inscribes within the concept of biopolitics.
95. Friedmann, *La puissance et la sagesse*, 48–49.
96. Friedmann, "L'homme et le milieu naturel," 112.
97. Friedmann, *La puissance et la sagesse*, 42.
98. As he concisely puts it in *La puissance*, "Can we suppress, or at least reduce, the Disequilibrium which thus results for human beings? And if so, by what means? These are some of the questions to which this book will attempt to respond." Friedmann, *La puissance et la sagesse*, 23. We can in some sense read *La puissance* as Friedmann's final attempt to answer the positive political and ethical questions his concrete sociological research had been posing to him his entire life.
99. As in the case of dehumanization, there are strong echoes of Marx in this context, though I think that it is telling and important that Friedmann again does not

invoke either the notions of *Entfremdung* or *Entäusserung* here. See note 58 for a more detailed discussion of that resonance and the ways that it does and does not figure into my own project here. As I noted earlier, I do not take either concept to be simple stand-ins for the early Marx's "alienation." Rather, on my reading, Friedmann's terms are much simpler and more straightforward descriptions of the experience of industrial labor.

100. Friedmann, *Industrial Society*, 212.
101. Friedmann, *Industrial Society*, 390.
102. Friedmann, "L'homme et le milieu naturel," 106.
103. Friedmann, "L'homme et le milieu naturel," 114.
104. Friedmann, *Industrial Society*, 263. We may again hear the early Marx echoed here: "So much does objectification appear as loss of the object that the worker is robbed of the objects most necessary not only for his life but of his work." Marx, "Economic and Philosophic Manuscripts of 1844," 72.
105. Friedmann, *Industrial Society*, 241.
106. Friedmann, "L'homme et le milieu naturel," 106.
107. As he says, "No one, then, can deny that human labor involved many repetitive and subdivided operations before the time of mechanization." Friedmann, *Industrial Society*, 132.
108. Friedmann, *Industrial Society*, 209.
109. Friedmann, *La puissance et la sagesse*, 23.
110. Friedmann, *La puissance et la sagesse*, 108.
111. Friedmann, *La puissance et la sagesse*, 23.
112. Friedmann, *La puissance et la sagesse*, 28.
113. As he puts it in one of the final sections of *La puissance*, "Discovering a New Sense": "Today, in a world in which different civilizations are being rapidly standardized from one antipode to another, across continents, in an ineluctable movement that grinds down traditional differences, I cannot understand how it is possible to speak of "rediscovering the sense of life." It is not a question of rediscovery or revival, but of new discovery." Friedmann, *La puissance et la sagesse*, 403.
114. Friedmann, *La puissance et la sagesse*, 17.
115. Friedmann, *La puissance et la sagesse*, 97. See also his cautious endorsements of many of the other technological facts of contemporary life, and the potential for human flourishing that they can carry with them, but which are so often dismissed outright: "It is necessary to study, with a sympathy denuded of any superiority complex, in accepting the potential values of a 'mass culture,' entirely different from that of classical humanism, the goods of cultural consumption diffused by the mass media." Friedmann, *La puissance et la sagesse*, 115.
116. Friedmann, *La puissance et la sagesse*, 19. Many thanks to Marie McDonough for her help in translating this passage.
117. Friedmann, *Industrial Society*, 384. See also his concluding remarks on mechanization, Friedmann, *Industrial Society*, 389.
118. Friedmann, *La puissance et la sagesse*, 109.
119. Friedmann, *La puissance et la sagesse*, 42.
120. Friedmann, *La puissance et la sagesse*, 404.
121. Friedmann, *La puissance et la sagesse*, 118.
122. Friedmann, *La puissance et la sagesse*, 114.

2. GEORGES FRIEDMANN

123. Friedmann, *La puissance et la sagesse*, 116.
124. Friedmann, *La puissance et la sagesse*, 124.
125. Friedmann, *La puissance et la sagesse*, 117.
126. Friedmann, *La puissance et la sagesse*, 102.
127. "The fundamental traits of a technological milieu comparable to that of the Western societies had already appeared within the socialist patrimony." Friedmann, *La puissance et la sagesse*, 116.
128. Friedmann, *La puissance et la sagesse*, 117.
129. Friedmann, *La puissance et la sagesse*, 117–118. It should be noted that these conclusions are formulated by someone well aware of the damage inflicted by the Cold War on the Soviet project.
130. "Labor, such as it is carried out every day by the masses of workers, of employees, constitutes a vast terrain in which the 'conditioning' of human beings by our new milieu takes place." Friedmann, *La puissance et la sagesse*, 114.
131. Friedmann, *La puissance et la sagesse*, 124.
132. Friedmann, *La puissance et la sagesse*, 98.
133. Friedmann, *La puissance et la sagesse*, 118.
134. Friedmann, *La puissance et la sagesse*, 408.
135. Friedmann, *La puissance et la sagesse*, 118.
136. Friedmann, *La puissance et la sagesse*, 119.
137. Friedmann, *La puissance et la sagesse*, 122. Or as he says a page later, "It is not a question of human beings learning to become God, but rather learning to become human." Friedmann, *La puissance et la sagesse*, 123.
138. "But are these reflections, these regrets, in vain? Are we, today, given our mental and physical constitution, the state of our nervous systems and the state of our relationship with our new environment, capable of controlling these same machines, of actually dominating and subjugating them? Only at the end of this book will I attempt to discern the price of such an effort, and to determine the conditions under which, and the culture within which, we human beings may finally reveal ourselves as superior to our own works." Friedmann, *La puissance et la sagesse*, 68.
139. Roughly, "Where may we 're-source' ourselves?," Friedmann, *La puissance et la sagesse*, 179–281.
140. Friedmann, *La puissance et la sagesse*, 181.
141. Friedmann, *La puissance et la sagesse*, 183–213.
142. Friedmann, *La puissance et la sagesse*, 214–227.
143. Friedmann, *La puissance et la sagesse*, 228–247.
144. Friedmann, *La puissance et la sagesse*, 179–281. Friedmann had some kind of firsthand knowledge and personal relationship of all of these traditions and their practitioners. Catholicism was the "principal religion of France, the country which so liberally welcomed my parents." Friedmann, *La puissance et la sagesse*, 183. His own background was Jewish; he did not simply encounter Indian religions secondhand, but engaged well-known Hindu practitioners directly beginning with his time in Toulouse; and Marxism was a lifelong companion, one that occasioned its fair share of both crises and revelations. Of course, the questions raised by the fact that Friedmann places "Marx, Marxisms, Communisms," and "militant revolutionaries" in general, in this explicitly religious company are many, and their answers again require greater attention than I can provide here.

145. See Friedmann, *La puissance et la sagesse*, 359–360; Hadot, "Spiritual Exercises," 81. Recall Hadot's query in "Spiritual Exercises": "With the exception of the last few lines, doesn't this text look like a pastiche of Marcus Aurelius?" Note that Friedmann does not use the general term "Oriental" that Hadot invokes but rather refers to the "Vedantic" and "Hindu Spirituality." Friedmann was rather familiar with the forms of Indian thought that were available to him—and indeed, Indian history and politics, which he reflects on at length in this section of *La puissance*. See Friedmann, *La puissance et la sagesse*, 222, and part 3, chap. 3, "Hindu Spirituality," 228–247.
146. See Friedmann, *La puissance et la sagesse*, 273.
147. See Friedmann, *Journal de guerre*, 280–291. It seems likely that for whatever reason Hadot never read Friedmann's *Journal*, or at least not these passages, as it certain that Hadot would have loved them and would have just as certainly had something to say about them.
148. Friedmann, *Journal de guerre*, 280.
149. "The difficulty is to accept science and technology, to mobilize the moral forces necessary to master them (thanks to a new wisdom), without lapsing into mysticism, whether Jewish, Christian, Muslim, or Vedantic." Friedmann, *La puissance et la sagesse*, 222.
150. Friedmann, *La puissance et la sagesse*, 409. Regarding the film Friedmann references, see Evald Schorm, dir., *Každý Den Odvahu* [Courage for every day], 84 minutes (Czechoslovakia, 1964).
151. The human and ecological wages of emerging forms of extractivism, for example, tied in complex ways to genuinely promising green technologies, persist and all proliferate new yet recognizable forms of immiseration, tied so clearly to new categories of experience.
152. Friedmann, *Journal de guerre*, 289, entry of June 24, 1940.

3. MICHEL FOUCAULT: FROM THE ANALYTICS OF POWER TO THE CARE OF THE SELF

1. Foucault, *The Hermeneutics of the Subject: Lectures at the Collège de France, 1981–1982*, trans. Graham Burchell (New York: Palgrave Macmillan, 2005), 252.
2. Foucault, *The Hermeneutics of the Subject*, 252.
3. Foucault, *The Hermeneutics of the Subject*, 252.
4. Foucault, *The Hermeneutics of the Subject*, 250.
5. See Foucault, *The Hermeneutics of the Subject*, 251. There is perhaps nothing more modern, after all, than a fragmentary reconstitution of Greco-Roman antiquity.
6. Foucault, *The Hermeneutics of the Subject*, 251.
7. See the introduction.
8. Foucault, *The Hermeneutics of the Subject*, 12–13.
9. Foucault, *The Hermeneutics of the Subject*, 209.
10. Foucault, "On the Genealogy of Ethics: An Overview of a Work in Progress," in *Essential Works of Michel Foucault, 1954–1984*, vol. 1, *Ethics: Subjectivity and Truth*, ed. Paul Rabinow (New York: New Press, 1997), 271.
11. It seems likely that there is great overlap between the "cult of the self" and conversion from revolution, though these themes again remain unexplored.

3. MICHEL FOUCAULT

12. Foucault describes his views on the role of intellectuals, and thus why he himself avoids prescriptive claims to an almost absurd (and to many annoying) degree in a number of interviews and shorter reflections. These answers and the principles that they reveal are fascinating and require further elaboration and, arguably, popularization, as this constitutes one of the greatest, if subtle, spaces of misunderstanding within Foucault's oeuvre. For greater detail regarding his views on this issue, see, for example, the following: Michel Foucault, "The Political Function of the Intellectual," *Radical Philosophy* 17 (Summer 1977): 12–14.; Michel Foucault and Gilles Deleuze, "Intellectuals and Power," in *Language, Counter-Memory, Practice: Selected Essays and Interviews*, ed. D. F. Bouchard (Ithaca, N.Y.: Cornell University Press, 1977), 206–217; Michel Foucault and Michael Bess, "Interview with Michel Foucault, 3 November 1980," in *About the Beginning of the Hermeneutics of the Self: Lectures at Dartmouth College, 1980*, ed. Henri-Paul Fruchaud and Daniele Lorenzini (Chicago: University of Chicago Press, 2016), 128–138; Michel Foucault and François Ewald, "The Concern for Truth: An Interview by Francois Ewald," in *Politics, Philosophy, Culture: Interviews and Other Writings 1977–1984*, ed. Lawrence D. Kritzman (New York: Routledge, 1990), 255–267. Foucault's clearest statements are to be found in the November 3, 1980, conversation with Michael Bess republished in *About the Beginning of the Hermeneutics of the Self* (see pp. 137–138 in particular), and in the interview with François Ewald called "The Concern for Truth" (see pp. 265–267) originally published in 1984.
13. Foucault and Ewald, "The Concern for Truth," 265. Following this point, Foucault also concludes the conversation by explaining, again, why he is not a relativist. In this exchange, we can also see the distinction between the "specific" and "universal" intellectual at play, as elaborated in Foucault, "The Political Function of the Intellectual," 12.
14. Foucault and Bess, "Interview with Michel Foucault, 3 November 1980," 137–138.
15. As he says, critique is "genealogical in its design and archaeological in its method." Michel Foucault, "What Is Enlightenment?," in *Essential Works of Michel Foucault, 1954–1984*, vol. 1, *Ethics: Subjectivity and Truth*, ed. Paul Rabinow (New York: New Press, 1997), 315.
16. In archeological texts like *The Order of Things*, Foucault referred to this as the "historical *a priori*." See Michel Foucault, *The Order of Things: An Archaeology of the Human Sciences* (New York: Vintage, 1994), 172.
17. See Michel Foucault, "Nietzsche, Genealogy, History," in *Essential Works of Michel Foucault, 1954–1984*, vol. 2, *Aesthetics, Method, and Epistemology*, ed. Paul Rabinow (New York: New Press, 1998), 370.
18. It is of course clear that Foucault is by no means neutral regarding institutions like the prison, the psychiatric institution, or the confessional, for example, even as the purpose of his major analyses of such institutions goes far beyond illuminating the subtle details of their particular horrors. If critique is meant to be nonprescriptive, it is by no means "nonnormative," and Foucault does not claim otherwise. As is clear, to so much as identify the historical–conceptual ground to be cleared is to take up a normative position, though it is primarily and consistently a negative one. This is in part what Foucault means by "problematization," and it is quite an undertaking on its own. Still, explicit moral or political principles, positive injunctions, given prescriptive projects, or a direct theorization of some criteria of judgment is

3. MICHEL FOUCAULT

typically fleeting at best across his work. Take it or leave it, however, the general ambiguity in these areas is tied to the tasks of critique and genealogy and a principled rejection of a top-down view of the role of intellectuals.

19. I do not highlight Foucault's arguments for attempting not to step outside of the critical role to claim that there "really is" a crypto-normative set of principles at play in Foucault's work. This is because Foucault himself would be the first to say that there is no great insight in such a claim, as it is obvious that normativity is simply a feature of our discursive reality. To so much as choose a project is to make a normative judgment, after all. Rather, I emphasize Foucault's general reticence to pass judgment, or at least not too much judgment, to demonstrate the rather striking contrast when it comes to the above-sampled descriptions of particular historical iterations of the "care of the self" within his genealogies.
20. See introduction, section II, "What is the Spiritual?"
21. Foucault, *The Hermeneutics of the Subject*, 13.
22. To hold the view that Foucault somehow abandoned politics, or the analytics of power, or that he somehow adopted a kind of political moralism as Friedmann defines it, one must conceptualize the relationship of ethics to politics in the way that I argue Foucault rejects (or, at very least, that rejection is a consequence of the coherence of his overall argumentation). Indeed, three of the primary misreadings of Foucault's ethics are all the arguable result of this misunderstanding: views that see a "break" from politics to ethics; views that read strange and strained accounts of moralistic politics into Foucault's later work; or more simply, views that would read forms of ethical reductionism, spiritualism, or moralism into Foucault.
23. Frédéric Gros, "Course Context," in Michel Foucault, *The Courage of Truth: The Government of Self and Others II: Lectures at the Collège de France 1983–1984*, ed. Frédéric Gros, François Ewald, Alessandro Fontana, Arnold I. Davidson, and Graham Burchell (New York: Palgrave Macmillan, 2011), 346.
24. Foucault, *The History of Sexuality*, vol. 1, *An Introduction*, trans. Robert Hurley (New York: Random House, 1978), 88–89.
25. The "repressive hypothesis" is initially introduced in Foucault, *The History of Sexuality*, 1:10, but Foucault elaborates it over the course of the text. See especially pp. 83–85. In the "Method" chapter, Foucault negatively defines his own use of the term "power" against what amounts to the repressive hypothesis: "But the word *power* is apt to lead to a number of misunderstandings—misunderstandings with respect to its nature, its form, and its unity. By power, I do not mean 'Power' as a group of institutions and mechanisms that ensure the subservience of the citizens of a given state. By power, I do not mean, either, a mode of subjugation which, in contrast to violence, has the form of the rule. Finally, I do not have in mind a general system of domination exerted by one group over another, a system whose effects, through successive derivations, pervade the entire social body. The analysis, made in terms of power, must not assume that the sovereignty of the state, the form of the law, or the over-all unity of a domination are given at the outset; rather, these are only the terminal forms power takes." Foucault, *The History of Sexuality*, 1:92.
26. Foucault, *The History of Sexuality*, 1:11.
27. Foucault, *The History of Sexuality*, 1:83.
28. Foucault, *The History of Sexuality*, 1:89.

29. Foucault, *The History of Sexuality*, 1:82.
30. See Michel Foucault, "The Ethics of the Concern for the Self as a Practice of Freedom," in *The Essential Works of Foucault 1954–1984*, vol. 1, *Ethics, Subjectivity, and Truth*, ed. Paul Rabinow (New York: New Press, 1997), 282.
31. Foucault, *The History of Sexuality*, 1:83.
32. Foucault, *The History of Sexuality*, 1:85.
33. Foucault, *The History of Sexuality*, 1:10.
34. Foucault, *The History of Sexuality*, 1:10.
35. Foucault specifies this term briefly in the text: "The aim of the inquiries that will follow is to move less toward a 'theory' of power than toward an 'analytics' of power: that is, toward a definition of the specific domain formed by relations of power, and toward a determination of the instruments that will make possible its analysis." Foucault, *The History of Sexuality*, 1:82.
36. Foucault, *The History of Sexuality*, 1:94.
37. While this view is generally well known and more or less understood, we must be clear even now: none of these terms are synonyms for "good." As Foucault very famously puts it to Dreyfus and Rabinow, "My point is not that everything is bad, but that everything is dangerous, which is not exactly the same thing as bad." Foucault, "On the Genealogy of Ethics," 256.
38. Foucault, *The History of Sexuality*, 1:12.
39. I owe this language to Arnold I. Davidson, who used it often to describe what Foucault was up to in his signature course on *The History of Sexuality* at the University of Chicago, for which I served as course assistant in 2013 and 2018. For further exploration of what this phrasing might mean, in ways that are far clearer to Anglophone ears than that of Foucault in Franglish (mis)translation, see Ian Hacking's "Making up People," in Ian Hacking, *Historical Ontology* (Cambridge, Mass.: Harvard University Press, 2002). See also Arnold I. Davidson, *The Emergence of Sexuality: Historical Epistemology and the Formation of Concepts* (Cambridge, Mass.: Harvard University Press, 2001).
40. In many ways, the histories of the vibrant characters that populate Foucault's works are the histories of how it came to be so much as possible for such forms of life to populate our world.
41. Michel Foucault, "The Subject and Power," in *Essential Works of Michel Foucault, 1954–1984*, vol. 3, *Power*, ed. Paul Rabinow (New York: New Press, 2000), 326. Note that although this text initially appeared in 1982, it very much demonstrates the persistence of Foucault's core theoretical concerns in *La volonté*, though texts like *Discipline and Punish*, and well beyond into the so-called "ethical" period. Michel Foucault, *Discipline and Punish: The Birth of the Prison* (New York: Vintage, 1995).
42. Foucault, "The Subject and Power," 327.
43. Foucault, "The Subject and Power," 340.
44. Foucault, "The Subject and Power," 341.
45. Foucault, "The Subject and Power," 341.
46. Michel Foucault, *Society Must Be Defended: Lectures at the Collège de France, 1975–76* (New York: Picador, 2003), 28.
47. Foucault, *Discipline and Punish*, 18.
48. Foucault, *Discipline and Punish*, 16.
49. Foucault, *The History of Sexuality*, 1:60.

3. MICHEL FOUCAULT

50. As he puts it in "The Subject and Power": "[Power] categorizes the individual, marks him by his own individuality, attaches him to his own identity, imposes a law of truth on him that he must recognize and others have to recognize in him. It is a form of power that makes individuals subjects. There are two meanings of the word 'subject:' subject to someone else by control and dependence, and tied to his own identity by a conscience or self-knowledge. Both meanings suggest a form of power that subjugates and makes subject to." Foucault, "The Subject and Power," 331.
51. Foucault, *Society Must Be Defended*, 28.
52. Foucault, *Society Must Be Defended*, 29–30.
53. Foucault, *Society Must Be Defended*, 30.
54. "It seems to me that power must be understood in the first instance as the multiplicity of force relations immanent in the sphere in which they operate and which constitute their own organization; as the process which, through ceaseless struggles and confrontations, transforms, strengthens, or reverses them; as the support which these force relations find in one another, thus forming a chain or a system, or on the contrary, the disjunctions and contradictions which isolate them from one another; and lastly, as the strategies in which they take effect." Or, in other words, "The omnipresence of power: not because it has the privilege of consolidating everything under its invincible unity, but because it is produced from one moment to the next, at every point, or rather in every relation from one point to another. Power is everywhere; not because it embraces everything, but because it comes from everywhere. And 'Power,' insofar as it is permanent, repetitious, inert, and self-reproducing, is simply the over-all effect that emerges from all these mobilities, the concatenation that rests on each of them and seeks in turn to arrest their movement . . . [Power] is the name that one attributes to a complex strategical situation in a particular society." Foucault, *The History of Sexuality*, 1:93. Thus, as he puts it in "The Ethics of the Concern for the Self as a Practice of Freedom": "I scarcely use the word *power*, and if I use it on occasion it is simply as shorthand for the expression I generally use: *relations of power*." Foucault, "The Ethics of the Concern for the Self as a Practice of Freedom," 282–283.
55. Foucault, *The History of Sexuality*, 1:95.
56. A brief gloss of the OED gives the following definition of power in the context of physics and mechanics: "15. a. Any form or source of energy or force available for application to work, or applied to produce motion, heat, or pressure; *spec. (a)* mechanical force applied to overcome a resisting force such as weight or friction." "power, n.1," *Oxford English Dictionary Online* (Oxford University Press, September 2011, http://www.oed.com.proxy.uchicago.edu/viewdictionaryentry/Entry/149167). This physical conception is also useful, because it helps demonstrate the ultimate neutrality (in normative ethical and political terms) of Foucault's idea of power.
57. Foucault, *The History of Sexuality*, 1:96.
58. Foucault, "The Subject and Power," 342. Or, as Foucault puts it elsewhere, "It should be noted that power relations are possible only insofar as the subjects are free. If one of them were completely at the other's disposal and became his thing, an object on which he could wreak boundless and limitless violence, there wouldn't be any relations of power. . . . This means that in power relations there is necessarily the possibility of resistance because if there were no possibility of resistance

(of violent resistance, flight, deception, strategies capable of reversing the situation), there would be no power relations at all." Foucault, "The Ethics of the Concern for the Self as a Practice of Freedom," 291.

59. Foucault, "The Subject and Power," 342.
60. We may call that a state of domination perhaps, but it is again anything but a relation of power in the strict sense. Unfortunately, there is neither time nor call to engage the even more complex question of the relationship between "states of domination" and relations of power just here, especially as Foucault's definition of "domination" does vary slightly in different conversations. Suffice it to say for now that Foucault is ready to admit that states of domination can and indeed do exist: "Slavery is not a power relationship when a man is in chains, only when he has some possible mobility, even a chance of escape." Foucault, "The Subject and Power," 342. However, it should be noted that this example must be taken metaphorically, as a way of attempting to imagine what a state of total domination of one subject over another might look like. Historically, slavery is not the best example, as Foucault himself has shown us precisely in analyzing the multiple forms that relations of power may take and the forms that resistance may take are just as varied and unpredictable. Foucault is slightly more abstract, and thus clearer, on this point in "The Ethics of the Concern for Self as a Practice of Freedom," when he characterizes domination as something like the absolute impossibility of any further management of conduct: "When an individual or social group succeeds in blocking a field of power relations, immobilizing them and preventing any reversibility of movement by economic, political, or military means, one is faced with what may be called a state of domination. In such a state, it is certain that practices of freedom do not exist or exist only unilaterally or are extremely constrained and limited." Foucault, "The Ethics of the Concern for the Self as a Practice of Freedom," 283.
61. Michel Foucault, *Security, Territory, Population: Lectures at the Collège de France, 1977–78*, ed. Michel Senellart, François Ewald, and Alessandro Fontana (New York: Palgrave Macmillan, 2007), 193.
62. Foucault, *Security, Territory, Population*, 194.
63. Recall that "governmentality" is *not* an inherently political term (or rather, calls into question just what we mean when we talk about the political), but is instead a blanket concept meant to bring together all of the ways in which human beings may be governed: the ethical government of oneself, the government of the family, the management of populations and individuals by state apparatuses, etc. It is worth noting here what Foucault says in "The Ethics of the Concern for the Self as a Practice of Freedom" on this subject: "I am saying that 'governmentality' implies the relationship of the self to itself, and I intend this concept . . . to cover the whole range of practices that constitute, define, organize, and instrumentalize the strategies that individuals in their freedom can use in dealing with each other. Those who try to control, determine, and limit the freedom of others are themselves free individuals who have at their disposal certain instruments they can use to govern others." Foucault, "The Ethics of the Concern for the Self as a Practice of Freedom," 300.
64. Foucault, *Security, Territory, Population*, 194.
65. Foucault, *Security, Territory, Population*, 194–195.
66. Foucault, *Security, Territory, Population*, 199.

3. MICHEL FOUCAULT

67. Foucault, *Security, Territory, Population*, 196.
68. Foucault, *Security, Territory, Population*, 197.
69. Foucault, *Security, Territory, Population*, 194.
70. Foucault, *Security, Territory, Population*, 204.
71. Foucault, *Security, Territory, Population*, 215. While I would insist that the question of the *marginality* of the raw materials of these different forms of counter-conduct is actually more complex, the point is taken.
72. See Arnold I. Davidson, "From Subjection to Subjectivation: Michel Foucault and the History of Sexuality," in *Foucault and The Making of Subjects*, ed. Laura Cremonesi, Orazio Irrera, Daniele Lorenzini, and Martina Tazzioli (London: Rowman & Littlefield International, 2016), 55–61.
73. For Foucault's detailed discussions of this concept and its relationship to the Delphic injunction to "know yourself," see, for example Foucault, *The Hermeneutics of the Subject*, 1–5; Foucault, "On the Genealogy of Ethics," 269.
74. Foucault, *The Hermeneutics of the Subject*, 15.
75. Foucault, *The Hermeneutics of the Subject*, 27.
76. Foucault, *The Hermeneutics of the Subject*, 15.
77. Foucault, *The Hermeneutics of the Subject*, 16.
78. Foucault, "The Ethics of the Concern for the Self as a Practice of Freedom," 282.
79. The practices in question include "for example, techniques of meditation, of memorization of the past, of examination of conscience, of checking representations that appear in the mind, and so on." Foucault, *The Hermeneutics of the Subject*, 11.
80. Michel Foucault, *The History of Sexuality*, Vol. 2, *The Use of Pleasure*, trans. Robert Hurley (New York: Pantheon, 1985), 29. This is the sense in which I have been using the term "ethics" across the course of this book, and it is not synonymous with "morality" or "moral codes," even as such codes may represent an ideal or standard according to which one engages in ethical self-cultivation.
81. Foucault, *The History of Sexuality*, 2:29. Now, to be clear, all of these terms—spiritualty, ethics, ascetics, subjectivation, the care of the self, etc.—can certainly be ambiguous and dynamic in their usage, and their proliferation very much raises the question of whether and how to distinguish them, if at all. However, to take the scalpel to this grouping and meticulously define each in reference to the others is a task in its own right, especially as Foucault himself offers little explicit help in that direction. What matters, I think, is that even if they are not exactly synonyms, all of these terms ultimately reference forms of the relationship of the self to itself, mediated and determined by practices—spiritual exercises, an "interior effort," or practices of self-overcoming—meant to bring about some transformation of the practicing subject. I will thus continue to use them in the ways that I have been, insofar as these practical, working definitions implied in these arguments more than suffice for my purposes.
82. Foucault, "The Ethics of the Concern for the Self as a Practice of Freedom," 291.
83. Foucault elaborates all of these distinctions, in detail and with examples, in Foucault, "On the Genealogy of Ethics," 263–265; and Foucault, *The History of Sexuality*, 2:26–28, respectively. While I cannot rehearse them all in detail here, this set of distinctions is extremely instructive for all of the conversations in this book. Note, however, that in the English translation of *The Uses of Pleasure*, *mode d'assujettissement* is translated as "mode of subjection," rather than "subjectivation."

I have kept to the use of "subjectivation" as it appears in "On the Genealogy of Ethics," as it clear that "subjection" means something distinct both in general and as it is used in *La volonté de savoir*. This distinction matters for my overall argument here.

84. As he puts it in "On the Genealogy of Ethics," "for instance, you can very well understand why, if the goal is an absolute purity of being, then the type of techniques of self-forming activity, the techniques of asceticism you are to use, are not exactly the same as when you try to be master of your own behavior." Foucault, "On the Genealogy of Ethics," 265.
85. Foucault, "The Ethics of the Concern for the Self as a Practice of Freedom," 288.
86. Here again, an insight and wording that I owe to Arnold I. Davidson, who came to a view consistently and compellingly repeated that "ethics does not replace politics" in his courses on Foucault whenever the specter of moralism invariably arose in our classroom conversations. It is my hope in this book to have shown why.
87. The Moses of the desert does not reach, or inhabit, the Promised Land, where he would presumably have become someone new yet again.
88. Just ask anyone who has ever walked a picket line or engaged in a mass movement, for starters.
89. Pierre Hadot, "Reflections on the Idea of the 'Cultivation of the Self,'" in *Philosophy as a Way of Life: Spiritual Exercises from Socrates to Foucault*, ed. Arnold I. Davidson (Oxford: Blackwell, 1995), 207. I have gone back and forth on Hadot's critique over the years, often thinking that he misunderstands Foucault. At the time of this writing, however, it is my view that Hadot is correct on this one: Foucault is indeed far too focused on the self, both in general and as a consequence of his own arguments.
90. At the time of this writing, a stand-alone article exploring this category as a whole is in production. I plan to systematically explore each of these concepts in a context that will allow such analyses time and space to both breathe in and fully exhale.
91. See Michel Foucault, *Subjectivity and Truth: Lectures at the Collège de France, 1980–1981*, trans. Graham Burchell (New York: Palgrave Macmillan, 2017), 34.
92. For context regarding Foucault's intervention on Iran, his reportage for *Corriere della Sera*, and the notion of "philosophical journalism" that he was attempting to enact, see Laura Cremonesi, Orazio Irrera, Daniele Lorenzini, and Martina Tazzioli, "Foucault, the Iranian Uprising and the Constitution of a Collective Subjectivity," *Foucault Studies* 25 (2018): 300–301. This piece originally appeared in Laura Cremonesi, Orazio Irrera, Daniele Lorenzini, and Martina Tazzioli, eds., *Foucault and The Making of Subjects* (London: Rowman & Littlefield International, 2016). For perhaps the most well-known book-length criticism of Foucault's Iranian intervention, see Janet Afary and Kevin B. Anderson, *Foucault and the Iranian Revolution: Gender and the Seductions of Islamism* (Chicago: University of Chicago Press, 2005); this text includes translations of almost all of the primary sources from Foucault's dispatches, including letters of response and critique. For a more recent and more evenhanded major work on Foucault and Iran, see Behrooz Ghamari-Tabrizi, *Foucault in Iran: Islamic Revolution After the Enlightenment* (Minneapolis: University of Minnesota Press, 2016). As Sabina Bremner notes, "Both books build much of their argument around their respective analyses of the

notion of political spirituality, although in opposite directions." Sabina Vaccarino Bremner, "Introduction to Michel Foucault's 'Political Spirituality as the Will for Alterity,'" *Critical Inquiry* 47, no. 1 (2020): 115n2. For two fascinating and rich interviews only recently published and translated, see Michel Foucault and Sabina Vaccarino Bremner, "Political Spirituality as the Will for Alterity: An Interview with the *Nouvel Observateur*," *Critical Inquiry* 47, no. 1 (2020): 121–134; Michel Foucault, Farès Sassine, and Alex J. Feldman, "There Can't Be Societies Without Uprisings," *Foucault Studies* 25 (October 2018): 324–350. Bremner's introduction to the former interview provides invaluable context as well. Finally, for two further generative pieces, see Talal Asad, "Thinking About Tradition, Religion, and Politics in Egypt Today," *Critical Inquiry* 42, no. 1 (Autumn 2015): 166–214; Bernard E. Harcourt, "Introduction to Foucault on Iran: Revolt as Political Spirituality," Columbia Center for Contemporary Critical Thought, Uprising 13/13 Seminar, December 11, 2017, https://blogs.law.columbia.edu/uprising1313/bernard-e-harcourt-introduction-to-foucault-on-iran-revolt-as-political-spirituality/#_edn1.

93. Michel Foucault, "What Are the Iranians Dreaming [*Revent*] About?," in *Foucault and the Iranian Revolution: Gender and the Seductions of Islamism* (Chicago: University of Chicago Press, 2005), 209.
94. Bremner's introduction to the interview and copious contextual notes are invaluable. Rather than attempting to recreate her excellent documentation here, I simply and strongly advise readers to closely engage the critical apparatus that she provides in both her introduction and the translated interview itself. See Foucault and Bremner, "Political Spirituality as the Will for Alterity"; Bremner, "Introduction to Michel Foucault's 'Political Spirituality as the Will for Alterity.'"
95. Foucault and Bremner, "Political Spirituality as the Will for Alterity," 121–122.
96. Foucault and Bremner, "Political Spirituality as the Will for Alterity," 124.
97. See Bremner, "Introduction to Michel Foucault's 'Political Spirituality as the Will for Alterity,'" 119; Cremonesi et al., "Foucault, the Iranian Uprising and the Constitution of a Collective Subjectivity," 299–300.
98. Pierre Hadot, *What Is Ancient Philosophy?* (Cambridge, Mass.: Belknap Press of Harvard University Press, 2002), 109.
99. I often wonder if this might be true on a strict "untranslated" deployment of Cynicism as a political intervention. Foucault himself speaks of the "style of existence specific to revolutionary militantism" in the nineteenth-century. Foucault, *The Courage of Truth*, 184. It is hard not to think of any number of twentieth- and twenty-first-century resonances here, with the vexed concept of "lifestyle politics" arguably the least of our concerns.
100. Foucault, *The Courage of Truth*, 184.
101. "We have tried to see how the practice of the true life, when it is pushed to its extreme consequence in the Cynics, and dramatized in a number of forms, becomes the scandalous manifestation of the other life. And this change, this turning round, this transformation of the true life into other life seems to me to have been the source and heart of the Cynic scandal." Foucault, *The Courage of Truth*, 269.
102. Foucault, *The Courage of Truth*, 287.
103. Foucault, *The Courage of Truth*, 286–287.
104. Foucault, *The Courage of Truth*, 183.
105. Foucault, *The Courage of Truth*, 184.

106. Foucault, *The Courage of Truth*, 184.
107. Foucault, *The Courage of Truth*, 186.
108. Foucault, *The Hermeneutics of the Subject*, 208.
109. See Pierre Hadot, "Epistrophe and Metanoia in the History of Philosophy," *Philosophy Today* 65, no. 1 (Winter 2021): 201–210 (originally published in 1953). Hadot revisits these themes in 1968; see Pierre Hadot, "Conversion," trans. Matthew Sharpe and Federico Testa, in *The Selected Writings of Pierre Hadot* (London: Bloomsbury Academic, 2020).
110. "It seems to me that we cannot understand revolutionary practice throughout the nineteenth century, we cannot understand the revolutionary individual and what revolutionary experience meant for him, unless we take into account the notion or fundamental schema of conversion to the revolution." Foucault, *The Hermeneutics of the Subject*, 208.
111. Michel Foucault, *Speaking the Truth About Oneself: Lectures at Victoria University, Toronto, 1982*, ed. Henri-Paul Fruchaud and Daniele Lorenzini, English ed. Daniel Louis Wyche, Chicago Foucault Project (Chicago: University of Chicago Press, 2021), 73–74.
112. The idea that what is good for the wealthy is somehow good for everyone is a paradigmatic example; cases of abuse would also fall under this category.
113. Cases like this are very much worth exploring through Foucault's framework in some other venue. They may touch on concepts like subjection and domination, which we have already seen, or they may invoke what he calls, in exceedingly rare language, cases of "objectification." On my reading, none of these existing concepts really cover these relations of what we might call abuse, though again this is a question for another time. As noted earlier, whether voluntarily or involuntarily "giving" to others in a way that amounts to the abnegation of the self is even a relationship of "care" at all is an open question. I take it, further, that there is in fact quite a close relationship between this form and its spiritualist inverse.
114. Paternalist ideologies, such as those public arguments that, say, states of enslavement or settler-colonial displacement are somehow educational, religiously redemptive, or the like for dominated people all come to mind here. As is well known, the long history of such practices and their attending discourses persists well into our present.
115. Foucault, *The Hermeneutics of the Subject*, 252.
116. Foucault, *The History of Sexuality*, 1:96.

4. THE PRACTICE OF DIGNITY: MARTIN LUTHER KING JR., SELF-PURIFICATION, AND THE MONTGOMERY BUS BOYCOTT

1. As is the case with several of King's publications at this time, *Stride Toward Freedom* is a book co-conceived and co-drafted with Bayard Rustin. Martin Luther King Jr., *Stride Toward Freedom* (Boston: Beacon, 1986). Indeed, Rustin's distinct literary voice and views on nonviolence are audible across *Stride Toward Freedom*, even as he wished his name not be included in the book. As noted by the King Papers Project, "Although Rustin helped draft much of King's memoir, *Stride Toward Freedom*, Rustin would not allow his name to be credited in the book, telling an associate:

4. THE PRACTICE OF DIGNITY

'I did not feel that he should bear this kind of burden.'" See "Rustin, Bayard: Biography, March 17, 1912 to August 24, 1987," Martin Luther King Jr. Research and Education Institute, https://kinginstitute.stanford.edu/encyclopedia/rustin-bayard. King's correspondence with Rustin regarding drafting and revisions to the book has been preserved by the King Papers Project; see, for example, Martin Luther King Jr., "Letter to Bayard Rustin, March 10, 1958," in *The Papers of Martin Luther King, Jr.*, Vol. 4, *Symbol of the Movement, January 1957–December 1958*, ed. Susan Carson Clayborne Carson, Adrienne Clay, Virginia Shadron, and Kieran Taylor (Stanford, Calif.: Stanford University Press, 1958), 380n1. I will return to Rustin's central, though underappreciated, role in Montgomery and beyond consistently throughout this chapter. I will also, however, for sake of concision, refer to "King" when referring to the text of works like *Stride Toward Freedom*.

2. *Browder v. Gale* was the case before the U.S. District Court for the Middle District of Alabama in which, on June 4, 1956, it was ruled that Montgomery's bus segregation laws were unconstitutional; the Supreme Court decision to uphold the district court's ruling was handed down on November 13, 1956, and the bus boycott officially ended on December 20, 1956. As King says, it would take about four or five days for the mandate to reach Montgomery. King, *Stride Toward Freedom*, 155. King also describes this incident in "We Are Still Walking," his contribution to *Liberation* magazine's December 1956 "Salute to Montgomery." Martin Luther King Jr., "We Are Still Walking," in *Daybreak of Freedom: The Montgomery Bus Boycott*, ed. Stewart Burns (Chapel Hill: University of North Carolina Press, 1997), 320.

3. King, *Stride Toward Freedom*, 155.

4. Claudette Colvin, "Transcript of Record and Proceedings, Browder v. Gayle, May 11, 1956," in *Daybreak of Freedom: The Montgomery Bus Boycott*, ed. Stewart Burns (Chapel Hill: University of North Carolina Press, 1997), 77.

5. King, *Stride Toward Freedom*, xxiv.

6. Indeed, we cannot so much as begin to understand the Montgomery boycott of 1955 without acknowledging the role of the Baton Rouge bus boycott of June 19–24, 1953, and the individuals and organizations that mobilized there. Baton Rouge, though much briefer and on a smaller scale, was well acknowledged by the Montgomery organizers to be a direct inspiration. Montgomery leaders like King, E. D. Nixon, and others, sought the insights of organizers like the Reverend T. J. Jemison, of Baton Rouge's Mount Zion First Baptist Church. See King, *Stride Toward Freedom*, 61–62. Similarly, it would be just as difficult to understand Montgomery without the backdrop of the far more famous and wide-reaching *Brown v. Board of Education of Topeka, et. al.* decision in May of 1954, which ended de jure segregation in public schools. Indeed, it would also be difficult to remove the Baton Rouge movement from the context of the *Brown* case, which bookended the former in some sense. (*Brown* was first argued in December of 1952, then again a year later in 1953, with the final decision handed down in May of 1954.) The Montgomery boycott also emerged against the backdrop of a longer tradition of activism, direct action, and legal intervention against segregation more broadly. Among these can be counted A. Philip Randolph's original March on Washington movement, which in 1941 pressured President Roosevelt to sign Executive Order 8802, desegregating the military. Not long after, in July of 1944, Irene Morgan, a mother of two traveling via Greyhound from Virginia to Maryland, was arrested for refusing to give up

her seat in the "colored" section of the bus for a white couple. This event resulted in the 1946 *Morgan v. Virginia* ruling, which outlawed segregation on interstate buses. The Morgan ruling, in turn, resulted in the 1947 Journey of Reconciliation, which inspired the 1961 Freedom Rides. These are just a scattering of the major legal events that framed the events in Montgomery in 1955 and 1956. There is no doubt that they played some role there, just as Montgomery would play a role in Birmingham, in the 1963 March on Washington, and so on.

7. For an account of the visit, see Sudarshan Kapur, *Raising up a Prophet: The African-American Encounter with Gandhi* (Boston: Beacon, 1992).
8. For a brief timeline of Thurman's life, see Amanda Brown, "Howard Thurman Timeline," in *The Fellowship Church: Howard Thurman and the Twentieth Century Religious Left* (Oxford: Oxford University Press, 2021). For a more extensive chronology, see "Howard Thurman Chronology," Howard Thurman Papers Project, Boston University School of Theology, 2016, https://www.bu.edu/htpp/howard-thurman-chronology.
9. Howard Thurman, *Jesus and the Disinherited* (Boston: Beacon, 1996), 26.
10. Thurman, *Jesus and the Disinherited*, 27.
11. Thurman, *Jesus and the Disinherited*, 29.
12. Thurman, *Jesus and the Disinherited*, 31.
13. "Given segregation as a factor determining relations, the resources of the environment are made into instruments to enforce the artificial position." Thurman, *Jesus and the Disinherited*, 32–33.
14. Thurman, *Jesus and the Disinherited*, 31.
15. Thurman, *Jesus and the Disinherited*, 10.
16. Thurman, *Jesus and the Disinherited*, 13.
17. Thurman, *Jesus and the Disinherited*, 15.
18. Thurman, *Jesus and the Disinherited*, 48.
19. Thurman, *Jesus and the Disinherited*, 30.
20. Thurman, *Jesus and the Disinherited*, 35–36.
21. Thurman, *Jesus and the Disinherited*, 28.
22. Thurman, *Jesus and the Disinherited*, 18.
23. As I emphasize later, this is in no way to suggest, for example, that the Klan and someone like Howard Thurman have the same or even a similar theory of the subject. It is true that groups like the Klan, their predecessors during the period of slavery, and indeed the advocates of Jim Crow during King and Thurman's time did consistently deploy a paternalistic ideology regarding the "nature" of Black people. Such claims very often took an absolutist or "naturalistic" view to justify various acts of economic and political barbarism after the fact, and they consistently informed the kinds of tactics on display across texts like *Stride Toward Freedom*, *Jesus and the Disinherited*, and many others. This ideological history and its deployment are well and thoroughly documented, and I need not rehearse them here. What matters for now is that, as we will see later, it was at least in part a sense of "who the community is" that determined the forms of dehumanization that such groups attempted to deploy and on which they based their view of the outcome.
24. Thurman, *Jesus and the Disinherited*, 11.
25. Thurman, *Jesus and the Disinherited*, 39, 43.
26. Thurman, *Jesus and the Disinherited*, 40.

4. THE PRACTICE OF DIGNITY

27. Thurman, *Jesus and the Disinherited*, 43.
28. Thurman, *Jesus and the Disinherited*, 42.
29. Thurman, *Jesus and the Disinherited*, 43.
30. Martin Luther King Jr., "Letter from Birmingham Jail," in *Why We Can't Wait* (Boston: Beacon, 1963), 87.
31. Within the Gandhian tradition, writers such as Krishnalal Shridharani and Richard Gregg were enormously influential in general, and on Thurman and Rustin, and thus on King, in particular. In the case of Shridharani, for example, we can see that influence through the lens of this concept of "self-purification" quite directly. In his major 1939 work *War Without Violence*, Shridharani provides a detailed schema that clearly represents a more extensive framework of the relationship between the many aspects of nonviolence than King or Rustin provide. This is especially striking in the way that *War Without Violence* treats ideas like "self-purification" in much greater detail than King does in the "Letter" or Rustin does in the "Lesson Plan" that I address later. Shridharani, along with figures like Gregg, was among the most influential popularizers and systematizers of Gandhian *satyagraha* in the West in the generation before King, whose influence on figures like Rustin and groups like the Fellowship of Reconciliation is clear. It is also clear that King is drawing on that tradition, both directly and in ways that are filtered through Rustin, in his explication to the Alabama clergymen. See Krishnalal Shridharani, *War Without Violence: A Study of Gandhi's Method and Its Accomplishments* (New York: Harcourt, Brace, 1939), 59. See also Gregg, *The Power of Non-violence* (New York: Fellowship Publications, 1944), 105.
32. King continues: "Negroes have experienced grossly unjust treatment in the courts. There have been more unsolved bombings of Negro homes and churches in Birmingham than in any other city in the nation." King, "Letter from Birmingham Jail," 87.
33. King, "Letter from Birmingham Jail," 88.
34. King, "Letter from Birmingham Jail," 89.
35. King, "Letter from Birmingham Jail," 88.
36. Michel Foucault, "The Subject and Power," in *Essential Works of Michel Foucault, 1954–1984*, vol. 3, *Power*, ed. Paul Rabinow (New York: New Press, 2000), 326.
37. I focus almost exclusively on the Montgomery movement, carefully bracketing the consequences of those shifts for the South and the United States as a whole, which would require a much more ambitious investigation, beyond the scope of this project.
38. King, *Stride Toward Freedom*, 14.
39. King, *Stride Toward Freedom*, 17–18.
40. King, *Stride Toward Freedom*, 16.
41. King, *Stride Toward Freedom*, 14–15.
42. King, *Stride Toward Freedom*, 14.
43. King, *Stride Toward Freedom*, 27.
44. King, *Stride Toward Freedom*, 28.
45. King, *Stride Toward Freedom*, 28.
46. King, *Stride Toward Freedom*, 24.
47. See the example of the Claudette Colvin incident, King, *Stride Toward Freedom*, 28–29.

4. THE PRACTICE OF DIGNITY

48. King, *Stride Toward Freedom*, 21.
49. As he says, "Even in areas—such as voting—where they would not really be accused of tampering with the established order, the educated group had an indifference that for a period seemed incurable." King, *Stride Toward Freedom*, 22.
50. King, *Stride Toward Freedom*, 24.
51. King, *Stride Toward Freedom*, 5–6.
52. King, *Stride Toward Freedom*, 7.
53. King, "Letter from Birmingham Jail," 92.
54. See, for example, Anna Holden's various interviews with white Montgomery residents. Anna Holden, "Report on MIA Mass Meeting, March 22, 1956," in *Daybreak of Freedom: The Montgomery Bus Boycott*, ed. Stewart Burns (Chapel Hill: University of North Carolina Press, 1997), 212–219.
55. King, *Stride Toward Freedom*, 23–24.
56. King, *Stride Toward Freedom*, 54.
57. Aldon D. Morris, *The Origins of the Civil Rights Movement: Black Communities Organizing for Change* (New York: Free Press, 1984), 52. Morris goes on to describe the central importance of the WPC in the Montgomery movement, including its support of Claudette Colvin, who had been arrested earlier the same year on March 2, 1955, for refusing to give up her seat. See Morris, *The Origins of the Civil Rights Movement*, 53. For more information on the WPC and its fundamental role in the boycott, see Jo Ann Gibson Robinson, *The Montgomery Bus Boycott and the Women Who Started It* (Knoxville: University of Tennessee Press, 1987).
58. Morris, *The Origins of the Civil Rights Movement*, 51.
59. Morris, *The Origins of the Civil Rights Movement*, 51, 298n20.
60. In fact, "Mrs. Parks had scheduled an NAACP Youth Council workshop to be held on December 4, 1955, but her arrest on December 1 canceled that function." Morris, *The Origins of the Civil Rights Movement*, 51–52.
61. See, for example, Eliot Wigginton, ed., *Refuse to Stand Silently By: An Oral History of Grass Roots Social Activism in America, 1921–64* (New York: Doubleday, 1991), 158–170.
62. Morris, *The Origins of the Civil Rights Movement*, 52, 298n22.
63. "On the evening of Mrs. Parks' arrest a bus boycott was also being discussed and planned by a group of black women who belong to the Women's Political Council (WPC). The WPC was organized by professional black women of Montgomery in 1949 for the purpose of registering black women to vote. Shortly after its inception it became a political force in Montgomery. Members of the WPC were especially prepared to play a role in organizing the bus boycott because of their previous experience. For example, in 1954 the WPC and other community groups met twice with Montgomery's City Commission and discussed the grievances of the black community regarding segregated buses. They informed the Commission that blacks were dissatisfied with standing over empty bus seats, boarding the buses by the rear door after paying fares in the front, and bus stops twice as far apart in the black community as in white neighborhoods. In response to these meetings the City Commission and representatives of the bus company acceded to the request that buses stop at every corner in the black community but refused to act on the other complaints." Morris, *The Origins of the Civil Rights Movement*, 52–53. Further, the WPC had supported fifteen-year-old Claudette Colvin after she was arrested

4. THE PRACTICE OF DIGNITY

on March 2, 1955, for refusing to give up her seat to a white person on the bus. The WPC "even began formulating plans to boycott the Montgomery bus line. These plans were dropped after it was learned that Miss Colvin was expecting a child out of wedlock." Morris, *The Origins of the Civil Rights Movement*, 53.
64. Morris, *The Origins of the Civil Rights Movement*, 54.
65. King began his pastorate at Dexter Avenue Baptist Church on September 1, 1954, and was elected president of the Montgomery Improvement Association (MIA) at the founding of the organization on December 5, 1955.
66. Morris, *The Origins of the Civil Rights Movement*, 54.
67. Morris argues that this newcomer status allowed certain individuals to take up successful leadership roles for these two primary reasons. This was true for King in Montgomery, Fred Shuttlesworth in Birmingham, C. K. Steele in Tallahassee, and Jemison in Baton Rouge, among others. See Morris, *The Origins of the Civil Rights Movement*, 43–44. Morris further elaborates the fortuitous set of combined factors that made King the ideal figurehead in Morris, *The Origins of the Civil Rights Movement*, 58–63.
68. Bayard Rustin, "Interview of Bayard Rustin by Ed Edwin, April 3, 1985," in *The Reminiscences of Bayard Rustin, No. 4: Interview of Bayard Rustin by Ed Edwin, April 3, 1985*, ed. Ed Edwin (Alexandria, Va.: Alexander Street Press, 2003), 138.
69. Morris, *The Origins of the Civil Rights Movement*, 51.
70. Morris, *The Origins of the Civil Rights Movement*, 62.
71. Morris, *The Origins of the Civil Rights Movement*, 62.
72. FOR was "organized in England in 1914. In 1915 the organization became the central pacifist organization in America. Many of the great architects of nonviolent protest in the United States—among them A. J. Muste, Bayard Rustin, A. Philip Randolph, James Farmer, Glenn Smiley, and James Lawson—received training from FOR." Morris, *The Origins of the Civil Rights Movement*, 157. From 1940 onward, A. J. Muste (1885–1967), a titan of twentieth-century American pacificism, served as executive director of FOR, and for a long time as a kind of father figure to Rustin, as well as a mentor to Smiley, Farmer, and other FOR members. In April 1942, James Farmer, then the field secretary for race relations, with the support of Muste, George Houser, and Rustin, founded the Congress of Racial Equality (CORE) as an outgrowth of FOR, which would become a major force within the civil rights era. See Morris, *The Origins of the Civil Rights Movement*, 157–159. See also John D'Emilio, *Lost Prophet: The Life and Times of Bayard Rustin* (New York: Free Press, 2003), 40–44, 53–55.
73. Smiley later described Rustin as his "American guru," from whom, "I learned practically everything that I knew at the that time of importance about nonviolence from Bayard . . . I would never have had the courage to have started . . . without the impetus that Bayard gave me." Glenn Smiley, foreword in *Nonviolence: The Gentle Persuader* (Nyack, N.Y.: Fellowship Publications, 1991); D'Emilio, *Lost Prophet*, 48.
74. Morris, *The Origins of the Civil Rights Movement*, 159.
75. Rustin had been invited by Nnamdi Azikiwe to visit Nigeria in June of 1953. To finance the trip, he had embarked on a six-month national speaking and fundraising tour. Following a talk to the American Association of University Women in Pasadena California on January 23, 1953, Rustin was caught by county police having sex with two men in the back of a car. He was sentenced to sixty days—the

first and only incarceration of his life that was not the result of nonviolent direct action. This event caused a rupture with Muste and the FOR, his trip to Nigeria was cancelled, and Rustin was forced to resign from the organization. D'Emilio, *Lost Prophet*, 190–193. It is worth noting that despite this break with Muste, Rustin's other "father figure," A. Philip Randolph, never abandoned him.

76. Morris, *The Origins of the Civil Rights Movement*, 159.
77. Jervis Anderson, *Bayard Rustin: The Troubles I've Seen, A Biography* (New York: Harper Collins, 1997), 187. See also Stewart Burns, ed., *Daybreak of Freedom: The Montgomery Bus Boycott* (Chapel Hill: University of North Carolina Press, 1997), 169, for more detail on Coretta Scott King's familiarity with Rustin and the relationship between Rustin and the King family.
78. Morris, *The Origins of the Civil Rights Movement*, 159.
79. Morris, *The Origins of the Civil Rights Movement*, 160.
80. Smiley, *Nonviolence: The Gentle Persuader*, 5.
81. Morris, *The Origins of the Civil Rights Movement*, 159.
82. See Rustin, "Interview of Bayard Rustin by Ed Edwin, April 3, 1985," 134–138.
83. Indeed, following Montgomery, "For the rest of the decade, Rustin applied himself to King's emergence as a national leader. He made himself useful in all sorts of ways. He introduced King to labor leaders . . . He drafted speeches and articles for King and provided line editing for King's own writing. Rustin helped prepare *Stride Toward Freedom*, King's account of the Montgomery bus boycott, offering comments on chapters and working with King's agent and publisher to help with the book's promotion." Their working relationship continued for years, with Rustin playing what D'Emilio can only describe as an "indispensable" role for King across an enormous range of campaigns and issues. D'Emilio, *Lost Prophet*, 266–267.
84. D'Emilio, *Lost Prophet*, 35.
85. Bayard Rustin, introduction to *Time on Two Crosses: The Collected Writings of Bayard Rustin*, ed. Devon W. Carbado and Donald Weise (San Francisco: Cleis Press, 2003), xxiii.
86. Rustin, introduction to *Time on Two Crosses*, xxiii.
87. See Rustin, introduction to *Time on Two Crosses*.
88. D'Emilio, *Lost Prophet*, 228.
89. D'Emilio, *Lost Prophet*, 229.
90. Rustin, *Time on Two Crosses*, 59. The song in question was "We Shall Overcome," now well known and associated with the movement.
91. Donald Ferron, "Report on MIA Mass Meeting, February 27, 1956," in *Daybreak of Freedom: The Montgomery Bus Boycott*, ed. Stewart Burns (Chapel Hill: University of North Carolina Press, 1997), 175.
92. D'Emilio, *Lost Prophet*, 229.
93. Rustin, *Time on Two Crosses*, 65.
94. Anderson, *Bayard Rustin*, 189.
95. "Smiley has told of attending many of the MIA's mass meetings after arriving in Montgomery. His responsibility was to speak fifteen minutes at the meetings, explaining the principles and techniques of nonviolence and persuading blacks that it was the method they should pursue." Morris, *The Origins of the Civil Rights Movement*, 160.
96. Bayard Rustin, "Lesson Plan on Non-violent Action (1941)," 1941, section II, series D, box 51, folder: FOR Bayard Rustin Files, Writings and Speeches 1941–1967,

4. THE PRACTICE OF DIGNITY

Swarthmore College Peace Collection, Fellowship of Reconciliation Papers, DG 013, McCabe Library, Swarthmore, Penn.

97. In the case of Smiley, as Morris puts it, "Smiley was delivering lectures he had presented hundreds of times as an FOR representative." Morris, *The Origins of the Civil Rights Movement*, 160.
98. Both versions are held in the Swarthmore Peace Collection: a two-page version from 1941 with the subheading "compiled by Bayard Rustin," and a four-page version dated "[194-]" and hand-labeled "Denver FOR." The primary difference between them is font size and spacing, but the Denver lesson plan does contain a handful of lines and points that do not appear it what seems to be the earlier version.
99. Rustin, "Lesson Plan on Non-violent Action (1941)."
100. Rustin, "Lesson Plan on Non-violent Action (1941)."
101. Indeed, anyone familiar with Rustin's work and political commitments would be justified in wondering if this text was added by a local FOR or CORE member, as it does not appear in the other version of the "Lesson Plan."
102. Section III, "Aims," states that "those who face conflict without violence have three aims. The first is concerned with *ends;* the others concerned with *means.* A.) To achieve social, economic or political gain; B.) To behave during the struggle as to gain the respect and sympathy of the exploiters; C.) To gain, by moral integrity, the sympathy and support of third parties and observers. Note: The violent struggle, by its very nature, makes the second aim impossible. Indeed, the one aim of those who use violence is to gain benefits with little or no regard for human personality." Rustin, "Lesson Plan on Non-violent Action (1941)."
103. Section IV also lists: "B.) Labor-capital disputes; C.) Denial of civil liberties; D.) Suppression of academic freedom, etc." Rustin, "Lesson Plan on Non-violent Action (1941)."
104. This passage also includes the statement that "*racial segregation* is based upon the superstition of inequality, for which there is no scientific, spiritual, or moral basis." Rustin, "Lesson Plan on Non-violent Action (1941)."
105. "Nonviolent direct action seeks to create such a crisis and foster such a tension that a community which has constantly refused to negotiate is forced to confront the issue. It seeks so to dramatize the issue that it can no longer be ignored. My citing the creation of tension as part of the work of the nonviolent resister may sound rather shocking. But I must confess that I am not afraid of the word 'tension.' I have earnestly opposed violent tension, but there is a type of constructive, nonviolent tension which is necessary for growth. . . . The purpose of our direction action program is to create a situation so crisis packed that it will inevitably open the door to negotiation." King, "Letter from Birmingham Jail," 89–90.
106. Rustin, "Lesson Plan on Non-violent Action (1941)."
107. Rustin's "Lesson Plan" essentially condenses Shridharani's schema in *War Without Violence* significantly, and King's "Letter" further condenses what Rustin preserves. Chapter 1 of *War Without Violence*, appropriately titled "How Is It Done?," includes twelve stages of *satyagraha*, rather than the four or five found in Rustin or King, in a more complex relationship to one another, and often more radical than the steps described in the American context. See Shridharani, *War Without Violence*, 27–64.
108. Rustin, "Lesson Plan on Non-violent Action (1941)."
109. Rustin, "Lesson Plan on Non-violent Action (1941)."

4. THE PRACTICE OF DIGNITY

110. As King famously describes the role of creative tension: "I must confess that I am not afraid of the word 'tension.' I have earnestly opposed violent tension, but there is a type of nonviolent, constructive tension which is necessary for growth. . . . The Purpose of our direct-action program is to create a situation so crisis-packed that it will inevitably lead to negotiation" (King, "Letter from Birmingham Jail," 88.)
111. Rustin, "Lesson Plan on Non-violent Action (1941)."
112. Rustin, "Lesson Plan on Non-violent Action (1941)."
113. Smiley, *Nonviolence: The Gentle Persuader*, 17.
114. Morris, *The Origins of the Civil Rights Movement*, 161.
115. Smiley, *Nonviolence: The Gentle Persuader*, 17.
116. Smiley, *Nonviolence: The Gentle Persuader*, 17–18.
117. In fact, Smiley's work in this direction was even more thorough: "Two days before Montgomery desegregated its buses, Smiley met with seventy sympathetic whites and conducted the same nonviolent workshops with them that had been held at the mass meetings. As those whites were trained to help integrate buses nonviolently, proof was provided to other whites that peaceful integration was possible." Morris, *The Origins of the Civil Rights Movement*, 161–162. An analysis of this practice among sympathetic whites would be fascinating in terms of understanding the role of political subjectivation within members of an *oppressive* group, though such work must be bracketed within the current project for want of space. For further details about Smiley's time in Montgomery and its place within FOR, see Glenn Smiley, "Memo to [FOR] Staff, April 7, 1956," in *Daybreak of Freedom: The Montgomery Bus Boycott*, ed. Stewart Burns (Chapel Hill: University of North Carolina Press, 1997), 250–253. See also Glenn Smiley, "Letter to Dr. Martin Luther King, April 13, 1956," pp. 253–254, in the same volume.
118. King, *Stride Toward Freedom*, 156. Note that a similar, though briefer and much more informal exercise was conducted by King in a kind of question-and-answer format at an earlier mass meeting in October. See Robert L. Cannon, "Letter to Alfred Hassler and Glenn E. Smiley, October 3, 1956," in *The Papers of Martin Luther King, Jr.*, Vol. 3, *Birth of a New Age, December 1955–December 1956*, ed. Clayborne Carson (Berkeley: University of California Press, 1997), 389–390.
119. Rustin, "Lesson Plan on Non-violent Action (1941)."
120. Smiley, *Nonviolence: The Gentle Persuader*, 16.
121. Morris, *The Origins of the Civil Rights Movement*, 161.
122. Lillian Smith, "Letter to Dr. Martin Luther King, March 10, 1956," in *Daybreak of Freedom: The Montgomery Bus Boycott*, ed. Stewart Burns (Chapel Hill: University of North Carolina Press, 1997), 203.
123. John M. Swomley, "Letter to Glenn Smiley, February 29, 1956," in *Daybreak of Freedom: The Montgomery Bus Boycott*, ed. Stewart Burns (Chapel Hill: University of North Carolina Press, 1997), 172.
124. Morris, *The Origins of the Civil Rights Movement*, 158–159.
125. Ferron, "Report on MIA Mass Meeting, February 27, 1956," 174.
126. Bayard Rustin, "Rustin to King: Memo on the Montgomery Bus Boycott, December 23, 1956," in *Daybreak of Freedom: The Montgomery Bus Boycott*, ed. Stewart Burns (Chapel Hill: University of North Carolina Press, 1997), 329. We can put aside for the moment Rustin's claim about the top-down nature of the school desegregation

4. THE PRACTICE OF DIGNITY

campaign; in either case, the view rehearsed here certainly reflects popular conceptions of both movements.
127. Rustin, "Rustin to King: Memo on the Montgomery Bus Boycott, December 23, 1956," 330.
128. King, *Stride Toward Freedom*, 42.
129. Ferron, "Report on MIA Executive Board 'Call' Meeting, January 30, 1956," in *Daybreak of Freedom: The Montgomery Bus Boycott*, ed. Stewart Burns (Chapel Hill: University of North Carolina Press, 1997), 129.
130. Ferron, "Report on MIA Executive Board 'Call' Meeting, January 30, 1956," 128–129.
131. King's statement here about being intimidated is unfortunately prescient, as this meeting took place from 11 a.m. to 2:35 p.m. on January 30, and the bomb was detonated on his front porch at around 9:15 that evening. Ferron, "Report on MIA Executive Board 'Call' Meeting, January 30, 1956," 129.
132. Ferron, "Report on MIA Executive Board 'Call' Meeting, January 30, 1956," 128.
133. Ferron, "Report on MIA Mass Meeting, February 27, 1956," 175.
134. Robinson, *The Montgomery Bus Boycott and the Women Who Started It*, 37.
135. Ferron, "Report on MIA Mass Meeting, March 1, 1956," in *Daybreak of Freedom: The Montgomery Bus Boycott*, ed. Stewart Burns (Chapel Hill: University of North Carolina Press, 1997), 197.
136. Ferron, "Report on MIA Mass Meeting, March 1, 1956," 198.
137. Holden, "Report on MIA Mass Meeting, March 22, 1956," 218.
138. King, *Stride Toward Freedom*, 42.
139. King, *Stride Toward Freedom*, 63–64. There are several recorded versions of this event, slightly different in detail, but generally identical. See also Robert J. Walker, *Let My People Go! The Miracle of the Montgomery Bus Boycott* (Lanham, Md.: Hamilton, 2007), 196, for a slightly more detailed account of this event. Walker names the woman as "an elderly seventy-year-old lady known affectionately as 'Sister Pollard,'" though neither King nor Robinson identify her.
140. Robinson, *The Montgomery Bus Boycott and the Women Who Started It*, 60. King also recounts what appears to be the same anecdote, as follows: "One elderly woman summed it up for the rest. When asked after several weeks of walking whether she was tired, she answered 'My feets is tired, but my soul is at rest.'" King, *Stride Toward Freedom*, xxx. It is sometimes suggested that the same woman, Sister Pollard, is being referred to in both anecdotes, and that it is in fact one story and one event, though this is unclear. Robinson also reports another event, perhaps apocryphal, but more comical than the story of Sister Pollard, though similar with regard to the changes that had come about through the practice of the boycott: "One December day a very aged black woman, who was struggling along on foot, walking with a cane, was overtaken by a bus with a lone black rider on it. The bus stopped at the stop sign just ahead of the old woman, to let the black passenger out. Seeing the situation, the crippled woman hobbled along faster toward the bus. The driver, thinking that the woman was hurrying to get on, seized the opportunity to show how courteous he could be to black people if they would only ride again. So he called out, in a very friendly tone, 'Don't hurt yourself, auntie, I'll wait for you!' With anger and scorn, the old woman pantingly, gaspingly called up to him as she hurried past the open bus door, 'I'm not your auntie, and I don't want to get on your bus. I'm trying to catch the ****** who just got off!' Then she drew back her

cane to strike the rider as he fled beyond her reach." Robinson, *The Montgomery Bus Boycott and the Women Who Started It*, 99.
141. Robinson, *The Montgomery Bus Boycott and the Women Who Started It*, 61.
142. King, *Stride Toward Freedom*, 45.
143. King, *Stride Toward Freedom*, 46. A reader has noted that Nixon's language of "fearless men" and "scared boys" can be read to exclude the major role that women played in organizing in Montgomery and beyond. Many issues arise here, and they stand in a complex relation to one another that I cannot do justice to in a note. I am in no position and I have no desire to try and excuse or attempt to explain away this very real concern, which I share. I am also uncomfortable attempting to handle, dismiss, or explain away the language of a major Black activist something like seventy years after the fact in a context outside of a specific and directed study on these themes. The only way forward is to address these questions in all of their challenge and complexity, even as such a study is simply impossible here. Still, several points are worth noting if in brief.

First, and as I have attempted to consistently emphasize, the fearlessness of countless women, whether in leadership or the rank and file, is vital to the Montgomery movement and the long civil rights era. Nixon himself, as I have emphasized, worked closely with Parks in the NAACP and continued to do so once the movement began. We must also reemphasize the fact that all of the defendants in *Browder v. Gale* were women, and again recognize the major role of Robinson and the WPC. It goes without saying that Parks herself, among many other Montgomery women, evinced a kind of fearlessness, indeed a kind of parrhesia, that has become iconic. I have tried my best to bring these figures forward across this chapter, even as there remains, as always, much more work to be done.

Second, and as King and many others discuss in detail, it is at the same time impossible to read Nixon's statement here without refence to the use of the word "boy" in the service of the dehumanization of Black men, and Black people in general, in this context. King speaks of this belittling usage often, and it is likely that the invocation would have resonated with those present at the meeting as Nixon spoke. Recall again the famous signs that read "I AM a man" during the 1968 Memphis santiation workers strike. The message in that case was, above all, one of humanization in the face of the explicit and tageted infantilization of Black workers, as is well known.

Whatever Nixon's intentions at the time, and regardless of whatever historical or linguistic account we may attempt to give, it is clear that these two themes of sexist exclusion and the tension around the use of certain terms by the forces of white supremacy, must be accounted for together in all their complexity, and despite whatever challenges and discomfort they raise.
144. King, *Stride Toward Freedom*, 74–75.
145. King, *Stride Toward Freedom*, 74.
146. Martin Luther King Jr. and Bayard Rustin, "Our Struggle," in *Daybreak of Freedom: The Montgomery Bus Boycott*, ed. Stewart Burns (Chapel Hill: University of North Carolina Press, 1997), 246. This text was in fact ghostwritten by Rustin for King, who "slightly revised Rustin's draft article on the bus boycott for publication in the second issue of *Liberation*. It was the first of numerous articles and chapter drafts that Rustin wrote for him." Burns, *Daybreak of Freedom*, 243.
147. King and Rustin, "Our Struggle," 247.

CONCLUSION: AUDRE LORDE—SURVIVAL, IMMEDIACY, AND POETRY AS A WAY OF LIFE

1. Audre Lorde, "A Burst of Light: Living with Cancer," in *A Burst of Light and Other Essays*, 40–133 (Mineola, N.Y.: Ixia, 2017), 131. See also Audre Lorde, *The Cancer Journals* (New York: Penguin, 1980).
2. Pierre Hadot, "Spiritual Exercises," in *Philosophy as a Way of Life: Spiritual Exercises from Socrates to Foucault* (Oxford: Blackwell, 1995), 82.
3. Lorde, "A Burst of Light," 130.
4. Perhaps predictably, we need look no further than the *New York Times* and a 2022 an article entitled "Investing in Real Estate as Self-Care"—an article that is not, in fact, a parody—to get a sense of the neoliberal uses of this term, evacuated of any moral or political substance, and constituting paradigmatic forms of ethical moralism and political spiritualism. See Jennifer Miller, "Investing in Real Estate as Self-Care," *New York Times*, July 29, 2022, https://www.nytimes.com/2022/07/29/realestate/investing-self-care-real-estate-women.html. For a similar view of "self-care" in the language of contemporary management and "entrepreneurial" discourse, we can look to a December 2017 article in *Forbes*, a comparably predictable source, entitled "Self-Care Is Not an Indulgence. It's a Discipline." Here, examples of "self-care" include "turning off the TV instead of watching another episode of 'The Crown' because the alarm is going off at 5am so you can get to the gym" and "Maintaining financial independence." Tami Forman, "Self-Care Is Not an Indulgence. It's a Discipline," *Forbes*, December 13, 2017, https://www.forbes.com/sites/tamiforman/2017/12/13/self-care-is-not-an-indulgence-its-a-discipline/?sh=747fd652feeo. Nice work if you can get it, but there is discipline, and there is discipline, I suppose. Ongoing critical readings of this kind of literature are all the more necessary as this language becomes more and more ubiquitous and thus ambiguous. For a more radical and generative conception of "self-care," grounded much more clearly and firmly in figures like Lorde and the concerns that guided her, see, for example, the forum on "Ethics, Theories, and Practices of Care" in *Debates in the Digital Humanities 2019*, ed. Matthew K. Gold and Lauren F. Klein (Minneapolis: University of Minnesota Press, 2019), chaps. 36–44, pp. 423–452. For a similar recent treatment of the concept of self-care, see Donna J. Nicol and Jennifer A. Yee, "'Reclaiming Our Time': Women of Color Faculty and Radical Self-Care in the Academy," *Feminist Teacher* 27, nos. 2–3 (2017): 133–156. Many similar treatments of this concept and related practices can be found in academic and activist literature too numerous to mention, but thankfully easy to find.
5. For biographical resources on Lorde, see Alexis De Veaux, *Warrior Poet: A Biography of Audre Lorde*, Array ed. (New York: Norton, 2004). For an exciting new biography of Lorde based on archival research, see Alexis Pauline Gumbs, *Survival Is a Promise: The Eternal Life of Audre Lorde* (New York: Farrar, Straus and Giroux, 2024). For a series of powerful reflections on Lorde's life and work by many who knew her, see Gloria I. Joseph, *The Wind Is Spirit: The Life, Love, and Legacy of Audre Lorde* (New York: Villarosa Media, 2016). The last includes contributions from figures like Sonia Sanchez, Angela Y. Davis, Assata Shakur, Barbara Smith, and Lorde's daughter Elizabeth Lorde-Rollins, among many others.

CONCLUSION

6. Lorde often reiterates this language in her written and spoken work, often when addressing others, especially those who do not share some or all of these forms of experience, and its emphasis and reemphasis plays a vital role in both grounding and elaborating so many of her interventions.
7. Lorde was a close friend and collaborator of Barbara Smith of the Combahee River Collective. In 1980, they cofounded Kitchen Table: Women of Color Press.
8. As she says, "I do not wish my anger and pain and fear about cancer to fossilize into yet another silence, nor to rob me of whatever strength can lie at the core of this experience, openly acknowledged and examined. For other women of all ages, colors, and sexual identities who recognize that imposed silence about any area of our lives is a tool for separation and powerlessness, and for myself, I have tried to voice some of my feelings and thoughts about the travesty of prosthesis, the pain of amputation, the function of cancer in a profit economy, my confrontation with mortality, the strength of women loving, and the power and rewards of self-conscious living." Lorde, *The Cancer Journals*, 1.
9. Audre Lorde, "A Litany for Survival," in *The Collected Poems of Audre Lorde* (New York: Norton, 2000), 255.
10. Lorde, "A Burst of Light," 133.
11. Once again, however, and as I must continue to emphasize, what makes something a mere surface-level invocation and what makes something a genuine and robust ethical–political intervention are rather more complicated questions.
12. Audre Lorde, *Zami: A New Spelling of My Name* (Freedom, Calif.: Crossing, 2001), 3.
13. As she puts it, "Self-preservation starts very early in West Indian families." Lorde, *Zami*, 22; regarding her mother, see also 17, 58. Later, she speaks of her teenage years in similar terms: "How meager the sustenance was I gained from the four years I spent in high school; yet, how important that sustenance was for my survival" (Lorde, *Zami*, 82).
14. Lorde, *Zami*, 103.
15. While I again cannot give a complete bibliography of secondary literature on Lorde here, new and familiar readers are strongly encouraged to see Keguro Macharia, "Survival in Audre Lorde," *New Inquiry*, August 25, 2017, https://thenewinquiry.com/blog/survival-in-audre-lorde. Another excellent account can be found in Alexis Pauline Gumbs, "Praise the Lorde: The Queer Survival of Audre Lorde," in Gloria I. Joseph, *The Wind Is Spirit: The Life, Love, and Legacy of Audre Lorde* (New York: Villarosa Media, 2016).
16. Lorde, *Zami*, 111.
17. Lorde, "A Litany for Survival," 255.
18. See Martin Luther King Jr., "Letter from Birmingham Jail," in *Why We Can't Wait*. (Boston: Beacon, 1963), 96.
19. Lorde, *The Cancer Journals*, 66.
20. See Pierre Hadot, Jeannie Carlier, Arnold I. Davidson, Marc Djaballah, and Michael Chase, "Is Philosophy a Luxury?," in *The Present Alone Is Our Happiness: Conversations with Jeannie Carlier and Arnold I. Davidson*, ed. Jeannie Carlier, Arnold I. Davidson, Marc Djaballah, and Michael Chase. Cultural Memory in the Present (Stanford, Calif.: Stanford University Press, 2011), 186–190. See also chapter 1, this volume.
21. I wish to thank Hélder G. Telo, who raised a number of important questions around these themes at the Philosophy as a Way of Life International Seminar on February

CONCLUSION

14, 2024, and further clarified those concerns and many of the source texts related to them in a private email exchange in May 2024. On these themes, we may think of key passages that contrast mere survival and the good life in dialogues like the *Crito* and *Gorgias*, or in Aristotle's *Politics*, and perhaps especially in book 10 of the *Nicomachean Ethics*. Taken as a whole, this last text certainly raises the question of the contrast and possible conflict between the best possible life understood as the life of philosophical contemplation and the life of politics, a noted historical tension between book 10 and the nine books that precede it. Of course, there are strong reasons to take a more complex view of book 10 on this set of issues, especially in reading it against books 1–9, as many have. Regarding this same tension between contemplation and leisure on the one hand and political life on the other, we might also think of certain passages from Plato, including book 7 of the *Republic*, *Theaetetus*, and several others. Thankfully again, these exegetical questions are beyond my concern here, and it suffices to note that this tension between the political life, "survival," leisure, and philosophical contemplation as a characteristic of the good life, do emerge and persist in the reception history of these and other texts.

22. Hadot et al., "Is Philosophy a Luxury?," 186.
23. As Seneca puts it in letter 91 to Lucilius: "So we must consider every possibility and reinforce our spirit against whatever could happen. Imagine exile, tortures, wars, and shipwrecks. Chance can take you from your country, or take away your country itself, it can drive you into the desert, and even this situation in which one is stifled by crowding can become a desert. Let us set the whole condition of human destiny before our eyes, and anticipate in our mind not what great misfortune often occurs but the greatest that can occur, if we don't want to be overwhelmed and dazed by these unaccustomed blows as if they were new; we must consider fortune in its full form." Seneca, *Selected Letters*, trans. Elaine Fantham (Oxford: Oxford University Press, 2010), 189–190.
24. Audre Lorde, "Age, Race, Class, and Sex: Women Redefining Difference," in *A Burst of Light and Other Essays* (Mineola, N.Y.: Ixia, 2017), 119.
25. Lorde, *Zami*, 70–71, 85.
26. Lorde was present at the March on Washington, though her experience there was telling. As she notes in "I Am Your Sister," emphasizing the role that Black lesbians have always played in major movements: "When I weaned my daughter in 1963 to go to Washington in August to work in the coffee tents along with Lena Horne, making coffee for the marshals because that was what most Black women did in the 1963 March on Washington, I was a Black Lesbian." In this same set of passages, she speaks movingly of supporting striking students at City College in 1969, as well as a number of other cases. Audre Lorde, "I Am Your Sister: Black Women Organizing Across Sexualities," in *A Burst of Light and Other Essays* (Mineola, N.Y.: Ixia, 2017), 14. Regarding her anti-apartheid work, see Lorde, "Apartheid USA," in *A Burst of Light and Other Essays*, 18–29. See also her reflections on working with South African groups like the Zamani Soweto Sisters in Lorde, "A Burst of Light," 97–103, entries of June 20–21, 1986; as well as groups like Artists Against Apartheid in Lorde, "I Am Your Sister," 15.
27. It is not entirely clear that this constitutes a technical term for Lorde, though it is certainly a descriptive one. See, for example, Lorde, *The Cancer Journals*, 1, 8; Lorde, "A Burst of Light," 109, 124.

28. Audre Lorde, "Poetry Is Not a Luxury," in *Sister Outsider: Essays and Speeches by Audre Lorde* (Berkeley, Calif.: Crossing, 2007), 36–37.
29. See chapter 3, section IV, "The Limits of Lost Concepts."
30. Audre Lorde, "The Transformation of Silence Into Language and Action," in *Sister Outsider: Essays and Speeches by Audre Lorde* (Berkeley, Calif.: Crossing, 2007), 41.
31. As Foucault says, "For there to be parrhesia, you recall—I stressed this last year—the subject must be taking some kind of risk [in speaking] this truth which he signs as his opinion, his thought, his belief, a risk which concerns his relationship with the person to whom he is speaking. For there to be parrhesia, in speaking the truth one must open up, establish, and confront the risk of offending the other person, of irritating him, of making him angry and provoking him to conduct which may even be extremely violent. So it is the truth subject to risk of violence." Michel Foucault, *The Courage of Truth: The Government of Self and Others II: Lectures at the Collège de France 1983–1984*, ed. Frédéric Gros, François Ewald, Alessandro Fontana, Arnold I. Davidson, and Graham Burchell (New York: Palgrave Macmillan, 2011), 11.
32. Lorde, "The Transformation of Silence Into Language and Action," 42.
33. Lorde, "The Transformation of Silence Into Language and Action," 42.
34. See Lorde, "A Burst of Light," 63, 56, respectively.
35. Lorde, *The Cancer Journals*, 51.
36. Lorde, *The Cancer Journals*, 52.
37. Or, as she says later, "Every woman has a right to define her own desires, make her own choices. But prostheses are often chosen, not from desire, but in default. Some women complain it is too much effort to fight the concerted pressure exerted by the fashion industry." Lorde, *The Cancer Journals*, 56, 58.
38. Lorde, *The Cancer Journals*, 54.
39. See Audre Lorde, "The Uses of Anger: Women Responding to Racism," in *Sister Outsider: Essays and Speeches by Audre Lorde* (Berkeley, Calif.: Crossing, 2007), 124–133.
40. Audre Lorde, "Uses of the Erotic," in *Sister Outsider: Essays and Speeches by Audre Lorde* (Berkeley, Calif.: Crossing, 2007), 54.
41. Lorde, "A Burst of Light," 71.
42. Lorde, *The Cancer Journals*, 67.

BIBLIOGRAPHY

Afary, Janet, and Kevin B. Anderson. *Foucault and the Iranian Revolution: Gender and the Seductions of Islamism*. Chicago: University of Chicago Press, 2005.

Anderson, Jervis. *Bayard Rustin: The Troubles I've Seen, A Biography*. New York: Harper Collins, 1997.

Anderson, Perry. *Considerations on Western Marxism*. New York: Verso, 1979.

Asad, Talal. "Thinking About Tradition, Religion, and Politics in Egypt Today." *Critical Inquiry* 42, no. 1 (Autumn 2015): 166–214.

Atzler, Edgar. *Körper und Arbeit. Handbuch der Arbeitsphysiologie*. Leipzig: G. Thieme, 1927.

Bremner, Sabina Vaccarino. "Introduction to Michel Foucault's 'Political Spirituality as the Will for Alterity.'" *Critical Inquiry* 47, no. 1 (2020): 115–120.

Brown, Amanda. "Howard Thurman Timeline." In *The Fellowship Church: Howard Thurman and the Twentieth Century Religious Left*, xiii. Oxford: Oxford University Press, 2021.

Burns, Stewart, ed. *Daybreak of Freedom: The Montgomery Bus Boycott*. Chapel Hill: University of North Carolina Press, 1997.

Cannon, Robert L. "Letter to Alfred Hassler and Glenn E. Smiley, October 3, 1956." In *The Papers of Martin Luther King, Jr.* Vol. 3, *Birth of a New Age, December 1955–December 1956*, ed. Clayborne Carson, 388–391. Berkeley: University of California Press, 1997.

Cavell, Stanley. *Cities of Words: Pedagogical Letters on a Register of the Moral Life*. Cambridge, Mass.: Belknap Press of Harvard University Press, 2004.

Collins, Steven. *Wisdom as a Way of Life: Theravāda Buddhism Reimagined*. Ed. Justin McDaniel. New York: Columbia University Press, 2018.

Colvin, Claudette. "Transcript of Record and Proceedings, Browder v. Gayle, May 11, 1956." In *Daybreak of Freedom: The Montgomery Bus Boycott*, ed. Stewart Burns, 74–77. Chapel Hill: University of North Carolina Press, 1997.

Cremonesi, Laura, Orazio Irrera, Daniele Lorenzini, and Martina Tazzioli, eds. *Foucault and the Making of Subjects. New Politics of Autonomy*. London: Rowman & Littlefield International, 2016.

——. "Foucault, the Iranian Uprising and the Constitution of a Collective Subjectivity." *Foucault Studies* 25 (2018): 299–311.

Davidson, Arnold I. *The Emergence of Sexuality: Historical Epistemology and the Formation of Concepts*. Cambridge, Mass.: Harvard University Press, 2001.

——. "From Subjection to Subjectivation: Michel Foucault and the History of Sexuality." In *Foucault and the Making of Subjects*, ed. Laura Cremonesi, Orazio Irrera, Daniele Lorenzini, and Martina Tazzioli, 55–61. London: Rowman & Littlefield International, 2016.

D'Emilio, John. *Lost Prophet: The Life and Times of Bayard Rustin*. New York: Free Press, 2003.

De Veaux, Alexis. *Warrior Poet: A Biography of Audre Lorde*. Array ed. New York: Norton, 2004.

Elden, Stuart. *Understanding Henri Lefebvre: Theory and the Possible*. London: Continuum, 2004.

Epictetus. *The Works of Epictetus. Consisting of His Discourses, in Four Books, the Enchiridion, and Fragments. A Translation from the Greek, Based Upon That of Elizabeth Carter*. Trans. Thomas Wentworth Higginson. Boston: Little, Brown, 1865.

Epicurus. "Letter to Menoeceus." In *The Art of Happiness*, ed. Daniel Klein. London: Penguin, 2012.

Ferron, Donald. "Report on MIA Executive Board 'Call' Meeting, January 30, 1956." In *Daybreak of Freedom: The Montgomery Bus Boycott*, ed. Stewart Burns, 128–130. Chapel Hill: University of North Carolina Press, 1997.

——. "Report on MIA Mass Meeting, February 27, 1956." In *Daybreak of Freedom: The Montgomery Bus Boycott*, ed. Stewart Burns, 172–175. Chapel Hill: University of North Carolina Press, 1997.

——. "Report on MIA Mass Meeting, March 1, 1956." In *Daybreak of Freedom: The Montgomery Bus Boycott*, ed. Stewart Burns, 196–199. Chapel Hill: University of North Carolina Press, 1997.

Foucault, Michel. *The Courage of Truth: The Government of Self and Others II: Lectures at the Collège de France 1983–1984*. Ed. Frédéric Gros, François Ewald, Alessandro Fontana, Arnold I. Davidson, and Graham Burchell. New York: Palgrave Macmillan, 2011.

——. *Discipline and Punish: The Birth of the Prison*. New York: Vintage, 1995.

——. "The Ethics of the Concern for the Self as a Practice of Freedom." In *Essential Works of Michel Foucault, 1954–1984*, vol. 1, 281–301. *Ethics: Subjectivity and Truth*, ed. Paul Rabinow. New York: New Press, 1997.

——. *The Hermeneutics of the Subject: Lectures at the Collège de France, 1981–1982*. Trans. Graham Burchell. New York: Palgrave Macmillan, 2005.

——. *The History of Sexuality*. Vol. 1, *An Introduction*. Trans. Robert Hurley. New York: Random House, 1978.

——. *The History of Sexuality*. Vol. 2, *The Use of Pleasure*. Trans. Robert Hurley. New York: Pantheon, 1985.

——. "Nietzsche, Genealogy, History." In *Essential Works of Michel Foucault, 1954–1984*. Vol. 2. *Aesthetics, Method, and Epistemology*, ed. Paul Rabinow, 369–392. New York: New Press, 1998.

———. "On the Genealogy of Ethics: An Overview of a Work in Progress." In *Essential Works of Michel Foucault, 1954–1984*. Vol. 1. *Ethics: Subjectivity and Truth*, ed. Paul Rabinow, 253–280. New York: New Press, 1997.
———. *The Order of Things: An Archaeology of the Human Sciences*. New York: Vintage, 1994.
———. "The Political Function of the Intellectual." *Radical Philosophy* 17 (Summer 1977): 12–14.
———. *Security, Territory, Population: Lectures at the Collège de France, 1977–78*. Ed. Michel Senellart, François Ewald, and Alessandro Fontana. New York: Palgrave Macmillan, 2007.
———. *Society Must Be Defended: Lectures at the Collège de France, 1975–76*. New York: Picador, 2003.
———. *Speaking the Truth About Oneself: Lectures at Victoria University, Toronto, 1982*. Ed. Henri-Paul Fruchaud and Daniele Lorenzini, English ed. Daniel Louis Wyche. Chicago Foucault Project. Chicago: University of Chicago Press, 2021.
———. "The Subject and Power." In *Essential Works of Michel Foucault, 1954–1984*. Vol. 3. *Power*, ed. Paul Rabinow, 326–348. New York: New Press, 2000.
———. *Subjectivity and Truth: Lectures at the Collège de France, 1980–1981*. Trans. Graham Burchell. New York: Palgrave Macmillan, 2017.
———. "What Are the Iranians Dreaming [*Revent*] About?" In *Foucault and the Iranian Revolution: Gender and the Seductions of Islamism*, 203–209. Chicago: University of Chicago Press, 2005.
———. "What Is Enlightenment?" In *Essential Works of Michel Foucault, 1954–1984*. Vol. 1. *Ethics: Subjectivity and Truth*, ed. Paul Rabinow, 303–320. New York: New Press, 1997.
Foucault, Michel, and Michael Bess. "Interview with Michel Foucault, 3 November 1980." In *About the Beginning of the Hermeneutics of the Self: Lectures at Dartmouth College, 1980*, ed. Henri-Paul Fruchaud and Daniele Lorenzini, 128–138. Chicago: University of Chicago Press, 2016.
Foucault, Michel, and Sabina Vaccarino Bremner. "Political Spirituality as the Will for Alterity: An Interview with the *Nouvel Observateur*." *Critical Inquiry* 47, no. 1 (2020): 121–134.
Foucault, Michel, and Gilles Deleuze. "Intellectuals and Power." In *Language, Counter-Memory, Practice: Selected Essays and Interviews*, ed. D. F. Bouchard, 206–217. Ithaca, N.Y.: Cornell University Press, 1977.
Foucault, Michel, and François Ewald. "The Concern for Truth: An Interview by François Ewald." In *Politics, Philosophy, Culture: Interviews and Other Writings 1977–1984*, ed. Lawrence D. Kritzman, 255–267. New York: Routledge, 1990.
Foucault, Michel, Farès Sassine, and Alex J. Feldman. "There Can't Be Societies Without Uprisings." *Foucault Studies* 25 (October 2018): 324–350.
Friedmann, Georges. Friedmann, Georges. *La Crise du progrès : esquisse d'histoire des idées: 1895-1935*. 6e éd. Paris: Gallimard, 1936.
———. *De la Sainte Russie à l'U.R.S.S.* Paris: Gallimard, 1938.
———. *Industrial Society: The Emergence of the Human Problems of Automation*. 2nd ed. New York: Free Press, 1967.
———. "L'homme et le milieu naturel: Panorama du nouveau milieu (1939)." In *Annales d'histoire sociale (1945), hommages à Marc Bloch II*, 103–116. Cambridge: Cambridge University Press, 1945.

BIBLIOGRAPHY

——. *Journal de guerre, 1939–1940*. Paris: Gallimard, 1987.
——. *Leibniz et Spinoza*. Paris: Gallimard, 1946.
——. "Machinisme et humanisme." *Europe*, no. 151 (June 1935): 437–444.
——. *Problèmes du machinisme en U.R.R.S. et dans les pays capitalistes*. Paris: Éditions sociales internationales, 1934.
——. *La puissance et la sagesse*. Paris: Gallimard, 1970.
——. "Travail et communion en U.R.R.S." *Europe*, no. 153 (September 1935): 58–80.
Friedrich, Horst E., and Barry L. Mordike. *Magnesium Technology: Metallurgy, Design Data, Applications*. Berlin: Springer Science & Business Media, 2006.
Gagarin, Yuri, and Vladimir Lebedev. *Survival in Space*. Trans. Gabriella Azrael. New York: Bantam, 1969.
Ghamari-Tabrizi, Behrooz. *Foucault in Iran: Islamic Revolution After the Enlightenment*. Minneapolis: University of Minnesota Press, 2016.
Gold, Matthew K., and Lauren F. Klein, eds. *Debates in the Digital Humanities 2019*. Minneapolis: University of Minnesota Press, 2019.
Goldschmidt, Victor. *Les "Dialogues" de Platon: structure et méthode dialectique*. Paris: Presses universitaires de France, 1947.
Gourné, Isabelle. "'Philosoviet' Commitments and a Sociological Stance Between the Two World Wars: Georges Friedmann's Political and Intellectual Role." *Sociologie du travail* 54 (2012): 356–374.
Gregg, Richard Bartlett. *The Power of Non-violence*. New York: Fellowship Publications, 1944.
Gumbs, Alexis Pauline. *Survival Is a Promise: The Eternal Life of Audre Lorde*. New York: Farrar, Straus and Giroux, 2024.
Hacking, Ian. *Historical Ontology*. Cambridge, Mass.: Harvard University Press, 2002.
Hadot, Ilsetraut. *Seneca und die Griechisch-Römische Tradition der Seelenleitung* [Seneca and the Greco-Roman Tradition of Spiritual Guidance]. Berlin, Walter de Gruyter, 1969.
Hadot, Pierre. "Ancient Philosophy: An Ethics or a Practice?" Trans. Matthew Sharpe and Federico Testa. In *The Selected Writings of Pierre Hadot: Philosophy as Practice*, 55–79. London: Bloomsbury Academic, 2020.
——. "Ancient Spiritual Exercises and 'Christian Philosophy.'" In *Philosophy as a Way of Life: Spiritual Exercises from Socrates to Foucault*, 126–144. Oxford: Blackwell, 1995.
——. "Conversion." Trans. Matthew Sharpe and Federico Testa. In *The Selected Writings of Pierre Hadot: Philosophy as Practice*, 93–104. London: Bloomsbury Academic, 2020.
——. "Epistrophe and Metanoia in the History of Philosophy." *Philosophy Today* 65, no. 1 (Winter 2021): 201–210.
——. "Forms of Life and Forms of Discourse in Ancient Philosophy." In *Philosophy as a Way of Life: Spiritual Exercises from Socrates to Foucault*, ed. Arnold I. Davidson, 49–70. Oxford: Blackwell, 1995.
——. *The Inner Citadel: The Meditations of Marcus Aurelius*. Trans. Michael Chase. Cambridge, Mass.: Harvard University Press, 2001.
——. *Introduction aux "Pensées" de Marc Aurèle*. Paris: Librairie Arthème Fayard, 1997.
——. "Jeux de langage et philosophie." *Revue de Métaphysique et de Morale* 67, no. 3 (July–October 1962): 330–343.

———. "Marcus Aurelius." In *Philosophy as a Way of Life: Spiritual Exercises from Socrates to Foucault*, 179–205. Oxford: Blackwell, 1995.
———. "My Books and My Research." Trans. Matthew Sharpe and Federico Testa. In *The Selected Writings of Pierre Hadot: Philosophy as Practice*, 33–42. London: Bloomsbury Academic, 2020.
———. *Philosophy as a Way of Life: Spiritual Exercises from Socrates to Foucault*. Ed. Arnold I. Davidson. Oxford: Blackwell, 1995.
———. "Postscript." Trans. Michael Chase. In *Philosophy as a Way of Life: Spiritual Exercises from Socrates to Foucault*, 277–286. Oxford: Blackwell, 1995.
———. "Reflections on the Idea of the 'Cultivation of the Self.'" In *Philosophy as a Way of Life: Spiritual Exercises from Socrates to Foucault*, ed. Arnold I. Davidson, 206–213. Oxford: Blackwell, 1995.
———. "The Sage and the World." In *Philosophy as a Way of Life: Spiritual Exercises from Socrates to Foucault*, 251–263. Oxford: Blackwell, 1995.
———. "Spiritual Exercises." In *Philosophy as a Way of Life: Spiritual Exercises from Socrates to Foucault*, 81–125. Oxford: Blackwell, 1995.
———. "There Are Nowadays Professors of Philosophy, but Not Philosophers." *Journal of Speculative Philosophy* 19, no. 3 (2005): 229–237. http://www.jstor.org/stable/25670570.
———. "The View from Above." In *Philosophy as a Way of Life: Spiritual Exercises from Socrates to Foucault*, 238–250. Oxford: Blackwell, 1995.
———. *What Is Ancient Philosophy?* Cambridge, Mass.: Belknap Press of Harvard University Press, 2002.
Hadot, Pierre, Jeannie Carlier, Arnold I. Davidson, Marc Djaballah, and Michael Chase. "Interpretation, Objectivity, and Mistakes." In *The Present Alone Is Our Happiness: Conversations with Jeannie Carlier and Arnold I. Davidson*, 61–74. Stanford, Calif.: Stanford University Press, 2011.
———. "Is Philosophy a Luxury?" In *The Present Alone Is Our Happiness: Conversations with Jeannie Carlier and Arnold I. Davidson*, ed. Jeannie Carlier, Arnold I. Davidson, Marc Djaballah, and Michael Chase, 186–190. Stanford, Calif.: Stanford University Press, 2011.
———. "Philosophical Discourse." In *The Present Alone Is Our Happiness: Conversations with Jeannie Carlier and Arnold I. Davidson*, 52–60. Stanford, Calif.: Stanford University Press, 2011.
———. "Philosophical Discourse as a Spiritual Exercise." In *The Present Alone Is Our Happiness: Conversations with Jeannie Carlier and Arnold I. Davidson*, 87–97. Stanford, Calif.: Stanford University Press, 2011.
———. *The Present Alone Is Our Happiness: Conversations with Jeannie Carlier and Arnold I. Davidson*. 2nd ed. Stanford, Calif.: Stanford University Press, 2011.
Harcourt, Bernard E., "Introduction to Foucault on Iran: Revolt as Political Spirituality." Columbia Center for Contemporary Critical Thought, Uprising 13/13 Seminar, December 11, 2017. https://blogs.law.columbia.edu/uprising1313/bernard-e-harcourt-introduction-to-foucault-on-iran-revolt-as-political-spirituality/#_edn1.
Holden, Anna. "Report on Mia Mass Meeting, March 22, 1956." In *Daybreak of Freedom: The Montgomery Bus Boycott*, ed. Stewart Burns, 212–219. Chapel Hill: University of North Carolina Press, 1997.
"Howard Thurman Chronology." Howard Thurman Papers Project, Boston University School of Theology, 2016. https://www.bu.edu/htpp/howard-thurman-chronology.

BIBLIOGRAPHY

Hurt, John Smith. "Spike Driver Blues (1928)." In *Avalon Blues: The Complete 1928 Okeh Recordings*. New York: Columbia Records, 1996.
James, William. *The Varieties of Religious Experience*. New York: Penguin, 1985.
Jean-Daniel, Reynaud. "Friedmann, Georges (1902-1977). Professeur d'histoire du travail (1946-1959)." In *Les professeurs du Conservatoire national des arts et métiers, dictionnaire biographique 1794-1955, A-K*, ed. C. Fontanon and A. Grelon, 544-549. Paris: Institut national de recherche pédagogique, 1994.
"John Henry." Library of Congress. https://www.loc.gov/item/ihas.200196572.
Joseph, Gloria I. *The Wind Is Spirit: The Life, Love, and Legacy of Audre Lorde*. New York: Villarosa Media, 2016.
Kapur, Sudarshan. *Raising up a Prophet: The African American Encounter with Gandhi*. Boston: Beacon, 1992.
King, Martin Luther, Jr. "Letter from Birmingham Jail." In *Why We Can't Wait*, 85-109. The King Legacy. Boston: Beacon, 1963.
———. "Letter to Bayard Rustin, March 10, 1958." In *The Papers of Martin Luther King, Jr.* Vol. 4, *Symbol of the Movement, January 1957-December 1958*, 380. ed. Susan Carson Clayborne Carson, Adrienne Clay, Virginia Shadron, and Kieran Taylor. Stanford, Calif.: Stanford University Press, 1958.
———. *Stride Toward Freedom: The Montgomery Story*. Boston: Beacon, 1986.
———. "We Are Still Walking." In *Daybreak of Freedom: The Montgomery Bus Boycott*, ed. Stewart Burns, 318-323. Chapel Hill: University of North Carolina Press, 1997.
King, Martin Luther, Jr., and Bayard Rustin. "Our Struggle." In *Daybreak of Freedom: The Montgomery Bus Boycott*, ed. Stewart Burns, 243-249. Chapel Hill: University of North Carolina Press, 1997.
Laugier, Sandra. "Pierre Hadot as a Reader of Wittgenstein." *Paragraph* 34, no. 3 (November 2011): 322-337.
Levinas, Emmanuel. "Heidegger, Gagarin and Us." Trans. Seán Hand. In *Difficult Freedom: Essays on Judaism*, 231-234. Baltimore, Md.: Johns Hopkins University Press, 1990.
Lorde, Audre. "Age, Race, Class, and Sex: Women Redefining Difference." In *A Burst of Light and Other Essays*, 114-123. Mineola, N.Y.: Ixia, 2017.
———. "Apartheid USA." In *A Burst of Light and Other Essays*, 18-29. Mineola, N.Y.: Ixia, 2017.
———. "A Burst of Light: Living with Cancer." In *A Burst of Light and Other Essays*, 40-133. Mineola, N.Y.: Ixia, 2017.
———. *The Cancer Journals*. New York: Penguin, 1980.
———. "I Am Your Sister: Black Women Organizing Across Sexualities." In *A Burst of Light and Other Essays*, 10-17. Mineola, N.Y.: Ixia, 2017.
———. "A Litany for Survival." In *The Collected Poems of Audre Lorde*, 255-256. New York: Norton, 2000.
———. "Poetry Is Not a Luxury." In *Sister Outsider: Essays and Speeches by Audre Lorde*, 36-39. Berkeley, Calif.: Crossing, 2007.
———. "The Transformation of Silence Into Language and Action." In *Sister Outsider: Essays and Speeches by Audre Lorde*, 40-44. Berkeley, Calif.: Crossing, 2007.
———. "The Uses of Anger: Women Responding to Racism." In *Sister Outsider: Essays and Speeches by Audre Lorde*, 124-133. Berkeley, Calif.: Crossing, 2007.
———. "Uses of the Erotic." In *Sister Outsider: Essays and Speeches by Audre Lorde*, 53-59. Berkeley, Calif.: Crossing, 2007.

——. *Zami: A New Spelling of My Name*. Freedom, Calif.: Crossing, 2001.
Lorenzini, Daniele. "Ethics as Politics: Foucault, Hadot, Cavell, and the Critique of Our Present." In *Foucault and the History of Our Present*, ed. Sophie Fuggle, Yari Lanci, and Martina Tazzioli, 223–235. London: Palgrave Macmillan, 2015.
——. "Must We Do What We Say? Truth, Responsibility, and the Ordinary in Ancient and Modern Perfectionism." *European Journal of Pragmatism and American Philosophy* 2, no. 2 (2010): 16–34.
——. "La vie comme 'réel' de la philosophie. Cavell, Foucault, Hadot et les techniques de l'ordinaire," in *La voix et la vertu. Variétés du perfectionnisme moral*, ed. Sandra Laugier, 469–487. Paris: Presses Universitaires de France, 2010.
Macharia, Keguro. "Survival in Audre Lorde." *New Inquiry*, August 25, 2017. https://thenewinquiry.com/blog/survival-in-audre-lorde.
Marcus Aurelius. *The Communings with Himself of Marcus Aurelius Antonius, Emperor of Rome, Together with His Speeches and Sayings*. Trans. and ed. C. R. Haines. Cambridge, Mass.: Harvard University Press, 1916.
——. *Meditations, with Selected Correspondence*. Trans. Robin Hard. Oxford: Oxford University Press, 2011.
Marx, Karl. *Capital*, Vol. 1. New York: Penguin, 1990.
——. "Economic and Philosophic Manuscripts of 1844." In *The Marx-Engels Reader*, ed. Robert C. Tucker, 66–125. New York: Norton, 1978.
——. "Theses on Feuerbach." In *The Marx-Engels Reader*, ed. Robert C. Tucker, 143–145. New York: Norton, 1978.
——. "Theses on Feuerbach." Trans. Clemens Dutt. In *German Socialist Philosophy*, ed. Wolfgang Shirmacher, 104–106. New York: Continuum, 1997.
Melnik-Duhamel, Catherine. "L'affaire Georges Friedmann: À propos de la publication de *De La Sainte Russie à l'URSS*," Mémoire de diplôme d'études approfondies (DEA), Institut d'études politiques (Sciences Po), 1986.
Morin, Edgar. "Préface: Il était minuit dans le siècle." In *La puissance et la sagesse*, by Georges Friedmann, 9–18. Paris: Gallimard, 1970.
Morris, Aldon D. *The Origins of the Civil Rights Movement: Black Communities Organizing for Change*. New York: Free Press, 1984.
Nelson, Scott Reynolds. *Steel Drivin' Man: John Henry, the Untold Story of an American Legend*. New York: Oxford University Press, 2008.
Nicol, Donna J., and Jennifer A. Yee. "'Reclaiming Our Time': Women of Color Faculty and Radical Self-Care in the Academy." *Feminist Teacher* 27, nos. 2–3 (2017): 133–156.
Patočka, Jan. *Plato and Europe*. Trans. Peter Lom. Stanford, Calif.: Stanford University Press 2002.
Rhodes, Richard. "Guernica: Horror and Inspiration." *Bulletin of the Atomic Scientists* 69, no. 6 (November 1, 2013): 19–25.
Robinson, Jo Ann Gibson. *The Montgomery Bus Boycott and the Women Who Started It*. Knoxville: University of Tennessee Press, 1987.
Roudinesco, Elisabeth. *Jacques Lacan & Co.: A History of Psychoanalysis in France, 1925–1985*. Chicago: University of Chicago Press, 1990.
Rustin, Bayard. "Interview of Bayard Rustin by Ed Edwin, April 3, 1985." In *The Reminiscences of Bayard Rustin, No. 4: Interview of Bayard Rustin by Ed Edwin, April 3, 1985*, ed. Ed Edwin, 55. Alexandria, Va.: Alexander Street Press, 2003.

———. "Lesson Plan on Non-violent Action (1941)." Swarthmore College Peace Collection, Fellowship of Reconciliation Papers, DG 013. McCabe Library, Swarthmore, Penn.

———. "Rustin to King: Memo on the Montgomery Bus Boycott, December 23, 1956." In *Daybreak of Freedom: The Montgomery Bus Boycott*, ed. Stewart Burns, 329–331. Chapel Hill: University of North Carolina Press, 1997.

———. *Time on Two Crosses: The Collected Writings of Bayard Rustin*. Ed. Devon W. Carbado and Donald Weise. San Francisco: Cleis Press, 2003.

"Rustin, Bayard: Biography, March 17, 1912 to August 24, 1987." Martin Luther King Jr. Research and Education Institute. https://kinginstitute.stanford.edu/encyclopedia/rustin-bayard.

Schorm, Evald, dir. *Každý Den Odvahu* [Courage for every day]. 84 minutes. Czechoslovakia, 1964.

Schwab, Françoise. "Vladimir Jankélévitch à Toulouse. 1940–1945. Une parenthèse inoubliable. La guerre." *Cités* 2, no. 70 (2017): 105–118. https://www.cairn.info/revue-cites-2017-2-page-105.htm.

Seneca. *Selected Letters*. Trans. Elaine Fantham. Oxford: Oxford University Press, 2010.

Shridharani, Krishnalal. *War Without Violence: A Study of Gandhi's Method and Its Accomplishments*. New York: Harcourt, Brace, 1939.

Simiand, François. *Cours d'économie politique professé en 1928–1929 : [2ème année]*. Paris: Domat Montchrestien, 1930.

Smiley, Glenn. "Letter to Dr. Martin Luther King, April 13, 1956." In *Daybreak of Freedom: The Montgomery Bus Boycott*, ed. Stewart Burns, 253–254. Chapel Hill: University of North Carolina Press, 1997.

———. "Memo to [FOR] Staff, April 7, 1956." In *Daybreak of Freedom: The Montgomery Bus Boycott*, ed. Stewart Burns, 250–253. Chapel Hill: University of North Carolina Press, 1997.

———. *Nonviolence: The Gentle Persuader*. Nyack, N.Y.: Fellowship Publications, 1991.

Smith, Lillian. "Letter to Dr. Martin Luther King, March 10, 1956." In *Daybreak of Freedom: The Montgomery Bus Boycott*, ed. Stewart Burns, 201–203. Chapel Hill: University of North Carolina Press, 1997.

Swomley, John M. "Letter to Glenn Smiley, February 29, 1956." In *Daybreak of Freedom: The Montgomery Bus Boycott*, ed. Stewart Burns, 171. Chapel Hill: University of North Carolina Press, 1997.

Thurman, Howard. *Jesus and the Disinherited*. Boston: Beacon, 1996.

Trebitsch, M. "Les mésaventures du groupe *Philosophies* (1924–1933)." *La Revue des reviews*, no. 3 (Spring 1987).

Turner, Ronald. "The Way to Stop Discrimination on the Basis of Race. . . ." *Stanford Journal of Civil Rights and Civil Liberties* 11, no. 45 (April 9, 2015): 45–88. https://ssrn.com/abstract=2592570.

Vatin, François. "'Machinisme,' Marxism, Humanism: Georges Friedmann Before and After WWII." *Sociologie du travail* 49 (2007): e16–e33. http://france.elsevier.com/direct/SOCTRA.

Walker, Robert J. *Let My People Go! The Miracle of the Montgomery Bus Boycott*. Lanham, Md.: Hamilton Books, 2007.

White, Frank. "Episode 107: The Overview Effect." *Houston We Have a Podcast*, hosted by Gary Jordan. NASA. 2019. https://www.nasa.gov/johnson/HWHAP/the-overview-effect.

BIBLIOGRAPHY

——. *The Overview Effect: Space Exploration and Human Evolution*. 4th ed. Reston, Va.: American Institute of Aeronautics and Astronautics, 2021.

Wigginton, Eliot, ed. *Refuse to Stand Silently By: An Oral History of Grass Roots Social Activism in America, 1921–64*. New York: Doubleday, 1991.

Williamson Brothers & Curry. "Gonna Die with My Hammer in My Hand (1927)." In *Anthology of American Folk Music*. Vol. 1, *Ballads*. Washington, D.C.: Folkways Records, 1952.

Wuthnow, Robert. *After Heaven: Spirituality in America Since the 1950s*. Berkeley: University of California Press, 1998.

INDEX

Abernathy, Ralph, 208–209, 213, 225, 228–229
abnegation, ethical-political, 21–23, 100, 132, 136, 139, 147, 175, 237–238, 294n113
Alabama State College. *See* Alabama State University
Alabama State University, 207–208
alethia, 151
American Federation of Labor, 113
Anabaptism, 179
anachronism, problem of, 79–80, 264n29, 268n87, 278n49. *See also* Hadot, Pierre
analytics of power. *See* Foucault, Michel
Anderson, Jervis, 214
anticipation, Howard Thurman on the degrading effects of, 190–191. *See also* Hadot, Pierre
apartheid, 247
Arbeitsphysiologie. See Atzler, Edgar
Aristotle, Aristotelianism, 48, 64, 66–67, 244, 306n21
armistice of 1940, 97, 130, 134, 139, 277n34
art of living, 52, 72
artisanship, 118–119
ascesis. *See* askesis

asceticism, 22–24, 34, 47, 162, 173. *See also* askesis
askesis, 47, 63–64, 68, 162. *See also* asceticism
assembly line, 122
assujettissement. See Foucault, Michel; subjectivation, political
astronauts, 84–86
attention to the present moment, as spiritual exercise, 65–66, 68. See also *prosokhē*
Atzler, Edgar, 281n74
Augustine of Hippo, Saint, 48, 264n27
Aurobindo Ghose, Sri, 261n2
automation, industrial, 2, 27, 37, 94, 97, 110, 120, 122–123
Axiothea of Phlius, 270n110
Azikiwe, Nnamdi, 299n75

Baton Rouge Bus Boycott, 209
becoming human. *See* humanization
biopoetics, 166, 236, 249
biopolitics, biopower, 166, 282n94
Birmingham, Alabama, campaign, 197–199
Bremner, Sabina Vaccarino, 167

Browder v. Gale, 182–184, 186–187, 221, 295n2, 304n143
Brown v. Board of Education of Topeka, 209, 295n6
"Burst of Light: Living with Cancer, A" (Lorde), 4, 236, 307n24
bus desegregation, 41, 215, 221–222, 225–225. See also *Browder v. Gale*; King, Martin Luther, Jr.; *Morgan v. Virginia*
bus segregation, 41, 182, 202–204, 207–208, 296n6. See also *Browder v. Gale*; King, Martin Luther, Jr.; *Morgan v. Virginia*

California Cult of the Self, 16, 21, 29, 144, 150
Calvinism, 179
Cancer Journals, The (Lorde), 236, 241, 243, 251, 305n1, 306n8, 307n27, 308n37
capitalism, capitalists, 27, 93, 101, 105, 121–122, 266n58
care: for oneself as an act of political warfare (*see* Lorde, Audre); of the city, 13, 20, 75–76, 105, 144, 152, 169, 186; of the community, 13, 31, 43, 92, 105, 152, 194, 198, 200, 231, 255, 296; of the other, 12, 30, 41, 43, 92, 105, 150, 152, 169, 174, 185–187, 201, 255; of the self, coterminous with care of the other, 12, 28–31, 41, 43, 74–76, 92, 105, 147, 150, 169, 175, 185–187, 201, 238, 240, 255; of the self, 2–4, 9, 14, 20, 28–29, 39, 41, 43–44, 76, 103, 143, 147–148, 150–152, 162–166, 174, 176, 178, 189, 201, 240, 243–244, 254, 256, 259n18, 259n27, 272n125, 287n19, 291n81; of the soul (*see* Patočka, Jan)
Carlier, Jeannie, 54, 77–78, 80
Cassou, Jean, 277n34
Cavell, Stanley, 5, 265n46
Chaplin, Charlie, 66
Charta 77, 5, 258n6, 273n2
Chase, Michael, 81–83
Christianity, 47, 49, 56, 59, 64, 82, 129, 131, 160–161, 173, 190
civil rights movement, American, 3, 41, 180, 185, 187–190, 198, 205, 210–211, 215, 231

Cold War, 86, 284n129
Coleman, Ornette, 270
collection of facts, as second step in nonviolent campaign, 198–199
Collins, Steve, 270n107, 270n112
Colvin, Claudette, 1, 186, 208, 298n57, 298n63
communism, communist party, 96, 101, 115, 129, 211–212, 273n2, 274n9, 276n28, 281n86
confession, practice of, 154–156, 269n107, 286n18
Congress of Racial Equality (CORE), 211, 218, 225, 299n72, 301n101
conservatism, 25, 101, 148
conservatism, American, 25
contemplation: as form of retreat, 22, 45, 92, 100; spiritual exercises of, 6, 45, 65, 66–69, 85, 240, 244–246, 255, 267n82, 269n107, 306n21
conversion: as outcome of spiritual exercises, 51, 128, 162, 172–173, 195, 264n37, 294n109; and revolution (*see* Foucault, Michel)
cosmic consciousness, 66, 268n295. See also view from above
cosmonauts, Soviet. See Gagarin, Yuri
Coste, Florent, 108, 133, 135, 278n52
counter-conduct. See Foucault, Michel
Courcelle, Pierre, 263n27
Cynicism. See Foucault, Michel; Hadot, Pierre

Davidson, Arnold I., 61, 71, 79, 87–88, 260n1, 263n21, 263n23, 288n39, 292n86
D'Emilio, John, 212
Derrida, Jacques, 258n6
Dexter Avenue Baptist Church, 201, 208, 214
dialogue, philosophical. See Hadot, Pierre
Diggers and Levelers, 173
Diogenes of Sinope. See Foucault, Michel; Hadot, Pierre
direct action, 3, 13, 21, 41–42, 197–201, 210–211, 216–221, 224, 234, 295n6

INDEX

disinherited, the, 34, 44, 74, 189, 190–196, 250
Dreyfus, Hubert, 144, 288n37
Dubček, Alexander, 273n2
Dubreuil, Hyacinthe, 112, 280n66

egoism, 19–23, 29, 31, 33, 136, 138, 146, 150, 244. *See also* Foucault, Michel; withdrawal, political
Elektron, incendiary, 107, 278n49
elites, problem of, 9–11, 34, 71–76, 92, 99, 137, 146, 175, 244, 271n113. *See also* specialists, problem of
Engels, Friedrich, 95, 275n26, 279n58
Epictetus, 1, 52, 67, 73, 264n32, 266n58, 272n118
Epicurus, Epicureanism. *See* Hadot, Pierre
ethics, relationship of to politics. *See* politics, relation to ethics
everyday life, 21, 23, 61, 72, 75, 87, 93, 99, 103, 116, 124–125, 137–138
Ewald, François, 145, 286n12–13
Executive Order 8802, 295

Farmer, James, 299n6
Fellowship of Reconciliation (FOR), 190, 211, 215–216, 225, 299n72, 299n75, 301n97–98, 301n101, 302n117
flakiness, spiritual, 15, 17
Ford, Henry, 112–114
Foucault, Michel: analytics of power, 39–40, 141, 150–157, 161, 165, 174; analytics of resistance, 156–162; biopoetics, 166; care of the self, ethics of (*see* care of the self); on collective vs. individual morality, 20, 144, 165; combative dirtiness, 170; conduct of conducts, 155, 158–61, 193, 203; conversion (distinct from counter-conduct), 160; of power, 164; counter-conduct, 159–161, 166, 187, 291n71; Cynicism, ancient, 168–169, 248, 250–251, 259n18; Cynicism, revolutionary, 168–173; Diogenes on (*see* Cynicism, ancient; Hadot, Pierre); problem of egoism and withdrawal, 19–23, 144, 146, 149; ethical substance, 163, 270n108; ethical work (*travail éthique*), 163, 270n108; forms of elaboration, 163; freedom, 158, 164, 290n60, 290n63; governmentality (*see* governmentality); know thyself, ancient injunction to, 291n73; mass movements, lack of analysis of, 41, 165, 178, 180; moral dandyism, 20–21, 144 (*see also* Hadot, Pierre); morality as distinguished from ethics, 3, 10, 162, 291n79; and the other life, 169, 170 (*see also* parrhesia); pastoral power, 159–161; political power, first or final point of resistance to, 13, 141, 149, 165, 178, 184–185; political spirituality, 134, 166–168, 172–173, 177, 292n92, 293n94; prescriptive reticence, 145–146, 166–174; relationship of the self to itself, on (*see* relationship of the self to itself); repressive hypothesis, the, 153–154, 287n25; coalescence of resistance into revolution, 157, 171; conversion from revolution, 172, 285n11; conversion to revolution, 144, 172, 294n110; and revolutionary life, 170–171; and revolutionary subjectivity, 41, 173–174; self-forming activity (*pratique de soi*), 163, 174, 177, 292n84 (*see also* practices of the self); subjection, 156, 161, 163–164, 175, 291n83, 294n113; subjectivation, 161–164, 173, 176, 179, 187, 201, 213, 220, 270n108, 291n81, 291n83, 302n117; mode of, 163, 270n108; technologies of the self, 2, 146, 166, 176–177, 192; and the true life, 168–170, 172, 249–250, 293n101
freedom, 45, 62, 64, 122, 195, 229, 252, 266n57, 272n125, 301n103. *See also* Foucault, Michel
Freedom Rides, 296n6
French, E. N., 208
Friedmann, Georges: and the *affaire Friedmann*, 96, 275n26; on contemporary media, 81–83; dehumanization, 98, 110, 111–114,

INDEX

Friedmann, Georges (*continued*) 118, 120, 126, 279n58, 282n99; despiritualization (*Entseelung*) of labor, 111, 118–119, 279n58; and early *marxisme naïf*, 26–30, 90, 101–105, 115, 125; exterior effort, 37, 91–94, 97–98, 100–103, 124–128, 131–133, 136, 138–139; Hospital Complimentary Unit, 37, 96, 107–109, 134–135, 276n32; humanization, 25, 50, 92, 114, 117–118, 122, 124, 126, 129, 131–132, 133, 136, 264n34; humans as superior to our works, 136–137, 282n91, 284n138; inferior to our works, human beings as, 113–114, 117, 131; interior effort, 2, 14, 29, 38, 46, 89, 91, 94, 96–104, 118, 120, 126–128, 131, 133–138, 139, 189, 201, 291n81; labor upon the environment as labor upon oneself, 123, 126, 133, 139, 281n85; leisure, question of, 105–106, 123, 245; on Marcus Aurelius, 129–130, 260n2, 282n86, 285n81; and mechanization (see *maschinisme*); milieu, new industrial and technological, 101, 103, 115–117, 123, 126–128, 131, 133, 136, 138, 165, 282n94, 284n130; moralism, definition of (see moralism); mystical comforts (*see* spiritualism); and natural milieu, 106, 115, 117–118, 133–165; on noiose, stupefying effects of, 112, 280n66; on nostalgia, problem of, 100, 103, 118–124, 127–128, 131, 136; scientific management, critique of, 111–114, 119, 126, 279n58, 280n72; spiritualism, definition of (see spiritualism); spiritualization of labor, 119; sociology of labor, 2, 36–38, 90–91, 93, 95, 97, 99, 111–119, 122–123, 125–126, 260n1, 274n13, 280n73, 283n107, 284n130; technological change, challenge of, 36–38, 93, 99, 100–103, 110, 116–117, 120–122, 124, 138, 198, 260n2; technologies of death, 107, 133, 278n49; USSR, relationship to, 2, 24, 36, 95, 114, 117, 124–125, 134, 140, 275n19, 275nn26–27, 276n30, 279n58, 281n81, 281n86. *See also* Great Disequilibirium; *Journal de guerre, 1939–1940*; "Technological Adventure of Human Beings in the Twentieth Century, The"

Gagarin, Yuri, 84–86, 272n135
Gandhi, Mohandas Karamchand, 3, 190, 197, 209, 212–214, 257n4, 297n31
Garan, Ron, 85, 273n137
genealogy, theoretical method of, 41, 104, 144–146, 149, 153, 172–173, 177, 179, 276n27, 286n15
Germany, in the Second World War, 96, 134, 139, 277n34
Gernika (Guernica), 278n49
God, gods, 63, 195, 223, 229, 284n137
Goldschmidt, Victor, 54, 266n56
good life, 44, 51–52, 244, 246, 307n21
goodwill, as ethical-political force, 96, 140, 216–217
Gorgias, 307. *See also* Plato
Gourné, Isabelle, 95, 273n7, 275n19
governmentality, 29, 139, 141–142, 148–151, 159, 179, 275n28, 290n63
grammar of fear. *See* King, Martin Luther, Jr.
Great Disequilibrium, 38, 94, 98, 103, 110–121, 124–126, 129–135, 260n2, 278n49, 279n58. *See also* Friedmann, Georges
Gregg, Richard, 257, 297
Gros, Frédéric, 151
Groupe Philosophies, 273n9, 279n58; roulette affair, 274n10
Guernica. *See* Gernika
Guterman, Norbert, 273n9; translation of Marx's economic and philosophical manuscripts, 279n58

Hacking, Ian, 288n39
Hadot, Ilsetraut, 49, 263n22
Hadot, Pierre: anachronism, on the problem of, 79–80, 264n29, 268n87; ancient philosophy, interpretation of, 48–53, 58, 67, 69–73, 76–77, 79, 87,

INDEX

261n6, 265n42; Christianity, 47, 56, 59, 64, 83, 261n6, 267n80, 269n107; Cynicism, ancient, 61, 64–65, 75–77, 259n18, 265n42, 268n93, 270n110, 272n125; descriptive project, 10, 34–35, 55–58, 80, 111; Epicurus, Epicureanism, 34, 52, 61–64, 67–70, 72–73, 81, 267n74, 268n93, 268n95, 269n103, 270n110, 271n113; on Foucault, 54, 165; on Friedmann, 46–47, 54, 56–58, 77, 80–81, 84, 88, 97–100, 129–131, 261n2; luxury, philosophy as, 271n1; on Marcus Aurelius, 47–49, 50, 55, 73, 78, 81–84, 129–130, 262n14, 263n21, 264n32, 268n95, 285n81; on moral dandyism, 16, 259n27 (*see also* Foucault, Michel); *parrhesia*, 168; philosophy as a luxury, the problem of, 63, 71–73, 244, 270n112; prescriptive project, 10, 34–35, 54–58, 60, 77–78, 80; sage, the, 52–53, 63–64, 113, 265nn45–46, 266n48; Skepticism, ancient, 61, 64, 69, 77, 269n103; spiritual exercises (*See* spiritual exercises); Stoicism, ancient, 34, 48, 50, 61–73, 77–78, 81, 245, 264n32, 268n83, 268n95, 271n113, 272n119
happiness, 24, 64–65, 67
hate, 190–192, 229, 233
healing, 53–54, 61, 111
Heidegger, Martin, 86
Henry, John, 113, 280n73
Highlander Folk School, 22, 207
Hinduism, 131, 261, 284–285
Hipparchia the Cynic, 270n110
Holt Street Baptist Church, 225
Houser, George, 299n72
human flourishing, 7, 22, 27, 37, 136, 241–242, 283n115
Humani Generis, 261n5
humanism, 90, 274–277, 280, 283
humanization, 25, 50, 92, 114, 117–118, 122, 124–129, 131–133, 136, 264n34, 304n143
Hurt, "Mississippi" John Smith, 280n73
Husserl, Edmund, 5, 258n6

"I AM a Man," signs reading, 205, 304n143
imagination, spiritual exercises of, 47, 66–67, 84, 245, 259n12
imaginative overflight, 66–67, 84, 269n95. *See also* view from above
India, 82, 246, 261n2, 277n34, 284n144, 285n145
indifference, Stoic principle of. *See* Stoicism
industrial psychology, 275n18. *See also* Atzler, Edgar
industrialization, 93, 106, 112, 114, 120, 122–124, 275n18, 283n99
inner armor, 195, 229. *See also* Thurman, Howard
International Space Station, 85
Iranian Revolution, 167–168, 177–179, 292n92, 293n97
Islam, 82, 267n80, 285n149

James, William, 10, 259n16
Jankélévitch, Vladimir, 277n34
Jaspers, Karl, 92, 128
Jemison, T. J., 295n6, 299n67. *See also* Baton Rouge Bus Boycott
Jesus, 190, 193–196
Jim Crow, 198, 205, 207, 296n23
Johns, Vernon, 203, 227
Jones, Rufus, 190
Josephus, Flavius, 267
Journal de guerre, 1939–1940 (Friedmann), 2, 37, 95–98, 104, 106–109, 129–135, 139, 260nn1–2, 261, 273–278, 275n26, 276n30, 276nn32–33, 277n34, 278n49, 278n52, 285, 285n147
joy, 63, 67, 86, 171, 226, 249
Judaism, 47, 82, 267n80, 284n144, 285n148

Kierkegaard, Soren, 266
King, Coretta Scott, 211, 300n4
King, Martin Luther, Jr., 35, 44, 185, 295n6, 299n65; care of the self, coterminous with the care of others, 31; collection of facts, practice of, 198

INDEX

King (*continued*)
(*see also* Rustin, Bayard); courage, practice of, 181, 183–184, 197; degenerating sense of "nobodiness" (*see* dehumanization, problem of); dehumanization, 21, 42 192–195, 198, 200–205, 296n23, 304n143; desegregation, 181, 187; on direct action, 3, 13,21, 41–42 197–201, 210–211, 216–221, 224, 234, 295, 300–301; elitism, problem of, 8, 11; fear, grammar of, 181–184, 193, 205, 231, 233; influenced by Gandhian tradition, 180, 297n31; home, January 1956 bombing of, 227, 303n131; influence of Howard Thurman, 44, 180, 189–190, 197 indignity, on the political problem of, 202, 206; Jim Crow (*see* segregation); Memphis Sanitation Workers Strike, 1968, 205, 304n143; MIA (Montgomery Improvement Association), role in, 208–209 (*see also* MIA); Montgomery Bus Boycott, 31, 33, 41–42, 180, 181, 185–187, 201, 206–207, 208, 225, 227–230, 303n140, 304n143; training in and strategic use of nonviolence, 30, 197, 206, 210–211, 217, 219, 223–225, 230–233, 302n118; positive vs. negative peace, 243, 301n105, 302n110; peace, varieties of, 243; relationship to Bayard Rustin, 23–234, 297n31, 300n83, 301n107, 302n126, 304n146; relationship to Reverend Glenn Smiley, 210–212, 294n1 (*see also* Smiley, Glenn); segregation, 41, 198, 201–205, 296n23, 298n49; self-purification, 3, 13–14, 16, 41, 134 180–181, 189, 197–201, 210, 219–225, 228–229, 234, 257n4, 297n31; spiritualism, problem of, 16, 21, 22, 32. *See also* "Letter From Birmingham Jail"; spiritual exercises; *Stride Toward Freedom*
King, Martin Luther, Sr., 190

labor: sociology of (*see* Friedmann, Georges); upon the environment as labor upon oneself, 151, 281n85 (*see also* Friedmann, Georges);
law: and injustice, 42–43, 183, 187, 198–201, 206, 213, 216, 228, 230–231 (*see also* "Letter from Birmingham Jail"); as model of sovereign power, 153, 154, 156, 287n25, 289n50 (*see also* Foucault, Michel); of an epoch, 115 (*see also* Friedmann, Georges); universal, of nature, 62, 66 (*see also* Hadot, Pierre)
Lebedev, Vladimir, 272n135
Lefebvre, Henri, 273n9, 279n58
Lesson Plan on Non-violent Action (Rustin), 42, 197, 215–221, 223–224, 297n31, 301nn102–104, 301n105, 301n107
"Letter from Birmingham Jail" (King), 3, 189, 197, 205, 215, 218, 219, 223, 297n32, 301n105, 302n110
Levinas, Emmanuel, 86
liberalism, 25, 101, 148, 199, 281n86
liberation, political and spiritual, 7, 21, 26, 30, 34, 45, 67–126, 147, 166, 186, 188, 191–192, 195–196, 238, 244, 247, 254
Lorde, Audre: and anger, 254, 306n8; apartheid, activism around, 247, 307n26; Australia, visit to, 250; cancer, 4, 241, 251–252, 255, 306n8; caring for herself as political warfare, 4, 15, 16, 32, 44, 237–238, 239, 242, 244; on death, 256; elitism, problem of, 11, 13; erotic, the, 255; flesh, to live one's battles in the, 241, 250; ice cream, segregation and, 246; illusion of safety, 44, 242–244; immediacy, 40, 44, 45, 240, 244–248, 255, 258; intersectionality, 4, 241, 306n7; life of, 305n5; March on Washington, role of women in, 307n26; parrhesiast, as, 45, 240, 248–253, 256; poetry, role and status of, 44–45, 236, 240–241, 244, 246–249, 251, 253–256; prosthesis, 251–253, 306n8; self-conscious life, 247, 306n8; self-indulgence, rejection of, 4, 15, 16, 22, 32, 175, 237–238, 244; self-preservation, 4, 237, 242–243, 306n13 (*see also* Lorde, Audre:

INDEX

survival); silence, transformation of into language and action, 246, 249, 251–254; survival, 240, 241, 242, 243, 249, 253; white feminists, parrhesiastic challenges to, 250–251. *See also* "Burst of Light: Living with Cancer, A"; *Cancer Journals, The*; "Poetry Is Not a Luxury"; *Zami: A New Spelling of My Nam*
Louverture, Toussaint, 272
love, 46, 92, 190, 197, 224, 229, 233
Loyola, Ignatius of, 47, 261n6
Lucilius Junior, correspondent of Seneca, 307n23
Lucretius, Titus Carus, 84
Luther, Martin, 117

Marcus Aurelius Antoninus, 245, 266n58. *See also* Friedmann, Georges; Hadot, Pierre
Marx, Karl, 2, 5, 29, 36, 95–96, 101, 115, 123, 125, 129, 258n8, 275n26, 277n42, 279n58, 281nn85–86, 282n99, 283n104, 284n144
Marxism, 26–28, 36–37, 90, 95, 100–101, 121, 129, 131, 273n9, 275n26, 277n42, 279n58, 281n86, 284n144
maschinisme, 2, 36–37 95, 97, 106–114, 118–119, 122–124, 274n11, 277n39, 278n45, 280n64, 280n66, 281n80, 283n107
meditation, spiritual exercise of. *See* Hadot, Pierre
Memphis Sanitation Workers Strike of 1968
metaphysics, metaphysical, 16–19, 23, 55, 82–83
MIA (Montgomery Improvement Association), 208, 211, 227, 231, 299n65
Michelet, Jules, 112, 280n64
Molotov-Ribbentrop Pact, 96–97, 130, 133, 275n26, 281n86
monasticism, 22–24, 64, 87, 244
Montgomery Bus Boycott, 210–211, 214–215, 225, 228, 298n54, 300n95, 302n117, 302n118. *See also* King, Martin Luther, Jr.

moral perfectionism, 3, 5, 196, 225, 265n46. *See also* Cavell, Stanley
moralism, political: definition of, 23–26; problem of, 13, 24–33, 37, 39, 40, 43, 45, 76, 92, 100–101, 103, 105, 116, 125–128, 139, 145, 149, 175, 188, 248, 260n37, 287n22, 292n86, 305n4
Morgan v. Virginia, 295n6
Morgan, Irene. *See Morgan v. Virginia*
Morhange, Pierre, 273n9, 274n10. *See also Groupe Philosophies*
Morin, Edgar, 97, 273n7, 277n34
Musonius Rufus, Gaius, 73, 173
Muste, A. J., 299–300n75, 299n72

NAACP (National Association for the Advancement of Colored People), 207–208, 298n60, 304n143
neoliberalism, 25, 266n58, 305n4. *See also* California Cult of the Self; moralism; spiritualism
Neoplatonism, 61, 64
New Age, 15, 18–19
Nixon, Edgar Daniel (E.D.), 185, 207–210, 213, 225, 227–228, 231, 233, 295n6, 304n143
nonviolence, 3, 30, 41–43, 180, 183, 188–190, 197–201, 207–212, 214–217, 219–225, 232, 254, 257n4, 294n1, 297n31, 299nn72–73, 299n75, 300n95, 301n105, 302n110, 302n117. *See also* FOR (Fellowship of Reconciliation); King, Martin Luther, Jr.; Rustin, Bayard; Smiley, Glenn; Thurman, Howard
Nonviolence: The Gentle Persuader. *See* Smiley, Glenn
nostalgia, problem of, 100, 103, 118–124, 127–128, 131, 136. *See also* Friedmann, Georges

overview effect, 84, 86, 272n136. *See also* White, Frank

Parks, Rosa, 185, 207–210, 225, 298n60, 298n63, 304n143
parrhesia, 45, 168, 221, 232, 240, 248–253, 304n143, 308n31

passions, therapeutics and aseksis of, 46, 51, 62, 109, 223, 254
pastoral power. *See* Foucault, Michel: counter-conduct
Patočka, Jan, 5, 258n6, 273n2
PCF (Communist Party of France), 36, 96, 134, 276n28
Pétain, Philippe, 97, 130, 277n34
Philo of Alexandria, 68, 267n80
pilgrimage, spiritual exercise of, 6, 225–231, 269n107
Plato, Platonism, 48, 64, 66, 74, 79, 129, 244, 265n46, 266n56, 271n113, 282n86, 307n21
Plotinus, 48
Plutarch, 66
"Poetry Is Not a Luxury" (Lorde), 247
politeia, 151
politics, relation to ethics, 9, 12–13, 29, 40, 91, 94, 102, 139, 149, 172
Politzer, Georges, 273n9, 276n28. *See also Groupe Philosophies*
Porphyry, 271n117
practices of the self, 1, 5–6, 32, 34, 36, 45, 54, 59–60, 74, 80, 94, 139, 146–147, 162–164, 180, 188, 199, 237–238, 255; collective, 35, 41, 137; contemporary, 8, 9–10, 88, 104, 138
Prague Spring of 1968, 273n2, 281n86

Quakerism, 190, 211
quietism, 22–24, 26, 75, 147, 173

Rabinow, Paul, 144, 288n37
Ramakrishna Mission, 261n2, 277n34
Randolph, A. Philip, 211–212, 225, 299–300n75, 299n72
reductionism, ethical-political, 13, 24–25, 28, 32, 102, 184. *See also* moralism; spiritualism
relationship of the self to itself, 3, 43, 196, 240–241, 248, 251, 290–291; as a circuit, 30, 40, 164, 241, 247, 253; Foucault on, 13, 141–142, 146, 148–149, 163–165, 174, 177–178, 180, 184, 290n63, 291n81

religion: belief, religious, 17, 18, 70, 177, 195, 197; conditions, religious, 9, 35, 50, 77, 160, 168, 179, 188, 212, 260n2, 265n48, 284n144; distinct from spirituality, 18, 167; life, religious, 15–16, 19, 170; practice, religious, 6, 9, 15, 31, 33, 43, 200, 244, 269n107; religious retreat, 21–22, 24, 128, 177; religious specialists, 9, 10–11, 34, 47, 73, 99, 137, 244; religious traditions, 64, 126, 129–130, 132, 161, 170, 173, 267n80, 281n86; religious violence, 7, 176
resistance, analytics of. *See* Foucault, Michel
Resistance, French. *See* Friedmann, Georges
retreat, political, 21–23, 31, 92, 100, 102, 127–128, 132, 136. *See also* moralism; quietism; withdrawal, political

revolution, 41, 46, 91, 106, 115, 246, 258n8, 272n118, 284n144. *See also* Foucault, Michel
Ricoeur, Paul, 258n6
Roberts, Chief Justice John G., 25, 260n36
Robinson, Jo Ann Gibson, 185, 207, 228, 230, 298n57, 303n140, 304n143
Rome, ancient, 46, 50, 59–60, 64, 78, 130
Rustin, Bayard, 185, 190, 193, 198, 205, 209, 225, 227, 231, 302n126; collaboration with King, 3, 182–183, 215, 233–234, 294n1, 300n83, 304n146; Lesson Plan on Non-violent Action, 42, 197, 215–221, 223–224, 297n31, 301nn102–n104, 301n105, 301n107; life and influence of, 3, 210–215, 299n72–75, 300n90
Ryazanov, David, 279n58. *See also* Marx, Karl; Stalinism; USSR

satyagraha, 297n31, 301n107
scientific management. *See* Friedmann, Georges
"Second" World, 93, 103, 105, 258n6, 278n49. *See also* USSR

INDEX

self-absorption, 21, 144, 147
self-care, 4, 9, 18–19, 237–238, 280n66, 304n4
self-change, 1, 5, 7, 9, 11, 22, 23, 30, 32–33, 101, 103, 139, 164–166, 178, 185, 187–188, 201, 234, 240, 258n8
self-purification. *See* King, Martin Luther, Jr.
self-transformation, 1, 3, 7, 43, 53, 166, 169, 171, 176–177, 179, 184, 195, 239–240, 247, 253, 256
self, attainable but unattained. *See* Cavell, Stanley
Seneca, 66, 245, 307n23
Shridharani, Krishnalal, 257n4, 297n31, 301n107
Siddeswarananda, Swami, 277n34
Simiand, François, 119
slavery, 72–73, 122, 270n110, 271n113, 290n60, 296n23
Smiley, Glenn, 210–215, 221–225, 299n72–73, 300n95, 301n97, 302n117. *See also* King, Martin Luther, Jr.
Smith, Barbara, 305n5, 306n6
Smith, Lillian E., 212, 224
socialism, 90, 93, 96, 105, 125, 275n26, 276n30, 284n127
socialism with a human face, 90, 125, 273n2
sociodrama, spiritual-political exercise of, 215, 221–224. *See also* Smiley, Glenn
Socrates, 1, 59–60, 74–76, 79, 265n45, 271n113, 272n119, 275n125
Soviet Union. *See* USSR
spaceflight, 84–86, 272nn135–136. *See also* Gagarin, Yuri; Levinas, Emmanuel
specialists, problem of, 9–11, 34, 72–74, 80–88, 99–100, 103, 137, 146, 185, 244, 262n12, 263n27, 270nn111–112, 271n113, 275n18, 276n32
spiritual demands, spiritual needs, 3, 10, 35, 37–38, 53, 57–58, 61, 70, 73, 80, 86, 88–89, 94, 105, 110, 112, 136, 218, 230; contemporary, 47, 57, 77, 80, 88–89, 102–103, 129–133, 138–139, 199–201, 218, 236, 253

spiritual exercises: anticipation, practice of 68–70, 207n23 (*see also* Thurman, Howard); as exegetical problem, 48–50; attention to the present, practice of, 65–68, 268n84; contemplation (*see* contemplation); contemporary, 34, 54, 57, 61, 76–84, 99; death, contemplation of, 56, 61–62, 68, 70; definition of, 6–11, 47–48, 51, 167; dialogue, philosophical, 6, 47, 55, 65–66, 75, 87–88, 266n56, 267n82, 306n21; dialogue with oneself, 47, 50, 75, 259n12; historical translation, problem of, 9–11, 34, 78–79, 82, 87, 99, 127, 135, 176, 236–237; *hypomnemata*, 50, 65; judgment, askesis of, 60–64, 68; meditation, practices of, 6, 47, 67–70; memory, practices of, 68–70; physics, ancient practice of, 66–67, 268n83 268n93, 268n95, 270n109; premeditation of evils, 34, 50, 68, 245; *prosokhē* (*see* attention to the present moment); self-examination, 68–69; spiritual but not religious, claim of, 15; view from above (*see* view from above). *See also* Hadot, Pierre
spiritualism, ethical: definition of, 15, 19–23; problem of, 13, 15–23, 26, 28–32, 37, 40, 43, 45, 56, 92, 100, 102, 118, 127–128, 131, 136, 139, 145, 149–150, 175, 244, 248, 287n22, 305n4. *See also* Friedmann, Georges
spirituality, 5, 31, 151, 163, 177, 264n36, 282n91; aesthetic misdirection, problem of, 14, 17, 147–148, 248; definitions of, 6, 49, 90, 102, 162, 163, 177; negative associations with, 14–19, 31, 243
Stalinism, 95, 124, 275n524, 276n30, 281n86
Steele, C. K., 299n67
Stocisim. *See* Hadot, Pierre
Stride Toward Freedom (King), 181, 183–184, 187, 223, 294n1

subjection, political: Foucault on (*see* Foucault, Michel); and political self-purification, 244; and segregation, 200–206
suffering, human, 6, 35, 52–53, 61, 63–65, 68–69, 72, 81–84, 121, 200, 220–221, 270n112, 285n151
Sunzi, 266n58
Supreme Court of the United States, 1, 25, 182–183, 186, 194, 223, 231, 295n6
survival. *See* Lorde, Audre

Taylor, Frederick Winslow, 111–114, 119, 279n58, 280n72. *See also* Friedmann, Georges: critique of scientific management
Taylorism. *See* Friedmann, Georges, scientific management, critique of; Taylor, Frederick Winslow
"Technological Adventure of Human Beings in the Twentieth Century, The" (Friedmann), 38, 93–94, 99, 104–110, 117, 120, 123, 125–126, 131–132, 135;
telos of spiritual exercises, 6, 9, 53, 58–60, 62, 77, 94, 104–105, 163, 173, 177, 200, 223, 265n48, 270n108, 282n91
Theosophy, 15
Thoreau, Henry David, 262n10, 265n46
Thurman, Howard, 3, 42, 44, 180, 185, 189–198, 200–201, 203–206, 210–211, 227, 230–231, 240, 242, 244–245, 250, 296n8, 296n23, 297n31

unattained but attainable self. *See* Cavell, Stanley
USSR, 2, 24, 36, 95, 114, 117, 124–125, 134, 140, 179, 275n19, 275n24, 275nn26–27, 276nn28–29, 279n58, 281n81, 281n86, 284n127

view from above, 11, 34, 47, 66–67, 84–88, 100, 103, 134, 146, 259n12, 268n86, 272n135
view from below, 11, 34, 76, 86, 88, 100, 103, 134, 138, 139, 146, 186, 223
violence, 7, 176–177, 182–183, 191–195, 206, 216, 219, 221, 226, 230–233, 287n25, 289n58, 301n102, 308n31

Wahl, Jean, 263n23
walking, 42–43, 183, 186, 207, 214–215, 224, 226–231, 252, 292n88, 303n140
War Without Violence. *See* Shridharani, Krishnalal
White, Frank, 84, 272n136
wisdom, 11, 21–22, 53, 59, 60, 63–65, 70, 92, 123, 236, 266n58, 285n149
withdrawal, political, 19–24, 29, 75, 144–146, 149–150. *See also* egoism; Foucault, Michel, egoism and withdrawal; quietism; retreat, political
Wittgenstein, Ludwig, 49, 263n23. *See also* Hadot, Pierre
World War I, 108–109, 134, 278n49
World War II. *See* Friedmann, Georges; *Journal de guerre*
WPC (Women's Political Council), 207–209, 225, 298n57, 298n63, 304n143. *See also* Robinson, Jo Ann Gibson
Wuthnow, Robert, 15–18, 21, 31

Yezhovshchina (Great Purge, Great Terror), 279n58
yoga, 15, 18, 31

Zami: A New Spelling of My Name (Lorde), 242, 246, 306n13

GPSR Authorized Representative: Easy Access System Europe, Mustamäe tee
50, 10621 Tallinn, Estonia, gpsr.requests@easproject.com

www.ingramcontent.com/pod-product-compliance
Lightning Source LLC
Chambersburg PA
CBHW031232290426
44109CB00012B/267